POLITICAL INTERNET

This book investigates the Internet as a site of political contestation in the Indian context. It widens the scope of the public sphere to social media, and explores its role in shaping the resistance and protest movements on the ground. The volume also explores the role of Internet, a global technology, in framing debates on the idea of the nation state, especially India, as well as diplomacy and international relations. It also discusses the possibility of whether the Internet can be used as a tool for social justice and change, particularly by the underprivileged, to go beyond caste, class, gender and other oppressive social structures.

A tract for our times, this book will interest scholars and researchers of politics, media studies, popular culture, sociology, international relations as well as the general reader.

Biju P. R. is Assistant Professor, Department of Political Science, Government Brennen College, Thalassery, Kerala, India. He is a writer, blogger and teacher with research interests in the Internet, politics and social change. He has written extensively on the interfaces of social media and politics in popular web journals, academic outlets and online news portals. He is a peer-reviewer for reputed journals such as the *Asian Journal of Communication* and contributor to *South Asia Politics*, and online outlets such as Merinews, India Opines and Countercurrents.org. He is the author of the books *Myth of Social Media Politics* (2016); *Intimate Speakers* (2016) and *Intimate Revolution: Cyber Sexuality in the Antiporn Nation* (forthcoming) and is presently working on a novel.

POLITICAL INTERNET

State and Politics in the
Age of Social Media

Biju P. R.

Routledge
Taylor & Francis Group

LONDON AND NEW YORK

First published 2017 by Routledge

2 Park Square, Milton Park, Abingdon, Oxfordshire OX14 4RN
52 Vanderbilt Avenue, New York, NY 10017

Routledge is an imprint of the Taylor & Francis Group,
an informa business

First issued in paperback 2019

British Library Cataloguing in Publication Data
A catalogue record for this book is available from the British Library

Library of Congress Cataloging-in-Publication Data
A catalog record has been requested for this book

ISBN: 978-1-138-21370-8 (hbk)
ISBN: 978-0-367-27959-2 (pbk)

Typeset in ITC Galliard
by Apex CoVantage, LLC

Gayu
You became my religion, when
I chase down my passion.

CONTENTS

ACKNOWLEDGEMENTS

On 15 August 1995, Videsh Sanchar Nigam Limited (VSNL) formally launched the Internet for the Indian public. I read this news in the local daily *Malayala Manorama*. This book has been more than two decades in the making ever since and writing it was a journey I travelled with family, colleagues, friends and many unfamiliar people. It was their stories and my experiences with them that I would tell.

I owe my deepest gratitude to following people for their valuable contributions.

To friends, friends of friends and their friends who shared their life stories on social media with me in the in-depth surveys conducted for this book.

To Gayathri, my world, for your love, unwavering support and beautiful smile after the critique of my first draft that told me I was on the way. I am fortunate to have brainstormed, critiqued, argued with and loved by you.

To 'F', 'L', and 'SA', who read parts of this manuscript and from whose comments I benefited a lot.

To professionals, whose ideas and arguments I have used in this book in connection with the three-day seminar on social media I organised from 13 to 15 September 2011 with financial support from the UGC.

To Geert Lovink who shifted my views fundamentally. On 26 March 2010, I contacted Professor Geert Lovink, Dutch-Australian media theorist and critic, whom I didn't know before, with a request for a comment on subject titled 'Consulting Public Sphere and Internet by Biju P. R., India, Kerala'. He was generous enough to reply to my enquiries, though I was unfamiliar to him. The email communication continued till 7 December 2012. I have hugely benefitted from his comments. Still I know him only as my email contact.

To Johanna Niesyto, research fellow at University of Siegen, Germany, with whom I am still personally not acquainted, who I contacted via email only over a period from 26 March 2010 to 5 December 2012 for comments on sections of this manuscript, who generously commented on it, from which I hugely benefited for the advancement of its theoretical side.

To Zeynep Tufekci, Harvard Berkman Center for Internet and Society; who introduced me to journals such as *New Media and Society* and *Information, Communication and Society*.

To Aakash Chakrabarty for reading my initial query on LinkedIn, later Antara Ray Chaudhary for her faith in this *book and for commissioning it at Routledge* and R. V. Rajesh copy editor.

I thank the anonymous referees for their useful suggestions.

To those people who did not become a part of the book, but continue to enrich my heart and thoughts and perhaps belong to another book.

To my parents, Rajamma and Raju, and my brother, Shiju, who have always been supportive and loving; though they claim to have no idea what I do, I nonetheless owe my small success to their constant support.

ABBREVIATIONS

AAP	Aam Aadmi Party
AICC	All India Congress Committee
AIDWA	All India Democratic Women's Association
BBC	British Broadcasting Corporation
BIS	Business Innovation and Skills
BJP	Bharatiya Janata Party
BPL	below poverty line
BSP	Bahujan Samaj Party
CD ROM	compact disc read-only memory
CII	Confederation of Indian Industry
COMET	Communication Plan for Election
CRY	Child Rights and You
CSO	civil society organisation
DIT	Department of Information and Technology
DIY	do-it-yourself
DNA	Daily News & Analysis
EDSA	Epifanio Delos Santos Avenue
EESC	European Economic and Social Committee
FGUSMGO	Framework & Guidelines for Use of Social Media for Government Organizations
FYP	Five Year Plan
G2E	government to employee
HCU	Hyderabad Central University
I&B	information and broadcasting
ICANN	Internet Corporation for Assigned Names and Numbers
ICT	information and communications technology
IIM	Indian Institute of Management
IIT	Indian Institute of Technology
IM	instant messaging

ABBREVIATIONS

INC	Indian National Congress
IPC	Indian Penal Code
IQ	intelligence quotient
ISRO	Indian Space Research Organisation
IT	information technology
LGBT	lesbian, gay, bisexual and transgender
MEA	Ministry of External Affairs
MIT	Massachusetts Institute of Technology
MMS	multimedia messaging service
MNS	Maharashtra Navnirman Sena
NBA	Narmada Bachao Andolan
NDTV	New Delhi Television Limited
NGO	non-governmental organisation
NOTA	none of the above
NRI	non-resident Indian
NSA	National Security Agency
OECD	Organisation for Economic Co-operation and Development
OGPL	Open Government Platform
OMG	Oh my god!
PFA	Public Finance Act
RSS	Rashtriya Swayamsevak Sangh
RTI	Right to Information Act
SARS	severe acute respiratory syndrome
SC	Scheduled Caste
SMS	short message services
SNS	social networking site
TRAI	Telecom Regulatory Authority of India
UPA	United Progressive Alliance
USA	United States of America
Wi-Fi	wireless fidelity
WWW	World Wide Web

INTRODUCTION

Political Internet is a distinct portrayal of the political trajectories of Indian Internet. The fascinating question is whether the Internet is in politics or politics is in the Internet or what is political about the Internet. The first question is that of application of Internet in political engagements, whereas the second question is concerned with who and how the Internet is owned or put it otherwise, the second question is all about political economy of Internet. The third question is more significant to Indian condition in the sense that by entering the Internet landscape many people are also entering into a rational political act. To a curious mind, these interesting questions regarding Internet in India is that of how to approach it. How should one approach the fundamental question on Internet, more particularly in a peculiar context of the social structure prevalent here? Social landscape in India is intervened by social facts such as castes, religions, languages, culture, class and gender. Therefore, individual behaviour and attitude is largely scripted by the invisible power of the social structures. For that reason, the role of Internet in bringing changes in the social structures and explicit human behaviour is a pertinent question.

Which of the analytical lens on technology does one prefer – digital dystopia or utopia on Internet? Those who prefer the former approach it with an inherent understanding that technology is corruptive, whereas those who prefer the latter perceive that technology is one of the solutions. The intriguing enquiry is that if Internet beat the raucous social structure or if the tumultuous social structure beat Internet. Anyhow, fundamentally there are few significant questions that fill in the approach by any means. Is Internet democratising India or re-feudalising it? Is there a public sphere facilitated by Internet? Will social capital get new channels of expression in social media platforms? Can social platforms fine-tune contentious politics? What are the changes Internet brings in the government deliveries to citizens? Are the elite corners of state apparatus such as diplomatic practices

1

and conduct of foreign policy unable to withstand the pulls of cyberspaces? How could people on social margins benefit out of Internet? Are the educational practices facilitated by cyberspaces more a political act for people on the social peripheries? Are cell phones the political choice in the cleavage-rich Indian society? Can social media situate a civil society of the private interest against excesses of state apparatus? The fundamental questions being furnished in the approach to Indian Internet have one underlying denominator. It is that there is an apparent fluid interplay between democratic engagements and social platforms in Internet. Direction of that correlation is fascinating to the intriguing mind of a democracy enthusiast. The focal point here is that to very many people, Internet is a political choice. People in Internet means a rational political act. It is principally an assumption in the sense that people migrating to social spaces through Internet platforms must be discoursed in the sense that Internet is a class-free, caste-abhorrent, minority-inclusive, subaltern-friendly, gender-neutral open social space. So naturally people in virtual spaces are more political than those in physical social spaces.

To address various questions raised on the foot lines of political Internet, one needs to look at the other way around. Characterising the nature of politics is itself an important step to understand political ramifications of Internet. The nature of Internet too is significant. The melting pot of both phenomena gives shape to political Internet. It is more significant in the sense that any discussion on Internet and political behaviour usually spills over into the unsettled social order in the modern idea of Indian state hailed down from the cultural past. However, what is less inspiring? Our shelves are already flooded with literature on both the questions, that is what is politics and what is Internet. To that respect, at the outset, guess that it neither attempts to define what politics is nor gives a meaning to what Internet is. Rather, political Internet specifically locates the political significance of Internet. It tracks if politics is in Internet or if Internet is in politics or if Internet is political in India. However, it doesn't mean an enquiry pertaining to politics of Internet or Internet politics for the reason that both are two distinct questions which in no way comes in the purview of this book.

Politics is amazing! It happens everywhere. To Aristotle politics is a levelling process where people engage in political act to make an ethical life in city state. According to the author of the book *Chimpanzee Politics* (1982), Frans de Waal, it happens even among chimpanzees. He observes that sexuality and power among chimpanzees are as complex as among human beings. B. Guy Peters sees it as principally concerned with governing and making of public policy.[1] Peter P. Nicholson views that the central province of any political act is the exercise of force.[2] Author Bernard Crick in the book *In Defence of Politics*[3] has the view that political act is a form of rule through which conciliation and cooperation are achieved by sidestepping differences in order to pursue a common purpose. For the author of the book *Politics: Who Gets What, When, How* (1936), Harold Laswell,[4] it is a question of power. He defines it as a social realm concerning the influence and the influential. For Adrian Leftwich, the editor of the book *What Is Politics?*, two things are important in understanding politics in a society. First one is that politics as an activity is concerned not only with public; rather, it is a universal aspect of human behaviour found among two or more individuals engaged in some activity at any scale, be it formal or informal and public or private. Second, if politics is an intrinsic aspect of human behaviour, when we understand human behaviour, we need to understand it politically.[5] So any understanding of politics therefore should also look at Internet as a social landscape. Internet is an important social avenue yet to be properly understood. The reason for such an assumption is that people preferring Internet at times is a rational choice particularly because of the social structure that apparently makes social mobility impossible. So people moving to Internet signifies a new social system where social mobility is possible. Your Facebook, WhatsApp, Twitter, LinkedIn, Blogger, WordPress, Skype, Viber and so on are more political for a society that still lives in the imagination of its past.

Internet is but a different social house. Modern metaphors are insufficient to comprehend the nuances of social spaces in it. Internet itself is a metaphor. The meaning conveyed through it is rarely comprehended in its entirety. There are many continents yet to be discovered in it. Many invisible tendencies with space-like mysteries are thought to be therein. For example, many physical metaphors were used to convey what Internet is when it was in its infancy. Those days, ordinary people were taught of the idea what Internet is with metaphors of the physical world. Just think of space to cyberspace, net to Internet, Window to Desktop and so on. Now, things are reversing. Allegories have boomeranged. Metaphors of Internet are now giving meaning to many things in the physical world. Internet is echoing back. It is on the background that billions of things from the physical world are going to be connected to Internet in the days ahead. Trees will have more digital roots and dogs will get more bits. Cars are more connected to Internet than human beings, and purchasing and consumer behaviour is more mediated by Internet than actual market. People call it Internet of Things (IoT). In the age of IoT, the whole social world looks different from the previous one. Big data is significant in such a social system. Enormous volumes of data in digital formats just because Internet has eased all forms of human life create enormous opportunities. Risk too!

Everything is in Internet – economy, culture, history, geography and sensory perception. Nothing is free from its reach. Amidst such a paradigm shift, one thing is more significant – that is political act and Internet. Politics and Internet are a significant interplay in the trajectory of social cleavages prevalent in India. Such significance is a more fascinating theme to discuss in the Indian context. As we know, India is a rigid society with many fundamental problems yet to be resolved and technology is looked after with hope. The common perception is that decades of constitutional experiments in democracy arguably did no favour to the citizens on the social margins. Ordinary people still look at democracy with much hope. In that respect anything that gives them a hope would be accepted as taken for granted. Any metaphors of change are welcome at least according to ordinary Indians. Internet is a taken-for-granted metaphor for them. Though there is no empirical evidence, ordinary people believe that digital technology is the saviour.

This book locates the much-hyped version of Internet popular among ordinary Indians. Based on the initial questions raised in the approach to Internet, the book takes neither dystopian nor utopian projections of Internet. Rather, it takes a more practical consideration pertaining to Internet. Few variables are analysed in that respect. They are drawn in view of tracking the political question involved in why people are in Internet. Social variables such as 'we' feeling and togetherness, associationalism and engaged publics, contentious politics, public sphere, diplomatic practices, learning processes and resistances are important indicators of political Internet. They are used in the analytical parameters to investigate if social space through Internet gives people an inclusionary public sphere, which were denied to them in the physical social world. Is Internet facilitating a 'we' feeling that ordinary Indians in the lower rungs of social hierarchy in India could not otherwise think? Will Internet give way to contentious politics in which opportunity structures facilitated by Internet were otherwise unimaginable? Is the 'friend power' in cyberspace a uniting tool for the people to react against discrepancies in society? Does it make sense to think that presence of diplomatic practitioners, institutions and functionaries in social media gives a more popular image to the conduct of foreign policy, which were otherwise an elite service in the ivory towers of the Indian state? In short, the state, democratic engagements, political deliberations, civil society, public sphere, social capital, contentious politics, diplomacy, expatriates, education and learning, resistances and social change are factors that come under investigation of political Internet. These factors remain largely changed by the phantom advances of technology. Certainly, such changes are going to have large-scale image-breaking effect on old social system prevalent in India. So people in Internet are of course a political act.

Indeed, Internet is a different social house for Indians. This book is an investigation into it. The political Internet is explored through participant observation, personal observation, in-depth interviews, closer examination of cyber behaviour of users, narratives of people in cyberspace, surveys and digital ethnography. Chapters following are pointers to the mechanics of social change in social media age. The evolution of political Internet! They are windows to the political question involved in Internet.

There are eleven subthemes in the manuscript for *Political Internet.* Each theme looks up on the manifestation of political Internet and its multifaceted interfaces with India's social and cultural undercurrents. This book is a timely intervention in sensitising academics, students of social science streams, scholars and professionals on social studies of technology and broadly Internet users, middle class and general interest clientele about the people power of Internet in India. It informs readers of the political significance of social media and its various manifestations.

Hundreds of video sharing platforms such as YouTube, over thousands of Facebook profiles, hundreds of online community pages, hundreds of blogs, randomly selected Tube sites and narratives based on in-depth interviews with people whom I met for this research formed the sampling frame in the study. Besides, for some chapters I have created many fake Facebook profiles, YouTube channels, Blogger accounts, cell phone numbers, Twitter profiles, Orkut accounts and a number of Gmail accounts. In this sharp and witty narrative, informed by the work of other writers, academics and reporters, as well as author's own wide-ranging research and interviews, the more political character of Internet is illustrated.

Notes

1 B. Guy Peters, 'Politics is about governing', in Adrian Leftwich (ed.), *What Is Politics*, Malden, MA: Polity Press, 2004, pp. 23–40.
2 Peter P. Nicholson, 'Politics and the Exercise of Force', in Adrian Leftwich (ed.), *What Is Politics*, Malden, MA: Polity Press, 2004, pp. 41–52.
3 Bernard Crick, *In Defence of Politics*, London: Weidenfeld & Nicolson, 1962.
4 Harold Laswell, *Politics: Who Gets What, When, How*, New York: McGraw-Hill, 1936.
5 Adrian Leftwich (ed.), *What Is Politics*, Malden, MA: Polity Press, 2004, pp. 100–101.

1

INDIAN INFOTOPIA

In this opening chapter, an extensive, though not exhaustive, theoretical account of the growth of Internet platforms as a tool of alternative communicative space and the linkages of such theories with Indian realities, particularly by people on the social margins, is documented. The focal argument is that as a liberating metaphor for people on the social margins, Internet must be looked after beyond the traditional instrumentalist and substantive agenda on social studies of technology. However, humanistic documentation of technological transformation of state and politics in India from academic points of view has not been an easy one, and its full implications are still unclear. Social Science in general and Political Science in particular are still diffident to view technology as worthy of discourse in Indian academia. Very few efforts were furnished in the past, that too with little public attention. In this background, this chapter makes an introductory approach to locate Internet as a site of discourse beyond the traditional empirical and instrumentalist perception of Internet. While doing so, the chapter does not altogether assume that Internet is not without negative repercussions, nor it proposes that technology is panacea for all the ills facing India. Internet is a bigger social house, which reproduces all the social architecture outside it such as caste, class and gender into the digital formats; it also intensifies its emancipating attributes to the people, at least the underprivileged. In this chapter, this position towards technology is extensively analysed based on three currents of technology discourse – dystopia, utopia and infotopia – which address the question of how to look at the trajectory of Internet and the underprivileged in the context of an extensive kaleidoscope of literary survey. This question is central to this chapter and probably the upcoming chapters.

Technology was in a contraposition in the political imagination of the Indian state. A section of Indian intelligentsia has seen it as a salvation philosophy and forecasted an element of transformatory effect in it. They contemplated technology as ending the torments of social structures in the near future. An equally important section anticipated it as inherently contravening to the social progress. The inception of the modern Indian state and its techno-rationalism was thus rooted in an intense ideological battle. In the twentieth century, political leadership and intelligentsia embraced technology, but as elsewhere in the world, it was too deep-rooted in either techno-dystopia or techno-utopia. Two stalwarts of Indian leadership therefore require special mention to contemplate on the techno-rationalism cultivated in modern Indian state. First prime minister and the builder of modern India, Jawaharlal Nehru, saw technology as a means to end perennial problems, while the father of the nation, Mohandas Karamchand Gandhi, anticipated the excrescence out of unnecessary pre-occupation with science and industrialism.

Nehru had an abiding faith in modern technology. He was convinced that the solution to India's fundamental problems such as social divides and economic backwardness lay within the vicinity of science and technology for progress. Heavy engineering, scientific research institutes and electric power were fundamental prerequisites for survival as a nation with a scientific temperament through which old problems could easily be solved, Nehru firmly believed.[1] Indeed, as an ardent advocate of industrialisation and enthusiast of modern science, Nehru believed in large-scale mobilisation of labour and capital as well as import of foreign technical expertise.[2] Nehru supposed that science alone could solve endemic hunger, poverty, insanitation, illiteracy and so on.[3] Technology would cut across all factors that divide India and thereby reconfigure a new India. Technology is then a salvation philosophy that could provide an alternative to India's ancient oppressive social systems. The fact is that science and technology exhibit no affiliation to ancient loyalties or reflect no caste, religion, language, regionalism, gender or any other social factors that divided India for centuries. Ramachandra Guha, a noted historian, in an article published in *Economic and Political Weekly* rightly observed that Nehru's educational and scientific policies could have made possible such an achievement, including the revolution in information and communications technology (ICT).[4]

Gandhi was a passionate opponent of modernity and technology who preferred pencil to the typewriter, loincloth to the business suit, the ploughed field to the belching manufactory and walking barefoot most of the time instead of bullock cart or modern automobiles. Had the Internet and Microsoft Word been invented in his lifetime, Gandhi would have found them abhorrent. He was against the de-humanising aspect of machinery. He believed that exposure to European industrial culture had depleted the rural India of its rustic beauty and innocence. Cotton manufacturing sector was an example, as the sector, due to its exposure to British cotton manufacturing industries, had lost its deep-rooted agrarian basis. Technology would impoverish people, he had anticipated.[5] Gandhi was certainly against all machinery designed for the exploitation of people, though he was not against technology as such.[6] For Gandhi, technology must improve productivity of workers, not displace them.

A major part of the philosophy of technology offers very abstract and unhistorical accounts of the essence of technology. Such accounts appear painfully lean compared to the loaded complexity revealed in social studies of technology. So far, technology has the distinguishing features which have normative implications that remain untapped in the Indian context. Technology studies are largely divided into two opposing schools of thought. Most essentialist philosophy of technology is critical of modernity. To a certain extent, they are even anti-modern. At the same time, most empirical modernist research on technologies ignores the larger issue of modernity and the normative implications of technology. Therefore, the empirical research on technology appears uncritical and even conformist to social critics. This chasm between essentialist and modernist on technology and the Indian state can thus be attributed to Gandhi and Nehru. Nehru's instrumentalist approach to technology was based on the common sense idea that technologies are tools standing ready only to serve the purposes of their users. Here technology is viewed as rather neutral. Gandhi had a rather substantive idea of technology and industrialism, which sees technology as creating a new cultural system of control. Bigger technological infrastructure erodes the essence of man, Gandhi believed. For example, massive passenger transportation projects such as aviation, metro and express corridors deprive man of their true essence. Travel has just become an economic affair, whereas many traditional and ritualistic things associated with travel have become secondary. This blind response implies the cultural implications of technology. This example can stand for a host of other issues in which the transition from tradition to modernity is judged as a progress by a standard of economic efficiency intrinsic to modernity and alien to tradition. Modernity as represented by Nehru and tradition as represented by Gandhi thus created an antagonistic technological infrastructure for the modern Indian state.

The ideological antagonism prevalent in the twentieth-century India over the technological infrastructure was contemplated ever since the First Five Year Plan (FYP). The politics of planned development in India has to say much about this ideological antagonism over technology. The First Five Year Plan (1951–56) aimed at bringing the country's economy out of poverty. It addressed mainly the agrarian sector, including investment in dams and irrigation. As poverty is more an agrarian phenomenon and majority of the Indians inhabit the sector, the modern Indian state committed itself to the cause of agrarian India. But there was a perception that as the agrarian economy is full of old social cleavages based on its commitment to caste, religion and other primordialities, it would finally inflate our old problems than wipe them out. The Second FYP (1956–61), therefore, stressed more on heavy industries. Industrial world represented a modern rationality and scientific temperament. Industrialisation marked a turning point in India's development as it has been more committed to progress than affiliation to ancient cleavages. Agrarian versus industrial, capital versus labour, rural versus urban and city versus village were at the heart of the idea of modern India. And the debate continues! The present arena of the debate is a new technology. It is the Internet and social media platforms, which for the last couple of years have been home to news, but they reflect both technological instrumentalism and substantivism.

The real question is the parameter at which Internet as a common man technology could be relooked, about which the modern Indian state has antagonistic perception. Here comes the critical theory of Internet in India. Despite their differences, Nehru's instrumental and Gandhi's substantive theories share a 'catch it or put down it' attitude towards technology. If technology (think Internet) is a mere instrumentality as Nehru views, then its design is not a political issue to be debated; only the range and efficiency of its application is the real issue. If technology is the vehicle for a culture of domination, it is apt to condemn technology. In both approaches, technology is destiny. Social study of Internet so far has not gone beyond instrumentalist and substantivist perception of technological infrastructure in the social study of Internet in the Indian academia. However, there is more to technology. Technology is shaped by the sociocultural context in which it is deployed.

For example, imagine events like India Against Corruption, Nirbhaya Campaign, hashtag feminism, cyber Dalit, long-distance democracy, Twitter activism, indeed an era of digital activism, online politics or cyber protest that captivate the imagination of the nation. It seems Internet has become a marketplace of ideas. It has transitioned from a platform for connection to a life support system, which an ever-increasing number of people take with them everywhere they go. Experts call it the Internet of Things. It means everything on the planet is 'Internetised'. In this scenario, political process in the same manner is influenced by Internet. India is no way behind this social science of Internet. Now the question comes in. Will people become rational political actors or Internet mediate our sensibilities. There are contrasting answers: utopian and dystopian. The Nehruvian techno-utopia finds expression in the digital India. Indeed, it is somehow the contribution of Nehru to modern India, they would argue. Therefore, technology is thought to be bringing benefits to the underprivileged just like what Nehru anticipated would bring in phantom changes in the ancient oppressive social systems and backwardness based on primordial loyalties.

On the other side, news from the digital technology is contemplating Gandhian perturbations. For example, mobile Internet services especially 2G, 3G and mobile communication, were blocked in the Indian state of Gujarat because the demand for OBC reservation by the Patel community turned violent. The protests were stirred by 22-year-old Hardik Patel, who led the agitation and was detained by Gujarat police, which activated a massive and violent protest in August 2015.[7] Here social technology is used for spreading hate and other primordialities, that too from the state where the greatest advocate of non-violence was born. Communal conflagration in Muzaffarnagar in Uttar Pradesh in 2013 had a social media root.[8] The clashes between the Hindu and Muslim communities in Muzaffarnagar district in Uttar Pradesh, India, between August and September 2013, resulted in at least 62 deaths including 52 Muslims and 10 Hindus and injured 93 and left more than 50,000 displaced.[9] Police in Uttar Pradesh found that social media mischief-makers found the new media an easy way to stoke communal violence anywhere in the state through objectionable messages in their posts. Social media platforms in Internet are increasingly used for hate, violence, anti-social activities, terrorism, gossip, rumour and so on, which mirror what Gandhi had anticipated, as technology would impoverish human being from progress. It upholds the assumption that technology robes the true essence of man. The ideological contraposition on technology to human being is thus reflected in Internet as a technology to human being in contemporary idea of the Indian state. The question is how to bring about a critical theory of technology.

A critical theory of technology charts a difficult track between Gandhian substantive dystopia and Nehruvian instrumentalist utopia of technology in the modern Indian state. The realities of technology are diverse and multiplicities of technological experiences could not be drawn to universally valid theoretical premises. A critical theory of technological infrastructure must engage far more directly with the question of technology than what is customary in its social studies.

The early Marxist Lukacs and the Frankfurt School took the first steps in this direction. Their theories of 'reification', 'totalitarian enlightenment' and 'one-dimensionality' show that the conquest of nature is not a metaphysical event, but one that begins in social domination. The remedy is therefore to be found in a democratic advance. That advance implies a radical reconstruction of the technological base of modern societies. Critical theory rejects the neutrality of technology and argues instead that 'technological rationality has become political rationality'.[10]

Critical theory argues that technology is not a thing in the ordinary sense of the term, but an 'ambivalent' process of development suspended between different possibilities. This ambivalence of technology is distinguished from neutrality by the role it attributes to social values in the design, and not merely the use, of technical systems. On this view, technology is not a destiny but a scene of struggle. It is a social battlefield, or perhaps a better metaphor would be a 'parliament of things' in which civilisational alternatives contend[11] (Latour, 1991: 194).

The citizen experience of Internet is diverse. Internet has crept into almost every aspect of Indian life, thus finding its increasing space in political deliberation too, just like what radio and later television achieved in democratic engagement. It is home to activists who challenge mainstream narratives. Politicians migrated to social networking sites. State apparatus increasingly resort to citizen deliveries through digital media platforms. Apps are developed for citizen deliveries by the governments. Here the moment comes to reflect more beyond Nehruvian romanticisation of science and technology and Gandhian scepticism on technology and modernity.

In fact, the social studies of Internet and politics in India are located in opposing currents of thoughts in its instrumentalist/deterministic and substantive aspects. Moreover, such debate is older. Internet and public sphere is an exhausted topic or to say it otherwise is a 1990 connection. It is now almost meaningless to think in terms of what role could Internet play in political sphere. The reason is very simple in the sense that literature on techno-sociality and techno-politics has advanced much in length and breadth. Deliberations on social media in politics have advanced a great extent in recent times to the extent that reading literature on social media is like an attempt to change a mountain. Maturing literature, therefore, often confuses social media enthusiasts. One must not confine to the ideological chasm between instrumentalist and substantivist approach to social media. Yet, two streams of technology literature should certainly be placed in discussions. It is appropriate to have a bird's-eye view of both techno-utopia and techno-dystopia on the background of Internet in democratic experiments or democratic experiments in Internet or both or whether Internet is an entirely different social arena at least according to the social groups end-noted in the narratives of mainstream Indian nation.

Serious pursuits of any of these models remain untapped in India. Many things related to social media need an analysis based on either of these models of analysis. Signing petitions on petition sites such as https://www.change.org/, http://www.petitiononline.com/, http://www.ipetitions.com/ and http://www.thepetitionsite.com/ against any social issues has been commonplace. Facebook communities in support of Koodankulam anti-nuclear movement in Tamil Nadu attracted a loose national coalition. Middle class are simply tweeting against corrupt political class. Are the mouse charmers doing anything meaningful to our democracy? The growing literature on the political function of Internet platforms, in fact, has a seesaw of their answers polarised. For the digital dystopians, social media is bound to spin around false promises, whereas it is emancipation for digital utopians. A plethora of dystopian and utopian configurations both elucidate the social media–powered mechanics of change in most cases in contradicting ways that do not carry any relevant point to the ground realities in India. Let us ask ourselves if it is sufficient to look at the Indian experience. Discussion on social media and political public has sharply bifurcated into two powerful and opposing streams of thought.[12]

Internet utopians have many testaments to their credit. *Being Digital* by Kevin Kelly, *Wisdom of Crowds* by James Surowiecki, Chris Anderson's *Long Tail*, Glenn Reynolds's *An Army of Davids*, Yochai Benkler's *The Wealth of Networks*, Clay Shirky's *Here Comes Everybody and Cognitive Surplus*, *Wikinomics* by Tapscott and Williams, *Crowdsourcing* by Jeff Howe and Dennis Baron's *Better Pencil* are just to name a few which remind us of the trumpet of digital era. There is something common in the literature: it is the faith in digital technology as bringing a new future. Analytical tools are in wide use among the televangelists of connection technologies for illustrating their emancipatory potential. For instance, 'Dragonfly Effect' by Aaker Smith and Adler, 'Cognitive Surplus' by Shirky, 'People Powered Uprising' by Tuffekci, 'Streetbook' by Pollock and 'Cute Cat Theory Talk' by Zuckerman, just to name a few, are important analyses of the power of connection technology bringing social changes in amazing ways. These are prophecies and popular terms bringing to light the diverse task social media platforms perform in Internet which include, among other things, usages like 'digitivism', 'tweetivism', 'cyberactivism', 'Internet advocacy', 'government 2.0' and 'Web 2.0'. Such words, though not found their place in the English dictionaries, have almost become cliché in popular imaginations.

On the other end of the gamut, digital sceptics have many authentications to their literatures, which are vehemently cynical of the liberatory potential of new media and connection technologies. Conceptual categories such as 'Net Delusion' by Morozov, 'Zero Comments' by Geert Lovink, 'Weak-tie' by Malcom Gladwell and 'Slacktivism' by Granovetter are popular in many corners. The unfaltering critique of digital communication platforms unleashed in the writings such as *Technopoly* by Neil Postman, Sven Birkerts's *Gutenberg Elegies*, Clifford Stoll's *High-Tech Heretic*, *Republic.com* by Cass Sunstein, Todd Gitlin's *Media Unlimited*, *Flickering Mind* by Todd Oppenheimer and *Cult of the Amateur and Digital Vertigo* by Andrew Keen are convincing. Steve Talbott's *Devices of the Soul*, *Big Switch* by Nick Carr, Lee Siegel's *Against the Machine*, *Dumbest Generation* by Mark Bauerlein, *Digital Barbarism* by Mark Helprin, *Distracted* by Maggie Jackson, *Tyranny of E-Mail* by John Freeman and *Shallows* by Nick Carr are also placed in the piling literatures on digital scepticism. They are trying to wake us from the nightmare into which we have been already sleepwalking on digital technologies of connection.

In the social study of Internet, in particular social media experiences of underprivileged from the vantage point of political deliberation and democratic engagement, one should adopt a strategy beyond traditional frameworks of technology analysis. The following section is a review of technology literature in order to have a portrait of Indian realities on Internet. While doing so, the focus is on unravelling the infotopia in the context of two opposing streams of digital technology literature as mentioned earlier. The underlying assumption, which gives synergy to this analysis, is the fact that incompatibility of foreign categories, variables and conceptual tools used to demonstrate an examination of the interplay between Internet and political engagement in India needs to be resolved. The attempt is to visualise an infotopia, i.e. an Indian perspective on social media public unique to India. It is to represent the lived in social media realities of Indians.

Digital ethnography

The social study of the connection between local culture and universally commanding technology are aplenty and contrasting. Before proceeding to analysis of connection technology in India, it is pertinent to understand why digital ethnography is significant to place technology in the idea of contemporary Indian democracy. The approach to virtual ethnography has been expanded and reformulated through new proposals such as connective ethnography, digital ethnography, netnography, ethnography on/of/through the Internet, cyber-ethnography, networked ethnography[13] and technography.[14] To answer the questions raised in the initial part, I have been deploying *digital ethnography*. I use digital ethnography here primarily as an explorative technique into the nuances of techno-social life. Therefore, I become YouTuber, Facebooker, Blogger and Tweeter on Internet. While doing so I plan to interact with social profiles pretending as if a natural collaborator, networker, follower, commenter and so on. Therefore, the primary method of exploration is digital ethnography, a method that requires us to participate in the phenomena one studies to understand them from the inside, while maintaining an outside perspective as well. To study YouTube, we become YouTubers. To study the blogosphere, we become bloggers. To study Twitter, we become tweeters, to study Facebook, we become a Facebooker, sometimes just a blog and other times a fake account in pseudo identity.

I plan to use a random sampling to identify social profiles. In doing so, data collected are subjected to social media analytics: interpretations of user behaviour in psychological parameters. Besides this, in some cases, data will be collected using a snowball sampling. It is because in some cases researchers will not be informed about some important social profiles, but will get information while meeting some new profiles. Participant observation and in-depth interviews are also devised with identified social profiles. Content analysis could be useful to get an analytical framework about certain net aspects. Grounded theories could be used in order to understand certain net behaviour. I will not have any information about certain things in net. Therefore, I do not develop any theoretical parameters to approach them in such occasions. Instead, certain things on the Internet need to be approached with a manifesto: tabula rasa. It is just like a blank slate, in which people are both the consumers and the producers of their experiences – something related to social constructivism.

Technologically embedded communication has become the usual aspect of daily life.[15] Thus the distinction between online and offline worlds is becoming less useful as activities in these realms become increasingly merged in our society and as the two spaces interact with and transform each other.[16] Yet there exist few qualitative enquiries with smaller portion of ethnographers. With the exception of few ethnographers, most ethnographic studies focus on offline social world.

This analysis of the ethnographic literature on technologically mediated phenomena suggests that digital ethnographers must alter their research techniques to accommodate the social changes, i.e. the current blending of offline and online worlds requires ethnographers to incorporate locally relevant, culture-specific categories to recognise the digitally mediated change mechanics. Just guess; writing took tens of thousands of years of evolution to become popular after humans articulated their first words. It took thousands more before the printing press and a few hundred again before the telegraph. Each new medium elicited a cultural change by redesigning how people could talk across time and space. Today, a new medium comes into view every time somebody creates a new web application every other time. New ways of connecting to others become easier through social media.

Each platform brings in new ways of cooperation, new kinds of groups and new ways of sharing and collaborating.

In general, the changes are too complex for simple surveys, interviews, mathematical models and focus groups to develop an understanding. Appreciating the complexities of this cultural shift requires total immersion in the subject. Approaches in the ethnographic study of the Internet have been varying and amazing by enormity in proposals in recent years. In virtual environments, social interactions present a challenge for social researchers and open up a new field for qualitative research that explores developing categories and conceptual tools reflecting indigenous and local context.

Digital ethnography includes a wide range of procedural approaches intended at answering the density of the object of research and the different ways in which this object has been assembled. Digital ethnographers or ethnographers of the Internet or of cyberspace have envisaged the need to answer very pressing questions such as how to use heterogeneous data (audio-visual data, text, SMS, MMS, comments etc. on social media platforms) in their analysis or how to coalesce research in front of the screen and in the digital sphere. They think about the big data where people make intimate speaks. A more important question addressed in virtual ethnography is the interfaces between social setting and the technological advancement. A study by Carey[17] tried to resolve the peculiar issue of technography as a way of investigation in reference to the ecological relations amongst environment, techniques and social agents without privileging any one of these in particular and aims at avoiding the anthropomorphism typical of actor-network theory as well as the perspective tendency to downplay power hierarchies. Digital ethnography intends to pay off the anthropocentric bias of ethnographic writing by placing a critical and moral emphasis on the ontologically constitutive role of land, water and air in culture and social interaction.[18]

Greschke's[19] study of ethnic group inhabiting a common virtual space in the World Wide Web (WWW) is an interesting one. While people inhabit physically on locations in different socio-geographical contexts, any focus on the research in a pluri-local and computer-mediated field is a challenge. In a provoking study, authors Adolfo and Ardèvol[20] argue that dialogical and situated ethical practice that takes into account every particular context when making any ethical decision during Internet research should be more apt in a local context while technology comes as a context. Muñoz[21] has undertaken an enquiry whether orthodox instruments and procedures of offline conventional researches are adaptable to the virtual context. Rybas and Gajjala[22] suggested that researchers studying the production of subjectivities in identity at the intersection of local/global and online/offline environments in techno-spaces must engage in the production of culture and subjectivity in a specific context.

Thousands of subcultures and countercultures exist within society where a dominant culture attains supremacy. Food, language, region, religion, caste, sexuality and ethnicity are examples. Virtual ethnographic studies executed in a variety of ways give importance to cultural diversities represented by subcultures and countercultures where a dominant culture prevails. Challenges of mediation, of online settings and shifts in distance or in time, here subsumed under the term *digital ethnography*, are all met in the course of trying to establish this engagement. It is necessary that undertaking exploration of the social media–powered mechanics of social change must pass through categories, conceptual tools reflecting particular subjectivity and moral emphasis, and should deviate from western hegemonising and homogenising analytical practices and terminologies.

Internet dystopia

What is the expanse of techno-scepticism? How is it relevant to discuss Internet and social media platforms in India? Does the Gandhian intellectual uneasiness with technology in the modern idea of Indian nationhood reflect up on the techno-scepticism grown over centuries? In fact, techno-scepticism is an old debate and somehow as old as Socrates, who started what may have been the first technology scare. In the book *Phaedrus*,[23] Socrates lamented the invention of writing, which 'creates forgetfulness' in the soul. Instead of remembering for themselves, Socrates warned, new readers of his age were blindly trusting in 'external written characters'. The library was ruining the mind, he believed. Books were ruining memories. The first techno-scepticism was thus born of Socrates.

Printing press only made things more badly. Gutenberg machine was lamented by some sections of people in modern era. In the seventeenth century, in *The Anatomy of Melancholy*, Robert Burton complained of the 'vast chaos and confusion of books' that make the eyes and fingers throb. The problem was the speed of transmission by 1890. One eminent physician blamed 'the pelting of telegrams' for triggering an outbreak of mental illness. Subsequently came in radio and television, which poisoned the mind with passive pleasure. Children, it was said, had stopped reading books with the penetration of television into our living room. Socrates would be pleased again!

Therefore, the sort of techno-scepticism born of Gandhi in the modern-era India is not new. It is still growing. Here it is right to reproduce briefly the Internet scepticism, which has grown into a powerful thought over the

16

last few decades after Internet and social media came in. What comes to any discussion on Internet scepticism at the beginning is the cultural critic Neil Postman's book *Technopoly: The Surrender of Culture to Technology*,[24] which was an interesting case to look at technology in a sceptic framework. Our culture is subservient to technologies in two ways: invisible and visible. Certainly, Internet would come under the banner of a visible coloniser. I am thinking about the compulsory punching system implemented in educational institutions in Kerala. Technopoly, a word Postman capitalises throughout the book, is a society which believes that one of the goals of human labour and thought is efficiency. The technical calculation is in all respects superior to human judgement. I have seen professors and employees of government queuing at punching time to mark their fingerprints. However, I am thinking beyond that. We have implanted seeds of a techno-rational society in which technological solutions are devised for human errors. For example, punching machine in government offices was introduced to check punctuality, sincerity and professional commitment among government employees. Ironically, by evening, a huge punching lineup is seen in offices. Employees are in a hurry to leave office. They are in a hurry to leave the office right at the office time, not bothering the work they are about to finish. Time is important. It gives a negative message that they are not using office time productively, let alone dissatisfaction among staff due to the technological solution executed by the employer, the government. Or another example of technological solution bringing harm is when employees bringing private motors to office. In a hurry to move home and office to and fro, most of us forget to heed attention to the price of environmental pollution. Our private choices have public causes. Therefore, rationalisation of technology has its own unintended consequences.

Sven Birkerts, author of *The Gutenberg Elegies: The Fate of Reading in an Electronic Age*[25], had an important contribution to techno-scepticism. He became verbal about the decline of reading culture in the age of digital technology. Sometime ago, one of my students was taking a seminar presentation on New Age technology. She was pointing to a story in which she narrated how technology has been deeply derailing the old system and reinstating a new system of learning, reading and information sharing. She narrated her personal experiences with Internet. When she was at school, she often takes at least a month in advance for the preparation of a seminar presentation as part of continuous evaluation. However, Internet changed everything when she was in her degree classes. She prepares seminar just by a night for the undergraduate courses. Internet is there. See, the change happened as one month of rigorous effort, reading and learning for a seminar has been eased by just a night's effort by a technology called Internet. Clifford Stoll in the book *High-Tech Heretic: Reflections of a Computer Contrarian*[26] believes that there is no substitute for a certain amount of hard slog when it comes to learning and that Internet cannot be a substitute for certain things in learning process. People are found going lazy about everything. Computer is a culprit. It makes people lazy and easy-going and makes them love only amateurism and entertainment. In *The Flickering Mind: The False Promise of Technology in the Classroom and How Learning Can Be Saved*, author Todd Oppenheimer[27] chronicles the ways in which computer technology in the schools has been an utter failure. Computers created a generation without thinking abilities but passive consumers.

The problems of technology have become a serious concern in the work of University of Chicago law professor Cass Sunstein's book *Republic.com* and updated version *Republic.com.2.0*,[28] which upheld that political deliberation through Internet is increasingly fragmented. He asked the question what happens to democracy and free speech if people use the Internet to listen and speak only to like-minded people and thoroughly rethinks the critical relationship between democracy and the Internet in a world where partisan political speak at social platforms has emerged as a significant political force. Here the observation is apt if you consider a society with strong social cleavages and social ostracisms. Internet too is a playground of old monopolies. At the same time technology writer Andre Keen has three books on Internet critique. In the book *The Cult of the Amateur: How Today's Internet Is Killing Our Culture*[29] he has placed social media in the context of debut success of amateurism where unskilled and non-professional talents are leveraging Internet at the cost of professionalism and culture. In *Digital Vertigo: How Today's Online Social Revolution Is Dividing, Diminishing, and Disorienting Us*,[30] Keen continued that critique of Internet in the sense that privacy is sold for market by digital companies without getting consent from the users. He warned of the danger of privacy loss in the age of Internet. *The Internet Is Not the Answer* is the latest book by Keen[31], who observes how Internet is creating inequality. In *Devices of the Soul: Battling for Our Selves in an Age of Machines*,[32] technology writer Steve Talbott observed that we have simply given power to technology while transferring almost all intimate information over to social networks and detaching from physical relations. Techno-rationality will ultimately destroy our human rationality while we replace technology to solve our human errors in the name of efficiency. Nick Carr, in the book *The Big Switch: Rewiring the World, from Edison to Google*,[33] recounted that utopia of equality would not materialise. Internet is moving away from many to few. Here the author also tries to unravel the issue of privacy in a world of interconnections.

18

Against the Machine: Being Human in the Era of the Electronic Mob, by Lee Siegel,[34] predicts the totalising effect of screen culture in our lives. Mark Bauerlein's noted book[35] *The Dumbest Generation: How the Digital Age Stupefies Young Americans and Jeopardizes Our Future (Or, Don't Trust Anyone under 30)* has the central thesis that the current generation is less accomplished and skilled than their predecessors. It was the result of their pervasive use of new media in the form of computers, Internet, cell phones, websites, blogging and Facebook. It is timely to reflect upon the writings in *Digital Barbarism: A Writer's Manifesto* by Mark Helprin,[36] which is a timely intervention on the subject of copyright issues in the age of cut-and-paste culture in Internet. Despite our wondrous technologies and scientific advances, we are nurturing a culture of diffusion, fragmentation and detachment. You will get this impression about connected world if you go through the pages of *Distracted: The Erosion of Attention and the Coming Dark Age* by Maggie Jackson.[37]

John Freeman,[38] an American literary critic, in the book The *Tyranny of E-mail: The Four-Thousand-Year Journey to Your Inbox*, has been vocal about the way in which emails are taking toll of our valuable time, which indeed changes the entire gamut of our social relations. Wisdom of the crowds indeed diminishes the importance and uniqueness of the individual voice. *You Are Not a Gadget* by artist and computer scientist Jaron Lanier[39] has been a timely intervention. He was looking at the implications that *digital Maoism* or *cybernetic totalism* has for our society. He observed that 'culture of sadism' has gone mainstream by way of anonymity, which has helped enable the darker side of human nature. Nasty, anonymous attacks on individuals and institutions have flourished. Nick Carr,[40] in *The Shallows: What the Internet Is Doing to Our Brains*, has gone farther in the scepticism of technology. We are losing our capacity for concentration, contemplation and reflection. William Powers, in Hamlet's *BlackBerry: A Practical Philosophy for Building a Good Life in the Digital Age*[41] (2010), has been critical of the technology we are using. We are born to check emails and our obsessive connectivity has effect on our brains and our very way of life. Catherine Steiner-Adair, EdD, and Teresa H. Barker's book *The Big Disconnect: Protecting Childhood and Family Relationships in the Digital Age*[42] has an interesting take on the effect of technology on kids and how to become healthy in an ever-changing technological world.

Here the lists of books mentioned are not exhaustive of the literary works on digital scepticism. However, they are useful to locate the dystopia on Internet.

Internet utopia

Utopians of the connected age gives you a different story of people who actually took part in the big changes of our time. Lesser participation makes bigger changes. Gone were the days when bloody struggles, street fights, arms, ammunitions and stone pelting created big changes for our parents and their parents. In his techno-future classic book *Being Digital* MIT Media Lab visionary Nicholas Negroponte[43] opined that business success depends on ability to convert products into digital forms. He predicted the digital age is coming and in his view, it cannot be denied or stopped. A good literature on the digital utopia could be seen in *Out of Control: The New Biology of Machines, Social Systems, and the Economic World*, where Kevin Kelly[44] examines the impact of the hive-mind model as it spreads into the scientific and technological communities. He demonstrates quite convincingly how the technological is becoming biological. In the book *The Future and Its Enemies*, author Virginia Postrel argues that future depends not on sticking to a centralised vision but to open-ended trial and error society. It resonates with a post-money, situational-ethic society.[45] Especially in the central chapter, 'The Tree of Knowledge', Postrel points to the rise of an open society which Internet could have created.

Crowd has a wisdom and according to James Surowiecki, wise crowds – independence, diversity of opinion, decentralisation and a way to aggregate the results – are of course good for collective actions. In *The Wisdom of Crowds: Why the Many Are Smarter Than the Few and How Collective Wisdom Shapes Business, Economies, Societies and Nations* James Surowiecki[46] says that crowd is smarter than elite few. People power is more powerful than those in the power. The mass will replace monopoly of the elite few. Internet helps people on the social walls to challenge the highhanded conventional elite lines. Crowd gets more visibility and acceptability through Internet. Internet is their liberating philosophy. Chris Anderson, in *The Long Tail: Why the Future of Business Is Selling Less of More*,[47] observes that 'The Long Tail' is really about the economics of abundance, an entirely new model for business that is just starting to show its power as unlimited selection reveals new truths about what consumers want and how they want to get it. However, it is not just a business model. People in connected age decide on who and when their leaders and every online act become a political choice.

Author Steven Johnson, in the book *Everything Bad Is Good for You*,[48] contextualises the case of Internet utopias by placing the core argument that popular culture is an IQ booster. Following Marshall McLuhan, Johnson observed that it is not the content but rather the interactive style of delivery (the 'medium') that engages us in a cognitive workout and ultimately results in the drastic IQ increases of post–World War II period. Internet is the latest addition in this process. Glenn Reynolds, *An Army of Davids: How Markets and Technology Empower Ordinary People to Beat Big Media, Big Government, and Other Goliaths*,[49] tells the great advantages of technology. Technology could empower individuals to determine their own futures and to defeat those who would enslave them. It elaborates how individuals, as opposed to large organisations, media and government, will become the primary moving force behind changes in journalism, politics, business, technology, charity, space exploration and overall human advancement. How exactly did David defeat Goliath? It was the technology of the slingshot which evened the playing field between the giant warrior Goliath and the undersized peasant boy David. Yochai Benkler, the Lillian R. Berkman Professor of Entrepreneurial Studies at the Harvard Law School, in the book *The Wealth of Networks: How Social Production Transforms Markets and Freedom*[50] observes the rise of networked information economy in which individual action oversteps proprietary strategies of the industrial economy and leads to social production. Well, it has significance for politics, economy, culture and society in Internet age. Peer production like Wikipedia and Linux allows user to generate content which are by any yardsticks political acts. It is people power coordinated through Internet, which challenges conventional monopoly of the industrial economy.

Clay Shirky's two books are important glue to the fact that technology has become a significant facilitator. In *Here Comes Everybody: The Power of Organizing without Organizations*[51] he investigates how groups are formed and operate in a networked society, exploring how new technology creates fresh modes of group formation. Internet helps us form groups effortlessly. Shirky, in *Cognitive Surplus: Creativity and Generosity in a Connected Age*,[52] argues that cognitive surplus was the outcome of the Internet, which was once made dormant by television. Don Tapscott and Anthony D. Williams's *Wikinomics: How Mass Collaboration Changes Everything*[53] and Jeff Howe's *Crowdsourcing: Why the Power of the Crowd Is Driving the Future of Business*[54] are manifestos that placed mass collaboration at the centre of organisational behaviour in the future. The power of many is more important than those few who had traditionally occupied power. Internet facilitates new togetherness because of the collaborative and sharing opportunities it provided to the people that were denied to them before.

Tyler Cowen's *Create Your Own Economy: The Path to Prosperity in a Disordered World*[55] shows what you can now do in the world of the Internet and new technology. Dennis Baron's *A Better Pencil: Readers, Writers, and the Digital Revolution*[56] places a narrative of the turn of digital scepticism in the contemporary social media age. Jeff Jarvis's *What Would Google Do?*[57] predicts how Google would become the future. Nick Bilton's *I Live in the Future and Here's How It Works*[58] makes a prophecy about how future exists in the present. Kevin Kelly, in the book *What Technology Wants*,[59] uses a concept called 'technium' which describes the evolution of technology into our culture.

As all technology belongs to a technological infrastructure in which many things coexist, Internet too is governed by a techno-sphere. In the infrastructure of human – technology interaction, any meaningful definition of Internet is insignificant without humans in it. The techno-sphere itself is a social system with individuals at the micro level and technology at the macro level. The individuals are humans in their social role as technicians, as producers and as users of technology. Producing and using technology is the self-organisational dynamic of such a techno-social system.[60]

Many are wary of Internet for its potential power in eroding characteristics that are essentially human, for instance, our ability to reflect, our pursuit of meaning, genuine empathy, a sense of community connected by something deeper than snarky or political affinity.[61] Many doubt if these instruments are 'social'. There is decidedly a prevailing faux about the camaraderie of Facebook and something illusory about the connectedness of Twitter. Many of us have opinions about technology that can be classified along the spectrum of being a 'techno-optimist' or a 'techno-pessimist', categorisations that reflect our general attitude about our technological past, present and future.

Moreover, many books, articles, terms and discussions associated with new media technologies and consequent social and political change potential of such Internet platforms have morphed to resurface as an American critical intellectual vocabulary from its various universities and media houses, which configure a global digital supremacy of America along with advancing a global homogenising political public. The vehement use of these intellectual western conceptual categories is so rampant in many of India's academic, media, civil society and popular circles.

Since most social media platforms are American, the values and social norms, which it reproduces, are American. The coverlet term 'Americanisation' has repeatedly been used to signify no more than a hypothesis regarding the genesis of a cultural example: media, dress, language, food, communication, mannerisms, lifestyle activism, foodism, cultural politics and so on, which may or may not be precise. It is applied arbitrarily within Indian media discussion to brand a collection of factors seen as threatening to nationalistic 'way of life', 'values' or 'identity'. This depreciatory use of 'Americanisation' sees India as adopting social practices and cultural values which putatively originate in the USA or specifically in 'Hollywood', 'Los Angeles' or some metonymic reference to that nation and its cultural production and soft power strategies.

Importantly, indigenising the debate about social media and its 'emancipatory' potential needs to be expanded to the attempt to developing a 'critical vocabulary' that equally reflects a 'critical mass' of intellectual concerns. Here comes trajectory of the term *infotopia*. It is obviously trying to locate an intellectual category at the interface of higher Internet culture and subsequent 'political public' in India with a higher concern for 'indigenising' categories and 'localising' analytical tools.

Social media: the Indian infotopia

How often do we know that many a discussion and categories underpinning 'social media–enabled changes' are useful to analyse native societies. Do we get a proper explanation for how in India people using social media for purposes that bring about a common cause can be traced in categories and concepts that Americans and Europeans and, to a degree, Africans discuss? Are the western categories and concepts really reflecting Indian realities in cyber sphere and digital natives?

Writers such as Burkhalter,[62] Ebo, Harcourt[63] and Stubbs[64] have examined the mechanics of reproduction of class, ethnicity, race and gender identities from offline to online. The fulcrum of digital media and political public debate worldwide resurfaced only to reflect some overriding intellectual 'categories of analysis' that are western. As discussed elsewhere about both the digital sceptics and optimists, most debate about social media–powered political changes and protest movements only imitated ever-expanding European and American intellectual vocabulary and conceptual tools that are detached from local settings of India.

Web 1.0 acted as a tool for cognition, Web 2.0 as a medium for human communication and Web 3.0 as networked digital technologies that support human cooperation. The latter is not yet fully in existence, but it shines forth in online cooperation systems.[65] The transformation from Web 1.0 to a Web 3.0 requires not a mere technological advancement but it is a social system based on evolution and a cooperative environment.

Technology must be defined contextually and locally by the particular technology and society relationship, said Tyler Veak at the *Symposium On Questioning Technology by Andrew Feenberg*.[66] In his trilogy[67] of books on the philosophy of technology, Andrew Feenberg has provided one of the most sophisticated theories of the technology–society nexus. For Feenberg, technology is the most important issue of our era. It is a major constituent of contemporary society and is intimately connected with politics, economics, culture and all forms of social and personal life. Technology can never be removed from a context, and therefore can never be neutral.[68] One of Feenberg's key contributions to theorising technology is connecting philosophically oriented social theory of technology with theories of democratisation. He notes that while technology is seen as a major power in contemporary society, it is often said to be incompatible with democracy. Feenberg, however, wants to demonstrate how technology can be part of a process of societal democratisation and how technology itself can be restructured to meet basic human needs. In this process, technologies should be created to help produce a more democratic and egalitarian society, thus focussing on the potential for the social reconstruction of society and technology.[69] This argument is relevant to this chapter.

For example, few people went to Calicut, a famous city in Kerala, for attending the entrance examination of a reputed central university in India. After the examination, one of them asked their friends, 'Shall we visit Focus mall?' – a shopping complex in the city. This story was shared by one of them in the undergraduate seminar programme. The presenter said people traditionally identify a place with certain symbols. Cultural artefacts, literary traditions, rivers, places and monuments are thus markers of that identity. Despite the country's ancient relics and architectural ruins rising over teeming cities, streets, rivers and roads, teenagers now hang out in malls, as it is a free public place with room to roam and access to a large crowd of people, something like a show business, exhibitionism. People have changed a lot. They are increasingly assimilated to a consumer culture, where they think they are born to purchase. So Focus mall is seemingly imitated as important for us more than the rivers or other traditional identities, in a place well known in the past. Therefore, malls have become souls of towns, restaurants their heart, hospitals their spirit, theme parks their vibrant charm, large constructions their name and physical objects their nerves.

Social media is a new addition to the commercialisation of our social architectures. Delhi was recently famous for its social media vigilance. At least according to the Aam Aadmi Party, it was true. Their social media campaign won the heart of the people. People believe that social media is a new connector. Middle class Indians are social media enthusiasts. Bangalore is famous for social media activism of ordinary people. Kerala has active social media denizens. Indian cities are profound social media social houses. Chennai and Mumbai are the heart of clicktivism.

Change is sweeping across India. Like the example mentioned, citizens increasingly identify social media with a new system. It is something very fascinating like the theme parks or the blockbuster movie you might be interested. Social media is like porn. Like car porn, movie porn, ad porn, cricket porn, book porn, now social media porn is an addiction. Be it AAP winning the assembly election at Delhi, anti-rape activism following Nirbhaya incident on 6 December 2012 or the anti-graft movement, social media is the winner. People think that it brought about changes. Social media gives hope to people. Ordinary Indians identify it with bigger changes.

People glorified it when Penguin withdrew Wendy Doniger's book. When Gail *Gayatri* Tredwell's book *Holy Hell: A Memoir of Faith, Devotion, and Pure Madness* was under controversy, which raised a shock wave following some allegations about a *math* in Kerala, people supported the author via social media. When media withdrew from reporting corporate exploitation and conspiracy, it was social media which gave public attention to injustices. Be it the Kiss of Love campaign, critique of government inaction or criminalisation of politics, people go instantly to social media and speak what they would feel about. It is a new way of heart speak, activism and citizen vigilance. An irrepressible band of new freedom seekers have gathered around Facebook for a nascent protest movement. They would speak against a broad spectrum of citizen concerns, injustices, unemployment, corruption and torture. They schedule social media for change. Believe that power of the people is greater than people in power. So social media is people's power.

The discussion on infotopia is at crossroads with dystopia and utopia concerning digital platforms. Social media has people power. On the other, it has also been a place of wicked games. Here at the trajectory of both social media for social good and social evil, young people often identify it with a new cultural metaphor. People think they were born to use it and speak through it. They would feel alienated if they are not able to use it. Using social media means digital citizenship, just like an electoral identity card in a constitutional democracy. In the electronic republic, digital citizenship gives them power to iconoclasm. Infotopia is the cultural metaphor of the electronic republic of our age. We are seduced by the archaic prophecies of techno-utopians and deserted by naysay of the techno-dystopians.

It is worth noting that social media is changing protest landscape in authoritarian political systems such as China despite state censorship and political repression. Increasing use of social media and diffusion of information is putting pressure on the government. Social media gives critical viewpoints that are lacking from nationalised media in authoritarian political regimes. So, when social media empowers citizens, it diminishes the state's ability to set the political agenda, despite Leninist traditions of control over information is upheld on the government agenda and state articulate the perspective that freedom of expression and information could pose a threat to their power.[70] Here comes the trajectory of ethno-perspective to digital technology.

More importantly, most of terms already popularised in western academia have placed the interface of social media and social change at the 'topple' down effect of political systems, which are anti-people. The rich vocabulary associated with analysing the emancipatory potential of social media is thus confined only to the 'liberal' question of 'political freedom'. The adoption of western discussion about the utopian and dystopian stipulations of social media's political power has widened the chasm between technological instrumentalists and substantivists.

A rich and powerful set of local narratives and experiences are important to analyse the social and political impact of digital technologies in India, which should emphatically avoid emphasis on western categories. There exists a strong reason to command a rich 'vocabulary' often reflecting local practices and indigenous characteristics. Importantly, indigenising the debate about social media and its 'emancipatory' potential needs to be expanded to the attempt at developing a 'critical vocabulary' that equally reflects a 'critical mass' of intellectual concerns. It is obviously trying to locate an intellectual category at the interface of higher Internet culture and subsequent 'political public' in India with a higher concern for 'indigenising' categories and 'localising' analytical tools.

Andrew Feenberg has developed a dialectical approach to technology that perceives both negative and positive uses and effects, while seeing technology as a forever-contested field that can be reconstructed to serve human needs and goals. As a result, he developed a position that falls neither into naive technological optimism nor into technophobia. Rejecting dystopic positions that would simply repudiate technology tout court, Feenberg argues that it is more productive to focus on its reconstruction rather than its vilification. Infotopia discussed in this chapter is reconstruction of Internet for the underprivileged Indians.

Conclusion

There is a 'democratic rationalisation' of technology as Andrew Feenberg has argued in his book *Questioning Technology*. The debate surrounding social media's liberatory potential in the social study of Internet confines only to the binary opposition between cyber 'optimists' and 'pessimists' that is less academic. The debate is highly polarised. It has almost become a cliché practice among media intellectuals and academics to criticise Internet and new media platforms for passion which bring about more harm than benefit. Nevertheless, the debate surrounding social media and its socially liberating role has been mired in serious trouble in the trajectory of binary debate.

Over the years, people are simply bashing social media and there are many evidence. They say it is used for gossip culture, hate campaign, casteist propaganda, communal riots, porn, middle class market, paid campaigns and so on. People madly attack social media for reasons that are not sound enough to disown the mass power of the medium. What motivated one to think social media in a sceptical note was that it had created unique problems in India. However, a whole bunch of social media enthusiasts believe that Internet could bring in what constitutional experiments did not achieve. At the same time, what is more worrying is that none of the previous models of analysis of social media actually reflects the Indian scenario. It is time to have a profound and realistic approach to a social media which could look at itself and its political significance in the context of cultural relativity, local situation and Indian particularities.

There is very important research gap in social media scholarship. In particular, there is no mention of social media and its political potential in the Indian context. Indian academics give no due respect to the fact that social media configures an important avenue for political communication and social change in India. This gap is at the centre of this theoretical exploration. Both Gandhian dystopia and Nehruvian utopia seep into relevance. Digital technology is more than a double-edged weapon. The point is how one might make use of it.

The dystopia or utopia does not seem adequately explaining the social media political interfaces in digital India. The dystopian projection of 'Net Delusion', 'Zero Comments', 'Weak-tie', 'Slacktivism' and Networks Without a Cause all address the digital activism in India without properly reflecting the complex 'flow' of people and society in the local context. This becomes more obvious in the complex interfaces of symbols like culture, language, food, dress, region and religion and rites. Utopian configurations such as 'Dragonfly Effect', 'Here Comes Everybody', 'People Powered Uprising', 'Streetbook' and 'Cute Cat Theory Talk' have acquired wider popularity; the idea of social media for political purposes steered by the western notions of human nature is out of way with the local cultures. Human society, especially in South Asian context, seems more emotional and attached to kith and kin than those of the rest of the world and in that complex attachment and emotional vibrancy, there is interference of local cultures, religion, language and so on. Neither utopia nor dystopia can sufficiently explain the Indian Infotopia since both are out of context with local cultures and social engagements.

Over the years, people are talking many things positive about social technologies. In places such as seminars, conferences, coffee shops, streets and television shows, social media enthusiasm is like a cult. If one criticises social media, it means swimming upstream against river flows. Television fame Shaili Chopra[71] calls it Big Connect. Technology writer Anuradha Goyal[72] tells about Mouse Charmers who make wonders with digital technology in a land which once was famous for snake charmers. Academic Pramod Nayar[73] observes it as a cultural shift. And he calls it Digital Cool to refer life in the age of smart technologies. Meenakshi Bharat and Sharon Rundle[74] call it Only Connect where life attains new forms in cyberspace. Everyone praise it. Are they sufficient? The following chapters try to give answers.

Democratisation of user-generated content on Internet has enhanced popular participation in the adventure of technology. It inserts agency into technical systems and provides openings for the democratisation of technology as such. Technology–society relationship is not unilinear. Certainly there is a significant degree of ambivalence in those relations. Here the chapter places the infotopia discussed in the Indian context. In the infotopia of Indian Internet, the underprivileged Indians benefit out of its democratisation potential. Technology is largely socially determined, which infotopia as a discourse on the multiple realities of citizen experiences on Internet exposes. Technology is neither good nor bad, nor is it a neutral force that can be used for either evil or good. It is a mirror of society. Infotopia just reminds the multiplicity of that technological experiences.

Notes

1 D. T. Khathing, 'Nehru and science and technology', in Raja R. Mehrotra, A. K. Agarwal, and S. Ganguly (eds.), *Nehru: Man among Men*, New Delhi: Mittal Publications, 1990, p. 143.
2 Willy, 'Industrialization, the Nehru style', 6 April 2012, <http://www.willylogan.com/?p=417#footnote_0_417>, accessed on 12 September 2015.
3 Anil Kumar Thakur and Debes Mukhopadhayay, *Economic Philosophy of Jawaharlal Nehru*, New Delhi: Deep and Deep Publications, 2010, p. xxi.
4 Ramachandra Guha, 'Verdicts on Nehru', *Economic and Political Weekly*, 7 May 2005, p. 1962.
5 Richard W. Bulliet, Pamela Kyle Crossley, Daniel R. Headrick, Steven W. Hirsch, and Lyman L. Johnson, *The Earth and Its Peoples: A Global History*, Vol. 1, 5th edition, Belmont, CA: Wadsworth Publishing, 2009, p. 751.
6 V. K. Natraj and Neeru Kapoor, *Gandhian Alternative*, Vol 4: Economics Where People Matter, New Delhi: Concept Publishing Company, 2005, pp. 105–106.
7 Express News Service, 'Gujarat mobile internet ban: Business takes a hit', *Indian Express*, 29 August 2015, <http://indianexpress.com/article/cities/

ahmedabad/mobile-internet-ban-business-takes-a-hit-2/>, accessed on 15 September 2015.

8 Ratan Mani Lal, 'Rising communal clashes in UP: Social media is to be blamed, says police', Firstpost, 1 July 2015, <http://www.firstpost.com/india/rising-communal-clashes-social-media-blamed-says-police-2321414.html>, accessed on 12 August 2015.

9 Bharti Jain, 'Government releases data of riot victims identifying religion', *Times of India*, 24 September 2013, <http://timesofindia.indiatimes.com/india/Government-releases-data-of-riot-victims-identifying-religion/articleshow/22998550.cms>, accessed on 1 May 2016.

10 Herbert Marcuse, *One-Dimensional Man*, Boston: Beacon, 1964, pp. xv–xvi.

11 Bruno Latour, *Politiques de la nature: Commentfaire entrer la science en démocratie*, Paris: La Decouverte, 1999, p. 194.

12 Pippa Norris, *Digital Divide: Civic Engagement, Information Poverty, and the Internet Worldwide*, Cambridge: Cambridge University Press, 2001.

13 Daniel Domínguez, Anne Beaulieu, Adolfo Estalella, Edgar Gómez, Bernt Schnettler, and Rosie Read, 'Virtual ethnography', *Forum: Qualitative Social Research*, 8 (3), September 2007, <http://www.qualitative-research.net/index.php/fqs/article/view/274/601>, accessed on 12 December 2013.

14 Phillip Vannini, Jaigris Hodson, and April Vannini, 'Toward a technography of everyday life: The methodological legacy of James W. Carey's ecology of techno culture as communication', June 2009, <http://dspace.royalroads.ca/docs/bitstream/handle/10170/165/TechnographyPreprint.pdf?sequence=1>, accessed on 13 November 2014.

15 M. Whitty, 'Liar, liar! An examination of how open, supportive and honest people are in chat rooms', *Computers in Human Behavior*, 18, 2002, pp. 343–352; M. Whitty, 'Cyber-flirting: Playing at love', *Theory and Psychology*, 13 (3), 2003, pp. 339–357; M. Whitty, 'Peering into online bedroom windows: Considering the ethical implications of investigating Internet relationships and sexuality', in E. A. Buchanan (ed.), *Virtual Research Ethics: Issues and Controversies*, Hershey, PA: Information Science Publishing, 2004, pp. 203–218; Clegg Smith, 'Electronic eavesdropping: The ethical issues involved in conducting a virtual ethnography', in M. D. Johns, S.-L. S. Chen, and G. J. Hall (eds.), *Online Social Research: Methods, Issues, and Ethics*, New York: Peter Lang, 2004, pp. 223–238; A. Vayreda, A. Galvez, F. Nunez, and B. Callen, 'Participating in an electronic forum: The difference gender makes', *Paper in the Proceedings of Conference on AoIR 3.0 Maastricht: Net/Work/Theory*, International Institute of INFONOMICS and University of Maastricht, Maastricht, the Netherlands, 13–16 October 2002; and C. Mann and F. Stewart, *Internet Communication and Qualitative Research: A Handbook for Researching Online*, London: Sage, 2000.

16 See the following writings to know more about these areas of scholarships. C. Haythornthwaite and M. M. Kazmer, 'Bringing the Internet home: Adult distance learners and their Internet, home and work worlds', in B. Wellman and C. Haythornthwaite (eds.), *The Internet in Everyday Life*, Oxford: Blackwell, 2002, pp. 431–463; M. Bakardjieva, *Internet Society: The Internet in Everyday Life*, London: Sage, 2005; J. Suoranta and

H. Lehtimäki, *Children in the Information Society*, New York: Peter Lang, 2004; D. M. Carter, 'Living in virtual communities: Making friends online, *Journal of Urban Technology*, 11 (3), 2004, pp. 109–125; and J. W. Salaff, 'Where home is the office', in B. Wellman and C. Haythornthwaite (eds.), *The Internet in Everyday Life*, Malden, MA: Blackwell, 2002, pp. 464–495.

17 J. W. Carey, *Communication as Culture: Essays on Media and Society*, New York: Routledge, 1989, p. 9.

18 Christian Fuchs, *Internet and Society: Social Theory in the Information Age*, New York: Routledge, 2008, p. 4.

19 Heike Mónika Greschke, 'Logging into the field – Methodological reflections on ethnographic research in a pluri-local and computer-mediated field', *Forum: Qualitative Research*, 8 (3), 2007. <http://www.qualitative-research.net/index.php/fqs/article/view/279>, accessed on 18 January 2015.

20 Estalella Adolfo and Elisenda Ardèvol, 'Field ethics: Towards situated ethics for ethnographic research on the Internet', *Forum of Qualitative Research*, 8 (3), 2007. <http://www.qualitative-research.net/index.php/fqs/article/view/277/610>, accessed on 18 January 2015

21 Rubén Arriazu Muñoz, 'On new means or new forms of investigation: A methodological proposal for online social investigation through a virtual forum', *Forum: Qualitative Social Research*, 8 (3), 2007. <http://www.qualitative-research.net/index.php/fqs/article/view/277/610>, accessed on 18 January 2015.

22 Natalia Rybas and Radhika Gajjala, 'Developing cyberethnographic research methods for understanding digitally mediated identities', *Forum: Qualitative Social Research*, 8 (3), 2007. <http://www.qualitative-research.net/index.php/fqs/article/view/282/619>, accessed on 18 January 2015.

23 The Phaedrus, written by Plato, is a dialogue between Plato's main protagonist, Socrates, and Phaedrus, an interlocutor in several dialogues.

24 Neil Postman, *Technopoly: The Surrender of Culture to Technology*, New York: Vintage, 1993.

25 Sven Birkerts, *The Gutenberg Elegies: The Fate of Reading in an Electronic Age*, Boston: Faber & Faber, 1994.

26 Clifford Stoll, *High-Tech Heretic: Reflections of a Computer Contrarian*, New York: Doubleday, 1999.

27 Todd Oppenheimer, *The Flickering Mind: The False Promise of Technology in the Classroom and How Learning Can Be Saved*, 1st edition, New York: Random House, 2003.

28 Cass R. Sunstein, *Republic.com*, Princeton: Princeton University Press, 2001.

29 Andrew Keen, *The Cult of the Amateur, How Today's Internet Is Killing Our Culture and Assaulting Our Economy*, London, UK: Nicholas Brealey Publishing Ltd, 2007.

30 Andrew Keen, *Digital Vertigo: How Today's Online Social Revolution Is Dividing, Diminishing, and Disorienting Us*, New York: St. Martin's Press, 2012.

31 Andrew Keen, *The Internet Is Not the Answer*, New York: Atlantic Monthly Press, 2015.

32 Steve Talbott, *Devices of the Soul: Battling for Our Selves in an Age of Machines*, Sebastopol, CA: O'Reilly Media Inc, 2007.

33 Nick Carr, *The Big Switch: Rewiring the World, from Edison to Google*, New York, NY: W. W. Norton & Company, 2008.

34 Lee Siegel, *Against the Machine: Being Human in the Age of the Electronic Mob*, New York: Spiegel & Grau, 2008.

35 Mark Bauerlein, *The Dumbest Generation: How the Digital Age Stupefies Young Americans and Jeopardizes Our Future (Or, Don't Trust Anyone under 30)*, New York, NY: Tarcher/Perigee, 2008.

36 Mark Helprin, *Digital Barbarism: A Writer's Manifesto*, New York: HarperCollins, 2009.

37 Maggie Jackson, *Distracted: The Erosion of Attention and the Coming Dark Age*, Amherst, NY: Prometheus Books, 2009.

38 John Freeman, *The Tyranny of E-Mail: The Four-Thousand-Year Journey to Your Inbox*, New York: Scribner, 2011.

39 Jaron Lanier, *You Are Not a Gadget*, New York: Vintage, 2010.

40 Nick Carr, *The Shallows: What the Internet Is Doing to Our Brains*, New York: W. W. Norton & Company, 2010.

41 William Powers, *Hamlet's BlackBerry: A Practical Philosophy for Building a Good Life in the Digital Age*, New York: Harper, 2010.

42 Catherine Steiner-Adair and Teresa H. Barker, *The Big Disconnect: Protecting Childhood and Family Relationships in the Digital Age*, New York: Harper, 2014.

43 Nicholas Negroponte, *Being Digital*, New York: Alfred A. Knopf, 1995.

44 Kevin Kelly, *Out of Control: The New Biology of Machines, Social Systems, and the Economic World*, New York: Basic Books, 1992.

45 Virginia Postrel, *The Future and Its Enemies: The Growing Conflict over Creativity, Enterprise, and Progress*, New York: Free Press, 1998.

46 James Surowiecki, *The Wisdom of Crowds: Why the Many Are Smarter Than the Few and How Collective Wisdom Shapes Business, Economies, Societies and Nations*, New York: Anchor, 2004.

47 Chris Anderson, The *Long Tail: Why the Future of Business Is Selling Less of More*, New York, NY: Hyperion, 2006.

48 Steven Johnson, *Everything Bad Is Good for You*, New York: Riverhead Trade, 2006.

49 Glenn Reynolds, *An Army of Davids: How Markets and Technology Empower Ordinary People to Beat Big Media, Big Government, and Other Goliaths*, Nashville, TN: Nelson Current, 2006.

50 Yochai Benkler, *The Wealth of Networks: How Social Production Transforms Markets and Freedom*, New Haven and London: Yale University Press, 2006.

51 Clay Shirky, *Here Comes Everybody: The Power of Organizing without Organizations*, London: Penguin, 2008.

52 Clay Shirky, *Cognitive Surplus: Creativity and Generosity in a Connected Age*, London: Penguin Press, 2010.

53 Don Tapscott and Anthony D. Williams, *Wikinomics: How Mass Collaboration Changes Everything*, London: Penguin, 2008.

54 Jeff Howe, *Crowdsourcing: Why the Power of the Crowd Is Driving the Future of Business*, New York: Crown Business, 2008.

55 Tyler Cowen, *Create Your Own Economy: The Path to Prosperity in a Disordered World*, Connecticut: Tantor Media, 2009.

56 Dennis Baron, *A Better Pencil: Readers, Writers, and the Digital Revolution*, New York: Oxford University Press, 2009.
57 Jeff Jarvis, *What Would Google Do?*, New York: Harper Business, 2009.
58 Nick Bilton, *I Live in the Future & Here's How It Works*, New York: Crown Business, 2010.
59 Kevin Kelly, *What Technology Wants*, New York: Viking Adult, 2010.
60 Wolfgang Hofkirchner, 'A critical social systems view of the Internet', *Philosophy of the Social Sciences*, 37 (4), 2007, pp. 471–500.
61 Bill Killer, 'The Twitter trap', *New York Times*, 18 May 2011, <http://www.nytimes.com/2011/05/22/magazine/the-twitter-trap.html?_r=0>, accessed on 8 December 2012.
62 B. Burkhalter, 'Reading race online: Discovering racial identity in usenet discussions', in M. Smith and P. Kollack (eds.), *Communities in Cyberspace*, New York: Routledge, 1999, pp. 60–75.
63 W. Harcourt, *Women@Internet: Creating New Cultures in Cyberspace*, New York: Zed Books, 1999.
64 P. Stubbs, 'Virtual diaspora? Imagining Croatia on-line', *Sociological Research Online*, 4 (2), 1999, <http://www.socresonline.org.Uk/4/2/stubbs.html>, accessed on 23 March 2006.
65 Celina Raffl, Wolfgang Hofkirchner, Christian Fuchs, and Matthias Schafranek, 'The web as techno-social system: The emergence of Web 3.0', in R. Trappl (ed.), *Cybernetics and Systems 2008*, Vienna: Austrian Society for Cybernetic Studies, 2008, pp. 604–609.
66 Tyler Veak, 'Whose technology? Whose modernity?: Questioning Feenberg's questioning technology', Symposium on Questioning Technology by Andrew Feenberg, 11th Biennial Conference of the Society for Philosophy and Technology, San Jose, California, 1999. [*Science, Technology and Human Values*, Spring 2000, pp. 238–242.]
67 The trilogies are Andrew Feenberg, *Critical Theory of Technology*, New York: Oxford University Press, 1991; *Alternative Modernity*, Berkeley: University of California Press, 1995; and *Questioning Technology*, New York and London: Routledge, 1999.
68 Feenberg 1999: 213.
69 Douglas Kellner, Review-article on Andrew Feenberg, *Questioning Technology*, New York and London: Routledge, 1999, <http://www.gseis.ucla.edu/faculty/kellner/kellner.html>, accessed on 21 April 2016.
70 Ashley Esarey and Xiang Qian, 'Digital communication and political change in China', *International Journal of Communication*, 5 (299), 2011, pp. 298–319.
71 Shaili Chopra, *Big Connect: Politics in the Age of Social Media*, New Delhi: Random House India, 2014.
72 Anuradha Goyal, *The Mouse Charmers: Digital Pioneers of India*, New Delhi: Random House India, 2014.
73 Pramod K. Nayar, *Digital Cool: Life in the Age of New Media*, New Delhi: Orient BlackSwan, 2012.
74 Meenakshi Bharat and Sharon Rundle, *Only Connect!: Short Fiction about Technology and Us from the Indian Subcontinent and Australia*, New Delhi: Rupa, 2014.

2

SOCIAL MEDIA VIGILANTISM

Ranjith, reputed film director in Kerala, India, raged a social media furore in August 2014. The perturbation was pertaining to the so-called 'social media vigilantism' recently showed by people against film fraternity.[1] He shared his anxieties about the uncensored public sphere resurfacing on Internet, which anonymous user profiles are misusing in order to dishonestly disparage every single movie creative people try to make. He complained while harshly criticising artistic work, cyber activists do not seem to bother about the efforts and energy being spent for making a movie. Many such criticisms are unhealthy and borne out of petty reasons. He meant people who post against films without true spirit on Facebook timelines are insane. The film director dubbed those who make harsh criticism of films and film stars in connected spaces are doing nothing, but making a kind of 'toilet literature'. The comment infuriated social media enthusiasts. Provoked out of the buzz, they retorted back at Ranjith through social media itself. Social media sites went viral on the matter and a perusal of the Facebook commentaries could be paraphrased in the following way.

Fan activists have the right to express their viewpoints on every film irrespective of whose film it is. Social media is the town square. Everyone will have place in it devoid of any social cleavages. Film lovers get an opportunity to criticise movies, which they might not get in previous media.

While venting on this, in a panel discussion on a prime time news hour debate, noted social media enthusiast V. K. Adarsh[2] said social media is a storytelling place – to voice their stories, pour ideas, paint grievances and recite feelings. Later on, he posted a comment against the views of director Ranjith on 27 August 2014 in Facebook, which got over 300 likes. Quite interestingly, while the debate was going on for some days, famous film actor Dileep on 4 September 2014 Facebook[3] post reported that he was mercilessly vilified on social media for the divorce issues with his wife Manju Warrier, who is an Indian film actress and dancer known for her award-winning performance in Malayalam films. She is regarded as one of the most successful leading actresses of the Malayalam film industry. Dileep complained that the social media enthusiasts forget the fact that he was a father and an individual, while vilifying him through social media trolls. These are not isolated cases of cyber mob lynching of celebrities, film stars, political class, youth icons, business tycoons, sporting icons, elites and authority. The cyber mob lynching of authority and elites started somehow when Shashi Tharoor raged the cattle class controversy in 2009 on Twitter.

The social media trolls have unwanted negative repercussions. Innocent people have been mob-lynched on cyberspace over the last few years. Ramachandra Guha, Shashi Tharoor, Ashis Nandy, Shobhaa De, Shaheen Dhada, Renu Srinivasan and others had to undergo the severe consequence of senselessness and pettiness of anonymous cyber mob on Indian Internet. Television anchor Sagarika Ghose was one of the early Indians to point the fact that Indian Internet has become a playground of saffron cadres. In a 2010 tweet, she supposed that Internet Hindus are like a swarm of bees who form their colonies. She often faces conservative Hindu attack for speaking on anything related to Muslims or Pakistan or Narendra Modi or any other thing sensitive to Hindu conservative wings in India. Of course, there is little space in Internet where one can freely express one's thoughts, or, put it otherwise, there is no more liberal space in Internet. In Gautam Adhikari's book *The Intolerant Indian*[4] the author shares a personal experience in publishing an op-ed article by Ashis Nandy on a topic related to the re-election of the Modi government in Gujarat following General Election in 2007. In a chapter titled 'Hindutva Hate Mails' in the book *Patriots and Partisans,* author Ramachandra Guha shared his experiences of saffron hate emails flooding his inbox. Guha says just less than 10 per cent of the total articles he wrote were about BJP, Rashtriya Swayamsevak Sangh (RSS) and other Hindutva issues. He claimed that these articles brought him into contact with a particular type of Indians – cyber Hindus. He identified five distinct types of hate emails illustrative of the *Homo Indicus Hindutvawadi* – a term used by Guha in the book.[5] It must not be overlooked while documenting social media vigilantism that authors, intellectuals, activists and even ordinary social media speakers are targeted for their activities inadmissible for right-wing cadres. Internet is undergoing a scrupulous ideological antagonism. One is an ardent cyber Hindu colony, which is more conservative, rightist and fascistic. Yet, it should not be taken to disown the public sphere which was venting angst against ills and pitfalls of the celebrated Indian democracy.

A recurrent debate in the field of media and culture studies pertains to the hegemony of corporate media and its cultural influence on audiences.

Earliest works of the School of Frankfurt have significantly influenced this question. Theodor Adorno and Max Horkheimer on *cultural industry*[6] or Walter Benjamin on the *mechanical reproduction of art*[7] addressed this question. This school of thought introduced a critical approach named the *cultural imperialism thesis*.[8] This analytical framework has seen worldwide communication inflows as a display of global media power. Emergence of Internet and social media provided information consumers with the opportunity to become *information producers* and to shape their own cultural environment. This assumption has indeed generated new perspectives on the question of cultural imperialism in the context of global media and culture industry. It led social scientists like Henry Jenkins,[9] Nicholas Negroponte[10] and Kevin Kelly[11] to think that the digital revolution empowers citizens with more freedom of expression and more influence on their cultural and political environment. On the other hand, some theorists such as Van Dijck,[12] Andre Keen[13] and Evgeny Morozov[14] argue that economic interests also drive digital media. Aside from the corporate interests likely to affect future sociological patterns of human life, online social interactions are potentially shaped by technological infrastructures. Unlike the traditional public sphere, new forms of public deliberation might be subjected to technological determinism. The question of technological determinism addressed by writers such as Turkle[15] had the predicted technology recreating social architecture. Pierre Bourdieu, sociologist, anthropologist and philosopher, analysed the application of communication technologies such as photography[16] and television[17] before the advent of the Internet. Technological devices are generally deployed to perform inborn sociological practices that have been inherited by the members of a specific culture or social class over time and history. According to Bourdieu, this phenomenon corresponds to the concept of *habitus*,[18] which reflects individuals' belonging to socio-economic environment as leading to the reproduction of power relationships through generations. In fact, the application of information and communication technologies can be interpreted as a manifestation of a social *habitus*, mainly conditioned by sociological parameters.

Consumers co-produce online information which suggests they contribute to shaping media content. However, they do not control the infrastructure through which online social practices take place. Rethinking cultural and media studies over the light of the digital era requires differentiating the medium (social media) from the media (mediated social practices). If online social practices are mostly determined by their technological infrastructure, they do not give users the opportunity to perform their social reality. In the opposite way, such social dynamics could only be artificial and limited by the technological facilities available. Van Dijck argues that the way social platforms are designed is conditioned by economic interests and intends to ensure that a large number of users provide content, creating opportunities for commercial transactions. From this perspective, economic parameters are most likely to affect the quality of social interactions as well as citizens' ability to debate rationally on public matters.

Having analysed it, the real question is, can digital media create an alternate public sphere for the underprivileged? Does it represent a public sphere in our age? In order to locate this, I was further exploring a plethora of literature in public sphere. The first to come to our mind is Habermas. Here we need a perusal of public sphere literature. While doing so, let us keep in mind that social public in Internet we are fond of is a place which cuts across the apparent social cleavages in India and thereby breaks the stigmatised, feudalised and hierarchical social order, where people get a new citizenship, which were generally denied by previous media, dominant textual narratives and power hierarchies.

Stories go viral on social media. Underprivileged citizens vent their angst against the system behind such stories. Be it vilification or glorification, one might consider that behind every social media story, there is an untold element. Previous media often overlooked such stories. Only social media could expose the hidden stories. Hence, social media give shape to a public sphere which is not a homogeneous monolithic overarching Habermasian one.

Social media vigilantism, which underprivileged citizens have been showing for the last couple of years, has configured a new kind of citizenship debate in India. One may call it digital citizenship. Social media stories to which user contents give shape are cue to this development. A principal entity that caters to this new citizenship debate is also the public sphere, which, despite being untouched by popular imagination, scholarship and academic curiosity, found a new sort of takers. One could have seen them in Facebook friend list, Twitter hashtag, YouTube comment thread and so on. They are known in different names across different social settings. One may refer to public spheres in different labels to pinpoint the one refurbishing beyond the Habermasian public sphere. Issue public, micro public, multiple public, counter-public, Islamic public, Dalit public and detailed examination of such alternative public spheres are examined elsewhere in this chapter.

Social media vigilantism is a decorous pattern of social media use, where ordinary citizens have been fond of showing pageant statesmanship. People show their citizen commitment in Internet, more profoundly than they were before. They take up events and issues of their interest. Be it Penguin withdrawing all published copies of the book *The Hindus: An Alternative*

History, a monograph by Wendy Doniger, an American Indologist, due to pressure from right-wing forces. Be it media in India showing no interest for bringing to public notice the truth about the allegation in a book, *Holy Hell: A Memoir of Faith, Devotion, and Pure Madness*, written by Gail Tredwell, which had shocking revelations about a human god in India. Social media vigilantism, that is people power coordinated through solidarity, was the only strategy available to underprivileged people to register their angst against media insensitivity and government apathy.

Social media vigilantism is significant for underprivileged and the social groups on the social margins. For them, it dispels the social cleavages and primordial loyalties that arbitrarily bestowed meaning to their everyday lives in the past. It has power to displace dominant social spaces, media sphere and textual narratives. Textual narratives in the past have become Brahmanic – be it Bollywood, mainstream media, apparatus of the state and business. They were also monopolies. What other than read/write web could offer one a space that is more expressive where underprivileged could streamline public vigilantism? Social media is a mirror that reflects Indian mind and it could destruct it.

Over the last couple of years, people from different social streams – film, sport, business, politics – have become more and more conscious of social media scrutiny by ordinary citizens from all walks of life about the public/private deeds of the icons, in particular elites and the political class. Icons too began to be critical of social media vigilantism. Film fraternity has become wary of this vigilantism on social media sites. They have become highly alert on all their deeds, be it public, private or personal. Social media enthusiasts watch you, believe it or not! Sports icons, films stars, business tycoons, political class and bureaucrats become cautious of the extreme levels of criticism in connected spaces. Why are icons, elites and influential people critical of social media vigilantism? Intolerance showed by them is a cue. Somebody is wary of social media vigilantism. People's voice becomes public opinion. Icons and stars are not in a position to tolerate social media vigilantism. For they did not face such a dilemma before.

Indeed, social media vigilantism in India has been a warning for celebrities, youth icons, film stars, sporting luminary, business tycoons and even the political class. Yes, beware, you are increasingly being watched by the mouse charmers of India. At least according to Shashi Tharoor it could be more acerbic. Political class is warier of social media enthusiasts. For the literary fraternity, it is a caveat and if there are disagreements, please just imagine what if author Chetan Bhagat would say about it, when he was brought down following his July 2014 'childish' remarks on Israel's attack on innocent Palestinians.[19] Traditional media is no more an exception to the social media vigilantism that at least according to Deepika Padukone, who raged a Twitter controversy with the *Times of India*, was true. The *Times of India* (@timesofindia) tweeted a photo of Deepika Padukone. It was from an event captioned 'OMG: Deepika Padukone's cleavage show'. Deepika's Twitter (@deepikapadukone) reaction to the *Times of India*'s tweet was: 'YES! I am a Woman. I have breasts AND a cleavage! You got a problem!!??' Very radical position. Personal is political. It went viral and #IStandWithDeepikaPadukone became India's top Twitter trend for hours on the same day. Ironically, an article analyzing the incident for BBC news written by Soutik Biswas quoted views of social scientist Shiv Visvanathan, filmmaker Shyam Benegal and journalist Shivam Vij. It communicates the idea that still traditional media formats depend heavily on gatekeepers. Chosen professionals, experts and elites still shape public opinions for the mass audience. At the same time, content produced by other than professional and experts challenge the role of media corporations and traditional intellectuals. Social media now acts as the citizens' channel for information.[20] Here few influential elites shaping the views for a majority of people still dominate previous media. Soutik Biswas for BBC News was doing the same thing – reinstating the old practice of retelling stories from the mount of monopolies. Social Media vigilantism stood up with Deepika Padukone. They were comprised of underprivileged, the middle class and feminists.

Social media vigilantism busted the class side of communicative spaces. It debilitated elitism of previous media. It helped more democracy. Now be it the *Times of India*'s cleavage controversy, or Chetan Bhagat's Israel comment, underprivileged have been newsmakers. They showed their political commitment. Their views and deeds are making headlines and even becoming policy parameter.

Social public

Vigilantism, which was not possible in the centralised hierarchised previous media, calls for a redefinition of public sphere conceptions. The growing emphasis is that social media scepticism overlooks non-western context in which it was operating. The sociocultural setting is important for any technology; considering social norms, social cleavages, social structure and dominant textual representations. It means de-westernisation of techno-social realities upon the instrumentalist/substantive perception of technological rationality of the Indian state. Social media realities of Indians are diverse and discursive. So social media vigilantism is an infotopia which democratises Indians' technological rationality.

Public sphere as a discourse has been documented well in the descriptions of technology as 'non-neutral' or a 'mirror of society' presented by both Kranzberg[21] and Lasch.[22] Technology acquires meaning when it is positioned within a particular discourse. For example, Kranzberg recognises technology as a historically relative construct that possess characteristics neither evil nor good inherent in it, but at the same time it is not neutral; rather, it is actualised within the historical context that delivered it. In the same way, Lasch outlines that technology mirrors the shortage, qualities and the optimism of a society. It means individuals are likely to respond to technologies to the discourse that surrounds it. The future of technology thus rests on the metaphors and language we employ to describe it, observe Gunkel and Gunkel[23] and Marvin.[24]

The discourse surrounding the political potential of new media could be relocated in the tension between the 'private' and the 'public', as articulated in Indian democracy. Online media lend themselves to several uses, but they acquire agency as they enable the re-negotiation of what is considered private and public in public life. A political opinion posted on a blog or a song uploaded to YouTube present an attempt to populate the private agenda. It also challenges the public, with privately articulated interests to a public agenda determined by others. In the truest form of democracy, negotiation of that which is considered public is considered private takes places within the public sphere only. Social media vigilantism referenced in the chapter puts proof for this argument

The modern public sphere, according to Habermas, plagued by forces of commercialisation and compromised by corporate conglomerates, produces discourse dominated by the objectives of advertising and public relations. Thus, the public sphere becomes a vehicle for capitalist hegemony and ideological reproduction. Naturally, a digital medium like Facebook and YouTube, with an infrastructure that promises unlimited and unregulated discourse operating beyond geographic boundaries, suggests a virtual reincarnation of the public sphere.

The new citizenship social media enthusiasts reconfigure is a new vigilantism. Questions are on the air as if the rational critical public debate, which once re actualised public sphere, would again resurface in the hybrid world of Internet and social media. How could one look at social media through the prism of public sphere? Social media has been extraordinary for online political activists and underprivileged for the question of right to expression. For that matter, it has exposed many scandals and news that the traditional media did not expose or failed to bring to public notice.

Growing social media vigilantism is the offshoot of the rising power of ordinary citizen to conduct public scrutiny of even the private deeds of elites, authority and ruling class in the connected spaces. Public sphere literature is significant enough to locate it. Many social media behaviours reconfigure a public sphere analogy.

Social websites have rechristened a Greek agora of contemporary time. The basis of modern representative democracy, i.e. deliberation and participation has been refined, when political class speaks to voters through platforms. Government is delivering services through channels of communication. For example, Narendra Modi, the prime minister of India, to push the Digital India initiative further, launched Twitter Samvad in March 2015. It was a collaboration between the Indian government and the digital company Twitter. The service will allow people to receive tweets as SMSes from government offices. As part of the initiative, citizens will be enabled first to know the government's actions by receiving political content in real time on their mobile devices anywhere in the country.

Let us contextualise public sphere in this discussion on social media. Certainly, public sphere debate originally initiated by German social theorist Jurgen Habermas[25] has gone into a sea of interpretations, following write-up such as Craig Calhoun's,[26] Dahlgren's[27] and J. D. Peters's.[28] Habermas himself has written extensively on the subject. A summary of the work goes like this. Habermas in his noted book on *The Structural Transformation of the Public Sphere*, published in 1962, had two major arguments, which include an in-depth analysis of the genesis of bourgeois public sphere in Britain, France and Germany in the late eighteenth and nineteenth centuries and an account of its degeneration in the twentieth century. The decline was due to the rise of spectator politics where media and corporate began to control the people. Thereby they mediate over the public sphere itself. The public sphere consisted of information and political debate via newspapers and journals, as well as institutions of political discussion such as parliaments, political clubs, literary salons, public assemblies, pubs, coffee houses, meeting halls and other public spaces where socio-political discussion took place. What Habermas called the bourgeois public sphere consisted of social spaces where individuals gathered to discuss their public affairs and to organise against arbitrary and oppressive forms of social and political power.[29] The thrust of the assumptions of Habermas is precisely that of transformation of the public sphere from a space of rational discussion, debate and consensus to a realm of mass cultural consumption and administration by corporations and elites in the twentieth century, says Douglas Kellner.[30] Indeed, re-feudalisation of public sphere in the twentieth century was a pointer to the fact that the powerful corporations control and manipulate the media and state.

Social media vigilantism discussed in the chapter relocates public sphere conceptions beyond Habermas's theorisation. Indeed, public sphere itself goes to a multitude of debate after Habermas. In brief, Habermas's idea of public sphere has some original parameters, which are core themes that reconfigure a social media public sphere, which I would call, somewhere else in the chapter, social public. This discussion does not wish to go into more intricate issues of public sphere debate. The focus is to connect public sphere with social media. To make such an analogy of social media public sphere, it is more appropriate to think about a public sphere beyond Habermas. Public sphere as homogeneous, monolithic and elephantine could not be a best bet to test public sphere in social media age.

A lot of literature has, indeed, gone further beyond Habermas and made extensive criticism on the point raised by him. Nancy Fraser observed that Habermas's public sphere was restricted in terms of class, gender and bourgeoisie.[31] It is fair enough to think that Internet represented the voices and concerns of gender, caste, class, regions and minorities. It provides spaces for coordination, sharing, information and coalition that can lead to a powerful movement. Deliberation, participation and contention have become almost ubiquitous since the inception of social media in democratic architecture.

Internet has given birth to multiple public.[32] Given the large number of people who use Internet, the possibility for multiple public spheres is relevant and unavoidable. Public sphere via social media can be global or local, smaller or larger. For instance, Erimbayer and Sheller[33] details a schema for approaching different types of publics and take account of three different dimensions of a public sphere. Instead of a single public sphere, there are rooms for many different kinds of spheres.

Along with multiple public, a 'counter public sphere' could re-emerge in social media. Counter-public has been a configuration on identity questions, which is standing in opposition to the overarching single homogenising public sphere dominated by conventional power structures.[34] For instance, Squires[35] details several types of counter-publics, focussing on African-Americans. Beneath an overarching public sphere, possibly many counter-publics could re-emerge under the pale shadow of the fading public sphere.[36] Dahlgren[37] has investigated 'issue publics'. These publics are organised around the issue of identity (guess, caste, gender, regional development or religion). Anderson[38] studied the Islamic public sphere, in which identity has been based on religion. Social media platforms thus give immense opportunity structure to identity framing and where all previously excluded social groups on the social margins get a legitimate space unhindered by social structures.

41

Many studies have raised important questions about its functionality and practicability[39]; in particular studies by Palczewski, Papacharissi and Poster are important. One common refrain is that Internet has the potential to form a public sphere or to assist the public sphere that exists, depending on the approach, but that this is no guarantee that such an outcome will occur. Three conflicting issues for Internet and public sphere have located by Papacharissi.[40] Zizi Papacharissi describes the emergence of a 'virtual sphere 2.0'.[41] Access and literacy are likely unequal. Internet audience will be likely shrinking. This would be similar to strict issue publics or Sunstein's *Daily Me* newspaper.[42] Third, online public could expose corruption by commercialism and infotainment as envisaged by bourgeois public sphere of Habermas. Manuel Castells stresses the novelty of this sphere.[43] Jean Burgess and Joshua Green argue that YouTube is a 'cultural public sphere'.[44]

The call for more research into the nuances of new media platforms to theorise a global public sphere and to reconsider the magnitude to which social media could further rational-critical debate and facilitate decision-making[45] is relevant in the context of social media vigilantism. There were novel attempts to look into the use of Internet for activism and deliberation.[46] Virtual sphere has largely been deployed to understand political dialogue on Internet significantly ever since 9/11 happened, elaborates a study by Khan and Kellner.[47] Nevertheless, there are profound differences between 'cafés' and the Internet, the social networking sites and agoras and Saloons of the past, New England Town halls and the social media town squares of the world.

The political significance of the public sphere theory of Habermas has been revitalised by the writing of critics in the information era. Instead of thinking about fragmentation of public debate and political polarisation, Internet has given birth to multiple public.[48] Given the large number of people who use Internet, the possibility for multiple public spheres is relevant and unavoidable. Considering multitude of interest reflected on Internet platforms, multiple public analogies could work for framing a public sphere approach to social media platforms.

One of the reasons why social scientists distinguish digital environments from the normative public sphere is because social technologies provide everyone with the opportunity to contribute to public discourses. To put it otherwise, factors likely to affect the rational social interactions and sustainability of public opinion in a digital world might reside in the fact that the online public sphere provides every citizen with the opportunity to express them publicly. It is one of the most significant differences between Habermas's model of a bourgeois public sphere and the online public spaces of the twenty-first century.

Given the context of an extensive literature on public spheres, using a 'multiple public sphere' framework is appropriate to understand the social media vigilantism resurfacing on social media actions through deliberation, participation and contentious claims. Manifestos reflecting issue public on Internet are revealing, for example, the right-to-die advocates,[49] use of new communication technologies by non-governmental organisations,[50] Greenpeace[51] and Sister Group online facilitating RTI movement in India[52] investigated relationship between the Internet and issue public.

Drawing from Habermas's original conception of public sphere, now it is apparently useful to propose a five-point[53] criteria for locating public sphere analogy resurfaced through user-generated platforms in Indian Internet. These factors are important in making sense of public space through social media platforms, which configure social media vigilantism in the Indian context. Most obviously, any public sphere must be (1) *discursive and deliberative* whether online or offline. In that deliberative space, everyone should get (2) *equal opportunity to be discussants.* This means the sphere should be inclusive and must not be any factors that expel those groups of people historically excluded from the development of national mainstream. Along with this, in the discursive open spaces, issues discussed are substantively (3) *political and civic* in nature. When everyone gets equal chance for discussing and deliberating issues that are political, (4) *ideas be based on their merit, quality and generality* and not by the perspective of the speaker. This means, such spaces offer (5) deliberative, open, participative, contentious spaces for all those social groups historically marginalised. The trajectory of social media vigilantism is significantly an attempt to torpedo the tradition-bound social structure. Certainly, the traditional Indian social landscape was not discursive, open, inclusive, political, meritorious and deliberative. The development of national mainstream has had its own impediments, especially those of feudal social order, social stratification and superstitious beliefs. Now, Internet platforms give opportunities to underprivileged people to change traditional public sphere and access to it.

What follows is an extensive citation of cases of social media vigilantism. Linkages between theories after Habermas and cases of vigilantism are attempted. In doing so, there was a deliberate attempt to draw cases relevant to this discussion. It doesn't mean that vigilantism is after all not without trolls and mob lynching. However, the focus of this chapter necessitates citations of cases only relevant to the hypothesis suggested in the chapter framework. The random selection of references was drawn on a snowball-sampling basis on a digital ethnography over a decade on Indian Internet between 2005 and 2015. Rather than documenting an authentic national database, more emphasis was given to narratives, personal experiences and user experiences.

Social media vigilantism

'Price of Petrol will be reduced from midnight of 14/15 August 2014 in the range of Rs 1.89–2.38 (Rs 2.18/litre at Delhi).' It was a tweet from Oil Minister Dharmendra Pradhan and the information was first officially released through Twitter. One might often feel it as nonconformist in a land where the current affairs were usually sourced through traditional media. However, such a bold decision by a Union Minister was significant since people increasingly use social media sites to source news, and what medium other than connected spaces could ruling establishment think of communicating with the citizenry, where growing monopoly and corporatisation of news industry makes them more apolitical.

In a television panel debate, R. Unni, a Malayalam post-modern short story writer and screen writer, has categorically stated 'social media is more than mere connection in a society, where you teach young girls how to pee in the toilets without making sound of urine mixing with water'. India is a best analogy befitting this sort of a cultural setting: a society with a very strong cultural norms and social controls on body, mind and freedom of expression, be it personal, sexual or public, a medium that has no censoring means many things. Therefore, it is timely to think that social media is a genie that unleashes a new cultural setting. Dr Achuthsankar S. Nair, Hon. Director, Centre for Bioinformatics, University of Kerala, for example, once in a seminar event held at Government Brennen College, Kerala on 14 September 2011 shared his social media experience. He pointed to a generation divide or indeed a social divide in social media age. He was saying that he saw students talking about voluptuous YouTube video comments among their circles. While discussing, there weren't any kind of gender gaps among them. They talk freely. However, the comments in question were most sensual, licentious and unprintable. He said senior citizens like him would not have such a talk even in very intimate circles. Elder generation does not talk things the social media generation does. Certainly, one's Facebook literature, ticklish YouTube commentaries, personal sex stories and erotic in blogging sites, status updates and style statements in Instagram are by any standards political choice. They are a new kind of citizenship. It could not be disowned for being a toilet literature or gossip culture. They represent a cultural shift.

The Editors Guild of India on 23 September 2014 asked the Narendra Modi government to extend access to media of government activities. They shared anxiety over deficit in transparency in the functioning of the government. Modi government was suggesting ministers and bureaucrats to use social media to engage with citizens. People often feel it confusing. What does it mean to say transparency in governance in a political setting where government repeatedly urges to be more and more an open government? A cultural shift is certain. At the same time, it is the conventional monopolies, elites and corporates that are largely reprimanding social media vigilantism, just like the film director, quoted initially, pointed out. Definitely, social public is a boundary that demarcates a cultural shift ensuing in Indian life.

Social media vigilantism is a political question. The unprintable words, the unspeakable ideas and the revealing photos once uploaded are more than fickle and thorny acts. They are more belletristic, questioning the cultural background of the nation in the past, which were highly oppressive to representation, expression and self-actualisation. The old methodologies and parameters could not grasp it. Old moral and ethical standards could not explain the new culture. The label 'toilet literature' therefore signified an entrenched mentality in the Indian mind, a cultural stereotype being propagated by the Brahmanic high culture. Therefore, calling them insane is also a mindset that typically represents an attempt to control them from making news of the nation and making the agenda of the time. Let us call them the new agenda setters. Those who oppose them are an organised syndicate who are afraid of losing their social power, colonies and monopolies.

Noted Congress leader Mani Shankar Aiyar on 18 January 2014 mocked the then potential prime ministerial candidate Narendra Modi of BJP and said, 'I promise you in twenty-first Century, Narendra Modi will never become the Prime Minister of the country. . . . But if he wants to distribute tea here, we will find a place for him, at the venue of the AICC meeting'. He was indirectly referring to Modi as a 'chai wala' Indian who came from a backward caste community who serves tea. This usage by Mani Shankar Aiyar itself portrays a taken-for-granted attitude prevalent among upper-caste Indians that they knowingly or unknowingly deploy against political opponents. It is a pointer to the fact that in 2014, our nation was highly feudal and hierarchical. It is still a stigma in India that lower-caste community getting into higher position in a society that is seemingly an anathema to those thinking they are worthy of their birth than others. It means one should do jobs to which one has virtue. Socially ostracised citizens and introverted and subaltern people who do not speak polished English of whom, Jawaharlal Nehru once called English-speaking caste, have been making news in the connected age. Narendra Modi became prime minister, and Aiyar lost the parliamentary seat in Tamil Nadu. Narendra Modi did not speak to traditional media but to social media, and data speak truth that social media vigilantism gave a good deal. Social media acts made news for Narendra Modi, which traditional media sourced largely for its prime time debates. See my discussion with the website of the Prime Minister of India.

> Dear bijugayu@gmail.com,
> Welcome to the official website of the Prime Minister of India.
> We look forward to your support and active participation in good governance. Share your views and feedback to help us serve you better.
> Thank You,
> PM India Website Management Team
> Welcome to PMO India
> no-reply@pmindia.gov.in
> Fri, Sep 26, 2014 at 5:25 PM
> 'Can u respond if I suggest, "plz sir, do something to increase broadband connectivity in our country?" '
>
> Author on 26 September 2014

What should one read just above is what is happening today's social media India. Just an email means many things. The communication between the official website of the Prime Minister of India at http://pmindia.gov.in/en/ and the authors on 26 September 2014 is testimony. Log on to email at @sampark.gov.in. On the email, one could see a new public sphere emerging. The Prime Minister of India is accessible in few clicks. One could interact with him on the link http://pmindia.gov.in/en/, know the Prime Minister on the link @ http://www.narendramodi.in/ and could ensure good governance with participation on the link MyGov @ http://mygov.nic.in/. At the centre of it, there is cyberspace. From local to national, for example, government is accessible and transparent to citizens. The public spheres in India developed in coffee houses, cafes, at town squares, in the media, in letters, books, drama and art in the past have now turned digital in the blogosphere, Twittersphere, Facebook and viral video sharing sites. They are engaged social publics leading to a new kind of digital citizenship. Here, inclusiveness, openness, participation and deliberation are mantras of new public sphere.

What happens when every day the institutions, the authority and communicative spaces one comes across do not connect with citizens' lived-in experiences and the most one feels alienated from the system. You would call it attention deficit, when particularly marginalised sections, minorities and vulnerable communities are not able to get proper representation of their lot that it deserves. Attention deficit is particularly severe in India and caste minorities, Dalit, third sex, women, victims of development projects and so on do not get their genuine grievances redressed, because the whole social system and more particularly political power are alien to them. Therefore, in the contemporary age, communicative spaces and public spheres that are more inclusive, more democratic and justifiable are necessary for an efficient democratic culture. Social media is just an answer to that. It gives digital citizenship to underprivileged and poorest citizens. Social media makes it possible to touch the untouched. By typing, doing and being, sexual minorities find their solidarity in connected spaces. While resolving issues such as distance, access, time, cost and quality, social media facilitates learning opportunities for marginalised people.

Not all spaces we know are equal. Particularly, Indian society structured by inequalities and dominant groups could have advantage since they create rules for communicative action. In this way, when a mainstream culture participates in a public sphere, marginalised groups participate through invisible publics. Civic plazas, multiplexes and market squares already exist, as there are numerous modes of mass media outlets. The critical question is: can social media provide a voice for traditionally expelled and marginalised groups, which they were not able to get in the previous media or in the previous public spaces?

The attention gap could be bridged as ordinary citizens get a storytelling space in read/write web. Thérèse F. Tierney,[54] the author of *The Public Space of Social Media*, examined the three ways of public: spatial, media and networked publics. The first worked on face-to-face communication, second on one to many communications whereas the third was a paradigm shift as it represented a communication culture from many to many. Indeed, Internet has had a huge role in bringing power back to the people.

For ordinary women, social media is space where they could find intimate citizenship. Women find an alternate sociability in Internet who once were expelled discussants in the communicative sphere in India. Feminist writers have suggested that Habermas's analysis of the public sphere has been an intensely privileged one and thus their curiosity has represented a critique of the male citizenship model of the public sphere theories. Instead, they have argued that the bourgeois public of the past was never the public as we thought it should be. Nancy Fraser has been one of the pioneers of such thinking. Fraser has powerfully argued that commensurate with bourgeois public, there were instances of a host of competing counter-publics, including nationalist publics, black publics, elite women's publics, popular peasant publics and working-class publics. There were competing publics from the start. More obviously, Dalits could find a new sort of identity assertion in connected spaces. This chapter surveyed plenty of social websites to explore the mechanics of change carried in the lives of Dalits. Dalits find it as an important social avenue devoid of any social cleavages. Internet is undergoing a sexual revolution. One cannot disown it as just for being a meagre side of Internet. Rather, sexual dissent and Internet are more than mere acts of profanity. Social websites are making far-reaching changes in the lives of sexual minorities and ordinary women who engage in sexual activism on Internet. They are developing twenty-first-century intimacies.

The thousands of platforms and the various user-specific platforms have a lot to do with the political action. For instances, discussion groups, chat rooms, alternative journalism, civic organisations, NGOs, grass-roots issue-advocacy sites (Berman and Mulligan 2003) and voter education sites[55] are choices that are more political. Therefore, social media is an image-breaking allegory. It has power to demolish the old system and bring in a more inclusive one. Social media is a metaphor that becomes iconoclastic when people power brings big changes via networked public.

Exciting individual experiments are already born of read/write web. Now Indians are at an important technological infection point. Most of our traditional social system in the past has been designed by social structures, which had entrenched social hierarchies. Let us call it Brahmanic literature, mainstream media owned by corporates, public sphere colonised by elites and upper castes and communicative spaces monopolised by feudal interests. The public spheres created by social structures thus were managed by codes, norms and rules designed for maintaining old systems. However, in recent years, a fringe group of actors, be it underprivileged, housewives, mothers, poorest, and even middle class, have now started challenging the old hierarchical cleavage-rich public.

What do underprivileged people's social media acts have in common? They leverage participatory media platforms to work together, to tackle a problem, to share stories and facts, to ask hard questions and then shape a judgement on which they can act. The user-generated platforms are in fact democratic spaces. The democratic structure of the platforms itself caters to generating ideas and perspectives that are more democratic and acceptable. This is because such social spaces never stand with those who speak and spread ideas. Instead, connected spaces are places of shared opinion, connected perspectives and democratic opinion. People using platforms for protest, civic activism, advocacy and networking are now influenced by those who put their own perspectives and ideas. Internet provides unparalleled opportunity structure and un-opinionated spaces to gather information, which is vital for identity framing leading to contentious politics.

What happens if underprivileged do things, which normally we would assume that they would not? In recent years with the democratisation of technologies along with several cultural and social forces, we are moving towards a new class of producers and creators. It is like a 'do-it-yourself movement'. Mass technologies enhance individuals create what one may call personal fabrications according to Neil Gershenfeld in the 2005 book *FAB*.[56] Therefore, with the advance of social technology at the personal level, friend power is the new mantra of movements. In the cyber age, in movements such as India Against Corruption, Occupy Movements, Arab Spring, movement participation occurs prima facie as a matter of social solidarities. Participation of the mob is thus unstructured. It helped politicise those depoliticised citizens in a significant scale. Underprivileged could fight for gender justice, corruption, violence, react against the inaction of ruling class, join forces against hazards in work place and sensitise public on social issues. This is possible just by technologies that work at the personal levels.

Kanwal Bharti,[57] Jaya Vindhayala[58] and Shaheen Dhada's[59] Facebook arrest were testimonials for personal fabrications that challenge the prevailing social structure, ruling dispensation and organised inaction of authority. Underprivileged and middle class citizens with less expertise in using most complex technology would easily learn to use it. In doing so, they are able to do things which they would not previously do. See Aseem Trivedi's[60] arrest for Internet cartooning, Ambikesh Mahapatra and Subrata Sengupta's[61] email arrest and Ravi Srinivasan's[62] Twitter arrest, and they are testimonials to the fact that middle class and poor citizens are able to make social fabrications in ways very unfamiliar to old systems. Sunandita Sur, a Cotton Hill College student from Odisha, whom I met on Facebook in one of my Facebook profiles used for research, found her learning potential in Facebook and Blogger platforms. In fact, young people like her represented a generation who would do things by their own. For the learners, social media technologies were their learning environment at home. ISRO scientist Vivek P. Nambiar says in Facebook that an auto-rickshaw driver's love for space scientist had motivated the driver for not charging auto fare, which becomes a viral story on Internet. If not Facebook, what other medium would tell us stories that we should know? Anna Hazare – led anti-graft movement and anti-rape culture activism in social media sites created outliers in Indian Internet. It could create social fabrications at personal levels and people could internalise the spirit of such movements only because of a technology that they would easily access. People use tweetivism, streetbook, clicktivism, e-signaturism, emailism, e-petitionism, YouTubism and so on to create a new sort of activism powered by personal technologies in the networked public.

Democratisation of technological rationality is almost rampant over the recent years. Technology has become mature enough by now, and dreams and aspirations of change were prevailing here for years. What then made poorest, middle class and so on in particular marginalised and underprivileged realise that time was ripe enough for doing change in online spaces? The answer lies in a cultural trend and it is 'do-it-yourself movement' (DIY) with a high-tech facet. Do-it-yourself movement is commonly used to describe the act of producing, creating, adapting or repairing something that lies outside of one's professional expertise. Change makers of social media age are not traditionally change makers. The book *DIY: The Rise of Lo-Fi Culture*, authored by Amy Spencer (2008), had the view that DIY movement would empower people to do things on which they would not have mastery.[63] For example, Amy Spencer had the view that self-publishing, be it blog or some other online platforms, could be empowering for anyone, in particular marginalised groups. It is important for them to be visible and self-publishing is just an intelligent tool for doing that.

In the last few years, the combination of social computing, online sharing tools and other collaboration technologies has led to a renewed interest and wider adoption of DIY cultures and practices. More than consumers of technology, citizens are makers, adapting technology to their needs and integrating it into their lives. The movement is about using anything one can get at one's hands to shape one's cultural identity. One's own version of whatever one thinks is missing in the mainstream culture. One can produce one's own art, record an album and publish one's own book. The enduring appeal of this movement is that anyone can be an artist or creator, or be part of the movement for activism, protest and change. The medium is mature enough. The point is to get involved.

One might have heard about 'long tail' effect in social media. It is a popular business talk among corporate. While talking about it, professionals in the business world think that one is going to raise a business campaign. The reason for business success is social media strategy. One might understand the fact that social media is good for contacting many people simultaneously. For example, travelogue books about mountain climbing like *Touching the Void* and *Into Thin Air* have made big publishing a sensation only because of a new economic model for entertainment and media industry.[64] Amazon was the imagination behind it. It created the *Touching the Void* a phenomenon by combining infinite shelf space with real-time information about buying trends and public opinion. The result was growing demand for a vague book. This is significant. Business has moved away from an age of scarcity to an age of abundance. One could call it the power of long tail effect. However, it has stories beyond mere business success.

Think about the underprivileged, poor housewives and unsuccessful beginners making use of long tail effect. Social media is their strategic device. However, social media bringing in long tail in our social life is something different from bloggers making gain traction via social media by preferring search words. Chandralekha's[65] YouTube song has been making her a reputed playback singer in Kerala. While doing so, not mere market strategy made her a big debut success. Rather, it was people power that drives it. Underprivileged, unlike those of traditional hit makers such as elites, ruling class and monopolies, are now able to make their own hits because Internet allows more space. Therefore, YouTube singer Chandralekha was a long tail in Indian Internet, which was able to break an old system of social apartheid and reinstitute a new system of social inclusiveness.

The amateur WhatsApp song of Aznia Ashmin, Rasha Salim and Ramlath Azeez[66] has become viral in the net, made big impacts in ad industry and the song appeared in a mainstream movie. The amateur song's success was not a deliberate business success; rather, it represented a new culture of localism representing their identity in connected spaces. The song was a beginning that stimulates similar other songs from local communities. The song was also a long tail but it rather hit on the immobile social structure.

Patrice Flichy[67] introduces the idea that Web 2.0 provides amateurs with the opportunity to contribute to their themes of interest, confront different opinions and find an audience. In that sense, amateurs acquire an influence that, not so long ago, was the exclusive privilege of professionals and experts. According to Flichy, this social recognition of amateurs is particularly significant in the field of arts, popular culture, science and politics. Here one could find the importance of social media vigilantism emanating from the fag end of social margins.

The long tail has more takers in Indian Internet, but not from business world only. It had been motivating Parvathy Shetty and Maithreyi Nadanappa to write an online petition on the eve of a rape incident at Bangalore city. Fascinatingly, mothers' online petitions have been prime time news in national media channels. Here, the inspiring story is that the long tail effect of social media is torpedoing the old social system of rigid hierarchy in India.

Online petition by Mamitha Bhandare has found its entry in the Justice Verma Committee report. It was also the long tail effect of social media by which ordinary citizens could fascinate the attention of policy makers. YouTube video of *Peruchazhi* Malayalam movie part 1 makes YouTube hits in just few days because of the ability to duplicate Internet traffic. While doing

so, underprivileged get greater online attention, which they would not previously get from traditional media. Therefore, the long tail effect in Indian
Internet is that social media could go through the rigid social structure
in India that could bring a more inclusion space for the ordinary citizens,
which they would not get in previous media. Social media users are active
participants on online deliberation. So, the elites of the cyber age are those
denizens of connected space who refurbish social media vigilantism.

Indeed, Habermas's conception of the public was 'bourgeois, white
supremacist, masculinist' and it was also inconsistent from the beginning.
We need to recognise models of public spheres where there is the proliferation of a multiplicity of competing publics, some of which are 'subaltern
counter–publics'.[68] It is significant since the public sphere accommodates
the kind of citizenship that ordinary citizens find in connected spaces. It was
in the connected spaces that Risana Faisal, who I met via a Facebook account
created for research, has found a new citizenship as she was increasingly
feeling that Facebook had been giving her a space devoid of old cleavages.
The unmarried woman feels a new identity in Facebook. Women divorcees
were feeling life as so rejuvenating in Facebook as they were getting a new
space sense there. Ordinary housewives were feeling that Facebook was
like a second life for them despite their life at kitchen. For ordinary women
bloggers, the blog platforms were self-publishing options when publisher
after publisher rejected one's poetry or story and Facebook became a space
for gathering audience for literary taste. Ambitious academics found new
identities through fantasies on connected spaces. In doing so, they were
believing the immense opportunities of Facebook for self-speak. Ordinary
women found virtual identity initially on Orkut and later on Facebook and
Skype. Mu Zimei phenomenon has been sweeping across Indian Internet.
A number of young people like Achoo Mole, who I met on Orkut, which
has closed operations in India, on Internet makes sexual exploration. Kalki
Subramaniam, a transgender activist in south India, writes about transgenders on a personal blog. Then what other than social media could provide
people the power to connect with others?

Multiplicity of public spheres is the immediate outcome of social media
vigilantism. One example of all these is in what we call the emergence of
sexual dissent whereby LGBT are developing their own visibility. In doing
so, they shift the margins and the boundaries of the wider society. Internet is just hitting into that. Social media is a new social house for doing
activism, finding solidarity and spreading awareness and bringing the mainstream culture to incorporate the voices of the unrepresented.

I would thus argue that there are multiple, hierarchically layered and
contested public spheres. For example, see the sex workers' public sphere,[69]

the gay public sphere,[70] an 'evangelical Christian public sphere' and the black public sphere.[71] I think the term *social media vigilantism* must learn to denote a plurality of multiple public voices and positions. Unlike earlier version of citizenship, which often floundered by marginalising and excluding certain groups, social media in public sphere debate could not imply one model, one pattern, one way or one voice. On the contrary, *social media vigilantism* is a loose term, which comes to designate an array of tale telling and a multiplicity of voices, in which new lives, new communities and new politics inhabit. This label fits into the contemporary empirical reality of the ethos of pluralisation.[72]

Social media has provided a new space for the unrepresented in our age. It facilitates an engaged public. The attention deficit, in which underprivileged and poor people are getting no attention in the system, is under a serious challenge. However, technological artefacts resolve attention deficit. People making use of vigilantism on Internet platforms have the ability to torpedo old social cleavages. Net also creates a producer public, which caters itself to its needs. Personal fabrication in which people find their own solution to their problems will be further boosted by net. In long tails and engaged citizenship where minorities, sexual dissenters, women, Dalits, caste minorities and other victims of development projects find their intimacy and citizenships, which they would not get in previous media. The change will go on. Our imagination would not be enough to understand it. The power of technology to effect change is beyond our comprehension. Social media is just a political choice. It is what we call political Internet. It is just a beginning. The beginning of vigilantism.

Use of the social media as an alternative medium becomes an asset or a harm, depending on how it is taken for use. Social media from this standpoint serves as a tool and does not contain the agency to effect social change. Individuals, on the other hand, possess varying levels of individual agency based on which they can make use of Internet to different ends. It is important to avoid both the substantive and instrumentalist viewpoint that online technologies are able to 'make or break' a public sphere. It is necessary to understand that technologies frequently push in assumptions about their potential uses based on the political, cultural, social and economic environment that brings them synergy. For that reason, it is not the nature of technologies; rather, it is the discourse that surrounds it guides how social media technologies are appropriated by a society as a public sphere.

Utopian rhetoric habitually extols the democratising potential of media that are new. Dystopian rhetoric conversely makes cautionary tales against enthusiasm regarding the democratising potential of social media. Others characterise the democratising potential of Internet as simply vulnerable.

Habermas himself doubts the democratising potential of Internet, as he saw it developing in a commercial direction, with a political orientation that was largely circumstantial (Habermas, 2006). This chapter examined the democratising potential of online media, as articulated through relevant theory, research and online practices. This chapter first traced dominant narratives on public sphere theories, beginning with an overview of the public sphere, examining models that oppose or supplement the public sphere and leading into assumption that examines the Internet as an alternative public sphere for the underprivileged.

A fluid kind of political dissent on Internet gives shape to the social media vigilantism. It regenerates a communicative sphere that can reconfigure a public sphere as an extension of the traditional bourgeois public sphere. Internet gives opportunities to more diverse and multiple voices to be represented. More importantly, it has provided space for those social groups that have historically been marginalised. Internet echoes the voices of gender, caste, class, regions and all minorities. It gives space for coordination, sharing, information and coalition that can lead to powerful movements. Deliberation, participation and contention have become almost ubiquitous since the inception of Internet.

Citizens organise criticism against the ruling class for their pitfalls. Through connected platforms, now old London coffeehouses, French saloons, New England town hall, local churches, town square and bumpy street corners, which once cemented public sphere, have been resurfacing with new wardrobe attire in YouTube, LinkedIn, WordPress and Tumblr. Now, the public spheres of digital age are bringing about a new kind of public sphere where the norms and preconditions of earlier public spheres are revitalised. In an age when people are more connected and plugged in the electronic republic, their sociability is also transforming into new horizons.

Application of public sphere theory to the social media discourses of the contemporary Indian democracy shows that one of the most significant differences between the emergence of the bourgeois public sphere and the liberalisation of an inclusive online public sphere lies in the intellectual leadership. When members of the bourgeois elite led publicity and public opinion in the period that preceded the modern Indian state, every citizen now has access to the public landscape. Interestingly this is probably the reason why digital technologies appear to be prominent in India, where social media contributed to break old social cleavages. Indeed, recent social media vigilantism proved to be led by people from all walks of life. In this regard, the historical changes currently occurring in Indian society might be a particularly appropriate reflection of the democratising culture of the technological rationality in India.

Notes

1 See <http://onlookersmedia.com/ranjith-stirs-protest/>.
2 See <https://www.facebook.com/VKadarsh>.
3 See <https://www.facebook.com/ActorDileep>.
4 Gautam Adhikari, *The Intolerant Indian*, Noida: Harper Collins India, 2011, pp. 21–22.
5 Ramachandra Guha, *Patriots and Partisans*, New Delhi: Penguin, 2012, p. 69.
6 Theodor Adorno and Max Horkheimer, *Dialektik der Aufklärung: Philosophische Fragmente*. Amsterdam: Querido, repr. 2002, *Dialectic of Enlightenment*. Trans. Edmund Jephcott, Stanford: Stanford University Press, 1947.
7 Walter Benjamin, 'The work of art in the age of mechanical reproduction', in Hannah Arendt (ed.), *Illuminations*, London: Fontana, 1968, pp. 214–218.
8 Jean Chalaby, 'Beyond national-centrism: Thinking international communication from a cosmopolitan perspective', *Studies in Communication Sciences*, 7 (1), 2007, pp. 61–83.
9 Henry Jenkins, *Convergence Culture: Where Old and New Media Collide*, New York: New York University Press, 2006.
10 Nicholas Negroponte, *Being Digital*, New York: Alfred A. Knopf, 1995.
11 Kevin Kelly, *Out of Control: The New Biology of Machines, Social Systems, and the Economic World*, New York: Basic Books, 1992.
12 Jose Van Dijck, *The Culture of Connectivity: A Critical History of Social Media*, New York: Oxford University Press, 2013.
13 Andrew Keen, *The Cult of the Amateur, How Today's Internet Is Killing Our Culture and Assaulting Our Economy*, London: Nicholas Brealey Publishing Ltd, 2008; and Andrew Keen, *Digital Vertigo: How Today's Online Social Revolution Is Dividing, Diminishing, and Disorienting Us*, New York: St. Martin's Press, 2012.
14 Evgeny Morozov, *The Net Delusion: The Dark Side of Internet Freedom*, New York: Public Affairs, 2012; and Evgeny Morozov, *To Save Everything, Click Here: The Folly of Technological Solutionism*, New York: Public Affairs, 2013.
15 Sherry Turkle, *Alone Together: Why We Expect More from Technology and Less from Each Other*, New York: Basic Books, 2012.
16 Pierre Bourdieu, *Un art moyen*, Paris: Les Editions de Minuit, 1965.
17 Pierre Bourdieu, *Sur la télévision: Suivi de l'emprise du journalisme*, Paris: Liber, 1996.
18 Pierre Bourdieu, 'Structure, habitus, power: Basis for a theory of symbolic power', in Nicholas B. Dirks, Geoffrey H. Eley, and Sherry B. Orthrer (eds.), *Culture, Power, History: A Reader in Contemporary Social Theory*, Princeton: Princeton University Press, 1993, pp. 155–199.
19 See the report at <http://www.dnaindia.com/india/comment-chetan-bhagat-tweets-in-support-of-israel-gets-defensive-after-causing-major-outrage-2002894>.
20 See the report, Bollywood cleavage row shows India's 'crass' side, available at <http://www.bbc.com/news/world-asia-india-29306346>.

21 M. Kranzberg, 'The information age: Evolution or revolution?', in B. Guile (ed.), *Information Technologies and Social Transformation*, Washington, DC: National Academy Press, 1985, pp. 35–53.

22 C. Lasch, *The Culture of Narcissism*, New York: Norton & Co, 1979.

23 D. J. Gunkel and A. H. Gunkel, 'Virtual geographies: The new worlds of cyberspace', *Critical Studies in Mass Communication*, 14, 1997, pp. 123–137.

24 C. Marvin, *When Old Technologies Were New*, New York: Oxford, 1988.

25 J. Habermas, *The Structural Transformation of the Public Sphere: An Inquiry into a Category of Bourgeois Society*, Cambridge, MA: MIT Press, 1962/1989.

26 C. Calhoun (ed.), *Habermas and the Public Sphere*, Cambridge, MA: MIT Press, 1992.

27 P. Dahlgren, 'Media and the transformation of democracy', in B. Axford and R. Huggins (eds.), *New Media and Politics*, London: Sage, 2001a, pp. 64–88; and P. Dahlgren, 'The public sphere and the net: Structure, space, and communication', in W. L. Bennett and R. M. Entman (eds.), *Mediated Politics: Communications in the Future of Democracy*, Cambridge: Cambridge University Press, 2001b, pp. 33–55.

28 J. D. Peters, 'Distrust of representation: Habermas on the public sphere', *Media, Culture and Society*, 15 (4), 1993, pp. 541–571.

29 See a brief of Habermas and the theory of public sphere by Douglas Kellner, *Habermas, the Public Sphere, and Democracy: A Critical Intervention*, <http://pages.gseis.ucla.edu/faculty/kellner/papers/habermas.htm>, accessed on 12 January 2014.

30 Ibid.

31 Nancy Fraser, 'Rethinking the public sphere: A contribution to the critique of actually existing democracy', in C. Calhoun (ed.), *Habermas and the Public Sphere*, Cambridge, MA: MIT Press, 1992, pp. 109–142.

32 The ideas of multiple publics have been found more attention in the writings of R. Asen and D. Brouwer (eds.), *Counterpublics and the State*, New York: State University of New York, 2001, and Dahlgren 2001b.

33 M. Erimbayer and M. Sheller, 'Publics in history', *Theory and Society*, 27 (6), 1998, pp. 727–779.

34 Fraser 1992; and C. Palczewski, 'Cyber-movements, new social movements, and counterpublics', in R. Asen and D. Brouwer (eds.), *Counterpublics and the State*, New York: State University of New York, 2001, pp. 161–186.

35 C. Squires, 'Rethinking the black public sphere: An alternative vocabulary for multiple public spheres', *Communication Theory*, 12 (4), 2002, pp. 446–468.

36 N. Garnham, 'The media and the public sphere', in C. Calhoun (ed.), *Habermas and the Public Sphere*, Cambridge, MA: MIT Press, 1992, pp. 359–376.

37 Dahlgren 2001a.

38 J. Anderson, 'New media, new publics: Reconfiguring the public sphere of Islam', *Social Research*, 70 (3), 2003, pp. 887–906.

39 C. Palczewski, 'Cyber-movements, new social movements, and counterpublics', in R. Asen and D. Brouwer (eds.), *Counterpublics and the State*,

New York: State University of New York, 2001, pp. 161–186; and M. Poster, 'Cyber democracy: Internet and the public sphere', 1993, <http://www. humanities.uci.edu/mposter/writings/democ.html>, accessed on 6 April 2014.

40 Z. Papacharissi, *A Networked Self*, London: Routledge, 2010.

41 Zizi Papacharissi, 'The virtual sphere 2.0: The Internet, the public sphere, and beyond', in Andrew Chadwick and Philip N. Howard (eds.), *Routledge Handbook of Internet Politics*, New York: Routledge, 2009, pp. 230–245.

42 Cass R. Sunstein, *Republic.com*, Princeton: Princeton University Press, 2007.

43 Manuel Castells, *Communication Power*, Oxford: Oxford University Press, 2009.

44 Jean Burgess and Joshua Green, *YouTube*, Cambridge: Polity Press, 2009.

45 Craig Calhoun, 'Information technology and the international public sphere', in Douglas Schuler and Peter Day (eds.), *Shaping the Network Society: The New Role of Civil Society in Cyberspace*, Cambridge: The MIT Press, 2004, pp. 229–251.

46 Barbara Warnick, *Rhetoric Online: Persuasion and Politics on the World Wide Web*, Frontiers in Political Communication, Vol. 12, New York: Peter Lang Publishing, 2007; Diana B. Carlin, Dan Schill, David G. Levasseur, and Anthony S. King, 'The post-9/11 public sphere: Citizen talk about the 2004 presidential debates', *Rhetoric and Public Affairs*, 8 (4), 2005, pp. 617–638; Victor W. Pickard, 'Cooptation and cooperation: Institutional exemplars of democratic Internet technology', *New Media and Society*, 10 (4), 2008, pp. 625–645; and Steffen Albrecht, 'Whose voice is heard in online deliberation? A study of participation and representation in political debates on the Internet', *Information, Communication and Society*, 9 (1), 2006, pp. 62–82.

47 Richard Khan and Douglas Kellner, 'New media and Internet activism: from the "battle of Seattle" to blogging', *New Media & Society*, 6 (1), 2004, pp. 77–95.

48 Asen and Brouwer 2001, and Dahlgren 2001b.

49 T. McDorman, 'Crafting a virtual counterpublic: Right-to-die advocates on the Internet', in R. Asen and D. Brouwer (eds.), *Counterpublics and the State*, New York: State University of New York, 2001, pp. 187–210.

50 M. Mater, 'A structural transformation for a global public sphere? The use of new communication technologies by non-governmental organizations and the United Nations', in R. Asen and D. Brouwer (eds.), *Counterpublics and the State*, New York: State University of New York, 2001, pp. 211–234.

51 P. R. Biju, and O. Gayathri, 'Towards online activism and public sphere in India', *Indian Journal of Political Science*, ISSN No. 0019–5510, 72 (2), June 2011, pp. 477–488.

52 Anuradha Rao, '"Sister-groups" and online-offline linkages in networked collective action: A case study of the right to information movement in India', *The Electronic Journal of Information Systems in Developing Countries*, 52 (7), 2012, pp. 1–17.

53 P. Dahlberg (2001) has proposed six criteria that an online space must meet in order to consider it as a public sphere. They are autonomy from state and economic power; exchange and critique of criticisable moral-practical

validity claims; reflexivity; ideal role taking; sincerity and discursive inclusion and equality. However, it feels as if Dahlberg focusses more on an overarching single public sphere and less on one sphere within a multiple public sphere framework.

54 Thérèse F. Tierney, *The Public Space of Social Media: Connected Cultures of the Network Society*, London: Routledge, 2013.

55 P. Levine, 'Online campaigning and the public interest', in D. M. Anderson and M. Cornfield (eds.), *The Civic Web: Online Politics and Democratic Values*, Lanham, MD: Rowman & Littlefield, 2003, pp. 47–62.

56 Neil Gershenfeld, *Fab: The Coming Revolution on Your Desktop—from Personal Computers to Personal Fabrication*, New York: Basic Books, 2005.

57 Dalit scholar Kanwal Bharti was arrested by Uttar Pradesh government for a Facebook comment. Later, the Supreme Court of India on 16 August 2013 sought an explanation from the Uttar Pradesh government for arresting Kanwal Bharti for allegedly writing a post on Facebook in support of suspended IAS officer Durga Shakti Nagpal.

58 Jaya Vindhayala, the state general secretary and a senior woman activist of the NGO outfit People's Union for Civil Liberties (PUCL), was imprisoned by a court in Andhra Pradesh on 13 May 2013 for posting comments on the social networking site Facebook against former Andhra Pradesh chief minister and Tamil Nadu governor K Rosaiah and Congress MLA Krishna Mohan from Prakasam district.

59 A 21-year-old woman from Mumbai, Shaheen Dhada, wrote something on her Facebook timeline against the call for bandh observance following the natural death of a powerful 'politico' in Maharashtra, Bal Thackeray, founder of the Shiv Sena party. The comment led to her arrest under controversial provision of the Section 66 (A) of Indian IT Act.

60 Aseem Trivedi, a Kanpur-based cartoonist, was arrested in Mumbai on 9 September 2012 under Section 124A (dealing with sedition) of the Indian Penal Code. The arrest was on charges of sedition for posting obscene content on his website, *Cartoons Against Corruption*, a cartoon-based campaign mounted to support the anti-corruption movement in India. Subsequently a ban was placed on his website by BigRock, an Internet Corporation for Assigned Names and Numbers (ICANN)-accredited Internet domain name registrar and web hosting company, after receiving a complaint from Crime Branch.

61 Ambikesh Mahapatra, a teacher with the Chemistry Department of the Jadavpur University, and his neighbour Subrata Sengupta, had allegedly forwarded cartoons mocking policies of Bengal chief minister and Trinamool Congress supremo Mamata Banerjee to nearly 65 recipients. The police slapped IPC Sections 500 (punishment of defamation), 509 (making obscene gesture to a woman), 114 (abettor present when offence is committed), and Sections 66 A and B (sending offensive communication) of the IT Act 2000 on the professor, who was arrested on 13 April 2012.

62 Puducherry entrepreneur Ravi Srinivasan, on 20 October 2012, tweeted against Karti Chidambaram, the son of Congress leader P. Chidambaram, that 'he has amassed more wealth than Vadra'.

63 Amy Spencer, *DIY: The Rise of Lo-Fi Culture*, New York: Marion Boyars Publishers Ltd, 2008.

64 To know more about long tail concept, see Chris Anderson, 'The long tail', Wired, 10 October 2004, <http://archive.wired.com/wired/archive/12.10/tail.html>, accessed on 24 October 2014.

65 Chandralekha is a YouTube icon in Kerala. She became a popular playback singer when non-resident Indians copiously commented and shared a song uploaded to YouTube by her cousin while she was singing the hit song 'Rajahamsame' from the popular movie *Chamayam*.

66 Law College students Aznia Ashmin, Rasha Salim and Ramlath Azeez used to exchange messages without having to pay for SMS on WhatsApp. However, their amateurism in composing a song with local slang on a usual college day became a big hit. They just uploaded a song sung by them only to make fun of one of their friends who was absent on the same day. The song became viral in WhatsApp and the trending hit rap song 'Maahile Penpillere Kandikka' had gone into the film *Oppana* by hit director Aashiq Abu in Kerala.

67 Patrice Flichy, *Le Sacre de l'amateur, Sociologie des Passions ordinaires à l'ère numérique*, Paris: Seuil, 2010.

68 Nancy Fraser, *Justice Interrupts: Critical Reflections on the Post-Socialist Condition*, London: Routledge, 1997, pp. 75–81.

69 Kamala Kempadoo and Jo Doezema (eds.), *Global Sex Workers: Rights, Resistance and Redefinition*, London: Routledge, 1998.

70 Eric O. Clarke, *Virtuous Vice: Homoertoticism and the Public Sphere*, Durham, NC: Duke University Press, 2000.

71 Black Public Sphere Collective (ed.), *The Black Public Sphere: A Public Culture Book*, Chicago: University of Chicago Press, 1995.

72 William Connolly, *The Ethos of Pluralization*, Minneapolis, MN: University of Minnesota Press, 1995.

3

ENGAGED PUBLIC

The country was disturbed when Sunitha Krishnan, a campaigner and co-founder of Prajwala[1], purposefully made public a rape video involving six unidentified men sexually torturing a girl. While doing so, she had an intention to track the identity of the perpetrators of the crime. 'I have received more than eighty Indian videos of unreported rape incidence through Shame the Rapist online campaign', later she claimed in Point Blank, an interview programme on Asianet News Channel on 23 February 2015 at 10 p.m. She claimed online campaign could help track the identity of perpetrators of rape culture and could bring justice to victims. Consequently, one of the six criminals has been identified after the release of the video.

In doing so, Sunitha was targeting a new audience and news consumers perhaps having less trust in government, politically apathetic and indifferent to traditional media formats. Their numerical strength is increasing, though miniscule minority at present. The role of civil society institutions in this changing social milieu should not be overlooked, in particular the interplay between technological infrastructure and civil society architect. In this background, it is timely to raise questions: does Internet help politicise the apolitical? What makes Internet-based click activism different from the old style of protest where class, gender, sexual identities and so on mobilise people for a particular cause? Is it advisable to think that the same mobilisational tactics, strategies and identities are still relevant in Internet age? Is cyber activism making recourse to old identities? Is there any difference between the functionalities of old activism and new activism of the cyberworld? Can social media make younger generation sympathetic to society? Are civil society spaces leveraging social networking sites such as Facebook, Twitter and YouTube? Why connection technologies are political for the underprivileged people? Whether poorest become political on connected space in a manner unmatched by the conventional modus operandi of political channels? To answer these questions raised, engaged public has been used as an analytical model in the chapter, which reframes an approach that befalls neither instrumentalist nor substantive perceptions of Internet. For the underprivileged technology is neither dystopia nor utopia nor neutral; rather, technology's social significance is decided by the socio-political location in which technology is deployed. Here, one may put in place Sunitha Krishnan's attempt to track the identity of perpetrators of crimes by illegally sharing rape video, which is a punishable offence under the Indian Penal Code (IPC).

A thin margin between digital infrastructure and social architecture has deterritorialised myriad forms of life. The blurring line between offline and online confounds whether technological infrastructure is placed in social architecture or vice versa. In the trajectory of life in bits, social engagements are transparent as never before. For example, sometime ago, my wife said some of the faculties in my college were in an academic tour programme. I was wondering! She is well updated on almost everything that happens around my college. 'How did you come to know?' I asked. 'Facebook; it gives every bit of information in our network. Everybody update this and that over to Facebook – the fish you bought, the side dish prepared for the dine, the new sari purchased for friend's wedding reception and so on', she replied.

Connected space is the new avenue for social relationship, as social relationships is fragmenting in the physical social world along with declining social capital. Being connected is a political choice. Therefore, engaged public is about being social and cultivating political vigilance in the age of Internet. More significantly, civic activism gets profoundly new takers from the fag end of the social margins and for them social structure is oppressive, whereas Internet is representing an emancipatory genie. It is an innovative narrative space, where personal fabricators, *Daily Me*,[2] long tails,[3] new agenda setters, producer public, amateurs, intimate speakers and eco-chambers[4] are becoming iconoclast.

Profound changes are taking place in the mobilising strategies in non-party political domains.[5] For example, following Anna Hazare–led anti-graft movement and Delhi gang rape on 16 December 2012, studies have found that social media facilitates a new sort of civic action in Internet.[6] Researchers Valerie Belair-Gangon, Smeeta Mishra and Colin Agur,[7] in a joint study, argue that emerging storytelling spaces on Internet have reflected the growing resentments of middle classes, the intellectuals, activists and journalists. The basis of their conclusion is a case study on the Delhi gang rape and its social media dimensions.

Connected spaces form new political identities. How could a social media enthusiast come to experience this new identity? Just think about that

Manesar plant in Haryana. It is a pride place for the famous Maruti Company, a household name for cars among middle class. In India, in 2012, it was in news, but not for good reasons. There was violence by employees, which resulted in the murder of a staff. We knew that in factory setting, what gives collective mobilisation is class solidarity. The Marxist notion of class struggle works profoundly here. Means of production and relations of production decide mode of production and in a factory system, which, in fact, is a mode of production, working-class solidarity leads to collective action. Theorist call classes a univariant collectivity. The only channelising force that motivates workers to agitate is their perceived notion of class exploitation. Manesar plant incident was somehow a 'class' act.

Similarly, caste is a social force that gives collective action consciousness at least for caste minorities. Caste system is hierarchical. It decides one's status. Lower castes in the hierarchy have been exploited by castes in the upper layer. Therefore, there were caste identity assertions all across India against caste discrimination. Such agitations were fuelled by the pain of discrimination, in particular among the lower castes. Like class, caste was also a univariant collectivity, which gives agitational consciousness to caste minority.

When it comes to gender, there were both cultural and biological aspects that influence the agitational consciousness. For instance, All India Democratic Women's Association (AIDWA), a leading women's organisation in India, calls for change in class relations, which is significant in bringing in changes in gender relations. The assumption is that when class problems are settled in, women's problems would naturally follow a resolution. Some other people, on the contrary, would tell that when you give economic power to women, their problems would end. At the same time, they are insignificant for autonomous feminist collectives. For them gender issues are neither class questions nor a question of economic empowerment. They would argue that change in social structures would bring in positive changes in their lives. The point is that women's problems are cultural. Hence, there were significantly many dimensions in the mobilisation of women then. Therefore, people would tell that gender is a bivalent collectivity. It is both a class and cultural question.

Just imagine NBA, a reputed environmental collective in India, which agitates against construction of big dams in the name of development projects that displaces people and destructs our ecosystem. What motivates people, in particular tribals become part of the ecological collective, is perceived notions of their ecological proximity: an identity that is related to a particular place and cultural setting. Here, environmental activism is a perceived notion of cultural identity in relation to tribals in forests. Tribal population in forests is thus a univariant collectivity.

Nancy Fraser[8] best described the said notions of univariant and bivariant collectivities as persuading people to either agitation or violence. The question of being political in the age of Internet is neither of them. Internet is a new social avenue that gives people new identities unlike those of notions such as bivalent or univariant collectivities. If so, engaged public is telling that be it working class, women's or ecological movements such as NBA; collective identities have mobilisation tactics. People participate when they find their lot is at stake. In the past, identity assertions were thus an offshoot of social structures that create troubles to life. Grievances were at the heart of most collective action programmes. However, in contemporary times, collective action is different. If it is about cyber activism, they have significant makeovers.

In Internet age, underprivileged people are increasingly coming to terms with the fact that they have a medium to do protest. There were inspiring stories from the Philippines that four-day SMS had dethroned Joseph Estrada from power. There was news from Arab countries that people's movements were in full swing that shook the foundations of many undemocratic governments. World over it was famously called the Arab Spring, a people's power movement that called for democracy. Social media was their platform. Occupy Wall Street, India Against Corruption, Nirbhaya and UK Uncut are examples of social media–embedded engaged public. In doing so, many ordinary people, who were not part of mainstream narrative, became part of collective action. It is an attribute of cyber identity.

Hashtags were trending on Twitter when injustices are reported. 'To question or not to question, that is the question' was the text of speech by historian Romila Thapar published in *Mainstream Weekly*. It was about the decline of public intellectualism in India. Personal Twitter feeds of many ordinary Indians were flooded with link to the article, comments and refutations. Rupa Subramanya's (@rupasubramanya) casteist tweet was trending on 28 November 2014. Her tweet against lower-caste house cleaner was notified on my Facebook page from Shivam Vij, a journalist working for the online news http://scroll.in/. Twitter was flooded with comments against her. She tweeted, 'Nothing to do with caste, but I for one don't allow my maid who cleans the washroom to cook. Basic hygiene. Not ancient Hindu scripture.' People said her tweet was a troll. Author Chetan Bhagat (@chetan_bhagat) tweeted his opinion on Israel and human rights violations in Middle East region. Funny comments on Facebook against his comment were notified and one among them pointed that 'it is likely to be your intelligence if you are a Chetan Bhagat kind of book reader'. Internet is going to be a citadel of click activism. It is habitual to act against an injustice if one has a medium. One need not risk blood and flesh on the street doing activism. It is the nature of modern activism and it should be.

Internet age is different from the old one. To distinguish it from other protest collectives familiar to us, the term *engaged public* is used. It is lifestyle politics of the digital citizens. There were new kinds of citizenship in connected space. Internet provides belonging and citizenship to new identities, such as digital citizenship to those underrepresented citizens, sexual citizenship to sexual minorities and intimate citizenship to citizen who look for alternative spaces for desires and intimacies.

Associational lives

Civil society organisations, which embrace social movements, NGOs, think tanks, media outlets, trade unions, faith-based charities and community-based organisations, represent, of all voices, those voices overlooked by the government and the private sector. The description of the term *civil society* has a rich scholarly inheritance[9] and it commonly refers to the notion that members of society come together to engage on issues of concern to society at large. For the purpose of analytical feasibility, each study has used the term *civil society* in their ease; for example, in a study titled *Making the connection: Civil society and social media*, Suw Charman-Anderson viewed civil society as a form of associational life, a good society and as an arena for public deliberations.[10] The term *civil society* was defined as the realm of private voluntary association, from neighbourhood committees to interest groups to philanthropic enterprises of all sorts in a study report prepared for the European Economic and Social Committee (EESC) by Semantica Research.[11]

Civil society comprises all those non-market and non-state actors outside the family. Yet, the development of civil society space in India was entirely different from those in the western world.[12] The western conceptions of civil society hold no significance and analytical potential in the Indian context. Hegel's nineteenth-century notion of civil society included the market, whereas contemporary concepts tend to regard civil society as a non-profit sector. Gramsci regarded civil society as an arena where class hegemony forges consent, while much contemporary discussion treats civil society as a site of disruption and dissent.[13] Between Marx and Gramsci, the latter initiated and added some crucial components to the understanding of civil society. Civil society not only transmits or inculcates established practices or beliefs; it is also a site of social contestation, in which collective identities, ethical values and alliances are forged. The public sphere as located in civil society provides a communicative sphere. Social media holds great significance as it facilitates a communicative sphere for civil society engagements.

Nonetheless, in the final analysis, the concept of civil society is rather ambiguous and means different things to different people in different national context, says Lehmbruch.[14] Any scale now accepts the concept of civil society in modern political science as an intermediary between the private sector and the state. Thus, civil society stems from the state and economic distinction. Equally important is that it is not the same as family-life society. Civil society, as Larry Diamond[15] defines, is the realm of organised social life that is open, voluntary, bound by a legal order or a set of shared rules.

The twentieth-century emphasis on civil society was informal networks, initiatives and social movements, as distinct from more formal voluntary associations and institutions. Social movements articulate new concerns and projects and generate new values and collective identities. The concept of civil society recently slices up two distinct senses. One is to indicate a set of societal movements, initiatives, forms of mobilisation, and the second one is to refer to a framework of settled institution rights, associations and publics. Civic groups include academic institutions, business forums, clan and kinship circles, consumer advocates, development cooperation initiatives, environmental movements, ethnic lobbies, foundations, human rights promoters, labour unions, local community groups, relief organisations, peace movements, professional bodies, religious institutions, think tanks, women's networks, youth associations and more.

Civil society sphere is an important element of our vibrant democracy where an active citizenship restructures governance in this part of the world. The fact is that India hosts an NGO base (estimates vary, depending on the source) between one and two million. Roughly 1.5 million NGOs are operational in India, says IndianNGOs.com's estimate. Yet, one estimate puts the figure at over 30,000.[16] The nuances of civil society enormously vary across time and place.[17] The contemporary usage tends to contrast civil society and the state. Until the 1990s, people's movements, NGOs and voluntary initiatives did not fall in the category of 'civil society' in the Indian context. The first major attempt at defining civil society in India came from a series of studies published in early 2000. The early studies about the development of civil society in India help to understand the diversity of civil society in that it describes its history and various strands.[18] Civil society comprises individual and group initiatives for public concern.[19] It implies that only those associations which establish openness of entry survive and stand by ecumenical criteria of citizenship turn up part of civil society. It also signifies that any association that excludes persons because of ethnicity, class or religious persuasion is clearly not a part of civil society.[20] Simply, civil society clubs together a massive amount of associations around which society freely organises itself and which signify a broad array of interests and concerns, illustrates a study by the OECD.[21]

There were three strands in the development of civil society in India, pre-independence, post-independence and post-reform phases.[22] However, there were sharp differences in civil society in value and content in these phases.[23] In the pre-independent phase, civil society space metamorphosed into a working-class movement, Indian National Congress (INC), and peasant uprisings, such as the Moplah revolt in 1921. Outside the INC, there were also other forms of social movements. During the post-independence period, the civil society space has reflected many ups and downs. The civil-rights movement was absorbed into the edifice of the new state. Its leaders became the architects of India's modern institutions. Nevertheless, disappointment towards a state that failed to fulfil its promises on basic rights prepared the field for groups challenging the government. The 1975–77 Emergency led to the creation of the civil liberties movements, often described as the origin of contemporary civil society. The Emergency had a refreshing effect on civil society which after 1977 witnessed an increase of activities within traditional social movements such as peasants, workers and students. It also found vigour amongst the so-called new social movements, including environmental groups and women's organisations.[24]

Over the years, civil society has reflected the emergence of expansive alliances whose power lies in their ability to use different tools of advocacy. They bring together very different groups and individuals ranging from affected communities, to activists, academics and celebrities. The biggest of these movements is the Narmada Bachao Andolan (NBA). Such alliances remain powerful social actors. They have emerged around a variety of issues: on the right to food, or on the rights of construction workers and homeless people, to give only a few examples.

Two important trends are worth mentioning. First, since the 1990s, identity-based groups have gained visibility and influence. A second trend adds to this sobering picture: a network of right-wing organisations whose activities range from social welfare to quasi-militias. The network draws on a tradition of communal and religious welfarism that reaches back to the early ages of people's actions before Independence. Nevertheless, it adapts itself to a programme aimed at capturing political power.

One noteworthy change in the post-reform period is the development of a more numerous and affluent middle class. This has changed the profile of civil society's membership. Once the realm of elites devoted to changing an unjust system, civil society in post-reform period turned up increasingly middle class whose aspiration for change derives from its own experience of hurdles and constraints. The development arguably contributes to embolden and empower civil society. Given the group's relative wealth and its presence in urban centres, it enjoys a visibility in the media and in political debates that the poor do not have.

To conclude, an important change in recent times has been the development of a diverse media. Today, a couple of odd news channels and an array of newspapers and radio channels are competing for news. This development helps civil society publicise an increasing number of issues, and build pressure around topics such as corruption or failures of justice. Yet, it also has limitations. Journalists are concentrated in a few cities. Their absence in remote areas means that issues in rural or peripheral regions are generally underrepresented. Similarly, readership and audience influence their coverage. It is widely felt that issues mirror according to the interest of a middle class urban audience. Civil society activism in India spreads across a wide array of social variables in the post-reform period. Activism occurs in a myriad of practices such as campaign to right to food, right to employment, right to health, right to education and right to information, says Neera Chandahoke.[25] Anna Hazare–led anti-graft movement has been a boost for civil society movements, and this was particularly due to its influence among urban middle class and Internet is so popular in this strata. Civil society organisations range from Rotary and Lions Clubs and organisations of the reactionary right that have large networks across the country, to small fragmented grass-roots groups of idealistic youngsters selflessly working for the betterment of their community. People's movements not registered with the government, research institutes, local NGOs working on delivery or those focussing on advocacy and Indian chapters of international NGOs all claim to fall under the category despite their very different operational modes.

The massive development projects and infrastructure initiatives seen in post-reform period in India has contributed to a widening inequality. Now the people living under poverty, unemployment, water scarcity, drought famine, food crisis, poor environmental standards, quick urbanisation, violation of civil and political rights are widespread. Addressing such fundamental issues that India faces still attracts the attention of state, market, citizen and civil society space.[26] Yet a perusal of the civil society space reflects seesaw reactions from various corners. Due to the inherent social, religious, ethnic and economic cleavages of Indian society, the civil society is flooded with inequality and conflict, as noted in the current Indian debate.[27] It is apparent that the partial failure of the state to address social and economic needs has had effects not only on the levels of development but also on the quality and character of civil society.

Therefore, the role of social media need not look at instrumentalist or substantive perception of technology. Nor does it need to look at neutral towards the operational function of the agent who uses it. Social media's role in civil society is discursive, conditioned by the sociocultural location in which it is deployed for a function.

Social media and civic activism

Activism in the 1960s and in the twenty-first century is different. Corrigal Brown's[28] study of social movement has highlighted change in the working of protest and activism in contemporary time. The study finds even higher levels of activism in contemporary age compared to those of previous generations: generations of 1960s and 1970s, adored by some and criticised by others for an activism memorised as tumultuous and confrontational. The individual who participated in activism and engaged in protest in the 1960s and 1970s was different in degree and ways from youth of today. The rise of the Internet alone means that we live in a very different social and political context than we did activism and advocacy in the 1960s, or even in the twenty-first century. Those seeking to engage in social and political causes have a greater selection of issues to choose from and can move easily among them in the contemporary era. However, it is noted that while levels of political participation may be rising, much of the activism that occurs today are outside conventional groups. Civil society institutions being the early adopters of the Internet to enable activism have successfully used it to further their goals and conduct their activities. On the one side, Internet facilitates and supports conventional offline collective action in terms of organisation, mobilisation and transnationalisation. On the other hand, it creates new modes of collective action.

The growing penetration of broadband and cell phones has configured a new audience and thus a new activist ecology has been forming. New media and digital forms of organising protest have necessitated redefining the conventional way of conceptualising collective action.[29] The conventional methods of looking at civic activism seemed as if they were insufficient to understand the online forms of collective action. Internet is having a discursive implication on civil society despite users being in front of a computer screen.[30] Information and communications technology (ICT) such as cell phones, email, the World Wide Web and social media sites is changing the ecosystem in which activism and advocacies communicate, coordinate, collaborate, cooperate and demonstrate. Cell phone–coordinated protest against the World Bank, cell phone–powered People Power II demonstrations in the Philippines in 2001 and software built to circumvent state-sanctioned censorship[31] are examples of social changes in that direction through digital technology.

Social media holds greater political significance where information is power. The rise of social media has power to crush the uneven social space on economic, political and local levels by facilitating grass-roots organisation, civil society collectives and citizen initiatives. Internet has been useful in effecting the attention of media, government functionaries and public opinion. In the seminal article 'The Issue Network and the Executive Establishment', Heclo described a new form of political organisation: 'Issue-activists' and 'issue-experts' that were forming 'loose alliances' in which they defined political affairs by sharing information.[32] In the report 'Appropriating the Internet for Social Change', Mark Surman and Katherine Reilly distinguished the technical network, i.e. networked ICTs, the social network, i.e. coalitions of civil society organisations (CSOs) and the intermediate notion of the network as a site of info sharing.[33] It is important to identify 'collaboration' and 'publishing' as two important practices in which social media and civil society converge. The analogy holds significance in the Indian context also because both are not possible for people on the social walls, as they do not have space and time for sharing solidarity outside the traditional social hierarchy and not own a media of their own. Internet provides all that.

As a communications space, social media is empowering civil society. Internet-enabled practices have power in breaking time and distance barriers to facilitating collaboration and knowledge sharing among geographically distributed activist groups in India, say Hattangdi and Ghosh.[34] It facilitates a loosely related national alliance of people, and their collaboration is not through the similarity of issues they face but the knowledge they hold. Email, social networking, user content platforms, teleconferencing, audio conferencing, radio broadcasts, interactive voice response system, television lessons, audiocassettes, CD ROMs and interactive radio counselling and so on hold significance to civil society spaces in India. Digital platforms set in different civil society purposes in different parts of India.[35]

Social media platforms facilitate various levels of civil society empowering activities and rapid communication on a global scale. They facilitate access to information and knowledge and the sharing of information resources, lowering the barriers to publication and enabling groups and individuals to bypass traditional gatekeepers in media and publishing and helping the formation and maintenance of virtual communities of people or institutions with shared interests.[36] The last few years have witnessed proliferation of ICT and the exponential growth of CSOs.[37] The network is one of the prime conceptual, practical and technical sites where these two developments come together and form civil society as communicative practice.

The convergence between civil society and social media finds specific expression in two notions that frequently stir up the role of Internet in facilitating – the social network and the info-network.[38] An equally important dimension to link civil society and Internet is the concept of the issue network used to characterise a variety of political practices that add to and intervene in the representative politics characteristic of national democracies. The term has been taken up to describe the issue politics or 'lifestyle politics' pursued by grass-roots organisations and individuals in mobilising around affairs that affect people in their daily lives, from the environment to media ownership and gender issues.[39] The issue network concept stirs up professionalised practices of NGOs, most notably those of advocacy.

The notion of NGO serves to highlight the open-ended alliances working on common social, cultural, environmental, energy, humanitarian and new political issues as part of their attempts to put these issues on the agendas of political institutions and democratic engagement.[40] Political scientist Craig Warkentin[41] has argued that the importance of the Internet for civil society chiefly draws from the fact that as a transnationally implemented network technology, it provides a perfect forum for the social networks of global civil society. The Internet's inherent qualities facilitate the development of civil society's constitutive network of social relations. The notion of the social network foregrounds relatively unregulated or under-regulated relations and social networks arise in the exchange of information and things among people, in the absence of institutionalised relations among them or beyond or alongside such relations. As networks for information sharing, Internet typically conceived as flat, smooth and formless spaces, as in the work of Manuel Castells on the space of flows.[42]

Engaged public in India: dimensions

The following section is an extensive analytical description of survey data on Facebook, Twitter, YouTube, Blogs, websites, web portals, petition and signature sites, forums and personal narratives. Cases of citizen responses, group actions on Internet and civil society intellectuals and activists have been analysed. Based on this, it was found that underprivileged and subaltern social groups have rampantly been using digital platforms. User behaviours are linked with human rights, health activism, environmental campaign and civil protest. For example, information explosion helped spread awareness and linkages with issues such as human rights and health atavism and foster network. A crude search on Google using the keywords 'human rights' on 14 April 2013 provided 654,000,000 (0.60 seconds) pages. A search on 'human rights campaigns' produced 517,000,000 results (0.63 seconds). A number of NGOs are now online and publishing their materials online. International organisations, think tanks and advocacy groups upload large portions of their materials online, making research much easier than before and enabling ready access to texts of legislation, treaties, resolutions, reports by special rapporteur and other essential documentations. Academic and research journals offer at least some of their articles in digital formats. The diffusion of Internet, however, has also meant that finding relevant and user-specific materials is more difficult for those who are not already familiar with the major civil society issues: the problem of over-information.

As another example, over the years a number of NGOs in India have been active in the area of environmental protection. They have been in the fore-front of reforestation campaigns, lobbying against deforestation or overuse of pesticides in agriculture and questioning polluting industries. A Google search on the keywords 'environmental pollution' turns up 81,600,000 results (0.22 seconds) pages; a similar search on 'global warming' returns over 272,000,000 results (0.19 seconds), one on 'toxic waste' returns over 23,800,000 results (0.24 seconds), as on 07 May 2013. Environmental campaigning requires access to scientific information. The increasing tendency of scientific researchers to publish on Internet as well as in specialist journals makes it easier for environmental groups to locate the kind of information needed to underpin campaigns or to buttress and inform arguments to be used in offline discussions with legislators and companies. There are striking similarities between the way environmental and human rights activists use the Internet to disseminate information, publicise and conduct campaigns, email alerts and put together rapid-response campaigns.

Examples of online civic groups that facilitate consolidation and integration of the scattered network of civil society actors are aplenty. For example, IndianNGOs.org,[43] Civil Society Online,[44] Centre for Civil Society,[45] NGOsIndia,[46] Accountability Initiative,[47] India Civil Society[48] and the list goes on. At the end analysis, Indian Internet is the playground for civic groups and social media platforms; especially Facebook, YouTube, Blogger and Twitter are vehicles of civic activism.

Alternative space

Alternative space and civic activism come together. Indeed, they support each other. For the underprivileged, social media is an alternative space, and thus, they have been able to shake an old system of cleavages, oppression and unequal power relations. For example, Parvathy Shetty and Maithreyi Nadanappa started online campaign following allegedly rape of a six-year-old first-grade student at Vibgyor High School in Bangalore by the gym instructor. It got wider public attention.

What do you do when you wake up when the news around you, the media, music, movies, literature, culture and the television you consume do not represent you and you cannot connect with them? Certainly, you would think of creating your own. Creating an alternative communicative space – be it for women, Dalits, caste minorities, third sex, poor people and the oppressed – has been costlier and even unthinkable for various reasons in the past. In particular, broadcasting, publication and sourcing of income are difficult. Communicative apartheid is an old story; now social media – one would call alternative media – has become suddenly more accessible and affordable.

So far, there has been an upsurge of social media usage in India among the underprivileged, youth, Dalits, minorities and women, and it shows a shift towards digital publications. Slowly, ever so slowly, other possibilities are being imagined as well. For example, if one finds it difficult in doing so and more particularly if one thinks the alternative media space, where one has been doing his or her creativity and stories, to be unprofitable, the solution will be there, at least according to Indian and Cowboy[49] productions. *Stories from the Land*, a Podcast series, is a collection of indigenous community–sourced stories that connect indigenous people to place with the aim of reinforcing worldview, philosophies and teachings.[50] It means one of the most favourite things that often fascinated the imagination of people from the ancient to the modern is certainly an idea. Attempt to find alternative space has more takers in social media age. It is important, therefore, to understand the trajectory of alternative in connected age. Obviously, alternative has more takers in India, be it mothers, caste groups, minorities, Dalits, third sex, gender, media and the underprivileged.

It has facilitated a new kind of networking, which is otherwise not possible for the older generation. Major corporate entities have combined networked films, radios, news media and magazine businesses that can get in touch with every human being in the world. In relation to such monolithic and monopolised communicative spaces, there are examples of people drawing content from alternative news sources on Internet. Current affairs blogs, portals and websites have been found very significant in political reporting.[51] Many online media services such as Merinews.com,[52] and Mutiny[53] have substantial readerships.[54] They are not just media, but media entrenched in society.

Alternative media differs from mass media, says Christian Fuchs.[55] Alternative space reflects citizen journalism, critical with grass-roots structure, alternative distribution and critical reception. As an alternative space, social media platforms can offer spaces for the neglected interest by conventional media outlets. As an alternative space, Internet and social media platforms offer spaces for those neglected interest by conventional media entities. Ecological movements such as the NBA and India Against Corruption are extending a sphere of influence for civil society politics from offline to the so-called town square of the world. Alternative citizen media philosophies such as countercurrents.org, merinews.com and mutiny.in are offering a fleet of free spaces for digital activists, where one can attract an expanding audience. Alternative media on the Internet have diversified greatly. They have the potential to stimulate public debate.[56] Grass-roots networks are offshoot of increased Internet alternative space that has hybrid constructions. They include networking and the fluid circulation of efforts by independent individuals, professionals from mainstream media organisation groups, movement groups and networks of networks.

E-letters tend to be more effective than traditional campaigning. For instance, as on 11 January 2013 there were (signatories) campaigns like 'No to reservations in private sector and IIT/IIM/Medical colleges'[57] (30,465); 'India Against Corruption'[58] (21,383) and 'Tell the Prime Minister of India to stop supporting the violence in Burma'[59] (1,659). They are alternative spaces! For the ambitious writers who have learnt to reject rejections by big publishing labels, social media was importantly alternative storytelling space.

If more than 200 million people connected simultaneously, that too when it was able to bring in many changes over a short span of time, which constitutional democracy was not able to do for about six decades, it is a good idea. All this happens in a society which has been historically characterised by unequal social structure and cleavages; if so, what other than social media could then be a fertile soil for civic activism?

It is in this space YouTube singer Chandralekha became a famous playback singer. It was in social media that Law College students Aznia Ashmin, Rasha Salim and Ramlath Azeez were able to get their pastime fun song into the film directed by popular director Aashiq Abu. This song was also the basis for a lot of ad campaigns ever since in India Inc. It was in this space that ordinary homemaker Namita Bhandare's solo activism found a mention by the Justice Verma Committee. It was also in this space that AAP found its electoral success two times, and fund-raising activism possible. It was this space where NaMo campaign found its soothsayers among youth and successful electoral margin in General Election 2014.

Social media is, therefore, an alternative space, from where civic activism gets its synergy. India Against Corruption, Anti-rape activism, and third sex activism are testimonials. According to Kalki Subramaniam it was a space where she was able to effect transgender activism in India. Her blog was a testament to this direction of her thinking. As a space for activism, social media is an alternative space and a space that caters to civil society activism.

Virality, hashtags and trending

Viral politics is a sort of token support.[60] In Internet, virality is the tendency of a video, image, or piece of information circulated going rapidly and widely from one Internet user to another. The Facebook data team analysed the viral activity seen on events related to the Ice Bucket Challenge from 1 June to 17 August 2014. It was found that more than 17 million videos related to the Ice Bucket Challenge were shared on Facebook. These videos were viewed more than 10 billion times by more than 440 million people.[61] The concept, which one knows by now, consists of people dumping a bucket of ice water on their heads and challenging others to do the same and it is among the biggest viral hits in Facebook's history. The nature of the Ice Bucket Challenge is, in itself, essentially spreadable and it is easy to do, if you are being called out in a public forum and there is a chain letter–like 'pass it on'. In India, it was spreading like beehive among all circles.

Charity, donation and protest are now a mark of new way of doing civic roles in Internet. It has now become a way of social change in India. It is liberating for marginalised people who suffer the torments of discordant social system. Social media enthusiasts are vigilant and they react in connected spaces for things ranging from women, sexuality, corruption, third gender, political class, rights, violence, rape: the issues of intimate citizens.

If so, what makes it so special? It is devoid of any cleavages. Anything can go viral in Internet. For example, Kiss of Love become viral on social media landscape. In January 2015, Arundhathi and Rahul Pashupalan, who were part of the Kiss of Love movement, were present at the *JB Junction*, a television programme on Kairali Channel. Arundhathi, an activist and student at Hyderabad Central University (HCU), said that many women in the four walls of their house commented on their Facebook page, which was in support of the cause they represented. However, none of them was able to come in the public arena. They were afraid of the social morality prevailing in the society. What makes them connected with such a movement was Facebook. Facebook is, in fact, the space of the unheard and unreached. The point they were making was that Kiss of Love is not an isolated movement. It is part of the loosely connected nationwide mindset in India at present going invisible. Movements began to translocate from structure to cultural symbols.

The attack of a coffee shop by right-wing forces on allegation of flesh trade paved the path for a cultural protest in India. Social media sites were viral against the so-called moral policing in India. It was in October 2014 when the said right-wing youth coterie attacked the coffee shop at Calicut. A group of youngsters decided to observe kiss day on November 2 expressing freedom of love following this incident. The youngsters started a Facebook campaign. It was later called Kiss of Love protest, which was a non-violent protest against moral policing. Indeed, it started in Kerala and later spread to other parts of India, at least in Internet. The movement began when the said Facebook page called 'Kiss of love',[62] which had over one and a half lakh likes, asked the youth across Kerala to participate in a protest against moral policing on 2 November 2014, at Marine Drive, Cochin. Kissing their friends and loved ones in public places to protest moral policing was the agenda of the campaign, which to an extent was achieved by the group.

Just see the *Times of India* photo captioned 'OMG: Deepika Padukone's cleavage show' and the actress hit back irritably, tweeting: 'YES! I am a Woman. I have breasts AND a cleavage! You got a problem!!??'. The tweet went viral. People began to support Deepika Padukone against the sexist comment of the news outlet. For them social media is the alternate space to represent their sentiments and stories, at a time when the supposed stalwarts of our moral empire collaterally fail. Media is sensational. Political class is inactive. Right wing is scot-free. What would the citizen do?

Hashtags are a great way to start an activism or tweet a riot. It was not long back when Chris Messina created them. They come in handy and create a deeper impact. Their popularity by reuse becomes so high that they become more of a rage. That is the beauty of hashtags; they create virality in the content and they get viral. 'Vizhinjam Beach, a splendid site ruined by filth&garbage, which I will clean w/local residents tomorrow 25/10 at 11am', Shashi Tharoor (@ShashiTharoor) tweeted on 25 October 2014. It was a response to Prime Minister Narendra Modi's call. In his bid to make 'Swachh Bharat' (Clean India) a people's movement, Prime Minister Narendra Modi initiated a chain by inviting nine eminent personalities including cricket icon Sachin Tendulkar, Congress leader Shashi Tharoor, industrialist Anil Ambani along with several actors to spread awareness on cleanliness. The social media–savvy prime minister appeared inspired by the ALS Ice Bucket Challenge, which had gone viral recently, as he asked the celebrities to nominate nine more people to join the campaign and hoped that the chain would continue. Activism happens in social media. It is easy to do so.

Hashtags are ways of speaking for or against one electoral candidate of the other. They help commoners raise voice against an injustice or a crime or a sick government policy. For example, people in the last few years have been tweeting against rape, corruption, nuclear energy and so on, which shows their anger in public towards a government ideology, or public policy, or a tradition and so on. Speaking from a political point of view, #development, #governance, #communalism, #rape, #RapeCulture, #abortion and #anticorruption are some of the top trending hashtags.

Is our political establishment on the brink of total collapse? Is our political class detached from their electorate? Illusions of a detachment from everyday realities of social life almost become norm of political engagement. It happens and it is reality of Indian politics. People are dissatisfied. Political scenario in India is fast changing. There are no organised responses. Political parties are all united. Political classes have the same interest. They perpetuate their class interest. If things are going like this, what could be the possible future?

It is on social media people look for alternative when they are dissatisfied with the prevalent ruling establishment. Aam Aadmi Party's (AAP) strategy is an example of mob rule and crowd wisdom landing into a winning stream. For example, they formed a government for a few days in Delhi in 2014 and went out of power for want of majority. Again, they formed a government with near total win in the 2015 assembly election. It was social media which made its success so possible: For the poorest, social media is the new site of political opposition.

'Friend power' in social media is working. People find it as an alternative source of political opposition. Hashtags are emissaries of a new style of political speak. Timeline is the new field of crowd politics. Social media is the new site of mob politics. Over the last couple of years, what happened to the most haunted in the country and what was at the centre stage, be it India Against Corruption, Aam Aadmi phenomenon, Nirbhaya, anti-rape campaigns and so on? It was the nascence of intimate citizenship in Internet.

Resentments against political class is more registered on social media. The reason is that a new political tribe has resurfaced in India. They have metamorphosed into a tribe with their own value system, morality, prejudices, judgements, cultural symbols and civic ethos. Triumph of this political class is not a continuation of the old establishment. Old pillars such as the judiciary, parliament, civil service, political parties and media have metamorphosed into a new political culture. They are more interested staying in power by conniving with the media and propaganda machinery. While doing so, they are easily surpassing the hard test of governance. Here underprivileged people become helpless repeatedly. Symptoms of restlessness on social media are everywhere and one could see the decline in political values and commitment to society. Left to right, there were no differences between political outfits. In the celebrated books *The Triumph of the Political Class* (2007) and *The Rise of Political Lying* (2005) author Peter Oborne examined that members of the twenty-first-century 'political class' are isolated and self-interested. The modern political class thinks it could override constitutional conventions because it was elected by an ever-diminishing proportion of eligible voters and can go to extremes in making

76

decision. The analogy of Oborne is relevant and survives the test of time in India. A spectre is haunting everyday politics. It is the spectre of political class. The triumph of a new political class and a mobile army of political lies haunt us. The new story goes like this. The criteria for being a successful politician can no longer be the treasured ideals of the past. For a young citizen, ambitious to join politics, here is a blueprint for career path. First, there must be a dynasty to nourish you up. You must set yourself apart from your contemporaries at university by taking interest in politics. You should actively stone-pelt public offices and should have been imprisoned for some reason or the other – often a crime, rape or bribe. You must join a think tank or consult a researcher to become an upwardly rising Member of Parliament on learning. Before getting to the top position, you will have eaten, drunk and slept with people exactly like you, not only in politics but also in the media, public relations circles and advertising. You will talk a language the vast majority of your fellow citizens cannot understand and be obsessed with the marketing of politics rather than its content. You will notice that once in power, you can get away with behaviour that would have fascinated your predecessors.

Poorest citizens are finding solutions in technology. For the underprivileged, technology is a credible political opposition, though not in full swing. Technology is used to fill the void created by old pillars of democracy. For example, in the Siri Fort on 27 January 2015, US president Barack Obama said that India has been largely a connected society which uses technologies of connection such as Facebook, Twitter and WhatsApp. Countries across the world have begun to recognise the fact that we are a techno-savvy society. Now it is our own turn to realise that we are a techno-freak. Let us place social media as political opposition in this critical context or at least in the context of some of the actual events reported. Here social media exposes the mirror image of the real opposition.

Social media is a buzzing hive for the useless outrage according to the counter-reactionaries and obscurantists. They dub hashtag and timeline activism as vanity activism. However, for the iconoclast, social media is the lantern for the intra-urban exiles. How and why?

In the past, it took days, huge financial investment and human labour to communicate on issues, say, to report a crime, violence, sensitise the people on social issues and mobilise people. However, in the connected age, the mechanics of mobilising structure are different. One could make it easily communicated if one has social media skills. While doing so, the issue being circulated goes viral and attains sensitivity. A pattern is noticeable. The issue and responses by social media enthusiasts do have a common thread. They are, for instances, a reaction against an injustice, violation of rights, a sexist remark or something related to an issue least addressed by previous media. It is then addressed by social media enthusiasts and starts trending until they open up the sleeping system.

In the Internet age, it is misplaced to neglect the power of Internet Activism. It has become a way to share and promote a cause, report corruption, share sentiments and rage against discrimination and heinous crimes like rape. Internet has become a tool to fight against sexism, injustice, rapes, homophobia and rights. What makes it so important is the virality.

#Entevaka500 (#myshare500)

The symptoms of restlessness get its symbolic expressions in social technologies. Underprivileged people protest in novel ways unheard in the past. For example, a money order protest campaign was staged by noted film director Ashiq Abu in Kerala. A Facebook post on the Kerala liquor bar bribe issue went viral in social media. People started sending money orders to K. M. Mani, then finance minister of Kerala, demanding his resignation. The post was mockingly asking the public to go for a crowd funding. It was because of the financially poor situation of the minister. The minister was struggling to make both ends meet. 'Since our sir (K. M. Mani, usually called as Mani sir) is in a financial crisis and struggling to make ends meet we should cooperatively collect some more crores for him. As of my share, I am offering Rs. 500', he said in the post. Social media users sent 'money orders' to the minister, who was accused of corruption charges related to the 'bargate' controversy. What does it signify? Anger of the Aam Aadmi against organised inactivity of political order.

#Yesudas on Twitter and Facebook

Legendary singer K. J. Yesudas in October 2014 landed in a storm of reactions after he said women should not trouble men by wearing jeans, says a BBC report titled *KJ Yesudas: India singer criticised for 'sexist' jeans remark*.[63] He said, 'What should be covered must be covered. Our culture involves the beauty, which should be covered. Women should not trouble others by wearing jeans. When they put on jeans, men are tempted to look beyond that (jeans)'. 'Women's beauty lies in their modesty. They should not try to become like men. They should not force others to do unnecessary things by wearing jeans, which would give them magnetism', Yesudas added.[64]

Social media enthusiasts were making massive online reactions against the popular playback singer K. J. Yesudas for his allegedly controversial comment that warns women of their provocative dressing while suggesting women to use sari, which is more a conventional dress. Comments after comments, he was attacked for sexist suggestion and imposing dress code on women.

Thereby there was a view which was at the centre stage of the viral reactions in Internet. It was that his comment was an attack on women's sexuality and body. People got a platform in which they would be able to place their anger, sense of humour and political wisdom as they wish it to be.

Lalism

On 02 February 2015, National Games was inaugurated in Kerala. In the inaugural venue, there was a stage show named Lalism, which became a controversial issue for the social media enthusiasts by the same evening, which was a topic for the prime time debates in local channels. The accusation was that the said programme starring veteran Kerala actor Mohanlal had been a big flop. The fund allocation for the programme was allegedly over-invoiced and overstated. The programme was not useful for a nationwide audience in which songs in local language were sung. The accusation went viral. However, no media in the state raised a finger on it. No journalist put an interest in it. All media reported that there was uproar over the issue in social media sites. Noted iconoclast director Vinayan posted a Facebook campaign against Lalism some days even before the programme was set in motion.

Social media became an alternative political opposition in the said event. When money power, celebrity status and lobbying bypass basic values of democracy, only social media activism raised storms against evil doers. For example, there were interesting political satires against Lalism and the political machinery in the Kerala state, which the traditional media was supposed to do, but failed to do.

#LoveLetterMovement

A Love Letter Movement became another way of novel protest when the Hindu Mahasabha announced battle against couples who came out in public place on Valentine's Day in February 2015. Young people in Kerala steered a new protest by creating a Facebook page which gave signal that young people once blamed for political apathy now had become more political. Elder citizens also joined the bandwagon and some of them uploaded old fleet of their love letters. It had thousands of followers. Political satire and literary talents were on display. Valentine's anti-Hindu protest statement ഇന്ന് ഒരു പ്രേമലേഖന മെഴുതാന് വെരുന്നോ (Do you come to write a love letter) flooded Facebook. Indeed, Kerala lovers protested by writing love letters on Valentine's Day against Hindu fascist forces calling for action against lovers.

79

In each of these cases, viral engagement begins when a set of political entrepreneurs asks a broader public to take note of what they consider to be an important public issue. It has a pattern. First, the social entrepreneurs provide information about the topic that is new or unknown to much of the audience and that is presented as urgent and plainly unjust. Second, the entrepreneur develops a narrative or 'frames' the issue in a way that identifies the injustice at stake and so serves to locate the issue in the worldview of the audience and highlight its salience. Third, based on this new information set in a narrative of injustice, the entrepreneur asks their audience to take action. Digital technologies make viral engagement possible, first by dramatically lowering the costs of publishing, broadcasting and recommending appealing, say Archon Fung and Jennifer Shkabatur.[65]

In the social media explosion where news, connection and information travel fast, traditional data format has changed profoundly. Now, data formats have become unstructured. Data are transformed into social data as they are created by a staggering number of anonymous population. Propinquity of data has been immediate with quick access. The source of data has become unverifiable as they are derived from multiple sources. And above all, the data size is so big, which is referred to as big data by experts. The social physics of social media activism spill over into easiness, is access-free, is cost-free, is time-saving and has a global reach. Social networking sites have turned out to be an essential factor of almost any lobby group, social movement and contentious groups. Some of the most used digital advocacy tools include chats, websites, Twitter, Facebook, MySpace, email, blogs and texts. Too many social media platforms are available for a wide range of purposes. Underprivileged people engaging in Internet advocacy use but select few. Facebook, YouTube, blogs and Twitter are favourite among advocacy groups to build resources.

What is the nature of engaged social publics in social media age? Th!nking Indian,[66] a LinkedIn group, for example, is an active community that beats commercial media for the reason that it is more inclusive and participative. Why is this significant? Internet provides a uniquely engaged civic sphere, where decisions that shape our lives are freely debated and circulated. Internet communities built there are able to limit the power of corporations, bureaucracies and governments. In a globalised world that continuously undermines localised democratic institutions, Internet is an essential means for defending and extending participatory culture required for a successful democracy. An engaged public could proffer virtual advocacy such as sharing of information, networking, collaborating, online protest, email activism, publication of data and addressing new political concern virtually.

There are gaps that exist between the civil society groups and their demand for coordination and collaboration. Keeping this in mind, think that there are many online channels for political articulation and conduits of solidarity for ensuring concerted efforts from civic groups. Philip N. Howard, author of *New Media Campaigns and the Managed Citizen*[67] (2006) and *The Digital Origins of Dictatorship and Democracy*[68] has the view that twenty-first-century civil society institutions have been relying heavily on information infrastructure to strengthen civic conversation and so democracy would be strengthened.

Internet has represented the voices of ordinary citizens and organisations lacking strong resources. At least according to the report titled *Public Media 2.0: Dynamic, Engaged Publics*, by Jessica Clark and Patricia Aufderheide[69], top-down dissemination technologies that supported democracy are being increasingly taken over by a more citizen-centric media, which is characterised by at least five characteristics: choice, curation and conversation, creation and collaboration.[70] Underprivileged people coming over to the citizen media through different channels of access are recognising themselves as members of public. Let us call it an engaged public. In India, this sort of coming together would have more significance. It could enhance solidarity, information sharing, participation, inclusion and contentions. Here the people find a new identification with technology that is more liberating, which once they did not. Social media acquires relevance to civil society sphere only when it is able to exploit the potential of Internet in facilitating networking, collaboration, coordination and cooperation through which civic activism gets strengthened at least across the lives of marginalised, oppressed and impoverished. In the alternative spaces, intimate speakers thus find their citizenship. They make engaged public of the sort impossible in the past.

Notes

1 Prajwala is an NGO based in Hyderabad, founded in 1996 by Dr Sunitha Krishnan and Brother Jose Vetticatil; the organisation actively works in the areas of prevention, rescue, rehabilitation, reintegration and advocacy to combat trafficking in every dimension and restore dignity to victims of commercial sexual exploitation.

2 The *Daily Me* is a term popularized by MIT Media Lab founder Nicholas Negroponte to describe a virtual daily newspaper customized for an individual's tastes. Negroponte discusses it in his 1995 book, *Being Digital*, referencing a project under way at the media lab, Fishwrap.

3 It is used in retail and marketing to refer to the large number of products that sell in small quantities, as contrasted with the small number of best-selling products.

81

4 In media, an echo chamber is a situation in which information, ideas or beliefs are amplified or reinforced by transmission and repetition inside an 'enclosed' system, where different or competing views are censored, disallowed or otherwise underrepresented.

5 Aditya Nigam, 'The non-party domain in contemporary India', Paper prepared for the Project on State of Democracy in South Asia as Part of the Qualitative Assessment of Democracy Lokniti (Programme of Comparative Democracy), Centre for the Study of Developing Societies, 2008, <www.democracyasia.org/qa/india/Aditya%20Nigam.pdf>.

6 Swati Bute, 'The role of social media in mobilising people for riots and revolutions', in Bogdan Patrut and Monica Patrut (eds.), *Social Media in Politics: Case Studies on the Political Power of Social Media*, London: Springer, 2014, pp. 355–366.

7 Valerie Belair-Gangon, Smeeta Mishra, and Colin Agur, 'Emerging spaces for storytelling: Journalistic lessons from social media in the Delhi gang rape case', 8 April 2013, <http://www.niemanlab.org>, accessed on 16 June 2013.

8 Nancy Fraser, 'Social justice in the age of identity politics: Redistribution, recognition and participation', The Tanner Lectures on Human Values, Stanford University, California, 30 April–2 May 1996.

9 F. Fukuyama, 'Social capital and civil society', 1999, <http://www.imf.org/external/pubs/ft/seminar/1999/reforms/fukuyama.htm>; M. Castells, 'Communication, power and counter-power in the network society', *International Journal of Communication*, 1, 2007, pp. 238–266; M. Castells, 'Toward a sociology of the network society', *Contemporary Sociology*, 29 (5), September 2000, pp. 693–699; and M. W. Foley and B. Edwards, 'The paradox of civil society', *Journal of Democracy*, 7 (3), 1996, pp. 38–52.

10 Suw Charman Anderson, 'Making the connection civil society and social media', *Commission by the Carnegie UK Trust*, 2010, <www.futuresfor civilsociety.org>.

11 EESC, 'Study on social media and social networking as agents of participatory democracy and civic empowerment', The EESC Engages Organized Civil Society Organizations Online prepared by Semantica Research for European Economic and Social Committee, 15 October 2012, <http://www.eesc.europa.eu/resources/docs/qe-31-13-867-en.pdf>, accessed on 15 July 2014.

12 Sudipta Kaviraj and Sunil Khilnani, *Civil Society – History and Possibilities*, Cambridge: Cambridge University Press, 2001.

13 Jan Aart Scholte, 'Civil Society and Democracy in Global Governance', CSGR Working Paper No. 65/01, Centre for the Study of Globalisation and Regionalisation (CSGR), University of Warwick, Coventry, January 2001.

14 Gerhard Lehmbruch, 'Germany', in Yamamoto Tadashi (ed.), *Governance and Civil Society in a Global Age*, Tokyo: Japan Center for International Exchange, 2001, p. 230.

15 Larry Diamond, *Development Democracy: Toward Consolidation*, Baltimore: The Johns Hopkins University Press, 1999, p. 221.

16 B. S. Baviskar, 'NGOs and civil society in India', *Sociological Bulletin*, 50 (1), 2001, pp. 3–15.

17 J. L. Cohen and A. Arato, *Civil Society and Political Theory*, Cambridge, MA: MIT Press, 1992.

18 N. Chandhoke, 'Civil society', in A. Cornwall and D. Eade (eds.), *Deconstructing Development Discourse, Buzzwords and Fuzzwords*, Warwickshire: Practical Action Publishing, 2010, pp. 176–184; D. L. Sheth, 'Nation building and the making of civil society', in R. Bhargava and H. Reifeld (eds.), *Civil Society, Public Sphere and Citizenship*, New Delhi: Sage, 2005, pp. 384–401; and R. Tandon, *Voluntary Action, Civil Society and the State*, New Delhi: Mosaic Books, 2002.

19 Tandon 2002: 32.

20 N. G. Jayal, 'Situating Indian democracy', in N. G. Jayal (ed.), *Democracy in India*, New Delhi: Oxford University Press, 2001, pp. 1–49.

21 OECD, *Civil Society and Aid Effectiveness: Findings, Recommendations and Good Practice*, Publication Series, Paris: Better Aid, OECD Publishing, 2009.

22 Amir Ali, 'The evolution of the public sphere in India', *Economic and Political Weekly*, 30 June 2001, pp. 2419–2425.

23 Maia Ramnath, 'Two revolutions: The Ghadar Movement and India's radical diaspora, 1913–1918', *Radical History Review*, 92, Spring 2005, pp. 7–30; and Bipan Chandra, Mridula Mukherjee, Aditya Mukherjee, K. N. Panikkar, and Sucheta Mahajan, *India's Struggle for Independence*, New Delhi: Penguin Books India, 1989.

24 Gail Omvedt, 'Peasants, Dalits and women: Democracy and India's new social movements', *Journal of Contemporary Asia*, 24 (1), 1994; Ghanshyam Shah, *Social Movements in India – A Review of the Literature*, New Delhi, Newbury Park and London: Sage Publications, 1990, pp. 35–48; and Pramod Parajuli, 'Power and knowledge in development discourse: New social movements and the state in India', *International Social Science Journal*, 43 (1), 1991, pp. 173–190.

25 Chandhoke 2010.

26 'Society for participatory research in India', <http://www.pria.org/-media/1723-capacity-challenges-for-civil-society-in-india>, accessed on 7 May 2013.

27 Gurpreet Mahajan, 'Civil society and its avtars', *Economic and Political Weekly*, 15–21 May 1999, pp. 1118–1196.

28 Catherine Corrigall-Brown, 'Protesting more, but alone', <http://www.irpp.org/po/archive/nov12/corrigall.pdf>.

29 Bruce Bimber, Andrew J. Flaganin, and Cynthia Stohl, 'Reconceptualising collective action in contemporary media environment, international communication association', *Communication Theory*, 15(4), 2005, pp. 365–388.

30 ANUpoll, 'Public opinion on Internet use and civil society', Australian National Institute for Public Policy, April 2011, <http://lyceum.anu.edu.au/wp-content/blogs/3/uploads//ANUpoll%20report.pdf>.

31 Hacktivismo, 'Hacktivismo', 10 April 2003, http://www.hacktivismo.com/.

32 Hugh Heclo, 'The issue network and the executive establishment', in Anthony King (ed.), *The New American Political System*, Washington, DC: American Enterprise Institute for Public Policy Research, 1978, p. 104.

33 Mark Surman and Katherine Reilly, 'Appropriating the Internet for social change: Towards the strategic use of networked technologies by transitional civil society organizations', Information Technology and International Cooperation Program, Social Science Research Council, November 2003.

34 Ashish Hattangdi and Atanu Ghosh, 'Enhancing the quality and accessibility of higher education through the use of information and communication technologies', <http://www.iitk.ac.in/infocell/announce/convention/papers/Strategy%20Learning-01-Ashish%20Hattangdi,%20%20Atanu%20Ghosh.pdf>.

35 R. Sharma, 'Barriers in using technology for education in developing countries', *IEEE* Proceedings, ITRE 2003, International Conference, 11–13 August 2003, *Information Technology: Research and Education*, 2003, 0–7803–7724–9103; B. C. Sanyal, 'New functions of higher education and ICT to achieve education for all', Paper prepared for the Expert Roundtable on University and Technology-for-Literacy and Education Partnership in Developing Countries, International Institute for Educational Planning, UNESCO, 10–12 September, Paris, 2001; and I. Bhattacharya and K. Sharma, 'India in the knowledge economy – an electronic paradigm', *International Journal of Educational Management*, 21 (6), 2007, pp. 543–568.

36 J. Naughton, *A Brief History of the Future: The Origins of the Internet*, London: Weidenfeld and Nicolson, 1999.

37 Helmut Anheier, Marlies Glasius, and Mary Kaldor, 'Introduction', in Helmut Anheier, Marlies Glasius, and Mary Kaldor (eds.), *Global Civil Society Yearbook 2001*, Oxford: Oxford University Press, 2001, pp. 3–22.

38 Noortje Marres, 'Net-work is format work: Issue networks and the sites of civil society politics', in Jodi Dean, John Asherson, and Geert Lovink (eds.), *Reformatting Politics: Networked Communications and Global Civil Society*, London: Routledge, 2006, pp. 3–17.

39 W. Lance Bennet, 'New media power: The Internet and global activism', in Nick Couldry and James Curran (eds.), *Contesting Media Power: Alternative Media in a Networked World*, Lanham, MD: Rowman and Littlefield, 2003, pp. 17–37; and W. Lance Bennett, 'Ithiel Sola Pool lecture: The uncivic culture: Communication, identity, and the rise of lifestyle politics', *PS: Political Science and Politics*, 31 (4), 1998, pp. 740–761.

40 Margaret E. Keck and Kathryn Sikkink, *Activists beyond Borders*, Ithaca, NY: Cornell University Press, 1998.

41 Craig Warkentin, *Reshaping World Politics, NGOs, the Internet and Global Civil Society*, Lanham, MD: Rowman and Littlefield, 2001, p. 32.

42 M. Castells, *The Information Age: Economy, Society and Culture, the Rise of Network Society*, Malden and Oxford: Blackwell, 1996.

43 See <http://indianngos.org/>.

44 See <http://www.civilsocietyonline.com/>.

45 See <http://ccsindia.org/>.

46 See <http://www.ngosindia.com/>.

47 See <http://www.accountabilityindia.in/>.

48 See <http://indiacso.ning.com/>.

49 See <http://www.indianandcowboy.com>. Indian & Cowboy is an independent indigenous media company that creates, produces and publishes indigenous media projects across multiple platforms on the Internet and for broadcast media.

50 See <http://www.indianandcowboy.com/stories-from-the-land/>.

51 M. Bahnisch, 'The political uses of blogs', in A. Bruns and J. Jacobs (eds.), *Uses of Blogs*, New York: Peter Lang, 2006, pp. 139–149; Antony Mayfield, 'What is social media?', iCrossing, 2008, <http://www.icrossing.

co.uk/fileadmin/uploads/eBooks/What_is_Social_Media_iCrossing_ebook.pdf>; and K. D. Trammell, 'The blogging of the president', in A. P. Williams and J. C. Tedesco (eds.), *The Internet Election: Perspectives on the Web in Campaign*, Lanham: Rowman & Littlefield, 2006, pp. 133–146.

52 See <http://www.merinews.com/>.

53 See <http://www.mutiny.in/>.

54 Common Dreams NewsCenter, <www.commondreams.org>, lists (in left column) alternative media sources (and corporate media sources online). Other popular sites include AlterNet www.alternet.org, a project of the Independent Media Institute, WebActive <www.webactive.com and BuzzFlash Report www.buzzflash.com>.

55 Christian Fuchs, 'Alternative media as critical media', *European Journal of Social Theory*, University of Salzburg, Austria, 13 (2), 2010, pp. 173–192, <http://fuchs.uti.at/wp-content/uploads/altmedia.pdf>, accessed on 13 January 2013.

56 J. H. Downing, *Radical Media: Rebellious Communication and Social Movements*, Thousand Oaks: Sage Publications, 2001, pp. 27–35.

57 See <http://www.petitiononline.com/petitions/ps0424/signatures?page=2>.

58 See <http://www.petitiononline.com/petitions/06042011/signatures?page=7>.

59 See <http://www.petitiononline.com/burma123/petition.html>.

60 Kirk Kristofferson, Katherine White, and John Peloza, 'The nature of slacktivism: How the social observability of an initial act of token support affects subsequent prosocial action', The University of Chicago Press and Journal of Consumer Research Inc, 2013, <128.206.9.138>, accessed on 9 November 2013.

61 See the Ice Bucket Challenge on Facebook, 18 August 2014, <http://newsroom.fb.com/news/2014/08/the-ice-bucket-challenge-on-facebook/>.

62 See <https://www.facebook.com/kissoflovekochi>.

63 See <http://www.bbc.com/news/world-asia-india-29471518>.

64 See more at <http://indianexpress.com/article/india/india-others/indian-singer-yesudas-against-women-wearing-jeans/#sthash.UidfMGKV.dpuf>.

65 Archon Fung and Jennifer Shkabatur, 'Viral engagement: Fast, cheap, and broad, but good for democracy?', 1 October 2012, <archonfung.net/docs/articles/2012/ViralEngagement5.pdf>.

66 See <https://www.linkedin.com/groups/Th-nking-Indian-6649160?home=&gid=6649160&trk=anet_ug_hm>; it had over 700 members just within four months of its formation and is perhaps one of the leading discussion groups.

67 Philip N. Howard, *New Media Campaigns and the Managed Citizen*, Cambridge: Cambridge University Press, 2006.

68 Philip N. Howard, *The Digital Origins of Dictatorship and Democracy*, Oxford: Oxford University Press, 2010.

69 Jessica Clark and Patricia Aufderheide, 'Public media 2.0: Dynamic, engaged publics', Report by Centre for Social Media, School of Communications, American University, Washington, DC, 2009.

70 Ibid.: 6–7.

4

SOCIAL TOGETHERNESS

This chapter is an attempt to link social media landscape in the context of both India and the book title of Robert Putnam's seminal work discussing the state of social capital in the USA and Italy, *Bowling Alone: The Collapse and Revival of American Community*. It takes you to Robert Putnam's idea and explores if Internet platforms such as Facebook and Twitter are important channels of building 'we' feeling that Putnam overlooked, though not deliberately. There are tribes of people who form social capital in the rigid and feudalised social order in India. This form of social capital is a sort of linking capital. They do it by way of intimate speak. The title, *social togetherness*, decodes the mechanics of social capital both bridging and bonding, which facilitates a linking capital in Indian Internet, at least among the subaltern and minority groups. If so, it is interesting to understand whether there is a tribe feeling on social media age.

Conduits of expressions and channels of communications in social websites are making sense of a new sort of camaraderie and union. It is some sort of Internet togetherness. We have habituated to a new way of alone together in technological forms of life. With the connected sociality, we are able to be in touch with one another and connected to wherever we want to be. Yet, we remain alone in the shapeless, intangible horizon of the cyberspace. The little devices of connection help adapt our lives to a new form of detached attachment. In contemporary life, when we are together, each of us is in our own fluff, feverishly and anxiously connected to keyboards and tiny touchscreens. In the silence of connection, people are comfortable with other people carefully kept at distance. Texting, emailing and posting give us the identity we want to be. They are intimate speakers.

Unskilled manoeuvres of amateurs become great success stories on social media. This chapter investigates why social media helps unknown singers like Chandralekha whose song uploaded to YouTube gave her fame and recognition and why a WhatsApp viral song, sung by law college girl students, became a hit on social media. This chapter initially assumes that these success stories are outcome of India's social cleavages where success and social mobility are socially preordained even before birth. In such a society a platform like Facebook and YouTube gives visibility to the under-privileged on the social margins.

Any analysis of social media must be vigilant enough to consider dis-cursive territory in which social solidarity on social media challenges the cleavage-rich social architecture of mainstream social landscape where mainstream narrative is monopolised in favour of a Brahmanic supremacy. Solidarity on social media helps the underprivileged overcome misfortune in the traditional social architecture. Therefore, amateurism is an infotopia for the poorest.

Facebook, Twitter, YouTube, WordPress, websites and narratives of per-sonal experiences tracked over a decade on Internet signify that amateur-ism has many meanings in the connected age. It is confronted with socially determined technological artefacts. Therefore, instead of projecting it as mere occasions of first timers making debut success stories, it is apt to con-sider it as a philosophy that gives justification for crowd-pullers. Be it pho-tography, storytelling or videographs, poorest and underprivileged people create their own economy, audience and community standards. In particu-lar, marginalised communities, who had bad luck of being footnoted in the textual narratives of Sanskritised India, the clicks and finger touches one is making in the connected spaces are more political. The political Internet is counteracting with the heaps of social structure and in so doing, the poor-est are able to bulldoze the textual India that do not have films, arts, crafts, news, culture, music and stories of their own. A discursive social house on Internet brings oppressed people on cutting-edge advantage. What enables them more on a counter-cultural movement and even confrontational in the connected spaces is a new kind of solidarity and one could call it 'link-ing capital'. Peripheries are opposing mass culture and spreading their lot because Internet gives more solidarity, 'we' feeling and togetherness. Social media in particular caters to a new sort of togetherness that forms social capital of the sort, most overlooked by our public imagination, academic curiosity and media attention.

A series of recent studies on Internet and society interfaces, among many worrying findings, have found that women get more endorsements and recognition for their user behaviours on Internet. Women becoming more revealing and expressive on Internet have meaning more than amateurism. Dalit lodging solidarity in connected spaces is more than mere symbol-ism. Third sex gets more of 'we' feeling because political Internet has no heteronormativity. People are making sexual dissent in connected spaces.

What bring Dalits, women, sexual dissenters and third sex activists together is linking capital. It is more profound because Internet has been providing anonymity, uncensored free space and control-free access. The uncensored public sphere thus evolved has no social cleavages, which characterised our society since time immemorial.

Social togetherness is a deliberate use of a term that signifies a peculiar tendency that apparently tells one that mouse clicks and touchscreens have a spare meaning. Each click or touch conveys a story. Your lone encounters in monitors are bringing in a new solidarity. There are encouraging stories of lone encounters of the mouse charmers on Indian Internet. There are inspiring social media stories picked up from the social peripheries. Not that before Internet one was reclusive and cloistered, but rather in Internet age, loneliness as a terrible poverty is a thing of past, rather it is leveraged by connection platforms for new sort of togetherness.

Whom do I know on social media?

In the book *Making Democracy Work* and *Bowling Alone*, Robert Putnam[1] fetched attention to the role social networks and social trust play in improving the well-being of individuals, groups, communities and society. No one is Robinson Crusoe in the age of connectivity, particularly when social media user profiles in Facebook, blogs and so on are testimonials. It is assumed that one cannot think of opting to live alone in the age of hyper-connectivity since he or she needs someone else in order to make a living. A common maxim that sums up much of the usual wisdom about social capital is that it is not what we know but rather it is whom we know is important in life. Our friends and family constitute the final safety net, when we fall down during hard times. One would say that networks and norms of reciprocity mark the beginning of social capital.[2] As the physical object is to physical capital, knowledge is to social capital and it implies connections among individuals and the value accrued from this connection.[3]

Therefore, consider the networks (bonding, bridging and linking) of people one has in life and ask oneself, whom do I know? What am I willing to do for them? What are others willing to do for me? Hence, we need to have connections among people and organisations, build trust, generate ideas collaboratively, foster communication and make things happen in the community. Individuality flourishes when one has someone whom he or she can trust and rely on a name that is willing to spend time with you and a big shot that he or she knows will be there in time of need, give information or even lend finance without recompense. This someone and the resources they bring with them are social capital.

When one has become rich, gets reputation and attains followers, what happens if our sense of community has contracted? Indeed, it is an assertion often with much overstatement, but it would be reasonable to say that people find no time joining community, groups, voluntary associations and building social trust and networks as they spend more and more time in the office, daily commuting back and forth and watching TV alone at home. Socialising with neighbours and even family bothered little for the atomised individuals in that levels. The decline of community and trust in social space gives a sign of paucity of social capital, which once led people to bowl together, says Robert Putnam.[4] Decrease in the group membership, low political engagement, decline in civic activism and less informal relationships are both a cause and an indicator of a considerable decline in social capital. There must be some detrimental effects that declining social capital can have on the economic productivity of the nation and the emotional well-being of its inhabitants.

Strong-tie and weak-tie relationships are high-flying art in successful social life.[5] When emotions fly up in close relationship, it mirrors a strong tie between people. At the same time, relations with distant people, even anonymous and the only thing that tie up people that way are that of sharing of information in weak-tie relations.[6] Furthermore, when people interact across explicit and formal authority structure, a linking social capital mirrors between citizens and their law enforcement officers, bankers, teachers and health care providers.[7] Thus, linking social capital is simply a theoretical refinement of bridging social capital networks that incorporates only those connected across vertical power disparities, but it is more profoundly significant in a feudal society like India. Bridging relationships take shape within weak-tie relationships and those of bonding within strong-tie relationships. Bridging social capital, therefore, is a loose tie that can share information and bonding social capital is a strong tie with friends and family, which gives emotional support. In fact, while bonding capital activates 'getting by', bridging capital triggers 'getting ahead'.[8]

The central concepts of social capital, therefore, in any forms have three components: moral obligations and norms, social values (mainly trust) and social networks (mainly voluntary associations). Initially pioneered by sociologists,[9] the investigative concept of social capital, in fact, was a multiform thought now without a consensus among scholars.[10] Among the many, social capital reveals a community-level feature and each group or community tends to correlate each other with a degree of trust among members. Putnam unfolds that trust, norms and networks that facilitate coordinated actions shape up social capital. A World Bank study outlines it as the institutions, relationships and norms that figure out the value and measure of social interactions.[11] The rules, norms, obligations, reciprocity and trust embedded in social structures, social relations and institutional arrangements, which facilitate members to achieve their individual and community objectives[12], configure social capital. The essence of social capital is quality of social relations, says W. Stone.[13]

The principal utility of trust and connectivity is that family, individual and group bestow their ties to gain access to resources, confidence and benefits.[14] Social networks, norms and trust form a brand of capital and facilitate attainment of good jobs, peace, performances, well-being, strengthening political engagement, democracy and so forth. Even if some authors do attempt to link social capital to society at large, nearly all readings pertaining to social capital look at individual actors or small groups and their networks and trust levels. Thus, social capital has been seemingly a local network phenomenon.[15]

Winter[16] suggests that social capital encompasses mutual-benefit social relations characterised by trust and reciprocity. The trust and network aspect in social interaction has made considerable headway in development policy debates; for instance, World Bank proposes it as an important development tool[17] in social engineering. It is seen as a crucial factor for alleviating poverty and achieving societal development.[18] Management experts have regarded it as a way of thinking about organisational development and maintenance.[19]

For Grootaert[20] social capital is the glue that holds societies together. It has gained momentum as a wider paradigm for capturing the contributions of social elements in explaining a variety of individual and collective behaviours.[21] The category has been more useful while exploring numerous factors such as social mobility, competitive advantage in economic organisations, political participation, psychological and physical well-being.[22] It has been useful for the study of families, schooling and education to public health.[23] In organisational studies, social capital has been taken in the context of career success, inter-unit resource exchange, employee turnover rates, product innovation, enterprising and supplier relations[24] (Adler and Kwon 2002). Social capital enhances job opportunities since the power of weak ties found in bridging networks are more resourceful while seeking jobs, says Granovetter.[25]

The term *social capital* was first coined in a study of community, in which it came to be believed that social capital might enhance interpersonal networks, by providing a foundation for trust, network, collaboration and group activities.[26] Social capital is a wholly social construct that has emerged from a flood of jargon, but productive for exploring culture, politics, society and social networks.[27] Bargh and McKenna[28], meanwhile, criticise such a skewed representation of social media–powered social capital and contend that the methodology and findings of Nie are erroneous. On the other hand, some researchers discovered that online interactions supplement and may actually replace personal interactions.[29] In fact, several studies observing the effects of online interactions found positive effects on community interaction, involvement and social capital.[30]

Other studies confirm online interactions form positive connections, particularly bridging social capital.[31] On one side, scholars predict an increase in bridging social capital with social networking sites (SNSs) and observe that Facebook promotes the loudening of bridging social capital through the nature of the site itself.[32] SNSs promote the 'friending' of people whom one vaguely knows and sometimes indirectly through other people. This gives the user the possibility to create and maintain larger and diffuse networks, which result in an increase in the bridging social capital.[33] As another way, scholars predict an increase in bonding social capital through social media. Research shows that people add their offline social network to their online social network.[34] SNS becomes a tool for the maintenance of offline relationships, thereby increasing bonding social capital. Therefore, to sum up, an increase in both bridging and bonding social capital could configure in all social media–related networking, collaboration and contentious claim making.

American political scientist Robert Putnam's central thesis is that if a region has a well-functioning economic system and a high level of political integration, they are the result of the region's successful accumulation of social capital. Just as physical, financial and human capital is vital for an organisation, social capital is essential for individuals, says Nan Lin, a sociology professor.[35] In fact, the factors that connect and hold communities and social networks together effect modern life in an age of busy schedules, atomised life and meticulous oppressive social orders. Certainly, the following section of the chapter is an attempt to identify what kind of social capital and social media interplay could configure, considering the large social hierarchy prevailing in India coupled with a fleet of social cleavages, which indeed makes life so difficult for communities on the fringes of India cloistered and cosseted.

A lack of clarity has occurred over the exact meaning of the concept of social capital since reckless compassion over the jurisdiction of the term claiming anything socially beneficial as instance of social capital.[36] This discussion was to identify from a plethora of theoretical literature on social capital that trust, networks, norms, values and storytelling form the core attributes of identifying social capital 2.0 in the social media landscape in India. Social capital holds iconoclastic power, which could destruct the hierarchical social order. In the crippled social structures characterised by Dalit oppression, discrimination against minority and other forms of social cleavages in India social capital appears to be a citadel of emancipation.

Social capital and Internet

This section of the chapter is committed to bringing attention to the theoretical understanding on Internet and social capital analogy. Internet and social capital are a significant correlation in India. More significantly, from the vantage point of social stigma and social exclusion, this correlation in a virtual network is principally a metaphor. People forming beliefs, impressions, values and judgements about each other, particularly with a stranger with whom one could not personally interact before Internet, is a new form of sociality, a cultural shift, says K. H. Craik,[37] and genuinely that could be caustic to the feudal social systems. New media platforms facilitate formation of online as well as offline social capital.[38] Storytelling abilities that shape rich and thoughtful experiences among members of stigmatised community create trust and one could find it more considerable among such communities in India. Perhaps, according to experts, online social networks might not increase strong ties a person may have, say Donath and Boyd.[39] On the other hand, weak ties might increase due to digital technologies since they are most suitable for bridging relations across a variety of factors that have often been disabilities for social progress.

Facebook had a strong association with maintaining existing offline relationships, as opposed to meeting new people.[40] The strongest relationship, however, was between Facebook use and bridging social capital. The study also provides hint that Facebook might provide greater benefits for users who have low self-esteem and low life satisfaction along with facing oppression and social stigma.[41]

At the outset, therefore, let us imagine that there are both utopia and dystopia prevailing over it. Putnam himself has recognised that Americans hold varying levels of civic and political participation due to Facebook, Twitter and a plethora of 'civic technology'.[42] There were many attempts by researchers on analysing the effects of Internet on social capital. Thus, a seesaw of reaction prevails over the kind of social capital consequent to social media. Moreover, the direction of influence remains less clear and not sure about if social media could configure what kind of social capital, be it bridging or bonding social capital. Yet, social scientists agree that social media sites play input task in the expansion of social capital and it can function as a means to build bridging and bonding trust and network.

Built on the ideological and scientific foundation of Web 2.0 platforms,[43] sharing information through social media is resourceful and crucial for communication under some particular circumstances like disasters[44] and health-related events.[45] Different social media sites provide contents that are disparate, though addressing the same basic issue. Virtual communities through bridging social capital have been resurfacing on Indian Internet; for example, Facebook has become more useful for networking in protest events such as anti-graft movements, Save Mullaperiyar campaign, protest against the nuclear plant at Koodankulam and 16 December 2012 rape incident in Delhi. Here a linking capital destructs social cleavages.

N. H. Nie[46] argues that the Internet limits personal interaction and thus limits individual social capital, since users flip over and then vanish on the computer screen or touch pad at the cost of social relations in physical world. Internet could isolate individuals and reduce the time spent participating in social activities, especially if Internet users are mainly engaged in solitary usage (web surfing, news reading etc.). Paul Attewell, Belkis Suazo-Garcia and Juan Battle[47] showed that adolescents with a home computer spend less time practising sports or playing outside. Moreover, virtual sociability is not equivalent to traditional sociability: face-to-face interactions are typically richer than virtual interactions by email, chat or instant messaging.

To assume the effect of social media sites on social trust and network building among Dalits, women, third sex and sexual dissenters, there was a consensus among scholars that Facebook and other social networking sites have a beneficial effect on social capital.[48] Several studies have examined the influence of social capital and social support on Internet usage.[49]

Trust space and network

'The 2012 Delhi gang rape case',[50] a Facebook community (just one among the many on the same subject) with over 5,000 people marking like on it in August 2013, reflected the online sentiments prevailing against the brutal rape of a teenager. People react on Internet. They have no other spaces for showing their anger against political class.

Compassion, trust, sympathy and shared understanding brought people together in technology. In technological solutions that cut across barriers of time, distance and often culture, technology becomes an intimate friend. On issues such as Delhi gang rape and anti-graft movement, sentiments against the nuclear plant at Koodankulam have been the quintessence of technological solutions offered. Social disadvantage and stigma make people come together and social media provides a comfort zone and a form of solidarity.

Social media condenses barriers of costs, distance, network, geography and access for organising collective action. By facilitating communication and coordination across physical and social distance, technology invariably stimulates framing contention in novel ways. A recent example of social trust and network formed on Internet was reflected in an anti-graft movement. The Facebook community 'India Against Corruption' as of January 2013 received around nine lakh likes and three lakh talkings about this. On the issue, the community has posted over two thousand topics. This community page is a vivid description of the trust and network space forging in Indian Internet.

'India Against Corruption', the official Facebook page, reads 'Led by Anna Hazare, IAC is a mass movement by the citizens of India to curb corruption and create a just society. Send pics, news, videos to IACJournalist@gmail.com'.[51]

Equally important is the viral growth of online communities against corruption in line with India Against Corruption campaign. 'I Paid a Bribe', a Facebook community, describes: 'www.ipaidabribe.com is your space to share corruption-related experiences and uncovers the market price of corruption'.

The Facebook page had around 138,667 Facebook likes as of 23 August 2016. 'Fight Against Corruption', another Facebook community, describes: 'The government is fooling the citizens by not accepting the Jan Lokpal Bill. Are you aware of this Bill? Please spare sometime to know about it. It definitely matters each and every one of us'.[52]

The page had around 21,244 likes by 23 August December 2016. In addition, websites, portals and blogs committed to fight against corruption can equally create a collective action platform. What bring them together is their sense of 'we' feeling. It results in contentious politics on issues that are people's issues. Though not directly related to the participants, people become participants from their fiesta corner of home and comfort zones of office. Solidarity is what matters in social media age. A webpage available at http://acorn.nationalinterest.in posted a commentary on corruption titled 'Why Anna Hazare is wrong and Lok Pal a bad idea' on 14 August 2011 and received 740 tweets, 169 recommends in Google+, 58 shares in LinkedIn, 13,000 Facebook likes and 534 comments by 24 January 2013. The pull-out in the *Times of India*'s online edition, 'Anna Hazare's movement is anti-social justice, manuwadi', received 2,700 Facebook likes and 1,340 comments on 24 January 2013. 5th Pillar Corruption Killer received 2,527 like marks and posted 10 notes on corruption-related topics on their website and had seven lakh visitors as on 24 January 2013. Facebook community Anna Hazare had over six lakh likes and around seven thousand talkings about this on 24 January 2013. This happens with every protest collaboration on Internet. People share solidarity. I have just swished into the social profiles. Participants belong to varied socio-economic profiles. There are housewives, students, young people, senior citizens and others. They share sentiments. They share solidarity. Their social media behaviour just represented their mindset. It is their psychology. If no social media, what could have helped such apolitical and depoliticised citizens become more political about the country?

Internet has made possible much greater ease in networking. For instance, 'Save Mullaperiyar Dam, Save Kerala',[53] a Facebook campaign, had 17,430 likes as on 11 January 2013. Members share their solidarity in their timelines. Several networking platforms are active to support a cause, spread an idea, raise fund, express solidarity and so on in Indian Internet that shape up bridging and linking relations. Greenpeace India, which has 323,691 likes as on 23 August 2016, ensures quick network with digital activist on Internet is another example.[54]

Trust building, networking, collaboration and gathering of people who click alone have become easiest and attractive among young people. Online extension of several protest movements have focussed on specific issues such as child rights movements. Child Rights and You, a non-governmental organisation in India that caters to change the lives of underprivileged children, has social media presence in Facebook[55] (268,807 likes on 23 August 2016); it had a website,[56] a twitter profile[57] (6,388 tweets and 14,220 followers), a blog,[58] a YouTube channel[59] with 632 subscribers and a LinkedIn profile[60] with 6,881 connections as on 23 August 2016.

It is easiest to live in communities with strong trust than those with less, and in particular, it is profoundly significant if one was disempowered. When one turns receptive to fresh ideas, resources and new people, it links with different backgrounds and moves on to 'bridging' trust and networks.

Solidarity and storytelling

Solidarity, norms, values and storytelling could have a destabilising effect on social cleavages in connected age; thus social media sites become a mediating force. At least according to Vivek P. Nambiar, as reported in the local daily *Mathrubhumi* (26 September 2014: 10), social media sites draw up a new form of togetherness. The news was a Facebook post on 24 September 2014. As an ISRO scientist, he was off to his quarters in the evening on the day India's MOM (Mars Orbiter Mission) was successfully placed on Mars. He hired an auto rickshaw as it was raining. While fixing the rate at 45, he started talk with the driver. While confirming that his client is an ISRO scientist, the driver enquired if MOM could be operated after ten months. And the driver in a fun-packed reply said that if it were his auto rickshaw it won't start after one day. When Vivek was about to be dropped at his place, the driver was hesitant to accept the auto fare and said, 'Sir we are proud of our scientists'. He shared this story on Facebook the same day. Certainly, Facebook has become a storytelling place where people get new 'we' feelings.

The game has changed! One no longer needs to live in a broadcast age where one waits for the mercy of the editors where marketers could plainly buy people's attention. On social media, no one is connecting with consumers but with people. While doing so, the only thing that makes it so possible is same-interest stories. It has also changed how we can interact and solve problems. Therefore, norms and value systems could change. Old values will be replaced by philosophies that are more inclusive.

Adivasi communities in Kerala staged 'Standing-Up' protest in front of the government secretariat asserting their rights over the alienated land since 9th of July 2014. However, the state, media and the public made a mockery of the struggle and there was scant attention from the media. It was not news for the mainstream media, but Internet gave it a space. Social platforms channelled solidarity for the protestors at least from amongst the informed citizenry of educational institutions and progressive organisations. Students of TISS, a leading educational institution, gave their social support via www.indiaresists.com/ and posted their messages.[61]

Just think of intimate speak is why Internet is building solidarity, thereby bulldozing old structures. For example, it was a Facebook communication between a Pakistani citizen, Bilal Ahmad, and I, which underlined this chapter's assumption that solidarity is being built by channels of expression on social media. Once, Bilal Ahmad, one of my Pakistani friends, wished me on New Year Day 2014 and it was in Facebook. However, when I responded, he said that though the world has new year, new hopes, desires and expectations we have nothing new, for there are the same old 'American Drones' and the same old Pak Army operations full of every kind of cruelty and inhumane operations in mine locality FATA. I replied, 'I extend him my support and solidarity'. This communication was significant in the sense that what actually was spreading in mainstream media about both countries were misplaced notions. I have seen many leading Pakistan-based intellectuals and leading diplomats who have significant influence on Pak establishment, spreading stereotypes about India. As Pakistan is a society largely discoursed in three As – Allah, Army and America – their future is not prospective unless they are able to delete unwanted intrusion of these three things from their politics. I remember an interesting episode the day before Independence Day celebration in India on 15 August 2014, in a TV debate on national channel Times Now, when Arnab Goswami asked a question to Khurshid Mahmud Kasuri, a Pakistani politician who was the Minister of Foreign Affairs from November 2002 until November 2007 under President Pervez Musharraf. The question was how you feel about India as a Pakistani hardliner in Pak circle. Quite interestingly, he said, 'India is a Brahmin society. Half of its people live in abject poverty'. It means in Pak society anti-Indian sentiments are sold like pornography. Their politicians and decision makers are addicted to them. It is their only lucrative fortune-making model. People at the society level, however, are loving, caring, wishing and share a common heritage. Here comes the trajectory of linking social capital and thus ordinary people from both the countries interact at the society level using social media platforms.

Internet is an abode of conveying your message. Certainly, it could have more significance in respect of its ability in documenting solidarity for a cause, a challenge and a struggle. Matrimonial sites such as shaadi.com, bharatmatrimony.com, simplymarry.com, matrimonialsindia.com and jeevansathi.com offer young women a space for meeting prospective partners while breaking old social systems where women do not have a say in finding their partner. It was earlier just an agreement between parents. Now things are going to be changed! Dating sites such as indiandating.com, hi5.com, apundesi.com, datedosti.com, metrodate.com and india-match.com offer a space for getting like-minded people with whom one could make a relationship in an otherwise highly rigid social structure. It is letting young people to experiment their own friends, partners, meeting new people transcending cultural constraints and tradition-bound social order. With families, traditions, taboos and stigmas still curbing any socially intolerable expressions, the platforms are becoming new ways of channelising the otherwise hindered social expressions. Now, it is easiest to open account on chat sites such as chatrooms.co.in, indiachat.co.in, chatrooms.org.in, onlinechat.co.in, chat.oneindia.in, allindiachat.com and talkdesi.com and find new people, increase relationship, gossip what one feels to utter and put across anything to any extent.

For the queer such as lesbians, gay, transgender, bisexual and inter-sex groups, social media is the safest place ever to get in a wild land of hetero-normativity. The queer go in search of solidarity in connected spaces. Social websites to the cause of sexual minorities are aplenty and empower the marginalised sexual minorities. See social profiles of sahodaran.org, mingle.org.in/, bombaydost.co.in, pink-pages.co.in, planetromeo.com and wordpress.com/. I have digital ethnographic exploration on those profiles. When their user behaviours were closely observed, it was found that they are instances of digital citizenship and belonging for sexual minorities in India.

Social profiles are also catering to Dalit activism. They are able to create togetherness. In particular, linking capital could be more profound on Internet and plenty of platforms that cater to these purposes are thriving day by day. Websites such as navsarjan.org/, ncdhr.org.in, drambedkar.org and upliftthem.blogspot.in are particularly a political choice where subalterns are fast migrating, believing that their inferior social position could be challenged because Internet could build solidarity.

Information sharing

There is a compelling reason to make a new proposition that alternative media platforms are catalyst to a new kind of alone together. What is more significant is that it gives an opportunity structure to frame a new sort of identity that is otherwise impossible in a commercialised media space. Stop Rape Now!,[62] an online petition by Namita Bhandare posted on http://www.change.org, had 665,757 supporters by May-end 2013 and has been a huge success story because it offers a solid set of recommendations to those within the state machinery who can make a difference. The petition made its way to the Justice Verma Committee's offices.[63] Indians today are willing to hold the problems of gender-based violence and discrimination and realise that everyone has a part to play. There are enormous networking platforms to support a cause, spread an idea, raise fund, express solidarity and so on to easily network with digital citizens. Here the digital citizenship hasn't had any kind of offline prejudices and social cleavages. The only thing that makes them get together is their same-interest subjects. The rigid social structure could be demolished, they believe. Social media has iconoclastic power. It is an image-breaking metaphor. It could build solidarity. User profiles surveyed for this chapter give proof for this assumption.

Human rights activism, fund-raising, petitioning against violence and spreading awareness via publications reflect an emerging virtual solidarity. Besides sharing information, social media has use in maintaining social relationships with one's friends and other actors in his or her existing social networks, as well as to develop new relationships with a vast population of unknown people in the world.[64] A web of movements have come recently when new social movement issues have taken digital routes, so networks and information sharing show values of linking capital to reach out to the social walls where subalterns exist without their own textual narratives. They have no stories because they do not have a space. And social media will just give storytelling place.

Internet enables existing struggles and makes new actions possible. Many traditional environmental groups, feminists, human rights and other new movement groups have websites, social media presence on Facebook, Twitter, YouTube and profiles in other interactive platforms. Plenty of them organise through social media and provide websites with information, articles, news and plan of ways for people to get new information and more composite interaction.

Facebook, Twitter, LinkedIn and so on create new ties and keep in contact with existing ties, thereby gaining bridging and bonding social capital. At the most, they most profoundly get linking capital; this is particularly so because of social media and its enormous opportunity structure, so ordinary people could have a space without social stigmas and entrenched social cleavages. Internet and particularly online communities might contribute to enriching social capital on Indian Internet in the backdrop of a range of protests, networks and collaborative efforts reported. A host of issues raised online signify a new form of togetherness, sharing and trust existing among a whole lot of strangers and anonymous people.

Internet advocacy groups are increasingly using online platforms for various activities. They use platforms to support a public cause, to sponsor an issue, to defeat or win an agenda, to disseminate information and ideas and to communicate with supporters and allies. Internet is increasingly used for mobilisation of participants, sending messages to the public, creating online forums for discussions and raising funds. It helps them to get media attention as issues nowadays first become viral on social media and the mass media track it on cyberspace. Internet is also used for educating the public. Internet offers a wide range of platforms for materialising advocacy. Anyone could generate and place user contents online, and the underprivileged people could see and retort to posts by their friends as opposite to organisations.

New media reshape discussions and debates within and across groups, changing intergroup relationships and attitudes. Every day people make a click on their mouse for various reasons and 'knowingly' or 'unknowingly' they become part of a shared network of individual experiences. The Facebook community 'Delhi Protests VS Gujarat Protests' status update on 25 December 2012 received 251 likes, 615 shares and 44 comments as on 30 December 2012, just in five days.

The Facebook photo share reads that 'Rampant Discrimination with victims on the basis of caste. Why show mood-based outrage as per convenience? Why not show equal anger on all cases of Injustice and Crime? Why discriminate between victims of same Pain?'[65]

Another photo share in Facebook community 'I Hate LOnlinezz But It Lovez ME More' page update status on 27 December 2012 received 2,453 likes, 2,526 shares and 117 comments as on 30 December 2012.

The photo page comments that 'Girls are not toys, Girls are not for entertainment, Girls have equal right to live and enjoy, So plz Guys.. Only for your entertainment.. DON'T ENJOY HER'.[66]

The Facebook Community status update on 27 December 2012 received 198 likes, 229 shares and 24 comments as on 30 December 2012.[67]

An interesting Facebook photo share is 'Reality of Our Great Indian Corporate Media | Will INDIA benefit from such MEDIA?'

What is resurfacing in all the actions cited is group solidarity and con-solidation of inter-group network that could break away old prejudices and taboos. Whether for Dalits, women, against media corporatisation, they are a sort of informed reactions, which are different from most direct action programmes from offline in the past. As a new social space, new media cul-tivates fresh sentiments of togetherness that bring atomised digital citizens clicking alone into common platforms.

Satisfying human needs and wants remains the most important techno-logical challenge we face today. Examining the effective utilisation of widely available communication technologies for figuring social capital, both bonding and bridging claim the centre of attention for digital optimists. Internet better supports all these communities and encourages others in a way that increases social capital locally, nationally and internationally. We participate in such communities, regardless of our income, education, race, culture or gender.

Technology and social change go hand in hand since new technologies would undermine existing problems between people and their immediate social environment (Katz, Rice and Aspden 2001). The hoard of social trust, connectivity, norms and networks that people can draw upon to solve common problems strengthens democracy, politics and well-being of the nation. Trust and networks reflect the prerequisite of stable liberal democ-racy, says Francis Fukuyama.[68]

Those who were born after Internet easily endorse and those born before Internet are on a snail's pace to acknowledge that social media facilitates social capital. They are proper sticker to the biography of social seclusion and feudal order. We have educated the habit of cleaning social cleavages with technol-ogy we use. The move from conversation to connection is part of this.

Now, it is much clear that, be it bridging, bonding or linking, social websites are able to foment newer forms of social capital. It gives people a storytelling place. Users get a space for building solidarity in a rigid social structure. Trust, norms and networks are easiest since the wider popularity of platforms is amongst ordinary people. In fact, in an age where connectivity marks the health of democracy and well-being of a nation, what other than social media platforms could reconfigure networks, collaboration, 'we' space, trust and solidarity? It is a cost-free and a quick-access medium. Social media and social capital move on towards the same direction.

An armada of social media sites has achieved popularity recently for specific activities. These activities range from philanthropy to profit making. In between, it has been used for political engagement, advocacy, campaigns, information dissemination, business networks, collaboration and so on. Among these, one important feature that perhaps gets a boost is social capital among communities who were cosseted and secluded from the mainstream; they are intimate speakers. Trust and network are possible among stigmatised groups. And social media just facilitates political Internet.

Notes

1 R. D. Putnam, *Making Democracy Work: Civic Traditions in Modern Italy*, Princeton, NJ: Princeton University Press, 1993; and R. D. Putnam, *Bowling Alone: The Collapse and Revival of American Community*, New York: Simon and Schuster, 2000.
2 Putnam 2000.
3 B. Daniel, 'Building social capital in virtual learning communities', University of Saskatchewan, April 2002, p. 5, <http://etad.usask.ca/802papers/daniel/>, accessed on 18 April 2012.
4 Putnam 1993.
5 M. Granovetter, 'The strength of weak ties', *American Journal of Sociology*, 78 (6), 1973, pp. 1360–1380.
6 M. Granovetter, 'The strength of weak-ties: A network theory revisited', *Sociological Theory*, 1, 1983, pp. 201–233.
7 S. Stretzer and M. Woolcok, 'Health by association? Social capital, social theory, and the political economy of public health', *International Journal of Epidemiology*, 33 (4), 2003, pp. 650–667.
8 X. De Souza Briggs, 'Doing democracy up close: Culture, power, and communication building', *Journal of Planning and Education Research*, 18 (1), 1998, pp. 1–13.
9 James S. Coleman, 'Social capital in the creation of human capital', *American Journal of Sociology*, 94, 1988, pp. 95–120; and Ronald S. Burt, *Structural Holes: The Social Structure of Competition*, Cambridge, MA: Harvard University Press, 1992.
10 Steven N. Durlauf, 'On the empirics of social capital', *Economic Journal*, 112, 2002, pp. 459–479; and Charles Manski, 'Economic analysis of social interactions', *Journal of Economic Perspectives*, 14, 2000, pp. 269–295.
11 World Bank, 'What is social capital?', 2000, <www.worldbank.org/poverty>.

12 Deepa Narayan, *Voices of the Poor: Poverty and Social Capital in Tanzania*, Washington, DC, USA: World Bank, 1997.
13 W. Stone, 'Social capital, social cohesion and social security', Paper presented at the International Research Conference on Social Security, 2000, <http://www.aifs.gov.au/institute/pubs/papers/stone2.html>.
14 N. Lin, *Social Capital: A Theory of Structure and Action*, London: Cambridge University Press, 2001, p. 19; and P. Bourdieu, 'The forms of capital', in J. G. Richardson (ed.), *Handbook of Theory and Research for the Sociology of Education*, New York: Greenwood Press, 1986, pp. 241–258.
15 C. L. Prell, 'Social capital as network capital: Looking at the role of social networks among not-for-profits', *Sociological Research Online*, 11, 2006, <http://www.socresonline.org.uk/11/4/prell.html>.
16 I. Winter, *Towards a Theorised Understanding of Family Life and Social Capital*, Melbourne: Australian Institute of Family Studies, 2000, p. 1.
17 C. Grootaert, 'Social Capital: The Missing Link?', Working Paper 3, World Bank, Washington, DC, 1998.
18 D. Eade, 'Editorial', *Development in Practice*, 13 (4), 2003, pp. 307–309.
19 D. Cohen and L. Prusak, *In Good Company: How Social Capital Makes Organizations Work*, Boston, MA: Harvard Business School Press, 2001.
20 Grootaert 1998: 1.
21 P. S. Adler and S.-W. Kwon, 'Social capital: Prospects for a new concept', *The Academy of Management Review*, 27 (1), 2002, pp. 17–40.
22 N. Lin and B. H. Erickson, 'Theory, measurement, and the research enterprise on social capital', in N. Lin and B. H. Erickson (eds.), *Social Capital: An International Research Program*, New York: Oxford University Press Inc; 2008.
23 Adler and Kwon 2002.
24 Ibid.
25 Granovetter 1973: 1368.
26 J. Jacobs, *The Death and Life of Great American Cities*, London: Penguin Books, 1965.
27 B. Daniel, R. Schwier, and G. McCalla, 'Social capital in virtual learning communities and distributed communities of practice', *Canadian Journal of Learning and Technology*, 29 (3), Fall 2003, p. 3, <http://www.cjlt.ca/index.php/cjlt/article/view/85/79>.
28 J. A. Bargh and K. Y. A. McKenna, 'The Internet and social life', *Annual Review of Psychology*, 55, 2004, pp. 573–590.
29 B. Wellman, A. Q. Haase, J. Witte, and K. Hampton, 'Does the Internet increase, decrease, or supplement social capital? Social networks, participation, and community commitment', *American Behavioral Scientist*, 45 (3), 2001, p. 436.
30 A. Kavanaugh, J. M. Carroll, M. B. Rosson, T. T. Zin, and D. D. Reese, 'Community networks: Where offline communities meet online', *Journal of Computer-Mediated Communication*, 10 (4), 2005, <http://jcmc.indiana.edu/vol10/issue4/kavanaugh.html>, accessed on 27 April 2008.
31 N. B. Ellison, C. Steinfield, and C. Lampe, 'The benefits of Facebook "friends": Social capital and college students' use of online social network sites', *Computer-Mediated Communication*, 12 (4), 2007, article 1, <http://jcmc.indiana.edu/vol12/issue4/ellison.html>, accessed on 30 August 2009.

32 J. Lewis and A. West, 'Friending: London based undergraduates' experience of Facebook', *New Media Society*, 11, 2009, pp. 1210–1229.

33 N. B. Ellison, C. Steinfield, and C. Lampe, 'Spatially bounded online social networks and social capital: The role of Facebook', International Conference on Communication Association, Dresden, 2006.

34 A. Lenhart and M. Madden, 'Teens, privacy, and online social networks', Pew Internet and American Life Project Report, 2007, <http://www.pewinternet.org/pdfs/PIP_Teen s_Privacy_SNS_Report_Final.pdf>, accessed on 3 June 2011; and M. Vergeer and B. Pelzer, 'Consequences of media and Internet use for offline and online network capital and well-being: A causal model approach', *Journal of Computer-Mediated Communication*, 15, 2009, pp. 189–210.

35 Lin 2001.

36 Rory J. Clarke, 'Bowling together', *OECD Observer*, OECD, 24 March 2003, web, 2004, <http://www.oecdobserver.org/news/fullstory.php/aid/1215/Bowling_together.html/>, accessed on 10 January 2011.

37 K. H. Craik, *Reputation: A Network Interpretation*, New York: Oxford University Press, 2009.

38 Adler and Kwon 2002.

39 J. Donath and D. Boyd, 'Public displays of connection', *BT Technology Journal*, 22 (4), 2004, pp. 71–82.

40 Ellison, Steinfield, and Lampe 2007.

41 J. Horrigan, *Online Communities: Networks That Nurture Long Distance Relationships and Local Ties*, Washington, DC: Pew Internet and American Life Project, 2001.

42 T. H. Sander and R. D. Putnam, 'Still bowling alone? The post-9/11 split', *Journal of Democracy*, 21 (1), 2010, pp. 9–16.

43 A. M. Kaplan and M. Haenlein, 'Users of the world, unite! The challenges and opportunities of social media', *Business Horizons*, 53 (1), 2010, pp. 59–68.

44 L. S. Palen, S. Vieweg, S. B. Liu, and A. L. Hughes, 'Crisis in a networked world features of computer-mediated communication in the April 16, 2007, Virginia Tech Event,' *Social Science Computer Review*, 27 (4), 2009, pp. 467–480.

45 W. Y. S. Chou, Y. M. Hunt, E. B. Beckjord, R. P. Moser, and B. W. Hesse, 'Social media use in the United States: Implications for health communication', *Journal of Medical Internet Research*, 11 (4), 2009, e48. doi: 10.2196/jmir.1249. <http://www.jmir.org/2009/4/e48/>.

46 N. H. Nie, 'Sociability, interpersonal relations, and the Internet: Reconciling conflicting findings', *American Behavioral Scientist*, 45 (3), 2001, pp. 420–435.

47 Paul A. Attewell, Belkis Suazo-Garcia, and Juan Battle, 'Computers and young children: Social benefit or social problem', *Social Forces*, 82 (1), 2003, pp. 277–296.

48 Ellison, Steinfield, and Lampe 2007: 1143–1168; P. U. Bhalchandra, N. K. Deshmukh, S. D. Khamitkar, S. N. Lokhande, S. S. Phulari, and A. R. Shinde, 'Understanding formulation of social capital in online Social Network Sites (SNS)', *International Journal of Computer Sciences*, 7 (1), 2010, pp. 92–96; S. Valenzuela, N. Park, and K. F. Kee, 'Is there social capital in a

social networking site?: Facebook use and college students' life satisfaction, trust and participation', *Journal of Computer-Mediated Communication*, 14 (4), 2009, pp. 875–901; and A. Kavanaugh and S. J. Patterson, 'The impact of community computer networks on social capital and community involvement', *American Behavioral Scientist*, 45, 2001, pp. 496–509.

49 Paul DiMaggio, Eszter Hargittai, Coral Celeste, and Steven Shafer, 'From unequal access to differentiated use: A literature review and agenda for research on digital inequality', in K. Neckerman (ed.), *Social Inequality*, New York: Russell Sage Foundation, 2004, pp. 355–400; Avi Goldfarb, 'The (teaching) role of universities in the diffusion of the internet', *International Journal of Industrial Organization*, 24 (2), 2006, pp. 203–225; and Ritu Agarwal, Animesh Animesh, and Kislaya Prasad, 'Social Interactions and the Digital Divide: Explaining Regional Variations on Internet Use', Robert Smith School Research Paper No. 06-024, 22 August 2005, <http://ssrn.com/abstract=796090> or <http://dx.doi.org/10.2139/ssrn.796090>, accessed on 22 August 2014.

50 See   <https://www.facebook.com/pages/2012-Delhi-gang-rape-case/315301411908352?ws&nr>.

51 See <http://www.facebook.com/Indiacor>.

52 See <http://www.facebook.com/IndianFightAgainstCorruption?fref=pb>.

53 See <https://www.facebook.com/savemullaperiyar>.

54 See http://www.facebook.com/greenpeaceindia?ref=ts&fref=ts>.

55 See <http://www.facebook.com/CRYINDIA>.

56 See <http://www.cry.org/index.html>.

57 See <https://twitter.com/CRYINDIA>.

58 See <http://blog.cry.org/>.

59 See <https://www.youtube.com/c/crychildrightsandyou>.

60 See <https://www.linkedin.com/company/cry>.

61 See <http://www.indiaresists.com/in-solidarity-with-stand-up-protest/>.

62 See <http://www.change.org/en-IN/petitions/president-cji-stop-rape-now>.

63 Justice Verma Committee was constituted to recommend amendments to the Criminal Law so as to provide for quicker trial and enhanced punishment for criminals accused of committing sexual assault against women. The committee submitted its report on 23 January 2013.

64 R. D. Waters, E. Burnett, A. Lamm, and J. Lucas, 'Engaging stakeholders through social networking: How nonprofit organizations are using Facebook', *Public Relations Review*, 35 (2), 2009, pp. 102–106.

65 Babasaheb Ambedkar's Page, <http://www.facebook.com/photo.php?fbid=413294412080006&set=a.130603050349145.32046.124340964308687&type=1&permPage=1>.

66 I Hate LOnlinezz But It Lovez ME More, <http://www.facebook.com/photo.php?fbid=509831319051028&set=at.207161535984676.60766.206974312670065.100001871217892&type=1&relevant_count=1&ref=nf>.

67 Babasaheb Ambedkar's Page, <http://www.facebook.com/photo.php?fbid=413807535362027&set=a.130603050349145.32046.124340964308687&type=1&permPage=1>.

68 Yoshihiro Francis Fukuyama, 'Social capital and civil society', 1999, 1, <http://www.imf.org/external/pubs/ft/seminar/1999/reforms/fukuyama.htm>, accessed on 16 January 2005.

5

'FRIEND POWER' IN RESISTANCE

In the political sphere, the significance of social websites is already well founded by political experiments recently in India. The question that emerges now is how could social media be used for purposes beyond election strategies. One significant aspect of this understanding is how these new channels of communications are affecting political resistance. Theorising resistance in the age of social media is increasingly relevant. Social media has generated a broad set of implications in resistance practices. It is also very difficult to locate them in one chapter or one book. Nevertheless, any attempt on resistance practices on social media age could never overlook one signifying idea. The significant locator in understanding resistance on social media is the contentious politics.

Contentions come in clusters, argued social theorists Charles Tilly and Sidney Tarrow[1] in the preface to the celebrated book *Contentious Politics*. In the social media age, when an act of protest is reported somewhere, it explodes into a larger one, triggering a spring of movements like the 'Arab Spring' or the 'Occupy' movement. In contemporary times, popular technology news that went like mythology is that a loosely networked, yet unrelated, episodes of Internet acts frame a new identity structure. It becomes a national coalition on Internet. The reason is that social media platforms provide opportunities for ordinary citizens to organise as if a collective actor, which they were not able to do with previous media.

The role of social media as a site of contentions has acquired vibrancy very recently. Growth of social media is not simply an improvement in communication apparatus; rather, it brings in a fundamental change in how people communicate not just between each other but also with political actors and democratic institutions. Social media facilitates clustering of political contentions. Oppressors are now more cautious of people's power of social media. It takes place on Internet. On Internet, contentions move on to a broader alliance. Often they are a clustering of differently related incidents, the Internet events. The only thing that gathers them is solidarity and will to share a common cause. One would rather call them identity framing on Internet. Ordinary people often try to exert power by contentious means against national states or opponents, says Sidney Tarrow.[2] Contentious politics occurs when they are often in league with more influential citizens and join forces in confrontation with elites, authorities and opponents.[3] Therefore, social media is not only a huge leap in efficiency of communication but is also a potential way to interact. SNSs allow people to choose whom to friend/follow. As a result of this people tend to follow or friend with those with whom they are familiar and comfortable.

It is a good time for intimate speakers[4] in the age of social connection. Resistance has found new dimensions in constant connection. *Social circle, network, connection, timelines, follow* and so on are their new buzzwords in the festive territory of connected space. Whether it is Facebook, Google+, LinkedIn or Twitter, what makes people gather around social platforms? This chapter identifies it as 'friend power'. It is the bond which is often treasured by most people on social websites. Social media is a new social house, where intimate speakers make it a theatre of resistance. They use it for resistance of a particular nature. 'Friend power' helps them do amazing things.

Turbulent times often give rise to mass resistance movements. One might have remembered the anti-feudal and anti-imperialist movements in the past. In recent times, movements for human rights, minority rights, series of protests against corrupt political elites, rape culture, ill effects of development inherent in capitalism and various political violence and ideological persuasions are examples for mass resistance.

What has become self-evident of the protest culture of contemporary time indeed began as an unintended consequence of the worldwide euphoria over Internet leviathan – unintended in the sense that inventors did not anticipate the kind of use leveraged by marginalised people. Twitter was never intended to be a tool of political resistance. Facebook was never thought to be a lethal weapon against corruption and other similar social evils. Google was never anticipated to be like a near-total solution for everything. YouTube was never considered in the initial days to be a powerful tool for political deliberations. It is the age of 'friend power'.

People express solidarity on Facebook. It is easy to do this. It does not make one risk blood and flesh on the street. People do it so generously. People call it slacktivism. However, the name does not warrant one to disown the mass power of social media. Supported by a dense social network and galvanised by culturally resonant, action-oriented symbols, contentious politics leads to a more sustained interaction with opponents. The result is the social movement, says Sidney Tarrow.[5] The point is that attitude polarisation or eco-chambers are culturally resonant metaphors that bring same-interest people together. When people like, share, reply on anything on social media spaces, they are doing it with an informed conviction that they want change in the way they desired so that they have friends in circles, solidarity in connection and people power in networks.

In institutional settings, like factories, organisations or mines, class is a hefty tool of social solidarity at the pedestal of belligerent social movements. However, for broader movements, class homogeneity was infrequent and could prevent solidarity. Therefore, what movements needed to be successful are strong informal networks and heterogeneous and interdependent social groups and localities. Thanks to the power of crowds! Class solidarity was a tool in swelling strikes and protest in the past, but it is much less important and it could be even counterproductive in the continual interactions with authorities that required constructing national social movements.[6]

Uttar Pradesh Police burnt Jagendra Singh, a social media journalist, alive for making a Facebook post against Ram Murti Verma, a state minister and a powerful Samajwadi Party politician at Shahjahanpur in Uttar Pradesh. On 30 May 2015, he had a series of Facebook posts, which accused Ram Murti Verma of gang raping a nursery worker with his henchmen, forcibly grabbing large tracts of land and high-level corruption. The following day, police raided his house and burnt him alive in front of his son. It happened in democratic India. What was the reason? It is the 'friend power' of an ordinary citizen. He used to speak about public issues to over 5,000 and more friends on Facebook.[7] Kanwal Bharti, Jaya Vindhayala and Shaheen Dhada's Facebook arrest, Aseem Trivedi's arrest for Internet cartooning, Ambikesh Mahapatra and Subrata Sengupta's email arrest, Ravi Srinivasan's Twitter arrest and S. Manikandan's blog arrest will provide evidence for that. They are political contentions in Indian Internet.

Street to social media: diffusion of contention

People do amazing things on social connections. They got a medium to speak. They use to tell stories through it. On 28 July 2014, a female Facebooker put a worrying comment on the declining media standard in India. In doing so, she had been bucketing examples from her student life at university. The media professionals she used to criticise were just postgraduate students in the journalism department at her university and were her contemporaries. An enthusiastic reading of her comments against them goes like this: the present-day media professionals had an ideal student life in the past, where they were courageous and committed. In fact, they have almost lost that courageous journalistic mind. In her view, media professionals in the talk shows and prime time news debates were acting as if they were directly from the field. She sarcastically asked where did they lose their journalism from, which has now almost become a show business where the likes of news anchors are making triumphant voices against panellists in prime time news hour debate. The paid news culture, glamour and channel owners interfering in media narratives all make it obsolete. Once they all had to learn Noam Chomsky and 'manufacturing consent'. Indeed, now they put it into practice. It is the so-called manufacturing of consent. But they are manufacturing consent for the show business they are doing. Brothers and sisters, where did you lose your enthusiasm and commitment to society? In fact, it is a thrilling satire on the Facebook comment that most of us have in mind when seeing the media culture. The comment generated a heated discussion, where users narrated how they stopped watching prime time news hour debate and talk shows on television. What she did on Facebook is not a rare incident. It is almost common in our social connections. Internet space is, indeed, ringing around the void created by previous media. Ordinary citizens use it and thus tell stories, which they draw from their lived-in experiences, memories, personal familiarity and neighbourhood.

Intimate speakers are leaderless. They are self-sustaining, auto evolutionary and spontaneous collectives. Leaderless resistance is a fundamental departure in the theories of organisation. Social media is their fiesta corner. They operate independently of each other in the social media age. Be it environmentalism, child rights, anti-rape activism or anti-graft, absence of leadership is fundamental to all. No one is a hero because everyone is hero. No one is a leader because everyone is a leader. 'Friend power' is like horse-power. It hits everywhere.

Prior to Internet, physical proximity usually determined one's associates, but now people are linked across great distances and national borders. They link the leaderless. Crowd is their substance. Wisdom of the mob leads them. A wide array of collective action groups from environment to electoral reforms have gone leaderless in the cyber age. As a political strategy, leaderless groups and lone individuals in movements against established adversaries have migrated to non-violent, peaceful insurgencies through social media sites. Leaderless revolution marked the latest phase in resistance politics in the cyber age. What motivated them was 'friend power'. Like waves of unknown faces behind Guy Fawkes masks, field activist culture moves as a mysterious tide.

In a much-publicised book, Cairncross[8] argues that with the rise of information technology and the consequent fall in communication, information and transport costs, distance will become less and less important. Extreme terms such as 'the end of geography' and the 'death of distance' vie with 'the revenge of distance' and 'geography returns' in attracting attention to an intriguing duality: the effect of the information society on our concept of geography. Geography would not matter in the connected age. As everything in our lives moved online, the best and brightest would scatter to the hinterlands, leaving only decaying urban wastelands in their wake. From the Arab Spring uprisings in Egypt, Tunisia, Libya, Syria, Bahrain, Kuwait, Algeria and Yemen in 2010, to Los Indignados in Spain, Occupy in London and New York in 2011, to Bulgaria, Brazil and Turkey in 2013, social websites have significantly contributed to increasing political participation.[9] Research showed that people who engage in protest activities are frequent users of social media.[10] *The Economist* announced in 1995 that the communication revolution would bring nothing less than 'the death of distance'.[11]

Internet made long-distance communication vividly quicker, easier and cheaper than ever before. It decreased the importance of geographic proximity in social interactions, transforming our world into a global village with a borderless society. Today, as people sit in their favourite places somewhere, in India or abroad, they can chat, text, view, share and exchange files or engage differently with friends or anyone anywhere across the globe.

Communication genres such as email, blogs, portals, news media, e-commerce and social media redefine notions of time/space. The time-related theory is 'temporal distance theory'; the space-related theory is 'media space'.[12] Internet and mobile media are getting rid of time and space limitations. Nicholas Negroponte,[13] in *Being Digital*, tells us of his firm conviction that in the digital world, previously impossible solutions become viable. People are connected anytime anywhere! They are doing many things at a time. There is a solution in connection.

One thing that is unique about online culture is the relative anonymity that comes with the territory of the Internet. By crossing computer screens or touchpad, people can leave their traditional social identities behind. They become relatively free from the underlying oppressive force of hierarchy based on gender, class and race. In connected spaces, anonymity is like digital condoms. One need not be either man or woman, upper or lower caste, middle or working class, or simply pretty or ugly looking. What makes connection experiences unique around social platforms is opportunity to fake oneself to hide identity.

When one is able to hide administrator status in chat, SNS, blogs and so on, one could diffuse contentions in amazing ways that can stand against authority, elites and oppressive elements. People are able to enhance solidarity in chat rooms. Women are able to build intimate citizenships in social networking sites because they have no patriarchy. Third genders go on cyberspaces because they have no torments of heteronormative sexuality. For protestors, activists and others, anonymity is the people power of the medium that could defy old and reinstate the new.

Resistance began to translocate from structural aspects to cultural aspects. Internet gives way to new cultural identities. Framing processes[14] in the Internet just provides that. Social media transforms the dynamics of collective action formation. For instance, it has become a coordinating, networking, cooperating and collaborating apparatus for a couple of political movements across a host of countries, which line across the broad political spectre. In Moldova, in 2009,[15] Agha-Soltan's death and subsequent anti-governmental demonstration in Iran in 2009[16] and YouTube video of Mohammed Bouazizi's self-immolation generating political unrest in Tunisia in 2010[17] were reported like dam effect of social media in collective action. Facebook page 'We Are all Khaled Said' that depicted Egyptian businessman Khaled Said's death after being beaten by police in Egypt had roughly four million Facebook users, representing about 5 per cent of the population, but Cairo's Tahrir Square became the symbol of social media's political power.[18] Cell phone–powered Second People Power Revolution in the Philippines; all showed the power of social media in effecting political changes across a broad spectrum of countries recently. The Occupy Wall Street, the Arab Spring and the UK Uncut are digital media–incorporated collective action programmes that raised convergence/divergence debate by focussing on how network structures at the international level affect policy outcomes, activist propaganda, advocacy and politics in native society.

Discussion resurfaces projecting social media as town square of India, 'India Against Corruption' as social media–powered Arab Spring and Jantar Mantar as Tahrir Square of India. Anna Hazare–led anti-graft movement gave a new label to social media, i.e. the 'Dragonfly Effect'[19] of India. Facebook was eulogised and predicted as India's Streetbook.[20] All these episodes prove that social media collaboration and application for advocacy and protest have become almost a ubiquitous means to achieve political goals everywhere on the planet from north to south and from west to east.

The ideas drawn from the social movement literature travel well beyond once we leave the offline world; it sounds a thrilling question. The propensity and capacity of the state for repression is the forerunner of contentions on social media.[21] In recent years, there has been a growing demand to look beyond the conventional social spaces to explore how popular contention unfolds in places like Facebook, Twitter and YouTube. Clearly, in the recent past new arenas have opened up at the local, national and transnational levels, and the social movements as well as other actors can sometimes take advantage of these new opportunities and arenas.[22] This chapter terms it as 'friend power' in resistance.

Lifestyle politics in the net

Togetherness leads to mass collaboration, and if one disagrees, at least according to the best-selling book *Wikinomics: How Mass Collaboration Changes Everything*, authors Don Tapscott and Anthony D. Williams[23] tell how Internet togetherness leads to mass collaboration. The power of Internet to bring in large collaborative efforts such as wikis becomes the source of the people power that drives *Wikinomics*. However, people power stories inspire people to go beyond the mere economic ramification of Internet, where ordinary people are making debut business success. There are fascinating stories of ordinary mothers from the kitchens that create prime time television debate. Local singers popularising their magnum opus, young storytellers making their successful debut, anonymous collaborators finding their solidarity, whistle blowers reporting the misconduct in public offices, academics spreading the value of gift culture using current affairs and other information blogs. All these coupled with user interface websites create 'friend power' resistance. Indeed, ordinary people's Internet stories are like folklores. How often do we know that the masses are making use of technology in ways that redefine the way we organised collective action, advocacy, fund-raising and lifestyle politics? The answer lies in 'friend power'.

Facebook, Twitter, LinkedIn, YouTube, Blogger and a fleet of social media platforms copy our lifestyle resistances. Fan activism, hobbyism, foodism, lifestyle politics and personal experience are rampantly reproduced on social websites. This means, individual life experiences such as our loneliness, issues with siblings, troubles in family, emotional life, personal tastes, private interest, eating habits, privacy behaviour and clothing styles all get vivid expression, diversification and consolidation via mediums such as Facebook and YouTube. 'Friend power' of the intimate speakers is important.

Every day, habitually we take up bit of ideological position in life. For example, we have love for our mother tongue. We promote the idea of buying and promoting 'Khadi' clothing. We support the idea that gender parity should begin in family. We love ideas of kitchen vegetable gardening as an alternative to imported vegetables. To save public education, people make call for government schooling. To save environment, we sensitise our children of the benefits of public transporting. We spread ideas of water and energy literacy in our homes. These are not isolated, rare episodes. Ideology of the everydayness has found expression on cyberspace. We are habituated to a convoy of soft ideological positions in everyday life that otherwise tag as lifestyle activism. Despite being fringe acts in our simple life, individual lifestyles result in iota of political dissent and pinch of individual resistance. It is rampant since the social world we inhabit infrequently sees class allegiances fragmented, political ideologies in crisis and at the same time cultural consumption increasing and loneliness terrifying in free time.[24]

With private and secretive password and username, privacy is to be like firewall protection and they are something like digital condoms. Now, caste, class, religious dogmas, race, ethnic affinity, status and a whole lot of mobility impediments seemingly remain unable to obstruct our newfound freedom on social websites. We are anonymous, fake, pseudo there and wander here and there, finding a sense of personal freedom, at least from taboo, social stigma, misogyny and ostracism. Of course, large and expanding sections of Indians moving to social websites are instances of political act, i.e. personal dissent, individual resistance and personalised political action. If not, how do we get a space of our own in an otherwise illiberal social hierarchy and immobile social physics?

India Against Corruption, an anti-graft movement in India, and the electoral victory of Aam Aadmi Party, indeed crowdsourced their mobilisation tactics by way of making open call to an undefined but large group of people. Social websites were their shelter. The new mantra of collective behaviour is mass collaboration or, to say, crowdsourcing. Author Jeff Howe[25] has chronicled the early adopters who used crowds to replace experts. Shaheen Dada, Ambikesh Mahapatra, Subrata Sengupta, Ravi Srinivsan, Aseem Trivedi, S. Manikandan, Jaya Vindhayala and a squad of social media–related episodes of arrest and legal fights were reminiscent of those early adopters of crowdsourcing in India. Their Internet behaviour replaced traditional change makers, while it took on the role of reforming moral crisis of the society. Intimate speak through comments, likes, shares and so on effect quick connection, easy access, choice and instant communication.

A new lifestyle politics is persuaded when an indefinable linkage between lifestyle politics and digital media resurfaces at the trajectory of 'friend power' politics. An economics professor at George Mason University has given a clarion call to make 'Your Own Economy' in the world of Internet using social media sites such as Facebook, Twitter and YouTube. In the social media age, one can decide which newspaper to read, TV news to watch and debate to participate, subscribe to select speeches on one's iPad, personalise blogs and receive feeds that suit one's distinctive tastes and participate in online groups and activities that also please one's own individualized, strange and even weird tastes. People do it all at a fantastically reduced cost and ease of access. Altogether, one could contribute to this hyper-personal network by adding user contents via one's own input and participation; for instance, one may write book reviews on Amazon.com, so that one could promote or defeat the book, post a movie review thereby creating or recreating its fate or post a car review and find its destiny.

Oftentimes families and individuals plan to watch movies when Facebook friends post comments on their Facebook timelines. Individual power of social media is iconoclastic. Friends on social connections indirectly influence our taste. *Cypherpunks* by Julian Assange[26] think it as ways to achieve societal and political change. These are not isolated cases. Many people do it. They source news from Facebook. Facebook is like the Wal-Mart of news in the connected age. It is becoming monolithic. However, they are most demanding at least according to intimate speakers.

The impending social space emerging at the trajectory of discursive territory and cyber culture embedded on Internet gives channels of expression. It is in our social web accounts, which have turned up a dustbin of fringe thoughts of habitual practices. From atoms to bits, liberally we have reproduced the otherwise not possible usual lifestyle practices. Wall posts, likes, share-it widgets and an expeditious list of interactive tools on Facebook have turned up making our stockpile of nihilism, scepticism, pessimism about capitalist consumerism and a whole bunch of globalised products. Tweet, retweet, follow and a new set of connection platforms on Twitter mirror our notions about healthy lifestyle, anxieties of obesity fear, sugar sensitivity and blood pressure aversion and health activism in online spaces.

It is commonplace, we go behind lifestyle advocacy blogs, shop-it-easy web portals and so on. A collection of connection platforms now reminds about a healthy lifestyle that tells us about how small concerns of life have become a huge sort of political dissent against unashamed corporate culture and brutish consumerism. Internet guru Clay Shirky forecasts the thrilling changes we will all enjoy as new digital technology puts our untapped resources of talent and goodwill to be used in the age of social media. Our untapped human potential that were almost lost due to watching sitcoms, films and other sit-there-and-consume-it mass media was the maggot of bygone decades. Television, Clay Shirky[27] writes in *Cognitive Surplus: Creativity and Generosity in a Connected Age*, has absorbed the lion's share of the free time available to citizens of the developed world. Young people are increasingly substituting computers, mobile phones and other Internet-enabled devices for TV. The time we free up from TV is our cognitive surplus. Of course, 'friend power' reinstates lifestyle politics on social web, which incorporates an armada of platforms to network based on personalised politics in the backdrop of the collateral falling of collectivised politics. It is indeed an outcome of the cognitive surplus.

Emailism, e-petitioning, digital collaboration, online fund-raising, online publishing tools, bridging online capital via weak-tie network and a surfeit of new forms of digital collaboration replicate our lifestyle politics on Internet. 'Friend power' is a neologism that we meaninglessly and blatantly deploy to extend the personal as political. We do it on Internet because it does not require much effort, cost and so on, and we need not risk blood and flesh on bumpy streets and town squares for doing activism. We habituated to this new water bubbles. We migrated to the tiny devices we have. We occupied connected spaces even in our bit of leisure time.

The world we live in and work came to recur new forms of meaning making, i.e. veganism, bicycle and pedestrian culture, raw foodism, ethnic food activism, call for government schooling, love for mother tongue, thoughts about alternative energy like wind and solar, lamenting bandh and hartal, sensitising on hand-made 'Khadi' clothing and so on. It is one of many versions of what we may call lifestyle politics. People might say it is an ideology of living day to day in accord with the planet and humankind. This ideal entails sewing own clothes, composting, bicycling, growing and canning our own vegetables, buying products only from recycled materials and so on. Equally important is the question if we know our lifestyle based on personal is political and choices based on ideologies we practice every day have been reproduced in the social websites we are using. Extensive survey over a decade's time found that user profiles regretted the McCulture that has been cultivated, Cocacolonisation our youth fascinated, Wallmarting resurfaced in local supermarkets and Hollywoodisation films reproduced. People simply create social profile pages for protest and fight injustices the way they think they should.

Erik Qualman,[28] author of *Socialnomics*, says that consumers and the societies that users are creating online have profound effects on our economy and the businesses that operate within it. Social search, social marketing and social commerce are making traditional marketing strategies obsolete. At the same time, let us imagine the profound impact of social media creating social lifestyles in connected space cannot be disowned.

Your friends, their friends and my friends now constitute a way of redefining and addressing social conflict in highly complex societies. The cultural change of everyday life, interpersonal politics, specifically gender relations and lifestyle practices all have resurfaced in a new form of cultural politics. Now all movements are centreless and decentred. Now the big question comes in: what happens to collective action, if it happens in a society coaxed by microphysics of power, i.e. everydayness of life. Contentious politics, cultural politics, lifestyle politics, personalised politics and now a large group of cultural terminologies are reconfigured to diffuse the cultural chemistry of new class, new power and new movements. The hidden networks of groups, secretive meeting points and circuits of solidarity all reformulate profoundly the image of a new political actor: YOU, i.e. the individual.

Collective action is taking place in terms of 'I' replacing the 'We' paradigm characterised by common traits and solidarity. Opposed to the vertical hit making process, horizontal, individualised politics gives shape to a new form of movement and solidarity. To Chris Anderson it is a long tail. 'Friend power' is a long tail. Now unsolicited decision to participate in contentious politics characterise all contemporary movements. With the surge of lifestyle politics of everyday acts and with the sweeping penetration of individualised political dissent, leadership factor in movements began to diffuse to new dimensions. The functional role of leadership within movements has become partially delegitimised. The role of social web in making contemporary movements amorphous and nebulous is strong. Now, social web forms a labyrinth of social action and tribe of leaderless acts. At the centre of this, the solo individual life memories, experiences, choices and grievances attain primacy.

In the everyday practices, individuals undertake many things with political resistance in mind. Lifestyle choices situated in close relation to issues of identity and consumption have profound significance in diffusing opportunity structures. *Lifestyle* is a term used within the discourses of sociology and marketing to refer to a coherent body of practices adopted by individuals, which may include the routines incorporated into habits of dress, eating, modes of acting and favoured milieu for encountering others. Individuals increasingly organise social and political meaning around their lifestyle values and the personal narratives that express them.

Mature and grown-up individuals constrained by the tradition, stereotypes, orthodox family structures, social status, family honour, patriarchal social system, gender disparity at home, romance castration at households, friendship, fear of family members and the peeping culture of kith and kin are able to find a solace in the social web. The call to protect our privacy, person, autonomy and individual agency from the unacceptable compulsions of class position, status, gender trouble and patriarchy is the primary concern of the modern protestor. It is very common among the educated, singles, troubling housewives, the middle class, professional elites and even normal idealised and glorified housewives to move on to Facebook, Twitter and so on to find an expression of self, cultivate a new identity and find the pleasure and beauty of the world we live in. We may refer this as lifestyle activism, i.e. individuals making personal political choices in an otherwise rigid social space. Atoms are not bits as a sea distance radiates between the two in the referral case of a particular class of people who afford frequently to clicktivism.

'Friend power' is a meticulous lifestyle practice that is able to include a horde of post material values on Internet such as consumer protest, new social movements, anti-nuclear advocacy, contentious politics, human rights activism, civil rights advocacy, anti-capitalist struggles, gender sensitisation, anti-graft movement, rape victim activism and so on. Nevertheless, personalised politics acquired newer forms on issues that are new and unprecedented. User-generated platforms have co-opted lifestyle practices that give off a set of discursive sites with new movement perspectives. A host of issues discussed on social media platforms, recently, for instance, ecology, human rights, freedom of expression, resentments against corruption, strike and 'bandh', are few parameters where social media has been used to mobilise and protest in novel ways which fall in the perspective of lifestyle politics in India.

The shared networks of individual experience represent criteria for refurbishing 'friend power' protest, i.e. lifestyle politics in the phantom diffusion of contentious politics across a broad range of political subjects in Indian Internet. Social fragmentation and the decline of group loyalties have given rise to an era of personalised politics in which personally expressive individual action frames displace collective action frames in many lifestyle causes. The group-based identity politics of the new social movements that arose after the 1960s still stays alive, but the age of Internet has seen more mobilisations that are diverse in which individuals have been mobilised around personal lifestyle values to engage with multiple causes such as freedom, inequality, development policies, environmental protection, work, human rights and so on.

Thus, accompanied by the development of highly affluent groups, the middle class, urban rich, educated professional elites, the new structuring has given rise to the growth of a marginalised and deinstitutionalised subaltern in the fringe margins of Indian society. There are now an increasing number of unemployed, partially employed, and casual labour, street-subsistence workers, street children, and members of the ghettos, groups that have been interchangeably referred to as urban marginals, urban disenfranchised and urban poor. The recent new social restructuring seems to have intensified and extended their unmitigated operation, network and collaboration.

116

Marginalisation of a large segment of middle classes is novel about this era. Slum dwelling, casual work, under-the-table payment and street hawking are no longer just the characteristics of the traditional poor but also spread among the educated young people with higher status, aspirations and social skills, government employees, teachers and professionals. The mechanics of urban middle class in the Indian cities respond to the larger political, social and economic processes that affect their lives.

The mechanics of action and networks should be active in all of these different occurrences, even though they are different in kind, where collective action, politics and contentions interact with each other on Internet. For many years, politics was associated with images of middle-aged men with privileged backgrounds and most people think that politicians were out of touch with the real people. However, in recent years the media has enabled people to get closer to politicians and become more involved in politics, so are Internet and social websites.

The cultural, political and economic climate of the contemporary India produces a context in which individualised tactics of resistance co-exist with collective identities and shared desires for social transformation. The loosely related, yet different, sets of incidents give shape to a new public in Indian Internet. Primary associations and face-to-face interactions are primarily thought to be sites of solidarity for social movements in the past. Class, race, caste, etc. give solidarity for movements to take pace. However, connection opportunities provided on Internet give power to underprivileged people to diffuse social movements into a new political public based on new solidarities. It is worth to call those variously unrelated, yet loosely connected, incidents, which provided a broad social coalition on Internet as 'friend power'.

Contemporary nihilist activists position their personal lifestyles within strategies of radical political resistance. Early thought has popularised that contentious politics has been an expression of mentality of crowd, of anomies and of deprivation. In present-day life, contentions are outcome of opportunity structure, which Internet provides. Identity framing, that is new solidarity giving shape to new identities in the realm of contemporary movements, gives shape to a new form of lifestyle politics based on everydayness. Opportunity structures on Internet diffuse variety of issue publics to form movement of a national character. Such issue publics have a loose networked structure. Here participants who are not directly implicated, but with a desire to be part of the solution, have been active participants of the movements from their comfort corners. Internet just gives opportunity structures to underprivileged people to be active members of the networked public on Internet.

Lifestyle politics is that which is individualistic. Today, the new social agenda focusses on the nexus between lifestyle choices and political resistance in the sense that personal is political. Attempts by people to enact their political beliefs in their daily lives have become commonplace in contemporary Indian culture, in spheres ranging from shopping habits to romantic attachments. Drawing on feminism and other movements that claim the personal is political, the radical anarchist activists position their own lifestyles within projects of political resistance. A range of lifestyle practices, from consumption, personal style to sexual relationships, to ideological position on life choice, and a whole lot of habitual doings affect a set of political dissent of the middle class.[29]

Lifestyle practices are communicative; just like any community, they have self-identification and group membership; identity performance, community cohesion and distinction are factors that fuel lifestyle activism. Many people seem to think that it is possible to change the world by wearing clothes that they have woven, buying organic food, riding a bicycle or making other sustainable changes in the lifestyle. While admitting that we have not eaten at McDonalds in years and that most of our clothes have been bought from the Khadi showroom of local self-government institutions, we do not have any illusions that making socially aware consumer choices is enough on its own. Now to fight against war, sweatshops, terror or environmental devastation, it is necessary to participate in organised mass struggles which not only can win partial gains but also can eventually take on the root cause of these problems, which is capitalism.

The personal and the political are one. Lessons learned in one arena may have applications in another. The conditions that allow for sustainable personal lifestyle changes are the same as those that allow for sustainable political changes: love and freedom, not fear, repression and coercion. In both arenas, fear may work in the short run but is usually counterproductive in the long term. Joy of living is a more powerful and much more sustainable motivator than fear of dying, both politically and personally.

Creating an alternative subculture or lifestyle is the preferred choice of resistance to the effects of capitalism, state-sponsored violence, development-related displacement and rehabilitation and so on. From greed to over-consumption, from destruction of the environment to worker exploitation, a solution will occur with a simple process of alternative consumption or lifestyle. Daily consumers are convinced that where they spend their dollar counts in supporting various causes.

The enormous popularity of Web 2.0 lifestyle technologies such as what-to-buy-now blogs, what-to-cook-healthy portals, what-to-wear fashion blogs and why-I-am-against-nuclear-energy communities tells us how to fashion our life to fine-tune our planet for sustainable life. The shopping and style guide apps available for smartphones and good book-read apps on tiny devices demonstrate that millions of people want the expertise of life-accomplish authorities. These lifestyle technologies are so appealing; millions of people search for, share and subscribe to the RSS web feeds of life-conduct gurus.

Contentious politics on social websites are theatres of resistance because organisers use contentions to exploit political opportunity structure to create collective identities. Such collective identities are being created through significantly a combination of correlations. They are many in number: leaderless resistance, shrinking of distance and time, anonymity, virility, opportunity structures, framing, emailism, e-petition, e-signatures, clicktivism, tweetivism and streetbook. Identity framing on Internet is bringing people to a dense network for sustained interaction with authority. Unlike traditional parties or lobbyists, who have money and power, ordinary people have nothing in common but a temporary coincidence of claim against others. It brings about the underprivileged people in confrontation with elites or authority. Therefore, social media has provided incentives to the poorest people to take part in contentions on Internet who would otherwise stay at home.

In modern world, it is interesting to know when people get to the street risking life to make claim against authority demanding rights and justice. Early scholars have pinpointed that contentious politics has been expression of mentality of crowd, of anomies, of deprivation. In contemporary life, political contentions are outcome of opportunity structure, which Internet provides.

Notes

1 Sidney Tarrow and Charles Tilly, *Contentious Politics*, Boulder, CO: Paradigm Publishers, 2007.
2 Sidney Tarrow, *Power in Movement: Social Movements and Contentious Politics*, New York, NY: Cambridge University Press, 2011, p. 28.
3 Ibid.
4 A term often used in the book to refer to any form of informal and intimate engagements between users outside the normal channels of communication on Internet platforms.
5 Ibid.
6 Gerald Marwell and Pamela Oliver, *The Critical Mass in Collective Action*, Cambridge: Cambridge University Press, 1993.
7 'Watch: Journalist burned alive by police for a Facebook post against State Minister', *The Logical Indian*, 12 June 2015, <http://thelogicalindian. com/story-feed/exclusive/watch-journalist-burned-alive-by-police-for-a-facebook-post-against-state-minister/>, accessed on 16 June 2015.

8 F. Cairncross, *The Death of Distance*, London: Orion, 1997.
9 Y. Theocharis, W. Lowe, J. Van Deth, and G. Albacete, 'Using Twitter to mobilise protest action: Transnational online mobilisation patterns and action repertoires in the occupy Wall Street, Indignados and Aganaktis-menoi Movements', 41st ECPR Joint Sessions of Workshops, Mainz, Germany, 2013.
10 A. Breuer and J. Goshek, 'Online media and offline empowerment in democratic transition: Linking forms of Internet use with political attitudes and behaviours in post-rebellion Tunisia', Annual Meeting of the International Communication Association (ICA), 2013, <http://papers.ssrn.com/sol3/papers.cfm?abstract_id=2180788>, accessed on 12 February 2014; K. E. Pearce and S. J. O. C. Kendzior, 'Networked authoritarianism and social media in Azerbaijan', *Journal of Communication*, 62 (2), 2012, pp. 283–298; and S. Valenzuela, A. Arriagada, and A. Scherman, 'The social media basis of youth protest', *Journal of Communication*, 62 (2), 2012, pp. 299–314.
11 'A connected world: A survey of telecommunications', *The Economist*, <http://www.economist.com/node/598895>.
12 Sang-Hee Kweon, Kyung-Ho Hwang, and Do-Hyun Jo, 'Time and space perception on media platforms', Twelfth Annual Convention, University of Alberta, Edmonton, Alberta Canada, *Proceedings of the Media Ecology Association*, 12, 2011, pp. 25–48.
13 Nicholas Negroponte, *Being Digital*, New York: Alfred A. Knopf, 1995.
14 Framing processes refer to 'the collective processes of attribution, interpretation, and social construction that mediate between opportunity and action' (see Doug McAdam, John D. McCarthy, and Mayer N. Zald (eds.), *Comparative Perspectives on Social Movements: Political Opportunities, Mobilizing Structures, and Cultural Framings*, Cambridge: Cambridge University Press, 1996, p. 2).
15 Nathan Hodge, 'Inside Moldova's Twitter Revolution', *Wired.com. Condé Nast Digital*, Web, 8 April 2009.
16 Ramtin Amin, 'The empire strikes back: Social media uprisings and the future of cyber activism', *Kennedy School Review*, 10.15350215 (2009), pp. 64–66, *ProQuest*, Web, 21 February 2012.
17 Simon Cottle, 'Media and the Arab uprisings of 2011: Research notes', *Journalism,* 12 (5), 2011, pp. 647–659.
18 Middle East, 'Social media outwit authoritarianism', *Oxford Analytica Daily Brief Service*, 9 February 2011, *ProQuest*, Web, 16 February 2012.
19 The Dragonfly Effect comes from the fact that the dragonfly is the only insect that can fly in any direction when its four wings are working together. The dragonfly itself is a symbol of happiness, new beginnings or change in some cultures that has embedded with social media.
20 Facebook is pretty much the GPS for the 'spring' revolution; see John Pollock's review on Egypt and Tunisia.
21 McAdam, McCarthy, and Zald 1996: 23–40.
22 Donatella Della Porta, *I New Global*, Il Mulino: Bologna, 2003; and Donatella Della Porta, and Hanspeter Kriesi, 'Social movements in a globalizing world: An introduction', in Donatella Della Porta, Hanspeter Kriesi, and

Dieter Rucht (eds.), *Social Movements in a Globalizing World*, London: Macmillan, 1999, pp. 3–22.

23 Don Tapscott and Anthony D. Williams, *Wikinomics: How Mass Collaboration Changes Everything*, London: Penguin, 2008.

24 Pierre Bourdieu, *Distinction*, Cambridge, MA: Harvard University Press, 1984; and Klaus Eder, *The New Politics of Class: Social Movements and Cultural Dynamics in Advanced Societies*, Newbury Park and London: Sage, 1993.

25 Jeff Howe, *Crowdsourcing: Why the Power of the Crowd Is Driving the Future of Business*, New York: Crown Business, 2008.

26 Julian Assange, *Cypherpunks*, New York and London: OR Books, 2012.

27 Clay Shirky, *Cognitive Surplus: Creativity and Generosity in a Connected Age*, London: Penguin Press, 2010.

28 Erik Qualman, *Socialnomics: How Social Media Transforms the Way We Live and Do Business*, 2nd edition, New Jersey: John Wiley & Sons, 2013.

29 Laura Portwood Stacer, *Lifestyle Politics and Radical Activism*, New York: Bloomsbury Academic, 2013.

6

POCKET PUBLIC

Mobile phone and the
mechanics of social change

This chapter illustrates the magnitude to which cell phones have rekindled a public sphere in India that can be used to create a pocket public analogy. While doing so, the core assumption is that cell phones are importantly a political choice, which was the principal hypothesis across the book. In exposing the modus operandi of such a political act, the chapter has extensively used methods such as netnography, content analysis, personal reflection and social media analytics. Stories that people have come across about the mobile phone uses have been extensively sourced in this chapter. Countries experiencing mobile-related changes have also been sourced for reference in the chapter. In so doing, the chapter assumed a grounded theory that tells cell phones are bringing power to people that is important because it has power to destruct old problems in novel ways. The chapter maps the mechanics by which mobile phone becomes relevant for political engagement, civic activism and protest in India, while it is conforming to the fact that they are part of engaged public where citizens unleash civic activism on the go.

General Election 2014 was an Internet election; 2019 will certainly be a mobile election and 2024 is likely to be an engagement election. Predictions go like this. However, one thing that makes all this prediction possible in India is a tiny device: cell phone. It is going to be at the centre of a new connection revolution in India. It has destructive power that traverses many old problems and brings in solutions that our democracy was not able to provide for the last couple of decades. If you disbelieve, at least according to Indian journalist Shubhranshu Choudhary who bagged the prestigious Digital Activism Award, 2014, for his CGNet Swara project[1] that connects tribals in Chhattisgarh using mobile phones and Internet radio and the local tribal language Gondi to communicate with the outside world; it is going to be true.

Distinct patterns of cell phone use linked to civic and political act reconfigure a new thematic political public. One could think of our pockets and leather bags on which most of us carry the tiny gadgets; in particular smartphones are importantly like public spaces on the go. The keypads, swipe pads, push button beep and touchscreens, while on the go, engage in a wide array of citizen activism and have turned out to be the new city squares of connected age. Now it is time to opine that mobile phones seemingly cut across a range of social variables traditionally associated with marginality, be it caste, class, religion, gender, region and all other distressing social cleavages and it ensures social mobility across rigid social layers in ways that were not possible in the past. Women display more liberating power as cell phones could beat patriarchy. Dalits and caste minorities adopt cell phone activism since they facilitate quick access coupled with instant connection that defeats old cleavages. Sexual minorities could be verbal about the power of cell phone that they are able to leverage in order to get out of a closeted life in a heteronormative society. Working women and housewives say they could escape from misogyny and sexist oppression as cell phones give them more sense of protection and quick connection while on the go. From fish markets to skyscrapers, cell phones affect lives in unusual ways. M-governance to m-market and m-politics to m-health and with a plethora of mobile-affiliated rich terminologies, cell phones could bring in change. And more particularly mobile phones are a political act for the oppressed.

One cannot deny the fact that India is much more a mobile nation than we were four years ago. Switching to mobile phones is not just how we communicate with each other; it is also how politically engaging are we. More importantly, it is also about how they could pass across a plethora of factors traditionally thought to be part of marginalisation, oppression and dominant textual narratives and could destroy the social cleavages based on injustice and prejudice. According to TRAI, 1,051.88 million Indians had telecom subscriptions as of February 2016.[2] Among these, urban subscription was 608.42 million and rural 443.46 million. Overall teledensity in India was 82.89. Data indicate that rural India is emerging as the growth driver of telephones as mobile services subscriber base in rural areas has increased.[3] What is more striking about the TRAI report of February 2016 is that states with greater social cleavages were still lagging far behind the national level of telecom subscription base. For example, Indian states like Uttar Pradesh, Madhya Pradesh, Bihar, Jharkhand, Uttarakhand and Odisha have lesser subscription population-wise. Kerala, Punjab, Karnataka and Tamil Nadu have greater telecom subscription, that is over 100 per cent. There are important correlations: states with greater telecom density do have arguably greater social mobility than those that do not, and states that have not leveraged the destructive power of cell phones are still experiencing more incidents of caste subjugation, sexist attacks, patriarchal oppressions, gender discriminations and violence of different sorts in particular domestic. Indeed, the assertion is that cell phones do have political power that can beat old cleavages. And data prove that areas with greater teledensity are showing more social mobility than those that do not.

Indians are increasingly taking to smartphones and the number of such devices in the country touches millions every year with almost half of the users below the age of twenty-five. Youth is the potential mobile market. The dramatic growth in the usage of smartphones has been driven by a desire among users to stay connected and to have instant access to social networking sites, says a survey by research firm Nielsen.[4] One-third of the YouTube viewers, nearly 30 per cent, access video through their mobile and spend over fifty hours a month on the website. Over 70 per cent of YouTube viewers in India are under the age of thirty-five, while 72 per cent have a college degree or higher degree, says a Google online survey of more than 2,000 Indians, reported by NDTV.[5] Smartphone use in India is quickly becoming popular and over 900 million mobile phone users stay connected in India, says a Nielsen study.[6] Statistics on mobile users in India projected by different studies differ substantially.

Exploration towards the interplay between cell phone and civic engagements in the Indian context has been enthused by reports that many American, African and European nationalities are facing up to a new form of civic engagement spearheaded by cell phones and more importantly smartphones. The fast growth of mobile phone and subsequent popularity of cell phone–embedded social change mechanics sweep across civil society groups, NGOs, bureaucracy, Election Commission, contentious groups and the state in general. Now, a new public resurfaces through and you may call it 'pocket public' that is certainly powered by cell phones. The political public shepherded by mobile technologies shatters the social anthropology of India that is otherwise unimaginable in the past. People talking on their cell phones on street corners, in airports and restaurants and in virtually all other public spaces is almost usual. How many among us perceive that those cell phones themselves constitute public spaces? Yes, they are and many studies confirmed it.

Studies confirm that mobile phone and public sphere are interconnected. Most remarkably, individuals who express higher levels of ease with mobile telephony and use it for information exchange have a propensity to be more active in civic and political engagement than those who report being less comfortable with the mobile technology.[7] Using instances of the Chinese SARS outbreak of 2003, London bombings of July 2005 and the South-East Asian tsunami of December 2004, Janey Gordon[8] argues that the mobile phone is challenging conventional sources of information. At various levels, cell phones have been catering to spectacular socio-political purposes; thus, a new power relations drift up in mobile use that deeply confront the inharmonious social structures and uneven power relations between different social classes especially in terms of caste, gender, religion, region, language and other social differences. The reach and effect of cell phone that is destroying old social structure has been reflected in some of the very recent incidents reported in rural India. The way in which 'community institutions' in India deal with cell phones is evocative of the power of mobile phones and the destructive power it has. Villages such as Siwan, Sunderwadi, Dausa and Anjuman have recently attempted on 'Talibanising' cell phones while giving them a gender dimension.

A village council in eastern India has barred women from using mobile phones, telling that they 'corrupt the social atmosphere' by encouraging women to elope with lovers.[9] Many 'Manuwadi' decisions of panchayats and district councils have been reported where the decisions of the council members have showed the deep-seated patriarchy prevailing in rural India. Here cell phones have destructive power, which the conservatives and the patriarchal mindset are alarmed at when women use them. This ancient mindset in an age when India sends Mars Orbiter Mission is sending a chill across our spine. Village councils in states like Bihar, Haryana, Uttar Pradesh and Rajasthan have showed this ancient mindset towards social technologies. Whilst the whole nation is talking about how to compose public spaces friendly and safer for women, some 'community institutions' have emerged with plans to work out the trouble by taking women out of the public sphere overall. Yes, it indirectly is playing out the fact that cell phones are bringing in change, power and liberation to women, Dalits, third sex and caste minorities, and this is even disturbing the advocates and perpetrators of old cleavages.

Siwan district has banned the use of mobiles and wearing short dresses by school and college girls in Bihar. The decision came along with Sunderwadi panchayat, Kishanganj district, in Bihar deciding to penalise a fine up to Rs 10,000 for girls using cell phone.[10] A ban on the use of mobiles was imposed by a panchayat of Dausa in Rajasthan in November and in Uttar Pradesh in July 2012.[11] In 2013 the Anjuman Muslim Panchayat in Udaipur's Salumber municipality debarred girls from using mobile phones.[12] The strange decisions of the community institutions are redolent of a 'Manuwadi' power relation reflecting old cleavages and patriarchal mindset that is still alive in digital India.

The political potential of cell phones, along with 'manuwadi' decisions of village councils in India, was signified by the recent hate campaign via SMS against Northeast people residing in South India. The government limited the number of SMSs and MMSs messages to five per day from each prepaid account on 17 August 2012. Then the situation was reviewed on 24 August, and the number was increased to 20 per day. Government withdrew the 15-day ban on bulk SMSs and MMSs on 30 August. The government censorship has a direct connotation to the political potential of cell phones in India.[13] It is clear that cell phone has political dimension, and our use of cell phone is certainly a political act in many ways.

Use of SMS, MMS and Internet-related mobile platforms for citizen engagement has led to m-government applications, and it has fabulous potential to augment democratic processes. Largely, m-governance platforms have been set in many states in India in various levels and have been adopted by different departments for delivering citizen services in the most critical areas such as agriculture, health information and price information, and the Election Commission too uses them for smooth conduct of voting process. For example, a study on the use of mobile phones by rural community health care workers under India's National Rural Health Mission scheme primarily by women whose main role is to aid pregnant women in childbirth has showed that there were four key benefits accruing out of m-health initiatives. Mobile phones are opportunity provider, capability enhancer, social enabler and knowledge generator.[14]

At the same time, mobile has been a favourite platform for contentious groups to organise collective action, mobilise supporters and generate awareness on contentious issues. Greenpeace India has been an ancestor to text campaign and their most referred mobile-powered activism was against the use of diesel in mobile towers in India. More than 70,000 concerned mobile users across India joined its public campaign to phase out diesel from telecom sector by sending SMS and faxes asking Sunil Mittal to endorse public commitment for implementation of Green Telecom directive issued by the Government of India.[15] To begin with, Greenpeace's first use of SMS in India was largely a fund-raising activity. As part of a drive to support people to plant trees, Greenpeace India sent out text messages proffering free saplings.[16]

Cell phones are iconoclast. They have image-breaking power. They bring in solutions to old problems. However, they also represent fundamental conflicts of civic life dramatically. Cell phones represent a sort of pocket activism, where they fill activism in our pockets and leather straps. Now, we carry lifestyle politics on the go with this device. The pocket public where we blatantly deploy pocket activism, m-politics, m-government to m-health has a definite biography. It has a larger technological architecture and social and political ramification deeply embedded in social structure.

Political power of cell phone

The 'Twitter Revolution' in Moldova[17] created a renewed interest in the role of new communication technologies in civil resistance and political protest activities. It is a new example in a growing list of events where such technologies played an important role in facilitating protests.[18] Twitter and other micro-blogging platforms represent a new phenomenon because they easily work across different types of communication technologies such as instant messaging, blogging and text messaging. This convergence of social technologies also draws attention to the widespread use of mobile phones for civil resistance, a factor often unnoticed by Internet enthusiasts in particular in India.

The role of mobile media in diffusion of political contention has manifested worldwide in the ways activists use it for coordinating street demonstrations, monitoring elections fund-raising and augmenting strategies for mobilising supporters. The use of mobile telephony and SMS, both by themselves and in coordination with Internet tools such as Listservs, blogs, meetup.com and online fund-raising, is still young, but has had significant impacts in countries like China, Ghana, Hungary, Italy, Egypt, Kenya, Korea, Kuwait, the Philippines, Sierra Leone, Spain and the USA.[19] Developing countries such as Turkey, the Philippines, Czech Republic, Bangladesh and Estonia have been successful in generating mobile services and solutions for m-governance. In Turkey, an application named Mobese facilitates effective communication between the central command unit and the mobile units for better law enforcement. Examples of successful m-governance services in other countries include bulk SMSs for health care, medication reminders, farm alerts and advices, exam results via SMS, parent communication, SMS for emergency, humanitarian relief and tax services.

The political power of cell phone has been widely referred to as the People Power demonstrations in the Philippines. For instance, mobile phones were a critical tactical tool in bringing down Milosevic[20] and Estrada in Philippines. In 2001, few days of dissent synchronised by text messages peacefully led to overthrowing of Philippine president Joseph Estrada from power on 17–20 January, popularly referred to as 'People Power II', which was possibly the world's first 'E-revolution': an alteration of government carried by new forms of ICTs.[21] Teddy Casino, one of the organisers of the SMS-organised *Epifanio Delos Santos Avenue* (EDSA-2) demonstrations that helped bring down the Estrada regime, was quoted by Shakuntala Shantiran in Focus Asia which underlined the continuing significance of text messaging in Philippines politics.[22]

In China, where political demonstrations are risky for participants, 12,000 workers went on strike in Shenzhen at the factory of a supplier of Wal-Mart; the migrant workers, who are unionised, organised coordination often through sending coded messages by cell phones, said a report in the *New York Times*.[23] Above all, cell phone has been successfully used to spread out critical news that has been concealed by governments. There are many examples for use of cell phones for activism, especially to spread messages and collaborate for collective action. In 2003, the Chinese government was trying to hide the news of an epidemic that was on the rise in rural areas. People used mobile phones to prevent the government from hiding information on the flu; the news of 'a fatal flu in Guangdong', however, reached over 120 million people within a few days.[24] The Chinese government reacted by admitting that there was, indeed, an outbreak and the administration also made it illegal to spread SARS rumour via SMS.

Arab Spring implies that social technology, text messages and video to social media sites accessed through cell phones are changing the way people living under dictatorships and authoritarian regimes.[25] Crimes committed by governments are reported quickly as they appear plainly. In Africa, mobile phones are spreading like firestorm, which means that Africans have connected to the world in a wholly diverse way than before. The world is becoming flatter because people communicate in parallel and it will continue. Fear of fraud was a motivation for the use of mobile phones in African elections. In Africa, cell phones have been used in instances to combat election fraud, and as political organising tools.[26] Mobile phones contributed not only to high voter turnout but also to the legitimacy of election results in Kenyan elections of 2002. Mobile phones gave better transparency of process, campaign effectiveness and reduction of fraud. Campaign groups developed cell phone number databases allowing people to contact each other and those at the polling stations to call for support when needed. Campaigns made use of short messaging services and election results were disseminated as soon as they counted, even in the most remote areas.[27]

Mobile phones played a key role in Kenyan elections of 2004. Kenya's electoral commission as well as local media used SMS services from cell phones to distribute news about polling. Voters used mobile phones to monitor the voting in more remote areas. Local radio stations even fielded callers who alerted the listening audience to 'the level of traffic at polling stations'.[28] There were reports that elections in Sierra Leone, Ghana and Kenya showed greater sensitivity towards the use of mobile as a weapon against electoral corruption.[29]

In Hungary, SMS became a political propaganda tool during elections. It is a country of 10 million, where 53 per cent of the population has mobile phones and 15 per cent Internet users; millions of mobile text messages and emails have been exchanged by party supporters.[30] In Italy, the 2004 election seemed complicated by the fact that the incumbent Prime Minister Silvio Berlusconi was also the country's largest media owner. One reader of the Smart Mobs blog, David Ture wrote about a horizontal SMS campaign for Berlusconi's party: 'The "SMS" (Sostieni Molto Silvio) campaign asks people to send SMS messages containing promotional sentences to five friends.' The Korean presidential election of 2002 was a defining moment for cell phone tactics in electoral campaign; many claimed that the use of Internet and SMS technology enabled an underdog candidate's followers to tip the election in his favour, says Jean K. Min, an editor for the Korean citizen-journalism site OhMyNews.[31] When the Spanish government attempted to blame the terrorist bombings at Madrid's Atocha train station on Basque separatists, thousands of citizens began circulating SMSs that questioned the government's version of events and summoned people to mass demonstrations across Spain. Ultimately, the opposition party won the elections.[32]

Spanish journalist Eva Dominguez says the most effective US electoral smart mobs were not organised at the grass roots but from the very top of the political hierarchy. Collective action can be mobilised and directed from above using mobiles. The Republican Party's chief strategist, Karl Rove, coordinated the 2002 Republican Congressional victories via his Black-Berry communicator. He used his BlackBerry to send messages even during meetings with President Bush, according to *Time* magazine.[33] In the USA, Democratic Party campaigners seem to be BlackBerrying, too, according to a *Washington Post* article shortly before the 2004 US elections. Dan Manatt, director of a Democratic political action committee aimed at candidates under forty, notes that the Internet and mobile phones are not instruments of persuasion aimed at converting voters to a cause, but are better used to 'preach to the choir' and help coordinate electoral campaigns, especially on election day. In particular, Manatt's group planned to equip their volunteers with mobile messaging devices such as BlackBerries for get-out the vote campaigns in congressional elections, allowing the volunteers to coordinate political activity at polling stations where otherwise they could not openly support a candidate.[34] John Collias, the field director of a Congressional candidate in Kentucky, noted that everyone is bouncing around so much on Election Day that it is common for the phone lines to be jammed and continues saying that BlackBerry is the ultimate firewall against that problem, and it has the potential to be very effective for them.[35] The Pew Internet and American Life study showed 88 per cent of registered voters owned a cell phone of some kind as of September 2012

129

and 27 per cent of the phone owners used the devices to keep up with campaign news or political issues in general.[36] *The Post* reporter Brian Krebs hypothesised that the BlackBerry preference might have started on Capitol Hill. After 9/11, all members of Congress were equipped with BlackBerries so they could communicate in an emergency. The Howard Dean campaign used the UPOC service as a kind of texting Listserv – campaigners could subscribe and broadcast SMS messages to other subscribers of specific campaign-related groups.[37] Smartphones are used by some voters in the USA as real-time fact-checkers or to post political messages to social networks, says the Pew Internet and American Life study.[38]

Cell phone and social change

The interplay between cell phones and democratic engagement and political dialogue projected in this volume as pocket public is one that is as an offshoot of mobile phones which despite its budding age has enhanced political participation and citizen participation. Now the question comes: Are cell phones encouraging political dialogue? Is mobile the next town square of India? Are smartphones commanding collective action?

Authors of the book *Cellphone Nation* Robin Jeffrey and Assa Doron have extensively engaged with the rise of cell phones in social change. To them, cell phones were a profit-doubling device for the famous fishing community in Kerala. Basic banking service facilities, or one might call M-banking, have been changing the lives of ordinary Indians. Ordinary traders and boatmen in the north Indian river ghats have found mobile phones useful in gathering pilgrims and tourists. Mobile phones have changed the farming communities in India in many ways. They also changed the political campaigns and voter engagements by political parties, and the electoral victory of Bahujan Samaj Party (BSP) in North India is an example. From politics to business, cell phones are now going to have far-reaching implications in contemporary India.[39] When geographical distances become cheaper than bicycle, people will have the luxury of cell phones. Here, oppressed and exploited people have found a new weapon that could reach out farther, faster and continuously. Even if you have no good road and modern transportation facilities, cell phones are bringing in quick access and what other device could bring you this comfort other than cell phones!

Many people have extensively surveyed this social change mechanics inherent in cell phones across the world. V. L. Rafael[40] in an article has observed that the fetish of communication suggested the possibility of dissolving existing class divisions. Though an overgeneralisation, in Indian case it has significance in many respects. On the other hand, Howard Rheingold

130

used the word *smart mob* as the analytical label in his book *Smart Mob*, which consists of people who are able to act in concert even though they do not meet or know each other.[41] Connectivity is important here.

Women empowerment gets more push and pull through cell phones in India. SMS has brought big changes in the lives of ordinary women. While women attain new freedom, the guardians of social order are increasingly under the shadow of fear. It is fascinating to see the trend that job information websites send job alerts to the mobile phone, text message alert for bank withdrawals from savings account and alerts regarding government services. From mobile banking to mobile politics, mobile phones have become a ubiquitous technology for the masses. With the economic reforms, new job avenues were reported in the enhancing market. Indian women have increasingly been getting on to newer social spaces facilitated by the machineries of the Indian state and ironically it is in a society that has yet to prove it is women-friendly in its social structure. The problem is that one would get a market system that gives more opportunities to women but is implemented in a social milieu that is still ancient in its attitude towards half of its population. The neoliberal market has, of course, produced a genderless market with the secular state in a new social avenue unrestrained by the witchcraft of social structure. Ever since, women began to benefit from a number of opportunities; in particular they get a social space outside the patriarchal system and oppressive social structure. With the cell phone, the curious family got a relief that their beloved are at a call away, if they are out of home as breadwinners, going for a job, going to office, going to banks and even at night shifts in metros. For daughters working in call centres, mobile phones let them keep in touch with their nervous families and provide a feeling of more security just by a device that is in a leather bag, pocket or palm.

In the post-reform India, cell phone has specific political significance. The sudden emergence of text messaging as a ubiquitous form of conveying messages has significant identification with a force that destructs old systems. It has attributes that attempt to foil the rigid social hierarchy in India. The mounting interconnection between mobile phones and Internet has made it possible for people to coordinate and organise political collective action with people they were not able to organise before, in places they were not able to organise before and at a speed they were not able to muster before. This mobile phone–enabled coordinating function has affected daily life in the form of what Ling calls 'hyper-coordination'[42] and what Rheingold calls 'smart mobs'.[43] Seriously, they are a second life for caste minorities. Cell phones are like a metaphor that destabilises old cleavages. Dalits, other caste minorities and even sexual minorities do not have sufficient money power to run their media but they would easily log on to social networking sites for storytelling and solidarity building. And cell phones are an important choice. It is an easily accessible, cheap and quick medium to be part of the connected age.

On the other hand, mobile devices provide an important access channel for governments to reach out to citizens and such devices are increasingly used to provide service and delivery information to citizens. The proliferation of mobile phones in India is shifting the political and social landscape, empowering people to source and share their own information and to have a greater say in what comes to public attention. The street use of mobile devices has started to affect the social physics and activist chemistry in India in ways which are not measured by any yardstick. Indeed, government and citizens, more particularly people on the social walls, could get a direct and face-to-face interaction with the government via cell phones which could also become an alternate mode of communication to traditional media corporates which are significant agenda setters and part of Brahmanic India.

The use of mobile media to incite and organise collective action, facilitate democratic engagement and furnish a thematic public space is only in its infancy. Yet it is significant considering the rigid social system in India. A random survey of published reports and personal communication surely suggests the frequency by which the contemporary mobile phone–assisted communication networks are enabling people to effect significant political changes. The turn of the twenty-first century has seen the rise of mobile phones as powerful devices that have transformed how ordinary people create and share information. Organisations and activists are harnessing the power of mobile technologies to improve and expand campaigns, better coordinate activities and demonstrations, and increase awareness about social issues, injustices, inequality and oppression. Activists, armed with either low-cost, basic mobile handsets or complex smartphones, are capable of instantly connecting with their network of colleagues and supporters.

Today we are living in the age of social web where the world is moving on the tips of our fingers. The new media technologies have changed the world drastically. Even the traditional print and electronic media have been influenced significantly by the new media technologies. The revolution in social technology has changed the pattern of political communication also. It has also affected civic engagement in unprecedented levels. The effect of new media technologies via cell phones on political behaviour, voting pattern, civic activism and destabilising old cleavages is the focal point of pocket public. The street use of mobile phone and the fast popularity of touch phone empowered by Internet have caused to bring in a new meaning to our collective behaviour.

Just as people have used alphabets and computers in both socially ben-eficial and socially destructive ways, mobile devices are being used to keep elections honest, to self-organise peaceful political demonstrations and to provide disaster relief services, and the same technologies and practices are also used to commit crimes, coordinate terrorist attacks and summon people to riots. These forms of collective action in the political sphere that have been instigated and abetted via mobile telephone during elections, demonstrations and riots are worth considering.

Mobile governance,[44] or m-governance, is the newest advancement in e-governance amidst the escalating recognition of sophisticated mobile technology such as Internet-enabled devices, wireless networks, palmtops, Wi-Fi, laptops, Bluetooth and mobile phones. This augmentation has taken India by hurricane effect with such technology reaching millions of homes, urban and rural. Kerala has been recognised in the 2012 edi-tion of the World Bank's publication for its m-governance activities. The 'M-Governance in Kerala' project covers over 60 government departments to utilise mobile technology to improve public service, strengthen pro-gramme efficiency and for better transparency and accountability. Kerala serves as a model for other states.[45] Kerala, having the maximum number of mobile phones in the country, is leading the m-governance initiatives and the state is implementing m-governance to let people avail services of 90 state government departments and agencies. M-governance, implemented by the Kerala State IT Mission, is the first of its kind in the country. Under the project, services of various government departments and organisations are enabled through an integrated service delivery and infrastructure plat-form, in a plug-and-play style. India can categorically take m-governance to a new level with development of mobile communication infrastructure and content.

Many mobile-related acts provide clue to the fact that India is fast mov-ing to a mobile republic. The growing use of cell phones to reconfigure m-government platforms is an example. The expanding mobile use is lead-ing to a connected mobile public. Mobile business and mobile activism are shaping both business practices, and contentious claim making, and they are double-edged. However, they provide insight into the growing inter-play between political public and mobile. Cell phone proffers a platform for citizen information; in particular, m-services (transactions and payments), SMS and other mobile applications are providing a channel of communi-cation between citizens and government. In short, cell phones enabling government-to-citizen transactions ultimately configure m-democracy initiatives and they are high on the dais of interplay between mobile and democracy. Things like m-administration, instant government to employee

(G2E) information and service are possible at any time. It doesn't matter if the data needed are on Internet or on their network or a portable device under their control. It can be accessed if you have a cell phone. Society is fast changing. There is a significant social shaping of technology. The mobile phone dimension of the change cannot be overlooked in this context.

Mobile public: Indian experience

Mobile device is fascination among youth and more importantly, it passes through the lives of underprivileged people regardless of age, gender and how much economic, cultural, social, symbolic and intellectual capital one holds. Youth obsession for mobile devices makes it a universally valid instrument for engaging in public discussions. Unlike personal desktop computers, smartphones have inherently enabling attributes such as mobility and individuality. Such transformative attributes endow it with the power to overcome spatial limitations. It is therefore not an exaggeration to designate smartphones as next-generation cyber public sphere as interplay between civic engagements and Internet is profoundly enhanced by smartphones in the days to come.

In the meantime, despite various kinds of media that includes networking technology, platforms of cyber public sphere have been limited to desktop computer for a long time. The power of mobile phones to create a public sphere has been unfortunately undervalued by mass media. More particularly mobile phone is the personal computer of India. Here mobile phone constitutes categories and variables in social sciences knowledge. It affiliates to a pocket public because of certain criteria. Mobile phone presents itself as the most important means of social communication due to 'mobility'. In a hierarchical and rigid society like India having greater social divides, inequalities and caste/class differences, cell phones have acquired a peculiar property of cutting across all barriers to social mobility and have become the symbol of a unifying force. From vegetable bazaars and fish markets to ivory tower dwellers, this technology has become a custom.

Individuality has greatly been recognised by the mobile technology since it gives many neglected groups to be able to live up to their expectations and aspirations. Mobile-enabled public space is mostly crucial in the sense that Indian mobile phone revolution is for the most part helping the poor, the remote, teeming millions, women and those who are appallingly at social margins and deliberately placed at social frontiers. Mobiles are being used to funnel demand for services and products to small farmers, vendors, plumbers, housemaids, electricians and fishermen. In remote areas of India, mobiles are used to hand out health information to poor rural women. In urban areas, they help sex workers and other vulnerable social groups. For many helpless women, cell phones are crucial to get help as they are vulnerable to assault, teasing or harassment. For women, they are significantly a channel of contact with law enforcement agencies when they are subjected to domestic violence. Mobile communications may be the preeminent way, or undeniably the solitary way, to arrive at peripheries of India's social landscape. Many studies reported that in a diverse country like India cell phones have greater social, economic and political values.

Patriarchal mindsets of the community institutions such as Khap Panchayat in north Indian countrysides are disturbed when women are increasingly using cell phones. They are afraid in the sense that women elope with strangers via cell phones, which are obnoxious to the patriarchal expectations about the modesty of a woman. In reality, the patriarchy is afraid of women getting jobs, earning money and, in many cases, doing it better than men do. They are afraid of India's other quiet revolution: the women's revolution. Cell phone is a supplement to a silent upheaval of women power breaking the social structure and social barriers. Primarily mobile phones are superior to desktops in many levels. First of all, it gives individuals a quick and easy access to the public sphere on the go. In addition, cell phones are more bedspreads to individuality. So that it carries important elements of Habermas's public sphere analogy.

Obviously universal service, which is necessary to bolster participation for public matters, gets recognition if you consider mobile as a social institution. As the debate between participatory versus representative democracy intensifies nowadays, cell phones will have winning arguments supplementing participatory politics. Ordinary people without any confusion could directly participate in the political decision-making process now. Civil society groups, NGOs, contentious groups, professional agencies and networks have deployed cell phones to avail funds from public. Micro-donations of Rs 10 to 50 to political parties are made with just an SMS, which can possibly revolutionise election funding in India. Greenpeace makes use of mobile phones to request its supporters for donation[46] from Rs 500 onwards. Major Indian political parties are by now making widespread use of the social networking sites such as Facebook, Twitter and YouTube, and are charming in brand advertising online with launching Nokia, Android, iPhone and Blackberry applications to succeed the hearts of the younger cohort.

Well-organised use of the Internet and the social media channels is made by the Election Commission in Uttar Pradesh and Bihar to help voters check their details in the electoral roll and locate their polling stations.

135

There is news that Bihar Election Commission decided to introduce mobile voting in the urban bodies' polls. Electors in northeast states could now use Google Maps to trace their polling stations and access other electoral information on the go by visiting the websites of Election Commission or state chief electoral officers.[47]

As reported by many media houses, the UPA government planned a Rs 7,000 crore scheme, 'A Phone in Every Hand', to give one mobile phone to every family living below the poverty line (BPL family) with free calls.[48] Nevertheless, whatever be the electoral gimmicks, there were many studies that reported that there is a close relation between mobile penetration and socio-economic growth. Despite, UPA government's 'A Phone in Every Hand' project was criticised as politically motivated, it is undisputed that when cell phones reach your homes and studies revealed that there is a close link between telecom density and economic growth.[49] Telenor[50] in Norway commissioned Deloitte to study the mobile and economic growth correlation in six markets: Malaysia, Thailand, Ukraine, Pakistan, Serbia and Bangladesh. It found that mobile phones provided the ability to communicate to those sectors of the community typically underserved by fixed line technology. It also enhances social inclusion by mobile telephony with a more positive impact on economic welfare, by increasing GDP and generating employment opportunities in both the mobile communications sector and the wider economy.

This is true in the case of India where mobile cuts across the social structure and rigid stratification that inhibit mobility and change. When Internet penetration is impeded by access and divide, mobile technology can obviously reach out to the people on the fringes. It has highlighted that farmers with mobile phones usually get better prices for their produce, and small and tiny shop owners can perk up their competence via mobile network. At the same time, many Indians still do not have mobile phones. Over 900 million SIM cards are in use in the country. However, unique users are around 600 million, roughly around 50 per cent of the country's population. While the urban markets are saturated, semi-urban markets are 70 per cent penetrated and rural markets only 40 per cent.[51]

The Election Commission of India planned to introduce mobile voting in the 2014 General Election in the large urban centres on an experimental basis by giving them a choice to vote from home or the office.[52] In addition, the Election Commission designed a coded SMS-based alert system to supervise the 2014 national elections. The plan was considered as a momentous step ahead from the 2009 elections when the body had introduced an online monitoring system called the Communication Plan for Election or COMET. COMET, which intended at building a database of mobile phone numbers of around 1.1 million poll officials deployed for General Election 2009 so that the poll panel could reach them swiftly, has transformed into a high-tech SMS-based alert system. The SMS-based monitoring system reduced the workload extremely.[53] The system was first used in the assembly polls in Uttar Pradesh, Punjab, Manipur, Uttarakhand and Goa in early 2012 and in Gujarat and Himachal Pradesh towards the year-end.[54]

If elections are the formal, socially contracted, legally controlled exercises of political power, street demonstrations are the informal, ad hoc, uncontrolled outbursts that can tilt elections, as they did in Spain, or unseat an elected leader, as they did in the Philippines. The street demonstrations that brought mobile communications and swarming tactics to the world's attention were the protests against the 1999 meeting of the World Trade Organization in Seattle, Washington,[55] famous as 'The Battle of Seattle'.[56] World over, the mobile technology has been found reaching out to social groups in novel ways that were previously not possible.

Now the question comes: can cell phones promote lasting political change, perhaps even a revolution? Can it be a town square, a public gathering, a loudspeaker, bumpy street and a 'public'? In many sense these questions found many solutions by connecting the recent change attempts powered by mobile technologies in India. The usefulness of mobile phones to facilitate political involvement and construct social change has long been disputed. Latest events in various parts of India in respect of cell phones and democratic engagement have again raised fresh questions about the role of cell phone technologies to create alternative public spheres and mobilise people for social action. In the Indian context, where access to Internet and digital technologies is marked by big divides, such as gender, age and class where the widespread uptake of mobile phones has led to sanguinity about the probability of exciting political participation and widening democratic engagement.

Mobile-powered social change theories recently formulated have largely tried to relate between mobile phones and participatory democracy, and argue that mobile phones not only transmit political information needed for rational deliberation in the public sphere, but also transgress cultural and social borders and hierarchies in the way they refashion identities and create informal economies and communicative networks. Cell phones assemble a public sphere on the go. It means underprivileged people could carry a public sphere on their leather bag or pockets. It is accessible 'where ever you are', if I quote from billboard campaigns of advertising agencies. A public sphere is possible in places like market, office, multiplex and tourist spots since cell phones give opportunities to connect to Internet at anytime, anywhere.

It is apparent that a cell phone is no more than just a phone; it is a multimedia tool used for social communication, networking and collaboration. Users could work together with music, pictures, videos, games, Internet, email, text messaging (SMS) and many things more every day. Indians send more than a billion text messages every day. Mobile phones affect political activity in novel ways. In a number of cases, mobile phone as a uniquely easy-to-use, cheap, accessible and personal communication device has been a key tool to facilitate mobilisation and collective action, drawing examples from many SMS campaigns, cell phone–powered activism, Internet connectivity via mobile phones and so on. The literature on collective action theory, mobilisation and diffusion theory and network society theory has been applicable to theorise cell phone–embedded public sphere, which draws some case studies as a starting point. Mobile teledensity data and recent mobile-related episodes and political activism indicate that a mobile public has just begun to emerge but is in the infancy. The mobile phones in our pocket or leather bag now carry with us a public sphere that is in tandem with us where we are!

Mobile phones have a social science. It has become an index of equality, justice and freedom in India. Social divides such as caste, class, gender, culture and region are defeated by cell phones. Across social groups mobile is the most acceptable and most sought-after device. Cell phones have drastically altered the potential for political organisation in India, quite often more markedly here than anywhere else has in the world. This is because of India's distinctive social structures of privilege and social discrimination and the means by which inexpensive cell phones can destabilise such unbending structures. Mass diffusion of cell phones has shaped promises that did not exist previously.

Pocket public: some reflections

Communication media, literacies and political governance have co-evolved for millennia. Much has been written about the role of print and literacy in the emergence of the democratic public sphere. A rich literature has grown around the role of the printing press in the Protestant Reformation and the emergence of constitutional democracies. Communication technologies and literacies possess a power that has on many occasions proved mightier than physical weaponry – the potential to amplify, leverage, transform and shift political power by enabling people to persuade and inform the thoughts and beliefs of others.

The same technologies and literacies can also organise, plan and coordinate direct political actions – elections, demonstrations and insurrections. It

138

may also be the case that they can be used to stifle, misdirect and demoralise those who would otherwise be involved in these activities. The power to persuade and communicate combined with the power to organise and coordinate and multiplied by the millions of mobile telephones and wireless subscriptions today poses a disruptive political potential that could equal or surpass that of the printing press, landline telephone, television or the Internet.

The ubiquitous tool for everyone from vegetable vendor to households will be the cell phones. India has moved from a society for whom phone was a luxury in the 1980s, to a society that now has the potential to make cell phone the next 'personal computer'. Cell phones constitute the next counter-public in India. In pockets or leather bags where one carry cell phones, a public sphere is hiding behind, so powerful enough to effect changes. Call it 'pocket public'. It is portable and accessible at fingertips at anyplace, anytime. More importantly, the pocket public is an offshoot of the potential of mobile phones to cut across a range of social variables that hamper mobility across social classes especially gender, caste, region, religion and other minority groups. In India, however, the pocket public will not be a public similar to that of youth public constituted by broadband India. Pocket public is spread over all age groups and all social groups different from the Internet public.

The rapid adoption of sophisticated cell phone platforms by a significant portion of the India's population is giving rise to spontaneous social experiments of varied forms. In the political sphere, the power of persuasion, organisation and coordination has been democratised throughout India by the availability of mobile telephones and text messaging. The examples cited throughout the chapter are neither exhaustive nor analytical. There are no guarantees that future pocket public will be peaceful or that democratisation of the power to organise collective action will lead to stronger democracies.

Cell phones lead to stronger democracy in the sense that they empower citizens in many respects. Cell phones configure popular demonstrations in protest events. Greenpeace has used cell phone activism against mobile towers. The capability of inexpensive and publicly visible monitoring and coordination of elections against fraud and its smooth conduct was facilitated by cell phones when the Election Commission of India used it in many states on an experimental basis. Mobiles have also resurfaced in the increased ability of volunteers to coordinate contentious challenges, fund-raising and the power to disseminate information that has been suppressed by political regimes and controlled by mass media. The integration of mobile phones into political engagement is still in its infancy in most parts of India that is constrained by a set of sociocultural tremors such as institutions, people and places, which adapt to and regulate the use of cell phones. Similar to those all new generation technologies that alter patterns of social life the mobile phone has been exposed to an ambush of condemnation and denigration for the ways in which it disrupts existing norms of propriety and social boundaries. Yet, mobiles are a political choice for ordinary Indians.

Notes

1 CGNet Swara is a voice-based portal, freely accessible via mobile phone, which allows anyone, people in the forests of Central Tribal India, to report and listen to stories of local interest. Reported stories are moderated by journalists and become available for playback online as well as over the phone (+91 8050068000).

2 See report, 12 March 2014.

3 See <http://india-cellular.com/MS-30–6–2014.htm>. Highlights of Telecom Subscription Data as on 29 February 2016, Press Release No. 26/2016, <http://trai.gov.in/WriteReadData/WhatsNew/Documents/Press_Release_no26_eng.pdf>, accessed on 23 August 2016.

4 PTI, '50% of smartphone users in India are under 25 yrs: Nielsen', 12 February 2013, <http://www.livemint.com/Politics/HYrKyOYLTMgzZgzosw12iM/50-of-smartphone-users-in-India-are-under-25-yrs-Nielsen.html>, accessed on 27 February 2013.

5 PTI, 'YouTube India viewers spend over 48 hours a month watching videos', *NDTV*, 13 February 2013, <http://gadgets.ndtv.com>, accessed on 13 August 2013.

6 Newswire, 'Smartphones keep users in India plugged in', 2 June 2013, <http://www.nielsen.com>, accessed on 13 August 2013.

7 Scott W. Campbell and Nojin Kwak, 'Mobile communication and the public sphere: Linking patterns of use to civic and political involvement', Department of Communication Studies, University of Michigan, <http://www-personal.umich.edu/~parkyo/site/paper%20abstracts/mobile_civic_ICA.pdf>, accessed on 17 August 2013.

8 Janey Gordon, 'The mobile phone and the public sphere: Mobile phone usage in three critical situations', <http://con.sagepub.com/content/13/3/307.abstract>.

9 Jason Burke and Manoj Kumar, 'Village bars women from using mobile phones', *Asian Age*, 6 December 2012, online, accessed on 25 February 2013.

10 PTI, 'Bihar panchayat bans use of mobile phones by girls', *Indian Express*, 3 January 2013, <http://www.indianexpress.com>, accessed on 27 February 2013.

11 Ibid.

12 Mahim Pratap Singh, 'Udaipur Muslim panchayat bans mobiles for girls', 11 January 2013, *The Hindu*, online, accessed on 27 February 2013.

13 Prasad Krishna, 'Indian mobiles go quiet amid SMS curbs', *The Centre for Internet and Society*, 27 August 2012, online, accessed on 25 February 2013.

14 Arul Chib, Cheong Yi Jiaa, Lee Lin Chieh Lynettea, N. G. Chiah Hwee Cheryla, Tan Chin Keea, and V. L. V. Kameswari; 'The hope of mobile phones in Indian rural healthcare', *Journal of Health Informatics in Developing Countries*, 6 (1), 28 January 2012, pp. 406–421.

15 Telecom Tiger, 'Sunil Mittal urged to take leadership to clean-up the telecom sector by 70,000 mobile users', 4 October 2012, <http://www.telecomtiger.com/PolicyNRegulation_fullstory.aspx?storyid=15819&section=S174>, accessed on 27 February 2013.

16 See more at <http://www.mobileactive.org/case-studies/greenpeace-india-sms-lead-generation#sthash.cE2NMDQS.dpuf>.

17 Evgeny Morozov, 'Moldova's Twitter Revolution', May 2009, <http://neteffect.foreignpolicy.com/posts/2009/04/07/moldovas_twitterrevolution>, accessed on 2 March 2013.

18 Manuel Castells, Mireia Fernández-Ardèvol, Jack Qiu Linchuan, and Araba Sey, *Mobile Communication and Society*, Cambrigde and London: MIT Press, 2007.

19 Howard Rheingold, 'Mobile media and political collective action', in James E. Katz (ed.), *Handbook of Mobile Communication Studies*, Cambridge, MA: MIT Press, 2008, pp. 225–240, <http://www.rheingold.com/texts/PoliticalSmartMobs.pdf>.

20 Fabien Miard, 'Mobile phones as a tool for civil resistance: Case studies from Serbia and Belarus', *Digi Active Research Series*, June 2009, <https://www.scribd.com/document/17352305/R-D-3-Mobile-Phones-as-a-Tool-for-Civil-Resistance-Case-Studies-from-Serbia-and>, accessed on 16 July 2014.

21 Julius Court, 'People power II in the Philippines: The first E-Revolution?', <http://archive.unu.edu/p&g/wga/publications/people_power_ii.pdf>.

22 S. Shantiran, 'Txt craze', *Star TV Focus Asia*, 2003, <http://focusasia.startv.com>, accessed on 2 March 2013.

23 H. W. French, 'Workers demand union at Wal-Mart supplier in China', *New York Times*, 2004, <http://www.nytimes.com/2004/12/16/international/osia/16china.html>, accessed on 2 March 2013.

24 H. Hoenig, 'Beijing goes high-tech to block Sars messages', *The New Zealand Herald*, 2003, <http://www.nzherald.co.nz/index.cfm?ObjectID=3507534>, accessed on 2 March 2013.

25 Soner Cagaptay, 'Can dictator survive new media?', *CNN World*, 10 February 2012, <http://globalpublicsquare.blogs.cnn.com>, accessed on 26 February 2013.

26 E. Zuckerman, 'My blog is in Cambridge, but my heart's in Accra', *Ethan's Weblog*, 2004, <http:// blogs.law.harvard.edu/ethan/2004/12/07#a626>, accessed on 2 February 2013.

27 B. Kagai, 'Mobile phone plays role in free Kenya elections', *Communication for Development News*, 2002, <http://www.comminit.com/C4DNews2003/sld-7120.html>, accessed on 2 March 2013.

28 E. Kalondo, 'Kenyans hold peaceful referendum after bitter campaign', *Monsters and Critics News*, 2005, <http://news.monstersandcritics.com/africa/article_1063516.php/Kenyans_hold_peaceful_referendum_after_bitter_campaigns>, accessed on 2 March 2013.

141

29 J. Black, 'Technology with social skills', *BusinessWeek Online*, 2003, <http://www.businessweek.com/technology/content/aug2003/tc20030819_4587_tc126 htm>, accessed on 2 March 2013.
30 E. Dányi and M. Sükösd, 'M-Politics in the making: SMS and e-mail in the 2002 Hungarian election campaign', in Kristóf Nyíri (ed.), *Mobile Communication: Essays on Cognition and Community*, Vienna: Passagen Verlag, 2003, pp. 211–232.
31 Cited in Howard Rheingold, 'Mobile media and political collective action', in James E. Katz (ed.), *Handbook of Mobile Communication Studies*, Cambridge, MA: MIT Press, 2008, pp. 225–240, <http://www.rheingold.com/texts/PoliticalSmartMobs.pdf>.
32 J. Adelman, 'U say u want a revolution: Mobile phone text messaging is evolving into a political tool', *Time Asia*, 2004, <http://www.time.com/time/asia/magazine/article/0,13673,501040712–660984,00.html>, accessed on 2 March 2013.
33 J. Carney and J. F. Dickinson, 'W. and the "Boy Genius"', *Time*, 2002, <http://www.time.com/time/ nation/article/0,8599,388904,00.html>, accessed on 2 March 2013.
34 B. Krebs, 'Technology shapes get-out-the-vote efforts', *The Washington Post*, 2002, <http://www.washingtonpost.com/ac2/wpdyn?pagename=article&node=&contentId=A2467–2002Oct9 &notFound=true>, accessed on 2 March 2013.
35 Ibid.
36 See the report 'US politics goes mobile, phones become tool: Study', 9 October 2012, <http://phys.org/news/2012–10-politics-mobile-tool.html>.
37 Z. Teachout, 'Dean wireless tops NASA wireless', Blog for America, 2003, <http://www.blogforamerica.com/archives/000435.html>, accessed on 2 March 2013.
38 See the report 'US politics goes mobile, phones become tool: Study', <http://phys.org/news/2012–10-politics-mobile-tool.html>.
39 Robin Jeffrey and Assa Doron, *Cellphone Nation*, Gurgaon: Hachette India, 2013, pp. 143–163.
40 V. L. Rafael, 'The cell phone and the cross: Messianic politics in the contemporary Philippines', *Public Culture*, 15 (3), 2003, pp. 394–425.
41 Howard Rheingold, *Smart mobs: The next social revolution*, New York: Basic Books, 2002, p. 168.
42 R. Ling and B. Yttri, 'Hyper-coordination via mobile phones in Norway, nobody sits at home and waits for the telephone to ring: Micro and hyper-coordination through the use of mobile telephones', in J. Katz and M. Aakhus (eds.), *Perpetual Contact: Mobile communication, private talk, public performance*, Cambridge: Cambridge University Press, 2001, pp. 139–169.
43 Rheingold 2002.
44 Accenture report depicts mobile governance as utilisation of all kinds of wireless and mobile technology services, applications and devices for providing services that benefit citizens, businesses and government units, <http://www.egovworld.org/pdf/Krishna_Prez_eGov2012.pdf>. A study by Khairiyyah Binti Mohd Noor (Malaysia), R K Bagga and K S Vijaya Sekhar says that m-Governance is a sub-domain of e-Governance and is not

a replacement for e-Governance, through which the governments deliver their services to the citizens using mobile devices, <http://www.csisigegov. org/ppt/mGovernance_trends_csi_oct2011paper.pdf>.

45 Praveen Rajpal, 'Mobile governance: With increased reach, it can become a tool of effective public-service delivery', *Economic Times*, 16 January 2012, online, accessed on 25 February 2012.

46 Greenpeace, a non-governmental environmental organisation, effectively uses mobile phones to raise fund. Its minimum individual contribution starts from Rs 500. I myself had to attend one such call from the organisation from the mobile number 91–8049134746. They requested me for a donation of minimum Rs 500. In addition, they educated me of their activities.

47 Kul Bhushan, 'Election Commission to use SMS alert system in 2014 Lok Sabha polls: Report', *Think Digit*, 8 January 2013, <http://www.thinkdigit. com>, accessed on 2 March 2013.

48 Amit Chaturvedi, 'Govt wants to gift phones to poor families: BJP mocks, but had suggested this first', NDTV, 8 August 2012, <http://www.ndtv. com/>, accessed on 2 march 2013.

49 Deloitte, 'Economic impact of mobile communications in Serbia, Ukraine, Malaysia, Thailand, Bangladesh and Pakistan', *Telenor ASA*, 2008, <http://www.telenor.com/wp-content/uploads/2012/03/Economic-Impact-of-Mobile-Communications.pdf>, accessed on 2 March 2013; and AT Capital Research, 'Bangladesh Telecom Sector: Challenges and opportunities', November 2010, <http://www.basis.org.bd/resource/Telecom-Challenges.pdf>, accessed on 2 March 2013.

50 Deloitte 2008.

51 Bhupesh Bhandari, 'Bhupesh Bhandari: A phone in every hand?', *Business Standard*, 17 August 2012, <http://www.business-standard.com>, accessed on 2 March 2013.

52 ANI, 'A new era of democracy', *Yahoo News*, 1 November 2012, <http:// in.news.yahoo.com>, accessed on 2 March 2013.

53 Bhushan, 8 January 2013.

54 IANS, 'EC to use SMS alert system in 2014 Lok Sabha elections', *Times of India*, 7 January 2013, <http://articles.timesofindia.indiatimes.com>, accessed on 2 March 2013.

55 P. Armond, 'Black flag over Seattle', *Albion Monitor*, 2000, <http://www. monitor.net/monitor/seattlewto/index.html>, accessed on 2 March 2013.

56 Organizers used mobile phones and websites to coordinate swarming – clusters of demonstrators who emerge from the general crowd to shut down traffic at specific locations at agreed times, then melt back into the crowd. Seattle police, unable to respond effectively to the new tactic, responded inappropriately – attacking innocent citizens while failing to achieve their objective of clearing out demonstrators (Reynolds 1999). The Seattle chief of police resigned after the incident. It appears obvious that the New York police closely studied the incident in preparing for their far more successful containment of demonstrators during the Republican National Convention in the summer of 2004. P. Reynolds, 'Eyewitness: The battle of Seattle', *BBC News*, 1999, <http://news.bbc.co.uk/1/hi/world/americas/547581.stm>, accessed on 02 March 2013.

7

INTERNET DIPLOMACY

Come citizens, diplomacy as an elite hierarchy is a thing of past! Now international relations have migrated to a pluralist digital age model. One may acknowledge it in many names: Twiplomacy, e-diplomacy, weiplomacy, digital diplomacy, YouTube diplomacy, Twitter diplomacy, online-diplomacy, Facebook diplomacy and so on. Internet is an integral part of diplomatic communications.[1] Contemporary global conditions are such that diplomacy anchored in statist line does not accurately capture the proper imagination of the diverse social forces that shape foreign affairs. Neither realist nor liberal paradigms are sufficient in explaining informal community forming in diplomatic arena. A discursive understanding is need of the hour. Critical theory offers appropriate framework for analysing rise and emergence of international relations and diplomatic practices more particularly in a normative context of technology. The rise of technological infrastructure necessitates incorporation of normative explanations for inclusion, participation and transparency in the conduct of interstate affairs. Taking into account the role of non-state actors and technological infrastructure in a Habermasian discourse to the study of diplomacy illuminates their potential for documenting non-territorial and informal political community in the conduct of foreign policy. Opportunity for an informal community through social media is so profound, as the inherent contradictions in global affairs in contemporary world call for change.

Max Horkheimer,[2] one of the founders of the Frankfurt Institute of Social Research established in 1923, coined the term *critical theory* in 1937. Critical theory is to endorse self-reflexive examinations of the experiences we have and the ways in which we make sense of our cultures, the world and ourselves. Critical theory refuses to identify freedom with any fixed forms of thought or institutional arrangements. It focusses scrutiny on the effects of power on the differential ability of actors to control their own circumstances.[3] In later years, the school failed to produce a systematic social theory. However, it combined a range of philosophical strands prevalent in social theorising. Prominent themes of political and social thought that it combined include historical materialism, cultural disenchantment, Freudian analysis and Hegelian dialectics, among other things. By the 1940s, many of the first-generation Frankfurt school thinkers began to counter the emasculation of critical reason, dialectics and self-conscious theory with a focus on the negativity of dialectics. The progressive platform of the Enlightenment or the project of emancipation from social and political oppression has been abandoned later by critics. Reason and social action in linguistics was resituated by Jürgen Habermas's communicative action[4] in the 1980s, which marked a vital turn in critical theory. It was during this time that international relations (IR) theorists drew on Habermas's theory and other critical theorists began to analyse the limits of realism, the dominant structural paradigm of international relations. Critical theorists sourced a long line of scholarship that extends from Marx and Gramsci[5] via the Frankfurt School to modern-day theorists such as Immanuel Wallerstein[6] and in IR, Robert Cox[7] and Justin Rosenberg[8] in order to resituate IR in a discursive context. However, the issues that underlie between unequal actors are differently situated, conditioned by socio-economic locality. To 'critical' scholars, world politics is marked by historically constituted inequalities, say, between core and periphery, north and south, developed and underdeveloped. To that end, liberal and realist approaches are seen as ideologies of inequality. First stages of this critical theory intervention in international relations included the seminal works of Robert Cox, Richard Ashley,[9] Mark Hoffman[10] and Andrew Linklater.[11] Linklater was instrumental in repositioning the emancipatory project in IR theory, combining various social and normative strands of critical thought, perhaps more than any other critical IR theorist. Critical interventions reflected an important 'third debate' in IR. Perhaps more importantly, critical theory stressed the need to take cognisance of the growing pluralism in the field of interstate affairs. Critical theorists explore what it meant for understanding and interpreting the growing complexity of global politics with the rising influence of technology, social media, human rights and democracy, and non-state actors. Increasing emphasis on promoting a 'rigorous pluralism' encompasses an array of critical investigations into the transformation of social relations, norms and identities in international relations. Here comes the trajectory of Internet diplomacy as important subthemes in the conduct of interstate affairs. It situates a discursive framework where local situations and normative understanding of global affairs demand for a new interpretation of diplomacy. Infotopia of technological rationality would thus confine neither to utopia nor to dystopia nor to neutrality; rather, it looks for how technology is experienced by underprivileged citizens in the socio-political locality.

So, what makes connection technologies so important in the conduct of interstate relations? The answer lies in the evolution of technology in the conduct of foreign affairs. Advancement in technology had a profound impact on the practice of statecraft. Smoke signals were oldest forms of communications, which were simplistic in design and execution that was used first in 200 BC to send messages along the Great Wall of China. In the twelfth century AD, Sultan Nur-ed-din built pigeon lofts and dove-cotes in Cairo and Damascus, where pigeons were used to carry messages from Egypt to cities as far away as Baghdad in modern-day Iraq. Telegraph is now an outdated communication system that was once used to transmit electric signals over wires from place to place and between nations. Before the explosion of cellular phones, there was what may be called landlines. Dial Up Internet, which was the archaic way to connect to the World Wide Web, was profoundly used in the conduct of interstate relations. Now it is the turn of platforms such as Facebook and Twitter.

Now what entered the realm of foreign policy? It is technologies of social connection which has direct influence on international relations in the twenty-first century. In the age of globalisation and Internet, top-down alleyway communications have almost become meaningless. In a new system of global communication network, technological social houses made governments just one of many stakeholders of foreign affairs. Increasingly unmanageable flow of information, indeed, altered the existing power and social structures of all societies and its relation with others. This change in fact calls into question traditional concepts of diplomacy and foreign policy itself.

This chapter explores how social media landscape and active engagement by members of civil society and underprivileged citizens informed of foreign affairs influence foreign policy makers' scope of action in India. Is diplomacy on social media a forerunner of global social media democracy? Will Internet democratise conduct of interstate affairs? Social media platforms are the new arenas of diplomacy and foreign policy execution. On Internet diplomacy, two things are very important: (1) Social media is facilitating diplomatic linkages between nation states, though on an informal level. (2) Citizen perception about diplomatic practices is fast changing. This chapter elaborates these two important aspects of cyber diplomacy. However, this discussion is not on the information imperialism and Internet governance. It is more about Internet and diplomacy with a special reference to the social landscape in India where diplomacy was thought to be an elite affair and ordinary citizens were not able to understand the jargons of foreign affairs in the past. However, it is not an exhaustive and an all-inclusive ramification of the connection technology and diplomacy but an elementary understanding of literatures on e-diplomacies and their growing linkages with selected cases in India.

Long-distance friendship through Internet

To the US secretary of state Hillary Clinton, social media is the new tools of the '21st-century statecraft' which is rapidly replacing fax telephones or diplomatic cables. Now social media is an important tool for government, political class, leaders, ministers and diplomats. In the near future, no one will be able to become a leader without digital followers and no diplomat will be well positioned to represent his or her country if he or she does not personally engage on cyberspace. And it is not the size of the followership that matters, but the quality of the conversations. This change is visible even at the level of citizen perspective about foreign affairs. Citizens of different countries are engaging beyond the political boundaries. If public diplomacy is all about a nation's interest well presented to a foreign nation and its people, the engagement between private citizens through connection technologies is of immense diplomatic opportunities for nation states.

The long-distance friendship that is evolving is influencing interstate relations in informal arenas and this perception was unearthed for the chapter by citing personal narrative of the author with citizens of different nationalities. Sometime ago, I got a comment on my Facebook cover page. The commenter was a national of Pakistan. He told me that the American drones had been hitting his native with human casualties thereon. I shared my solidarity with him. Everybody knows the irresolvable tug of war between India and Pakistan in diplomatic circles. However, it is not the reason that separates ordinary people from making friendship. We share goodwill and a common humanity. This humanity, which our political differences could not distance us, is the spirit of civilisations. Indians and Pakistanis meet informally on Facebook, Twitter and other places on Internet. Nothing distances us from sharing thoughts in connected space.

A US citizen called Cynthia Volkmann whom I befriended on LinkedIn said that she wanted to know my perception about Pakistan, as she was editing a book project for a senior Pak politician. I told her the story of Facebook comment by a Pakistani citizen and said we citizens do have no problems and that we are friends and sympathise with each other. However, what distances us is our political class and institutional apparatus. She was impressed and told me that she shared the same feeling about both the countries. She said she liked to join our league of imagined fellows of a common human heritage. I too was feeling camaraderie with this US citizen and we have become friends in connected space ever since.

As part of the research, once I sent a Facebook friend request to Andrei Shumilov, a Russian citizen and faculty in Institute for Social and Political Sciences (ISPS). What motivated me doing this was his profession. He worked as professor of political science. More interestingly, he asked me to write an article for *Polit Book*, a journal published by ISPS, of which he was an editor. Later, my article was published by the journal and the abstract was translated into Russian. It was all because I met him on Facebook!

Once Zhongshi Steve Guo, Associate Editor of *Asian Journal of Communication*, invited me to peer-review article submissions to the journal. I wondered how they got my profile. I had no previous connection with this Taylor and Francis journal, but they have got my profile from the Internet. Ever since, I have become a contact list for this Chinese citizen on their panel of peer reviewers.

What struck me most over the last couple of years was my email. Once I sent a seminar invitation to some scholars; I collected their emails from some Internet resources. However, I did not know any of those contacts before. Still, it was a wonder for me that Rainer Winter from Austria, a professor of sociology specialising in technology and society, came to attend our seminar, presented a theme paper and published it in our seminar proceedings. It was only this email that brought me in contact with several foreign nationals like Rainer Winter, with whom I shared a common humanity.

What signifies all across these stories of social media–based long-distance friendship? There is an interesting pattern of connection! In the connected space, private citizens are marching towards private citizens of other nations. Beyond the national governments, private citizens are also ambassadors of their nations. One might call them Facebook ambassadors or 'Twiplomats'. Facebook, Twitter, LinkedIn, Blogger and so on helped many people like this to be in contact with citizens of other countries. Nothing prevents people from meeting new people like this. While doing so, private citizens develop a cosmopolitan outlook, an international citizenship and mitigate national differences at individual capacities. There is something common to the stories just mentioned. They are instances of private citizens engaging with nationals of other societies on which political boundaries become meaningless. In this scenario, perception about other nations is cultivated by the behaviour of private citizens, not the public nation. This is one of the new arenas of the conduct of interstate affairs and nations must extend the jurisdiction and operational dynamics of diplomatic engagements to this nascent social space formed by the Internet. However, no conventional wisdom of modern statecraft or diplomacy understands this new relationship in connected spaces.

While nations distance from other nations on a range of things, which citizens could not properly understand, nationals are able to meet nationals of other societies. Technology is the new connector. This is also a harsh contradiction of our time. On the one side, political boundaries are becoming more and more rigid, whereas nationals of different societies are increasingly interconnected. However, our modern diplomatic practices neither understand it, nor foreign policy practitioners do properly execute it. It is in this technological turn in our human sociabilities Internet diplomacy is placed. It is a term often used to denote the rise of a new kind of diplomatic arena, which is coming over to social media platforms.

US Department of State was one of the early government bodies that recognised the growing importance of connected space in the foreign policy business. Go to its website and access the document titled '21st-century statecraft'.[12] Citing examples from the Arab Spring and the role of social media in disrupting authoritarian governments, the document emphasises 'Internet Moment' in foreign policy. Let us not forget the unscrupulous role of the US government in funding Internet activists operating in oppressive regimes. James Glanz and John Markoff reported the matter in a *New York Times* article on 12 June 2011.[13] The indisputable fact is that diplomatic arena has increasingly been influenced by Internet platforms.

The growing interplay between social media and diplomatic circles could be easily understood in the wake of conflict of interest between the Chinese government and Google. In 2010, there was an allegation by Google.cn that Chinese administration was violating its privacy policies. Remember, there was an equal interest showed by the US administration in the incident. Secretary of State Hillary Clinton warned that a 'new information curtain is descending across much of the world'. Indeed, she was pointing towards China's hackers targeting Google. Chinese government retorted aptly by saying that it was more concerned of the 'information imperialism' imposed on China. The term *information imperialism* was used by English-language-speaking Chinese newspaper *Global Times* in the context of privacy breach by the Chinese administration following Google's allegation.

Is the growing fascination with social media a mere sign of our desperation with other, profoundly more conventional instruments of diplomatic channels? It is certain that formal channels of diplomatic engagements are still popular and credible. Embassies, track, conferences and summit are time-tested and most enduring. It does not take us away from our immediate diplomatic objectives as important ways of wielding diplomatic prowess. Here social media as a tool of foreign policy has the unique advantage of being untested. It never fails and so it must be working. The question is whether it is information imperialism.

Studies corroborated that digital literacy projects and subsequent Internet-based pro-revolutionary activism have close connection. For example, in countries such as Kyrgyzstan, where a culture of communication practice helped a statewide revolution called Tulip Revolution in 2005, Internet projects cast shadow of doubts about a western imperialist project. Ramesh Srinivasan and Adam Fish[14] have documented the idea in a 2009 study. Adam Fish[15] in a 20 June 2011 write-up upheld that the US State Department and US-based philanthropic organisations had role in this sort of digital literacy projects. There were polemics about the Arab Spring. Anyhow, more empirical data are required before making any premature conclusion about US information intervention and US-backed operations of digital literacy in Syria, Tunisia and Egypt. The ideological position is that the US- and other western countries–promoted information intermediaries have incarnated into a new kind of imperialism in the informatic public sphere of the world.

Go to the website of the International Telecommunication Union (ITU) and check out the World Conference on International Telecommunications (WCIT) in Dubai, United Arab Emirates, from 3 to 14 December 2012.[16] Based on the above facts, there were some countries dissatisfied with the current practices of Internet Corporation for Assigned Names and Numbers (ICANN). The *New York Times* reported that a group of countries led by Russia and China was trying to use the deliberations to undermine the open spirit of the Internet. The *NYT* reported it as an attempt to topple down the true spirit of openness.[17] The fact is that there is a growing divide between the West and the rest on Internet governance. And there is growing diplomatic manoeuvre over Internet governance.

It is easy to see why a world in which young Indians embrace the latest technology funded by venture capitalists from Silicon Valley, while more prolific and established diplomats sit back, sip tea and take on a break from work. It sounds so appealing. However, is such a world achievable? Will Twitter and Facebook come to fill in the void left behind by conventional tools of diplomacy? Will the oppressed masses in cleavage-rich Indian nation join the barricades once they get unfettered access to Facebook and Twitter? Is social media the next step in the formulations of foreign policy? Here let us see social media tapping on the diplomatic functions of the modern Indian state.

Public and track diplomacies in Internet age

A world of informal layer of connection works with diplomatic consequences. Sometimes they are more powerful than the conventional way of
doing the basic business of diplomacy. Twitter, Facebook and so on are
significant tools for a new level of diplomatic engagement, though in an
informal manner, they have significance in the sense that nations are more
concerned about doing the foreign policy in a more informal way. They
represent a cultural shift from an old system of diplomatic engagements to
an endorsement of a new system of track diplomacy.

Track is more popular these days among diplomatic circles, as
people-to-people, business-to-business, media-to-media, society-to-society,
culture-to-culture and art-to-art interfaces are facilitating a new sort of intimate diplomacy between governments. This means such informal sources
of non-institutionalised channels of engagements are thought to have the
power what the traditional sources of diplomatic engagements do not have.
It ensures better understanding, more intimacy and broader coalition. Here
differences are reduced, suspicion is waning out and more engagements are
possible. However, what is being stated about track on Internet is different.
In the former case, it is more deliberate. It is steered by ruling dispensation.
In the latter case, it is more of an informal development.

Track on Internet is different as it is taking place in a discursive socio-
political locality. Technology facilitates it. It happens in ways how the
author has met US citizens, Russian citizens, Pakistani citizens, Chinese
citizens, Austrian citizen and others. This is a new way of cultural understanding of diversity and recognising it. A new kind of informal diplomatic
realm is taking shape on Internet. If the modern state is not able to understand the mass power of platforms in effecting interstate affairs, nations
are going to lose in connected age. As initially said, the USA was an early
adopter of this strategy. Now every diplomatic tweet counts. Every timeline
of foreign policy update has significance. Facebook and Twitter are new
sorts of diplomatic realm. Internet has been democratising diplomacy. And
more countries are joining the bandwagon.

Multi-Track Diplomacy is a conceptual way to view the process of
international peacemaking as a living system. It looks at the web of
interconnected activities, individuals, institutions and communities that
operate together for a common goal: a world at peace. Multi-Track
Diplomacy is an expansion of the 'Track One, Track Two' paradigm that
has defined the conflict resolution field during the past few years. Track
One Diplomacy is official government diplomacy whereby communication and interaction is between governments. Track Two Diplomacy is

the unofficial interaction and intervention of non-state actors. Social media is significant here.

In India, Internet is revolutionising the way in which we conduct public diplomacy.[18] Geoffrey Cowan and Nicholas Cull understand public diplomacy as 'an international actor's attempt to advance the ends of policy by engaging with foreign publics' giving proof of a very broad understanding of who public diplomacy's actors are. Joseph Nye believes it is 'diplomacy aimed at public opinion'.[19] While Josef Nye considers public diplomacy being about relationship building,[20] Matt Armstrong argues, '[p]ublic diplomacy involves understanding, influencing, developing relationships with and providing information to the general public and civic society abroad, in order to create a favourable environment for achieving national security, political, cultural and economic objectives'.[21] Anthony Pratkanis defines public diplomacy as 'the promotion of the national interest by informing and influencing the citizens of other nations'.[22]

Public diplomacy scholars have argued that diplomats should move from a one-way communication to a two-way communication model to be more effective.[23]Ministry of External Affairs in India embraces public diplomacy in Web 2.0, or public diplomacy 2.0. The ministry has a team of online warriors who post in English-language, Facebook commentaries, YouTube videos, blog and Twitter entries about ministry's activities. A number of Indian diplomats also blog or use Facebook or Twitter to reach out to people. The online presence of India's public diplomacy is a testimony to this. As initially pointed out 'public diplomacy 2.0' (also known as 'e-diplomacy', 'Facebook diplomacy' etc.) has been used in different terms.

The new arenas of diplomatic engagements

Literature on cyberspace and diplomatic arena is piling up.[24] Global affairs have come at a critical juncture in the age of connection technologies, and the effect of technologies of connection on international affairs is profoundly unpredictable. Middle East, North Africa and the Colour Revolutions that swept through Eastern Europe and Central Asia are living laboratories of how new communication technologies can have on the system of international relations. The increasing role of cyberspace in international affairs has brought into the picture new themes and new points of engagements for practitioners of global affairs in a challenging way. Networks and networked thinking, humanitarian needs, censorship, neutrality, terrorism, information ownership, privacy, cyberwars and rebellion are examples of such expanding list of new themes contributed by cyberspace to international affairs, which makes diplomacy more of a competitive space.[25] Information revolution is permanently changing the arena of international relations, says Shanthi Kalathil in the book *Diplomacy, Development, and Security in the Information Age*.[26]

The Arab Spring gave new inspirations to people across the world to bring in changes. Democracy remains appealing and underprivileged people are still willing to put their lives on the line to attain more democracy. Along with this, the venues of mass communication become more diverse and pervasive and so citizens become intellectually and politically empowered. The 24×7 news cycle has become outdated because it relied on a fixed number of information providers whose content could be monitored by policymakers with relative ease. Now information processing has become difficult for governments. Big data is so unmanageable and its processing requires trained professionals. Information sources are numerous and anonymous. Governments find it difficult to update on events and information. So, it lacks systematic ways to digest and judge information for future behaviour and actions. Therefore, a new arena has born of cyberspace with information overload.[27] Policymakers cannot be mere spectators. They have to act in time. However, the new field of act is different unlike the conventional field of conduct of international affairs. The field is more informed by platforms. YouTube videos produced by young Egyptians, Facebook updates of Iranians and tweets of a Tunisian give life to the new arenas.

In recent times, there were calls by practitioners of diplomacy to go beyond one-way, mass-media-driven campaigns to develop more relational strategies. Editors of the book *Relational, Networked and Collaborative Approaches to Public Diplomacy: The Connective Mindshift* say that relationships have always been pivotal to the practice of public diplomacy and that the relational dynamics are changing.[28] In fact, countries must be well cautious of the rise of the new arenas of international relations. Indian establishments are indeed far ahead of this shift.

'Think tanks and foreign services that shun social media are being left behind', says Rory Medcalf in an article posted in the *American Review*.[29] We are living in an era of social media diplomacy, commonly referred to as Diplomacy 2.0. In the social media age, diplomacy is re-energised in a way that people previously not related to the rank and file of diplomatic business now turned up to be critical contributors. It gives way to people's diplomacy, which according to conventional wisdom was an insignificant actor. Twitter profiles of India's diplomatic offices abroad have a good number of followers. Facebook is used as a community platform for sharing news, promoting Indian culture and engaging with the public. YouTube is used as a theatre of national imageries to growing consumers overseas. Indeed, social media greatly influences public diplomacy, says Jennifer Charlton in an article posted on the website of Canadian International Council.[30]

Welcome to the new world of e-diplomacy, which is called, more pompously, '21st-century statecraft' by experts in the USA. Historically, governments left diplomacy to the cagey and the discreet, who mostly met behind closed doors. Now they are also using Twitter, Facebook and YouTube. Much of this online activity is part of 'public diplomacy', which means government is communicating directly with the citizens of another country.

Nevertheless, e-diplomacy is an easy and cheap tool for other purposes, too, such as responding to disasters, to be in touch with nationals abroad, gathering information and managing relationships. According to *The Economist* magazine, foreign ministers getting the hang of social media are engaging virtual relations in cyber age.[31] E-diplomacy is the use of the World Wide Web and ICT to carry out diplomatic objectives. Though it is a broad definition which is hard to understand, it does not have any tendency to confuse e-diplomacy with social media platforms alone, says Fergus Hanson, non-resident fellow at the Brookings Institution's Foreign Policy program.[32] Text messaging, mobile technologies, Internet freedom, crowdsourcing capabilities, mapping software, tech camps and more are now used by the governments to extend their diplomatic reach to men and women otherwise excluded from public life in the country and beyond. So e-diplomacy is beyond social media. The power of ideas can create better results and transition traditional diplomacy to a new phase, where people are new players, and politicians and diplomats are not elites any longer.

India's citizen diplomacy in connected space

Any discussion on social diplomacy should begin from the biggest personal fabricator of social media in India: Narendra Modi, the prime minister of India. Just get a glimpse of his Facebook page at facebook.com/narendramodi. To the dismay, there was a sizable pattern of updates about his foreign cruise across different countries. Photos of Modi shaking hands with citizens of Nepal have thousands of likes. Many endorsed his address to the citizens at Fiji National University. Addressing the Australian Parliament, a photo of the G20 Summit speech titled 'Delivering Global Economic Resilience' has been favourites of his fan list. On 13 November 2014, Modi changed the cover page with a photo of ASEAN leaders. Interestingly what surprised was the comment section. There was an interesting comment by an Indonesian citizen, Claudia Henny. She commented that 'Nice to see all the leaders together especially our President of Indonesia Mr. Joko Widodo, PM of India Mr. Narendra Modi. I'm proud to be Indonesian.' A growing social media–based, diplomatic attaché has become significant if the growing online followers of leadership is taken into consideration. Though it is informal, it has the power to become influential. The social profiles of political class cater vehemently to this trend. Social diplomacy is increasingly becoming significant and as official as a foreign policy practice in institutionalised ways. In the days to come, if social diplomacy is not reckoned with official channels, believe it or not, nations are going to lose the test of the time.

Narendra Modi follows world's leaders and so they reciprocate. Our diplomats follow their counterparts in other parts of the world and so they reciprocate. Many among us do the same things. Many of your friends and their friends do follow leaders of other societies. So are the citizens of other societies that they follow our ruling class.

The first diplomat in India to reduce the 'iron curtain' between diplomacy and ordinary citizens was Nirupama Rao. Her Twitter replies to queries by 'Tweeples' during Libyan crisis, Somali pirates and other sensitive diplomatic issues marked the age of Internet diplomacy in India. *Deccan Herald* had a report on 2 March 2011 on the Twitter interaction between the diplomat and ordinary citizens.[33]

One might have never thought of seeing something from the elite corridors of diplomatic functionaries of the Indian state ever in life for the reason that it was always an ivory tower. Citizen perception about this elite empire was broken sometime ago. Several government bodies have been leveraging social media sites. However, the first government agency to join the social media was the Ministry of External Affairs in 2011. Visit the social profiles of India's public diplomacy of Ministry of External Affairs (MEA). See the social profiles, YouTube channel at youtube.com/user/Indiandiplomacy, Facebook at facebook.com/IndianDiplomacy, Instagram at instagram.com/indiandiplomacy, website at mea.gov.in, blogger at indiandiplomacy.blogspot.in/, Twitter at twitter.com/indiandiplomacy, Google+ at +IndianDiplomacy and Issue at issuu.com/indiandiplomacy. This elite institution is becoming more accessible to citizens or technology makes it so.

Rama Lakshmi,[34] who has been with *The Washington Post*'s India bureau, wrote an interesting piece titled 'Modi makes a lot of overseas trips, but is he a diplomatic failure with India's neighbors?' on 23 September 2015. She observed that Indian prime minister Narendra Modi's diplomatic aerobatics did not yield any result at least according to immediate neighbours in

Nepal and Pakistan. While making such an argument, the writer extensively cites Twitter responses from Nepal and Pakistan. The point is that in the age of constant connection, the real deal breaker in diplomatic engagements is social media.

Web diplomacy

Log on to webdiplomacy.net/ and the home profile describes it as 'A multiplayer web implementation of the popular turn-based strategy game Diplomacy'. The webpage has a Forum, 'A place to discuss topics/games with other webDiplomacy players'. There were many topics under active discussions such as Panama Papers and many other interesting discussions by forum members. The webDiplomacy game platform has over 70,000 members. This web app signifies the growing concern among various corners out there on the part of diplomacy-related players over disseminating web-based diplomatic information among Internet generation. The game apps on the web are aplenty. PlayDiplomacy.com is another example of online web app dedicated to promoting the diplomacy hobby, run by volunteers and funded by donations. Backstabbr.com is a modern web interface for the classic board game diplomacy. The online game apps on Internet point towards an apparent trend in making diplomacy, one held as a high political social realm down to earth. Many Indians are registered users of such game apps.

Apart from game apps, diplomacy and its institutional apparatus are vying for its real cyber presence over the last couple of years. More interestingly the official website of MEA has close to three crore visitors. What do all these signify? Social media presence of the MEA gives a new perception to citizens. It is also useful for government to reach out to citizens. One could call it Internet diplomacy. Visit mea.gov.in/in-focus.htm and download documents pertaining to the likes of Belgium visit, Washington DC visit, Saudi Arabia visit, Russia visit and Afghan visit. Publication of such documents over the websites signifies the External Affairs Ministry's commitment to speak to the particular audiences concerned.

S. N. Mohammed[35] has provided enough insight into how small countries are profiting from the web in multiple ways. For example, External Affairs Ministry's website is a clear example of self-presentation of India abroad. Web is a marketplace for image management in the age of Internet. Similarly, the website embassyindia.es is another example of image management abroad. The embassy website's useful links section embassyindia.es/useful-links provides a user abundant information about the web profile of many things that are Indian. Information pertaining to polity, economy, science and software, media, aviation, tourism and so on provides a new image of India abroad. Since Internet is interactive, informative and resourceful, it can be leveraged to create a better climate of relationship abroad. Moreover, for the underprivileged citizens, who were once end noted on the social peripheries, Internet provides enormous opportunity to be active participants in diplomatic engagements steered by cyberspace. So, for laypeople, technology on diplomacy is empowering.

The web has become a new combat zone among international state players to improve their nations' standing on almost everything under the sky. Diplomacy is generally thought to be state-sponsored propaganda activities,[36] designed to improve a nation's image among foreign audiences which is also known as public diplomacy,[37] and indeed has become a staple of modern international relations and more particularly with the rise of modern international broadcasting.[38] With the advent of the web, chronometer of image management has come to the forefront of interstate debates. Several studies have examined how nations have harnessed the power of the Internet to reach global audiences in ways unprecedented in history. However, equal weight should be given to the question how citizens inside the territory benefit out of web diplomacy. While communication apartheid and media monopoly privileged an elite few in the past, web has democratised diplomacy.

Twiplomacy

The web address twiplomacy.com/ is an interesting profile that would give one with hints on Twitter and its interesting implications for twenty-first-century diplomatic relations. Over the past years, foreign ministries and world leaders have used hashtags to promote specific issues. One could call it hashtag diplomacy. Twitter has become the channel of choice for digital diplomacy between world leaders, governments, foreign ministries and diplomats. Social media in general and Twitter in particular are no longer just an afterthought but an essential communication tool for governments to interact and broadcast 140-character messages.

An article posted on 17 October 2012 by Matthias Lüfkens titled 'The Digital Diplomat: Connected and on Twitter', published in *Canadian International Council*, reported that eighty-two countries' foreign ministries had Twitter accounts and forty-seven ministers of foreign affairs were personally on Twitter. Heads of states and governments are tweeting personally! Indian prime minister Narendra Modi (@narendramodi) follows prime minister of Russia Dmitry Medvedev (@MedvedevRussiaE), Brazilian president Dilma Rousseff (@dilmabr), prime minster of Australia

Malcolm Turnbull (@TurnbullMalcolm), prime minister of Sri Lanka Ranil Wickremesinghe (@RW_UNP), president of Mongolia Tsakhiagiin Elbegdorj (@elbegdorj), just to mention a few among many others.

The power of social networking site Twitter is that it connects people globally and brings citizens closer to their leaders. Diplomatic offices have migrated to Twitter. Citizens directly contact with embassies. Informal contact is possible. Many Indian embassies abroad have Twitter presence: Poland (@IndiaPoland), Egypt (@indembcairo), Kazakhstan (@indembastana), Mongolia (@IndiainMongolia), Kuwait (@indembkwt), Qatar (@IndEmbDoha), Madagascar (@IndembTana) and Bangladesh (@ihcdhaka), to name a few. The twitter accounts have some thousands of followers. The pages are also engaging and well updated.

The point is very clear. World leaders should follow each other on Twitter. If their countries have good diplomatic relations, Twitter is significant. Not following a peer on Twitter signifies a lot about the embittered relationship between two people. If one uses this analogy to the relations between two countries, it is more than an embittered relation. Not following someone back on Twitter is tantamount to a diplomatic catastrophe. It is not exaggeration to say that blocking someone on Twitter will soon be identical to breaking diplomatic ties. The days are not far when a Twitter argument might get out of hand and think of how just 140 characters could spark a war.

For those not yet convinced about the power of social networks, consider a lesson. If Twitter were a country, it would be ranked fourth, with more than half a billion registered users. People like Jack Dorsey are the unelected leaders of supra-national states, who are wielding more power than many world leaders. It is hardly surprising that world leaders now include trips to the tech giants in Silicon Valley on their official visits to the USA. 'Twiplomacy' is here to stay. Twitter has already made a massive impact on the way our leaders interact with each other. Diplomats connect with their host countries. Drafting a tweet is as much a part of the curriculum in diplomacy schools as writing government cables or diplomatic jargons. It is not to suggest that social networks like Twitter will replace face-to-face meetings between world leaders and government representatives. However, the Twitter connections between leaders will surely deepen and broaden existing relations with new audiences.

The *IndianDiplomacy* Twitter profile has over two and a half lakh[39] followers and the account has updates on a regular basis. Hashtag diplomacy is fascinating social media enthusiasts. Hashtags such as #CelebratingIndia, #IndiaConnect and #digitaldiplomacy were popular and were places of diplomatic tweets. In fact, the Twitter initiative has been appreciative especially due to its role during the Libya crisis. Along with updating relevant information about crisis, the profile helped Indians trapped in Libya to return home safely. The interactive platforms in a way were useful and hopeful for family and this was evident from the Twitter experience of the Ministry during the Libyan crisis.

Facebook diplomacy

Making friends on Facebook is a more significant diplomatic practice as diplomacy is more of marketplace competitions and margins of advantages. Diplomacy is now increasingly wrought down by technology. Facebook is significantly changing statecraft. Citizens and political leadership become Facebook ambassadors. Diplomatic officials are found to have used Facebook as a loudspeaker to contact and self-represent the country amongst the citizens across the world and comity of nations. Large Facebook pages clearly translate into large interactions; for example, India's Prime Minister Narendra Modi is the undisputed champion, with more than 215 million interactions on his Facebook posts in 2015, more than five times as many as the more popular Barack Obama campaign page, says a Burson-Marsteller study.[40] A closer look at the type of interactions shows that Narendra Modi leads in post likes and post comments. Indian prime minister Narendra Modi is undoubtedly the most effective world leader on Facebook, with huge interactions on each post. One of the highlights of Narendra Modi's social media engagement in 2015 was the 'town hall' meeting at Facebook's headquarters in California on 27 September with Facebook founder Mark Zuckerberg, which was live-streamed on the platform. During the 50-minute interview, Modi described in detail his vision of a digital government. Go to the page at facebook.com/IndianDiplomacy and spot over eight lakh likes by its followers. The page describes it as 'Official Facebook Page of India's Public Diplomacy'. More importantly, its updates are interesting. Timeline diplomacy in the page is creating enthusiasm. While going through the updates, there was something interesting. The verified Facebook page of India's Ministry of External Affairs had over 12 lakh followers by May 2016. The page has regular updates, which also receives hundreds of likes. Photos of diplomatic functionaries, events, talks, summits and so on are updated on the timeline. Facebook page of the official diplomatic institutions and their online activities are just a small picture of Facebook as a potential channel of informal diplomatic communication. Facebook is increasingly penetrating among citizens as a channel of diplomatic engagements at the informal levels.

Look at the *World Leaders on Facebook*, which is Burson-Marsteller's latest research into the question: how world leaders, heads of governments and international organisations communicate on social media?[41] The research builds on Burson-Marsteller's highly acclaimed annual *Twiplomacy* study. Initially it was focussed solely on Twitter. The 2016 study has been expanded to other social media platforms including Facebook, Instagram, YouTube, Google+ and more niche digital diplomacy platforms such as Snapchat and Vine. According to the Burson-Marsteller study conducted in early January 2016 on 512 Facebook pages, 87 heads of state, 82 prime ministers and 51 foreign ministers maintain personal pages on Facebook.[42] Barack Obama[43], whose follower list is close to five crore has highest followers on Facebook, is closely followed by Indian prime minister Narendra Modi,[44] whose likes are moving close to 3.5 crore on his personal page and 10.1 million likes on his institutional Prime Minister of India page,[45] which is in third position. Turkish president Recep Tayyip Erdogan (close to one crore), Egyptian president Abdel Fattah el-Sisi (over sixty-five lakh) and Indonesian president Joko Widodo (over sixty lakh) compete for the top 5 list of the most popular Facebook leaders. Burson-Marsteller study documented that 36 world leaders can boast more than a million likes on their respective Facebook pages.[46]

Facebook has become the channel for community engagement among world leaders. Many politicians discover social media as channels of communications during election campaigns. Barack Obama page, which was set up in late 2007 as an electoral tool for the former senator of Illinois, is an example. Since then, Facebook presence has become part of any social media political campaign and one of the best ways to engage with potential voters and citizens. Over 1.5 billion people have registered an account on the platform and among them 1 billion people are active on the social network every day. In 2015, the number of users on Facebook became even greater than the population of China. Given the global audience on Facebook, it comes as no surprise that governments and world leaders now have a presence on it.

While size does matter, it does not necessarily translate into increased engagement. To establish a correlation on engagement level, a ranking of page can be drawn on relative number of page post likes, comments and shares of each page of the leaders. Argentina's president Mauricio Macri[47] (close to forty lakh likes) is the undisputed 'Facebook president' with a high levels of engagement rate. Cambodian prime minister Hun Sen[48] (over forty lakh), Israel's Benjamin Netanyahu[49] (close to eighteen lakh), the Iraqi Prime Minister's office[50] (eighteen lakh), Brazil's Dilma Rousseff[51] (over twenty-eight lakh) and the White House[52] (over sixty-three lakh) all

160

enjoy engagement rates relative to their fans. India's prime minister makes a strong performance among the top 10 most engaged leaders with higher engagement rate despite his massive fan count.

Facebook pages of smaller courtiers have prolific pages. Presidency of the Dominican Republic was the most prolific Facebook page in 2015.[53] Governments of Botswana and the Philippines are almost as active, with many daily posts. Such profiles are using Facebook like a channel of governmental news service. Liking other Facebook pages is essentially an act of courtesy. While a like does not allow these pages to message each other privately, it makes it easier to follow the posts published on those pages. Politicians tend to like their respective political party, governments sometimes like all their ministries on Facebook and foreign ministries often like the pages of their embassies worldwide. A few foreign ministries also like the Facebook pages of embassies accredited in their respective capitals. Peer connection is so strong in the Facebook campaign page of Barack Obama, which is the most popular page liked by 21 of his peers and the White House is liked by 19 others. European Commission is second and the European External Action Service is in third place, on par with the White House, ahead of the French president and the French Foreign Ministry who are in fourth place. The Council of the European Union and the State Department share the fifth position. The UN is by far the most popular page with all world leaders, liked by 36 other pages, ahead of the European Parliament (25 likes) and NATO (15 likes).[54] A reading of peer page likes and peer connections on Facebook signifies the impending strategic significance of Facebook on foreign affairs as a channel of informal communication.

In the age of Internet, diplomacy is more engaged on informal channels. Here comes the significance of Facebook as a channel of diplomatic communication between non-state entities such as underprivileged people, non-state actors, NGOs and citizens abroad.

Video diplomacy

Over the last three decades, the Ministry of External Affairs, Government of India, has commissioned nearly 350 documentary films. The films portray various facets of life in India. Most documentaries focus on India's rich cultural heritages, values, its democratic and pluralistic society, its secular values, its vibrant economy, the innovativeness of enterprise of its people, the contributions of outstanding individuals to different walks of life and a host of other subjects. What happens if those documentaries are shared on YouTube? A fantastic idea and short versions of some of these films have been uploaded on to YouTube[55] and have proved to be hugely popular.

YouTube diplomacy has made some valuable inroads into citizen perception on the very institutions of the conduct of public diplomacy. It has certain merit. A single message can reach as many millions of connections as possible. Quick and easy access increases credibility and trust in diplomatic relations. It can be useful for both to tarnish and build reputations within seconds. Growing rumours could make diplomatic practitioners wary of YouTube vigilantism.

The YouTube[56] channel entertains users with a rich playlist, which contains documentaries for the last three decades produced by the MEA. The channel has uploads of the MEA that has close to five lakh views. The page had 1,403 video uploads by January 2014. A popular page, for example, *A La Cart!!! Food in the Streets of India*[57], had close to five lakh views by January 2014. Its Facebook[58] page had over one lakh likes.

Diplomacy in other platforms

The Blogger[59] page has comparatively very few followers, less than a hundred. It has also very few post from 2010 onwards. There were articles by some eminent scholars, which give a good sense of understanding about India, foreign policy and its various dimensions. What fascinates one, however, is the fact that such platforms are primarily used as a broadcasting medium, whereby a new culture of public perception about diplomatic institutions is created across the countries of the world as well among their citizens.

The Ministry of External Affairs has a profile on Google+.[60] It has close to eight lakh followers. The page is very active and regularly updated. Every diplomatic engagement gets mention in the profile page. With pictures and catchy phrases, it attracts a growing young audience as well as expatriates.

In Issuu,[61] a digital publishing platform, Public Diplomacy Initiative of India's Ministry of External Affairs has over a hundred publications with close to 500 followers. The platform has publishing programmes, which deliver plenty of information to social media enthusiasts. A good number of documents are available in the platform. Yoga in India, Climate Change, Indian in BRICS, India Perspectives and so on give us an idea about what the MEA gives a sense of ourselves to the world. They are well written, lucid, readable and understandable to those who are good at basics of English language.

MEA's Instagram profile has photo close to a hundred posts with close to a hundred followers. The Flickr profile of MEA has over 10,000 photo uploads. Photos have many views and comments. Though the number of photo uploads on Instgaram is small compared to activities carried on other social media platforms such as Facebook and Twitter, it is being seen by those people who should see it. A critical population is out there on Instgram that can be leveraged by the MEA for its diplomatic engagements abroad.

The MEA has gone mobile. It is interesting. It also has a mobile app,[62] called MEAIndia. It is available for download on App Store and Google Play Store. The iTunes app and Android app have some hundreds of downloads on mobile devices. Mobile app MEAIndia provides many services, such as passport, visa and consular assistance.

Future

If one read Palmer and Perkins, the determinants of foreign policy would be tangible and intangible forces. So are the famed aphorisms on foreign policy part of the conventional wisdom in the discipline. However, the prospect of foreign policy being tested via social media and cell phones remains untapped. It would be the future, a social future of diplomacy with more complex engagements.

There is a creative destruction of old ways of doing things. Social diplomacy is one among them. Such a practice will have greater significance. Boundaries between diplomacy, non-diplomatic channels of diplomatic practices and intelligence are all dissolving into a thin border.

Now barriers are breaking down, thanks to social media. When a crisis or event breaks across the connected space, personal fabricators on social media – Twitter, blogs, Facebook, YouTube and cell phones – help make a project with succinct meaning in a world of noise.

Many young amateur foreign policy commentators of the present day are likely to become foreign policy experts in the days to come. Today's trail blazers will become tomorrow's thought leaders. Social media is significantly a channel for them. At least they are innovators. This will raise serious challenge to many in the traditional diplomatic circles. It is the political Internet which gives power to amateur activists a space which otherwise they would not get.

If one does not navigate to timeline updates, if one does not tweet to the Twitter class, if one does not check out the YouTube comments of documentaries and films about international affairs, intelligence experts who believe secret is true and diplomacy is an elite business still in the age of Internet, he or she risks becoming primitive in the age of social media. Public diplomacy is fast getting acceptance among diplomatic circles as it is largely influenced by ordinary citizens who cross political boundaries in search of connection and mutual interest. It should also be extended to those social media diplomats who communicate with their counterparts in other parts of the world.

The fact is that in the twenty-first century, diplomacy could not overlook Internet. It influences diplomacy at two levels. One is that Internet as one of the channels of diplomatic engagements has the advantage of simplifying and increasing informal exchanges between the governments of the world. Second, Internet has changed citizens' perception about what constitute diplomatic practices and engagements.

Networked communication facilitated by the diffusion of cell phones is changing the way people communicate and replacing old power hierarchies in the process. Information not only travels instantly from almost anywhere on Earth, but is also democratised. Information is unfiltered by traditional gatekeepers like newspaper, radio or television editors. It is useful according to ordinary citizens who for centuries faced social divides and cleavages that are oppressive. Therefore, Twiplomacy, e-diplomacy, weiplomacy, digital diplomacy, YouTube diplomacy, Twitter diplomacy, online-diplomacy, Facebook diplomacy and other such neologisms are changing the traditional diplomatic environment and serious foreign ministries are trying to adapt themselves to them.

In the book *Real-Time Diplomacy: Politics and Power in the Social Media Era*, author Philip Seib,[63] professor of Journalism and Public Diplomacy and a professor of International Relations at the University of Southern California, vividly describes the old way of conducting diplomacy is anachronism in the age of constant connection.

Notes

1 Matthias Lüfkens, 'The digital diplomat: Connected and on Twitter', *Canadian International Council*, 17 October 2012, <http://opencanada. org/features/the-think-tank/essays/the-digital-diplomat-connected-and-on-twitter/>, accessed on 24 September 2015.

2 M. Horkheimer, *Critical Theory: Selected Essays*, New York: Herder & Herder, 1972.

3 Ecaterina Patrascu and Zahoor Ahmad Wani, 'Discourse of critical theory in the context of international relations', International Conference Rcic'15, Redefining Community in Intercultural Context, Brasov, May 2015, pp. 21–23.

4 J. Habermas, *The Theory of Communicative Action*, Vol. 1, Boston: Beacon Press, 1981.

5 A. Gramsci, *Selections from the Prison Notebooks*, New York: International Publishers, 1971.

6 Immanuel Wallerstein, 'The inter-state structure of the modern world system', in Steve Smith, Ken Booth, and Marysia Zalewski (eds.), *International Theory: Positivism and Beyond*, Cambridge: Cambridge University Press, 1995, pp. 87–107.

7 Robert Cox, 'Social forces, states and world order: Beyond international relations theory', *Millennium*, 10 (2), 1981, pp. 126–155.

8 Justin Rosenberg, 'Why is there no international historical sociology?', *European Journal of International Relations*, 12 (3), 2006, pp. 307–340.

9 R. K. Ashley, 'Untying the sovereign state: A double reading of the anarchy problematique', *Millennium: Journal of International Studies*, 17, 1988, pp. 227–262.

10 Mark Hoffman, 'Critical theory and the inter-paradigm debate', *Millennium: Journal of International Studies*, 16, 1987, pp. 231–250.

11 Andrew Linklater, *Beyond Marxism and Realism: Critical Theory and International Relations*, London: Macmillan, 1990.

12 US Department of State, '21st century statecraft', <http://www.state.gov/statecraft/overview/index.htm>.

13 James Glanz, and John Markoff, 'U.S. underwrites Internet detour around censors', *The New York Times*, 12 June 2011, <http://www.nytimes.com/2011/06/12/world/12internet.html?_r=0>, accessed on 13 July 2014.

14 Ramesh Srinivasan and Adam Fish, 'Internet authorship: Social and political implications within Kyrgyzstan', *Journal of Computer-Mediated Communication*, 14 (3), 2009, pp. 559–580, <doi:10.1111/j.1083–6101.2009.01453.x>, accessed on 14 July 2014.

15 Adam Fish, 'Information imperialism?' *Savage Minds*, 20 June 2011, <http://savageminds.org/2011/06/20/information-imperialism/>, accessed on 14 July 2014.

16 See <http://www.itu.int/en/wcit-12/Pages/default.aspx>.

17 'Global Internet diplomacy', *New York Times*, 12 December 2012, <http://www.nytimes.com/2012/12/13/opinion/global-internet-diplomacy.html?_r=0>.

18 Geoffrey Cowan and Nicholas J. Cull (eds.), *Public Diplomacy in a Changing World*, The Annals of the American Academy of Political and Social Science, Vol. 616, Thousand Oaks: Sage, 2008.

19 Joseph S. Nye, *Soft Power: The Means to Success in World Politics*, 2nd edition, New York: Public Affairs, 2004, p. 105.

20 Mark Leonard, Catherine Stead, and Conrad Smewing, *Public Diplomacy*, London: Foreign Policy Centre, 2002.

21 Matt Armstrong, 'Defining public diplomacy', *Mountain Runner*, 17 November 2008, <http://mountainrunner.us/2008/11/defining_public_diplomacy/>.

22 Anthony Pratkanis, 'Public diplomacy in international conflicts: A social influence analysis', in Nancy Snow and Philip M. Taylor (eds.), *Routledge Handbook of Public Diplomacy*, London and New York: Routledge, 2009, p. 112.

23 Richard Grant, 'The Democratization of Diplomacy: Negotiating with the Internet', Oxford Internet Institute, Research Report No. 5, November 2004.

24 See <https://ipdgc.gwu.edu/public-diplomacy-resources-issue-65>, accessed on 26 September 2015.

25 Sean S. Costigan and Jake Perry, *Cyberspaces and Global Affairs*, Burlington, VT: Ashgate, 2012.

26 Shanthi Kalathil, S. Arsène, D. Faris, S. Granger, J. Herlong, G. Hyman et al., *Diplomacy, Development, and Security in the Information Age*, Washington, DC: Institute for the Study of Diplomacy, 2013.
27 P. Seib, *Real-Time Diplomacy: Politics and Power in the Social Media Era*, New York: Palgrave Macmillan, 2012.
28 R. S. Zaharna, A. Arsenault, and A. Fisher (eds.), *Relational, Networked and Collaborative Approaches to Public Diplomacy: The Connective Mindshift*, New York: Routledge, 2013.
29 Rory Medcalf, 'The diplomatic tweet', *American Review*, <http://american reviewmag.com/opinions/The-diplomatic-tweet>, accessed on 22 September 2015.
30 Jennifer Charlton, 'Social media as a tool for public diplomacy', *Canadian International Council*, 17 October 2012, <http://opencanada. org/features/the-think-tank/comments/social-media-as-a-tool-for-public-diplomacy/>, accessed on 25 September 2015.
31 'Virtual relations', *The Economist*, 22 September 2012, <http://www. economist.com/node/21563284>, accessed on 26 September 2015.
32 Cited in, Andreas Sandre, 'E-diplomacy beyond social media', *Canadian International Council*, <http://opencanada.org/features/the-think-tank/ comments/e-diplomacy-beyond-social-media/>, accessed on 25 September 2015.
33 'Nirupama Rao breaks barrier, tweets on Libya and other crises', *Deccan Herald*, 2 March 2011, <http://www.deccanherald.com/ content/142448/nirupama-rao-breaks-barrier-tweets.html>, accessed on 7 December 2014.
34 Rama Lakshmi, 'Modi makes a lot of overseas trips, but is he a diplomatic failure with India's neighbors?', *The Washington Post*, 23 September 2015, <https://www.washingtonpost.com/news/worldviews/wp/2015/ 09/23/modi-makes-a-lot-of-overseas-trips-but-is-he-a-diplomatic-failure-with-indias-neighbors/>, accessed on 26 September 2015.
35 S. N. Mohammed, 'Self–presentation of small developing countries on the World Wide Web: A study of official web sites', *New Media & Society*, 6 (4), 2004, pp. 469–486, <http://dx.doi.org/10.1177/146144804044330>.
36 J. S. Nichols, 'Propaganda', in Donald H. Johnston (ed.), *Encyclopedia of International Media and Communications*, Vol. 3, San Diego, CA: Academic Press, 2003, pp. 597–606.
37 H. N. Tuch, *Communicating with the World: U.S. Public Diplomacy Overseas*, New York: St. Martin's Press, 1990.
38 P. M. Taylor, *Global Communications, International Affairs and the Media since 1945*, New York: Routledge, 1997.
39 See <https://twitter.com/IndianDiplomacy>.
40 Matthias Lüfkens, *Twiplomacy* and the *World Leaders on Social Media* series, Burson-Marsteller, January 2016. Burson-Marsteller is a leading global public relations and communications firm. *World Leaders on Facebook* is Burson-Marsteller's latest research into how world leaders, governments and international organisations communicate via social media. The research builds on Burson-Marsteller's highly acclaimed annual *Twiplomacy* study. Initially focussed solely on Twitter, <http://www.burson-marsteller.com/ what-we-do/our-thinking/twiplomacy-2016/twiplomacy-2016-full-study/>, the 2016 study is being expanded to other social media platforms

including Facebook <http://www.burson-marsteller.com/what-we-do/ our-thinking/world-leaders-on-facebook/world-leaders-on-facebook-full-study/>, Instagram, <http://www.burson-marsteller.com/what-we-do/ our-thinking/world-leaders-on-instagram/world-leaders-on-instagram-full-study/>, LinkedIn <http://www.burson-marsteller.com/what-we-do/our-thinking/world-leaders-on-niche-social-media-platforms/world-leaders-on-linkedin/>, YouTube <http://www.burson-marsteller.com/ what-we-do/our-thinking/world-leaders-on-youtube/world-leaders-on-youtube-full-study/>, Google+ <http://www.burson-marsteller.com/ world-leaders-on-google/> and more niche digital diplomacy platforms such as Snapchat <http://www.burson-marsteller.com/what-we-do/ our-thinking/world-leaders-on-niche-social-media-platforms/how-world-leaders-use-snapchat/> and Vine <http://www.burson-marsteller. com/what-we-do/our-thinking/world-leaders-on-niche-social-media-platforms/>, accessed on 23 August 2016.

41 Burson-Marsteller is a leading global public relations and communications firm.
42 Matthias Lüfkens, *Twiplomacy* and the *World Leaders on Social Media* series, Burson-Marsteller, New York, January 2016.
43 <https://www.facebook.com/barackobama/?fref=ts>, accessed on 5 May 2016.
44 <https://www.facebook.com/narendramodi/?ref=br_rs>, accessed on 5 May 2016.
45 <https://www.facebook.com/PMOIndia/>, accessed on 5 May 2016.
46 Matthias Lüfkens January 2016.
47 <https://www.facebook.com/mauriciomacri/>, accessed on 5 May 2016.
48 <https://www.facebook.com/hunsencambodia/?fref=ts>, accessed on 5 May 2016.
49 <https://www.facebook.com/Netanyahu/?fref=ts>, accessed on 5 May 2016.
50 <https://www.facebook.com/IraqPMMediaOffice>, accessed on 5 May 2016.
51 <https://www.facebook.com/DilmaRousseff/timeline>, accessed on 5 May 2016.
52 <https://www.facebook.com/WhiteHouse/>, accessed on 5 May 2016.
53 <https://www.facebook.com/danilomedinasanchez>, accessed on 5 May 2016.
54 Matthias Lüfkens January 2016.
55 See <http://www.youtube.com/indiandiplomacy>, accessed on 26 September 2016.
56 See <http://www.youtube.com/user/Indiandiplomacy>.
57 See <http://www.youtube.com/watch?v=bE-UF9bjhrA&list=TLWrfn63 6l0OKaLzu1_vJ4GeezjxLDidZS>.
58 See <https://www.facebook.com/IndianDiplomacy>.
59 See <http://indiandiplomacy.blogspot.in/>, accessed on 26 September 2016.
60 See <https://plus.google.com/u/0/+MEAIndia/posts>, accessed on 26 September 2016.
61 See Indian Diplomacy <http://issuu.com/indiandiplomacy>, accessed on 26 September 2016.
62 See <http://www.mea.gov.in/mea-mobile-app.htm>.
63 Philip Seib, *Real-Time Diplomacy: Politics and Power in the Social Media Era*, New York: Palgrave Macmillan, 2012.

8

EXPATS ON SOCIAL MEDIA

This chapter tries to excavate a few important questions such as how social media is used by expatriates to ease their transitions to new marketplaces of ideas, to relearn political and cultural socialisation and to reconstruct their social and cultural bond and identity with home country while adjusting themselves with social-economic profiles of the host country in a changing context. The underlying objective of this chapter is to locate the trajectories of Indian expatriates in Internet. While doing so, there are frequent uses of expressions such as *expatriates*, *diaspora*, *PIO* and *NRI*. It implies that such terms in the work are often used in a loose manner. Focus of the work is not to explain what are diaspora or expatriates Indians; rather, the spotlight of the discussion is on the interplay between Indians abroad and Internet and how the technological infotopia situate expatriates in digital revolution. The use of expats in social media is thus a more fluid label. The work eschews from hindsight of diaspora literatures. It uses contemporary documents, newspaper articles and personal accounts of the author to narrate the interplay between expatriate Indians and Internet. Over a hundred Facebook profiles, YouTube, Blogger, Twitter and websites are surveyed for the period between 2010 and 2015.

Expatriate Indians are a touch away! Diaspora is more emotional about the home country! So-called traitors, who appropriated taxpayers' money in forms of subsidised education from premier educational centres in India and later migrated to the USA and settled there are now looking back at the country! The brain drain is reversed now. People of Indian Origins (PIOs) are forming cyber communities and are finding belonging by shared interest with like-minded people in host countries while maintaining cultural bonds with home country. Non-resident Indians (NRIs) are more obsessed with developments in the home country. What makes these possible and what is reflected more visibly in all these incidents? It is Internet and social media platforms which are the new social house of the people abroad. Indian citizens abroad are leveraging social media sites, while Internet makes long-distance citizenship possible. In a shrinking world of globalisation and telecommunications, for expatriates who were once away from the home country, Internet is more a political option as their presence is more a question of identities and discursive practices.

Cultural belongings and political assertions in the age of Internet are profoundly transformed with new kinds of tools of engagement. Internet represented an arena for negotiating with a cultural past and umbilical bond for the diaspora. Self-publishers and self-broadcasters of the diaspora communities copiously make their community online. They portray emotional bond with home. They tell memories in an intimate way.

Profound changes are taking place in home country with the unparalleled contributions of expatriates. They finance projects, invest in economy, give jobs to citizens and collaborate with local entrepreneurs. Political class maintains contacts with diasporic communities, while government launches projects and start-ups for them. Among these contributions, one dimension need not be overlooked. Indians living abroad have found social media useful for interacting with home country, friends and family.

Social media, the town square of the world, has gained momentum over the chemistry of expatriates bonding with home country. This chapter is an initial forethought on homesick expatriates bonding with family and friends in India on social media, which indeed makes political boundaries insignificant. Based on an extensive literary survey on diaspora and Internet, this chapter attempts to give a preliminary portrayal of India's digital diaspora. While doing so, the people power of Internet is vividly exposed. For the expatriates, Internet is a discursive space for cultural belonging and political assertions. Therefore, Internet helps them redefine conventional notions of citizenship so as to make their home country more receptive to their claims. They achieve it through a transnational flow of information. Social media is thus a channel of representation and deliberation for the diaspora.

Theoretical reflections

Diasporas are communities of migrants from a homeland living in one or many host countries. It refers to the dispersal of any population from its original land and its settlement in one or various territories.[1] Although diaspora was originally associated with the exile of Jews from their historical homeland, suggesting forced dispersion and oppression in the host country, it is now used figuratively for minority expatriate populations who have migrated to new countries, such as political refugees, skilled labours, alien residents, professionals, immigrants, ethnic migrants and so on.[2]

Unlike any prior era in history, social technology allows expatriates to participate in the cultural and political life of homeland in unprecedented levels. Internet is inherently a special place for geographically dispersed people. These expatriates form cyber communities focussing on the land they have left. They organise informal cyber deliberations in elections in their homelands. They participate in the economic and cultural life of their homeland. Consequently, in politics, and cultural life, the twenty-first-century role of the state has been challenged by social technologies, which reduce barriers among states and improve communications among expatriate communities.[3]

Unfortunately, less scholarly attention has been paid concerning the potential role of expatriates as meaningful change agents in the social, political, cultural and intellectual atmosphere of the home country. There were some attempts in that direction, for example, Abdullah A Mohamoud's contribution of African Diaspora to policy dialogue[4] in African societies as well their role in conflict resolution and peace building.[5] In a study on Diaspora, development and the role of ICT, Joseph Guerson and Anne Marie Spevacek have observed that ICT can bring about an efficient, robust private-public framework that facilitates productive linkages between Diasporas and their home countries.[6] Indian and Chinese Diaspora are more active in Internet. Ruxandra Trandafoiu narrated the online cultural and political expressions of the Romanian diaspora, using websites based in Europe and North America in the book *Diaspora Online: Identity Politics and Romanian Migrants.*[7]

Expatriates could engage home country in a variety of ways such as advocacy, skill transfer, remittances, philanthropy and business investment.[8] Bhattiprolu Murti[9] in 2013 studied the interplay of Indian Diaspora and a website of the Ministry of Overseas Indian Affairs to facilitate investment facilities in India. Chinese Diaspora in Internet has been a focal theme in the study of Wenjing.[10] Eunkyung Lee[11] in a 2012 study explored an online community called www.MissyUSA.com, formed among female Korean immigrants in the USA as an example of a digital Diasporic space in the new media age. Ananda Mitra in a 2005 study using examples from a website for NRIs opined that the virtual space is offering the immigrants an opportunity to share their multifaceted identity narratives using their unique and non-editorialised voices.[12] In a paper on Diaspora and Internet, Myria Georgiou argues that Diaspora minority groups use the media in complex ways that feed back into their sense of cultural and political belonging. Diasporic groups represent some of the most significant minorities across European nation states. While living in and in many cases being citizens of European nation states, they also sustain political and cultural connections across boundaries, largely through the media.[13]

170

Numerous groups and individuals make use of online communities, including people who migrate transnational, like immigrants or ethnic minority populations. These groups are most likely to use the Internet to maximise the advantages of an online community.[14] Internet becomes a new interactive link both to homeland and host country and to Diaspora members.

A term is important here, i.e. *digital Diaspora*. A digital diaspora (also known as an 'e-diaspora' or 'virtual diaspora') is an electronic migrant community whose interactions are made possible through 'new' technologies of communication.[15] The 'virtual world' is ideally suited for connecting diasporas at the local and global levels. It provides a forum to exchange ideas, debate and mobilise opinion as well as support, friendship and acceptance between strangers, all of which aid in the cultivation of digital diasporas.

Research suggests that diasporas often use Facebook, Twitter and LinkedIn to build online communities that support integration in host countries, thus helping to fill the social void in participants' 'offline' life.[16] However, little is being explored in terms of diaspora contribution towards the home country.

There are grass-roots organisations active only in 'cyberspace', whose sole purpose is to network with diasporas scattered around the world. Known as cyber grass-roots organisations (CGOs), these organisations often solicit funds to advance socio-economic development in their homelands.[17] The linkages of the already documented works on the interplay between Internet and expatriates are useful to situate Indian expatriates.

The Indian experience

Non-resident Indians (NRIs) could access investment option just a click away with the launching of Overseas Indian Facilitation Centre[18] (OIFC) in joint partnership with the Ministry of Overseas Indian Affairs in association with the Confederation of Indian Industry (CII) in 2007. OIFC through its website and offices provides reliable data on investment opportunities free of cost. NRIs could access investment opportunities just through a mouse click.[19] Bhattiprolu Murti, in a study on digital media and Indian Diaspora, identified the future direction of research on Diaspora and social media would be to explore how Indian embassies engage with the country's Diaspora using major social media sites such as Facebook and Twitter.[20]

In a book titled *Indian Transnationalism Online: New Perspectives on Diaspora*, editors Ajaya Kumar Sahoo and Johannes G. de Kruijf say that online space gives a new space of engagement where transnationalism of the twenty-five million Indian Diaspora is acquiring new identities.[21]

Chandralekha was once a poor housewife in Kerala. Now her story is just like folklore song of poor becoming rich in Kerala or like the amateur success story of a debutante. She became a popular playback singer recently. How was it? It is a question one would get answer if one were part of the connected technologies and a roaming vagabond among social connections. Believe it or not, it was only because of YouTube! She became popular among the expanding homesick Internet expatriates from Kerala. NRIs copiously commented and shared an amateur song uploaded by her onto YouTube. She became famous by the viral video that expatriate Keralites liked and commented. The video was a song that she sung on the background of a hutlike house while holding her baby in her arms. If so, what does it mean to say expatriates in social media? Certainly, an important correlation, that Indians abroad are profusely migrating onto social websites to build 'bonding capital'. Technology is widely changing the way in which expats communicate with the home. They have become homesick intimate speakers in connected spaces. They make use of political Internet.

Sandra Samson was a higher secondary school girl. I found her on Google Talk (now Google Hangout). She said she had two Gmail accounts. She prefers to be online all the time. In an Orkut chat, when asked her, 'Why two Gmail accounts?', she replied, 'Well, one is to chat with friends and other one is to video chat with parents'. She was with her grandma. Her parents were in Africa. She used to chat with them late nights. However, she was not feeling loneliness of the usual school-going children in India whose parents are abroad and do not seem bothered about the absence of parents. Connection technologies filled in the void created by parents' pre-occupations with job and professional hazards. Technology is a connector. Expatriates are greatly using social technology to be in touch with their far-flung children, friends and relatives. Nevertheless, it is more like a bonding capital; thus nationals abroad are sustaining their relationship with the home country. They meet friends and relatives via technology.

Couples video-chat on Skype, parents call their children on Viber, siblings share photo and video on WhatsApp and Messenger and friends update events on Facebook. Expats now are increasingly feeling connected with home. For majority of Indians abroad, technology is like a second home, where they could reproduce memories, nostalgia, childhood, schools, college days, love affairs and so on. Social technology is like an intimate friend for them.

Undoubtedly, expatriates have more reasons to be in the platforms than the home country. It provides them a cost-free, quick access and cheap medium. In the medium, they keep to be active, on a round-the-clock basis, with their family at home. This is how Chandralekha became a playback singer through YouTube. This is how Sandra Samson is always online with her green icon never becoming idle. Technology gives them solution, a permanent one. Husband meets wife in Facebook. Expats vindicate their citizenship commitment in Twitter. Homesick citizens upload amateur videos on Facebook.

Nevertheless, it is more a linking capital also, where people, who otherwise do not make it to the mainstream social spaces due to structural factors, are able to make it to the centre of society. Undoubtedly, marginalised and poorest citizens have more reasons to be on the platforms than the well-off. For it offers them a cost-free, quick access and cheap medium where they keep in touch with beloved things and become active on a round-the-clock basis with their family at home.

People are a touch away! Several government bodies have been leveraging social media sites. The *Economic Times* reported that close to 10,000 NRIs had been on the Modi campaign during General Election 2014. Indians living in the UK, the USA, Europe and Southeast Asian countries had been in the election fray to steer the Modi campaign. Probably one could call them the *Amish Tripathi* generation of Indians who wanted to have change. To that direction, they have love for social media. Certainly, politicos are targeting the potential expat attachment for the home. They create social profiles and speak to them in ways that give political mileage.

Politicians are cashing in

Over last couple of years, the political class was most benefitting the online expats community support in India. If one goes through the social profiles of Narendra Modi, the prime minister of India, the answer is well clear. He has a huge fan base on Facebook, YouTube, Twitter, Instagram and so on. However, Narendra Modi is not alone in tapping overseas Indians. Politicians such as Shashi Tharoor and Narendra Modi have been expanding overseas follower bases. They have become the instant attention seekers. The immediate endorsement of expatriates helped them cash in. In fact, by strategy they represent Indian voices abroad among the expatriates. Perhaps, their targeted and strategic use of social platforms helps them cast a political billboard image abroad on Internet platforms. Most of Internet posts of Modi and Shashi Tharoor have frequent likes and shares among expatriate community. If you make a bird's-eye view of their Facebook timelines and tweets, it is apparent they are using social media as a loudspeaker to connect with expatriate Indians. The social media momentum, which Narendra Modi leveraged during his electoral victory in 2014 parliamentary elections, was more visible in the warm welcome and applause being extended by expatriate Indians to Modi when he was on a series of foreign tours.

Many known and unknown politicos are gaining the support; both moral and material, of expatriate Indians. AAP has been receiving majority of its online fund from the overseas Indians. It means political process and expatriate Indians are important correlations, which technology has mediated for the last couple of years.

Quite often, such online presence of expatriates is also an advantage to the government. Many government bodies have been leveraging social media sites. Yes, the first to join the social media fray was the Ministry of External Affairs in 2011. It has 884,000 followers on Twitter[22] and the account has updates on a regular basis. In fact, the initiative got appreciation especially due to its role during the Libyan crisis. It helped family and officials to reach out to expatriates who were caught in Libya. Based on the information posted on Twitter by their family members, platforms helped a two-way communication in times of crisis when access was almost difficult in a foreign country. Along with updating relevant information about the crisis, the profile also helped Indians trapped in Libya to return home safely. Platforms are useful and hopeful for family and this is evident from the Twitter experience of the ministry during the Libyan crisis. It has a YouTube[23] channel. The channel has uploads that has a considerable user base. The page had 1,403 video uploads by January 2014. A popular page, for example, *A La Cart!!! Food in the Streets of India*[24], had close to five lakh views by January 2014. Its Facebook[25] page has over one lakh likes. Its Twitter[26] page has close to one and a half lakh followers. It has a Blogger page too.[27]

Diaspora is more emotional about the home country! Individual online engagements lead to social gatherings. Self-publishers and self-broadcasters copiously make their community. Surveys of expatriates around the world display that social media has significance to the lives of expatriates living abroad. Over one crore PIOs and similar number of NRIs, as of May 2012, were available at http://moia.gov.in; now we have a huge expatriate base and obviously, they have rich resources. Saudi Arabia is home to a large number of expatriate Indians, especially citizens from Kerala, most of whom go in search of better jobs and opportunities. However, the loss of close family and friendship ties is undeniable. So is the bonding and strong-tie capital thereof. Thanks to technology, expatriates have now turned to modern communication tools such as Facebook, Skype and Twitter to be able to stay in touch with loved ones. The most evident reason for the rise in the social media trend is that it offers cheaper means of communication compared to landlines and mobile phones. In addition, the technology is instant which keeps people connected with the world round the clock. Overseas Indians are not so reluctant to leave their homelands anymore as technology has made the transition much easier.

Emotional bonds are consolidated

A Facebook video recently uploaded by a Gulf-based Indian user got whopping comments, likes and shares among a bunch of fellow national strangers both within and outside the country following a bus accident causing tragic deaths and human casualties in Malappuram district in Kerala. The content is an emotional speech by a homesick national requesting bus drivers in the state to be more vigilant on the road and be safe while driving! However, the comment threads indicate how emotional he was about the scenes and incidents in the state. A sweeping look at his Facebook Walls indicate all what he updated pertains to social and political affairs in the home state!

'Alakode vishengal' (News about Alakkode), a Facebook page pertaining to a remote area of Kerala, is popular among Diaspora of the region. The page updates almost about everything to the region from birth to death. A new way of alone together happens among nationals within and outside the country in the fifth estate. Social media platforms such as Facebook cater to this new spirit of social bond. Cherupuzha Times, a webpage steered by natives of rural area in Kerala, is a dedicated website for the cause of Cherupuzha area. The website updates local news pertaining to the region and has a large audience base among natives as well as people living abroad.

Although initial data showed that while email is still the most popular way for expatriates to stay in touch with far-off friends and family, an increasing number of people are finding more modern communication tools like Twitter and Skype indispensable for keeping up with the news from home. Facebook is popular for people abroad to stay connected with family and friends at home. Google+ and YouTube create a new social circle for the expatriates. Without Skype life could have become almost ironical, opines one of the New Zealand–settled Keralites via Gmail. Being connected is quite incredible. It helps families stay in touch, kids develop relationships with grandparents and friends stay updated, but it is not without some loss. Technology is bringing us closer together, but there is no chance that it could ever replace person-to-person, physical relationships.

A number of blogs and websites have already developed to the cause of expatriates living abroad; see http://www.expatsblog.com/, a webpage that gives information and guide to lives of expatriates all over the world. A webpage self-describing as 'for anyone moving or living abroad', http://

www.expatfocus.com/ provides a detailed list of blogs of people who write their life on foreign land. The government use of social media often lends a helping hand for expatriates and people abroad. In times of conflicts and humanitarian crises, government using social media has often provided a useful channel for expatriates to connect with relatives at home country.

Twitter and YouTube network has revolutionised political discourse and rewritten the rules of development dialogue in domestic society. Expatriates and Diaspora, previously expelled from the corridors of national mainstream, have been influencing policy outcomes in domestic society by their active participation on social media platforms that lead to discussion in the parent country. Therefore, social media paves way for building a strong bonding capital. This could be more helpful for the government to utilise the potential resources and rich experiences of expatriates for developing and building strong bonds.

Certainly, India is losing its trained workforce when its citizens become expatriates. At the same time, they also pump a huge amount of money back to home. E-commerce has been booming, as expatriates buy Indian goods through Internet. What does it then signify? Of course, generally NRIs prefer to buy property in India and social media helps them. Social websites for property exchange such as olx.in, quikr.com and trovit.co.in cater to the property needs of expatriates. Yes, it clearly indicates some social media trends. First, they want to come back to their motherland and when they come, they want to settle in here with a good property and house. However, it is difficult to generalise this assumption to all the Indians abroad. Some Indians go with an inherent ambition to settle abroad. Anyhow, Internet is a crucial tool in terms of financial transactions, property deals and other economic interactions, which bind the Indian expatriates to home. Internet is helping them form a bonding capital.

Students from India are travelling abroad in search of higher education opportunities. Their numbers are now increasing than ever before. The most preferred destinations are the USA, Australia, Singapore, Switzerland, New Zealand and the UK. Internet is helping student community in many ways. They can be in touch with their family members, meet friends, share feelings, seek help to solve the problems in terms of finance, study and adjust to the new climate. This is how Sandra Samson meets her parents abroad. Social media is her solution. Moreover, such students come with like-minded students and share knowledge in the subject of study. There are many student groups on Google+, LinkedIn, Facebook, Twitter, YouTube, MySpace and so on. They form communities according to their geographical location and interest.

Ditty was my neighbour, school- and collegemate. I remember he never showed a taste for studying abroad. However, sometime ago, I heard that he had settled in Australia. When asked, 'Why he did not come back to

176

India', his father said, 'Well he is comfortable there'. The father continued that they used to meet on Google Hangout. He showed his garden, vegetable plant and house, everything on video chat. Ditty is settled there with a good job, but his parents are in India and his root too. Technology would give them a solution. They could be in touch with everyone at home with this. For the Indian students in other countries Internet is a medium to seek help. As they cannot meet their family members physically, Internet provides the virtual relationship for both students and parents.

It is a commonplace assumption that Indians are fonder and deeply conscious of our rich cultural heritage. Certainly, they have been carrying the rich traditions, customs, practices, values and beliefs along with them. It is important to understand how the expatriates can maintain their cultural identity without losing their roots in different places and cultures. Indian festivals are celebrated across the world and these festivals are creating more interest in their own motherland. In the UK and the USA, the local Indian communities are playing an important role in making those festivals a success. Culture is a channel to bring Indian expatriates together. Internet provides an opportunity for expatriates to be in touch with their own culture. Internet plays key roles in building cultural bonding. It provides a platform to connect Indian Diaspora in the place where they are residing. It bridges the connection to share cultural affinity with India. Cultural capital of different geographical areas of our country, historical places, food culture, various languages and dress culture are visible over the Internet. It also enables sharing cultural life through video and audio. A person sitting in a western country can watch our festivals with the help of Internet. Many-to-many interaction has made this process much more effective. The cultural identity of Indian expatriates flourishes due to advancement in technology. Here physical distance is not a crucial issue. Websites maintain and promote the Indian culture among expatriates. See indianartsandculture.org, indiaculture.net, indiaculture.nic.in, bestindiansites.com/culture, saigan.com/heritage, culturopedia.com, indiancultureonline.com and thebestofindia.com, which cater to the cultural lives of expatriate Indians.

Information bonding

More importantly, social websites act as a source of information gathering. They are able to access any kind of communication such as newspapers, magazines, books, the broadcast media of radio, television and movies designed to reach the Indians. Internet is acting as an effective channel for information consumption. Internet provides an opportunity to Indian expatriates to access Indian mass media like e-newspapers, e-magazines, news channels, radio and television anywhere in the world. Though they are in different parts of the world, they could access various television and radio channels in their native language and can read e-newspapers and magazines in their language of interest or mother tongue. Therefore, this kind of attitude gives the feeling of belongingness with their motherland. Various news channels providing live news allow Indian expatriates to get to know the latest information about their motherland within no time. It is much faster than road, railway and air mode of communication. Well, Internet is going to shape a new bond. It is between expatriates and the home. Social platforms are certainly a connector.

Internet interlinks Indian expatriate community spread across the world. It interlinks them in many ways. To that respect, it has been able to demolish geographical barriers. With the rapid spread of technology, there were prophecies that upheld the thesis that geography or distance will be an ancient morsel. Richard O'Brien, British economist, futurist and author, has upheld the idea of end of geography in the book *Global Financial Integration: The End of Geography*.[28] The idea seems more significant if one thinks about the end of geography. Our expatriates, though away from home, could meet everyone on platforms. What makes them feel so? Technology is a new solution, a friend and a connector that brings in more attachment than separation. Journalist Frances Cairncross of *The Economist* in the book *The Death of Distance: How the Communications Revolution Will Change*[29] has been observing a technological revolution, where technologies such as telephone, television and the Internet are literally making everything everywhere. Technologies are changing the way we live, communicate and find our community identity. It is also significant for expatriates as they are able to communicate more intimately with their family. *Kenichi Ohmae* in a 1990 book titled *The Borderless World: Power and Strategy in an Interdependent Economy*[30] has been vocal about a world without borders. Borders are less relevant in interdependent economies. It gives an idea that distance is vanishing away with the connection technologies. They are also useful for the expats. Robert B. Reich in a 2001 book titled *The Future of Success: Work and Life in the New Economy*[31] upheld a similar view. In Internet-driven economies, no boundaries are a matter of challenge for interaction and no distance is a worry for collaboration. Jan Aart *Scholte* in a 2000 book, *Globalization*,[32] has been pointing out that there was globalisation of economic, social, political and cultural life. Technology seems facilitating such globalisation of everything everywhere. Thomas L. Friedman in 2006 wrote a book, *The World Is Flat*,[33] which was prophetic in the sense that it predicted that distance would not be a future hurdle for innovation.

What does all this literature tell us about future of the world? At least according to expatriate Indians, they are future modes of cultural bond and intimate relations, where they would meet and engage with friends in Facebook, life partner on Skype, parents on Viber, political class on Twitter or political developments in home country on YouTube. With the increasing popularity of technologies of connection, expatriates abroad are in no way a pain of separation or distance for the family.

Technology has demolished the political boundaries virtually. It has also been connecting people successfully. Expatriates talk about many things on Internet. They communicate many things. They are more concerned about the issues we face. On Internet, there is evidence that expatriates are more vocal about the home country. Poverty, minority rights, corruption, violence, crime, child labour, women empowerment, farmer suicide, environmental degradation, politicians, human rights and so on are the few topics which are usually discussed by expatriates on Internet. However, social togetherness is not just about expats using social media to get in touch with the home country. It has meaning beyond diaspora.

Conclusion

Expatriates know the value of social media for keeping in touch with loved ones back home. Twitter, Skype, Google+, Facebook, Blogger and YouTube are all very useful in sharing the highs and lows of relatives' living thousands of miles away. The profiles surveyed shared their feelings with social media and the potential of the medium to maintain bond with the home in myriad of ways. Respondents and social profiles said that they like to stay connected, stay updated and learn. They believed that it reassures them to know what their loved ones are up to, to share a laugh about a trending dog video or to celebrate even minor successes. Social media in their private lives are used for everything from sharing photos, to buying property on olx.in, to finding new recipes on sanjaykitchen.com or Mia kitchen,[34] to getting native news from local news online. Almost everything is available to learn via Google or somewhere else.

Social media is still a relatively recent phenomenon and the evolution of social media–based communities continues to flourish, but much remains to be learned from the study of timeless expatriates or alumnus especially in the age of unprecedented migration. Real or virtual communities are always people and not technological units or bits.

Social media has revolutionised the way expatriates and governments communicate and interact all over the world. This was what the survey of social profiles of Indians abroad was giving clue for the chapter conclusion. These days, the million-dollar question for India is how to use innovative social media strategies to engage expatriates in sustainable, continuing, result-oriented and cost-effective dialogue, particularly between the Indians abroad and the society in large. A few observations are made in the following based on the review of profile behaviour and ethnographic study of expatriate communities in cyberspace. Blogs, YouTube channels, Facebook, Twitter and Google+ were reviewed for the last five years from 2010 to 2015. Many platforms surveyed do not exist at all when this chapter was finished and new platforms have been born. It is thus not an exhaustive list of profiles or user behaviour but a qualitative documentation of the normative values that surround expatriates and political sphere of the home country.

Social media allows better engagement of expatriates in political process. Over a hundred Facebook profiles were analysed. Facebook profiles of expatriate Indians surveyed for the chapter have been constantly updating on timelines information pertaining to the home country. Majority of the updates of users are directly related to political affairs of the home country. Politicians in India are largely leveraging such profiles. Many profiles are politically engaging, sick of home country and engaging in dissent against what is going wrong in the country. Shares and likes are metrics of their involvement in the political developments in the home country.

Social media allows home country to rediscover the most prominent and successful members of expatriates, whose knowledge could be used to advance national initiatives and development projects. Social media helps solve the collective action problem faced by civil society. When it comes to engaging expatriates in national matters, the civil society sphere is able to appeal to the thematic social media public out there on Internet. They are easily dragging the homesick expatriates over to civil society issues and receive donations and moral and intellectual capital for civic activism. Since social media endows expatriates to have virtual access to government officials and politicians, their ability to directly influence the political public has increased.

The censorship of social media can have political costs. Regulating access to social media platforms can harm the relationship between governments and citizens living abroad because social media is viewed as one of the most important 'connector' to connect expatriates with their home country. Governments and civil society sphere need to chart their expatriates drawing information about diaspora distribution across the world. Based on the review of user profiles, it is apparent that government has to nominate an existing agency or create a new one so as to promote social media use for national matters among expatriates.

In short, social media is enhancing a strong bonding capital with expatriates. Governments, family, friends and expatriates are stakeholders in this process. However, serious attention needs to be given to the expatriate dimension of social media at policy level, which at present is conspicuous by its absence. We need to tap the potential of platforms more vigorously for bringing more changes via digital media platforms in the days ahead. Expatriates will, of course, benefit from social media, so are the family and government. Internet is political for the expatriates.

Now, it is time to think of an expatriate social media policy for the government. Exclusive government platforms dedicated for being in connection with people abroad becomes a necessity. Hope that the government will soon realise the potential of the platforms for effecting and reaching out to expatriates in a better way.

Notes

1 A. Alonso and P. Oiarzabal (eds.), *Diasporas in the New Media Age: Identity, Politics, and Community*, Reno, NV: University of Nevada Press, 2010, pp. 1–18.
2 C. Armstrong, *The Koreas*, New York: Routledge, 2007; R. Cohen, *Global Diasporas: An Introduction*, London: UCL Press, 1997; and W. Safran, 'Diasporas in modern societies: Myth of homeland and return', *Diaspora*, 1 (1), 1991, pp. 83–99.
3 Jon M. Garon, 'Revolutions and expatriates: Social networking, ubiquitous media and the disintermediation of the state', *Nku Chase Law & Informatics Institute*, <http://ssrn.com/abstract=2008024>, accessed on 27 September 2015.
4 Abdullah A. Mohamoud, 'The contribution of African diaspora to policy dialogue', *Amsterdam: African Diaspora Policy Centre*, October 2007, <http://www.diaspora-centre.org/DOCS/Migration Developm.pdf>, accessed on 27 September 2015.
5 Abdullah A. Mohamoud, 'African diaspora and post-conflict reconstruction in Africa', *DIIS Brief*, Copenhagen: Danish Institute for International Studies, 2006, <http://www.diis.dk/graphics/Publications/Briefs2006/mohamoud africandiaspora.pdf>, accessed on 27 September 2015.
6 Joseph Guerson and Anne Marie Spevacek, 'U.S.A.I.D., diaspora-development nexus: The role of ITC', Washington, DC, The United States Agency for International Development, 8 August 2008, pp. 1–32.
7 Ruxandra Trandafoiu, *Diaspora Online: Identity Politics and Romanian Migrants*, Brooklyn, NY: Berghahn Books, 2013.
8 J. M. Brinkerhoff, 'Creating an enabling environment for diasporas' participation in homeland development', *International Migration*, 50 (1), pp. 75–95.
9 Bhattiprolu Murti, 'India's use of digital media to engage with diaspora as part of its public diplomacy outreach: A case study analysis of the website of Overseas Indian Facilitation Centre', A Capstone Project, American University, Washington, DC, May 2013.

10 X. Wenjing, 'Virtual space, real identity: Exploring cultural identity of Chinese diaspora in virtual community', *Telematics and Informatics*, 22, 2005, pp. 395–404.
11 Eunkyung Lee, 'Digital diaspora on the web: The formation and role of an online community of female Korean immigrants in the U.S.', PhD Dissertation, The State University of New Jersey, New Brunswick, January 2012.
12 Ananda Mitra, 'Creating immigrant identities in cybernetic space: Examples from a non-resident Indian website', *Media, Culture and Society*, 27 (3), 2005, pp. 371–390.
13 Myria Georgiou, 'Diaspora in the digital era: Minorities and media representation', *Journal on Ethnopolitics and Minority Issues in Europe*, 12 (4), 2013, pp. 80–99.
14 B. Chan, 'Imagining the homeland: The Internet and diasporic discourse of nationalism', *Journal of Communication Inquiry*, 29 (4), 2005, pp. 336–338.
15 B. K. Axel, 'The context of diaspora', *Cultural Anthropology: Journal of the Society for Cultural Anthropology*, 19 (1), 2004, pp. 26–60; J. M. Brinkerhoff, *Digital Diasporas: Identity and Transnational Engagement*, Cambridge: Cambridge University Press, 2009; and A. Everett, *Digital Diaspora: A Race for Cyberspace*, Albany: SUNY Press, 2009.
16 D. Diminescu, M. Jacomy, and M. Renault, 'Study on social computing and immigrants and ethnic minorities: Usage trends and implications', *Joint Research Center Technical Note*, JRC55033, 2010.
17 L. A. Brainard and, J. M. Brinkerhoff, 'Lost in cyberspace: Shedding light on the dark matter of grassroots organizations', *Nonprofit and Voluntary Sector Quarterly*, 33, 2004, pp. 32–53.
18 The OIFC is a not-for-profit venture between a state agency, India's Ministry of Overseas Indian Affairs, and a non-state entity, the Confederation of Indian Industry (CII). The OIFC, with its headquarters Gurgaon, Haryana, near New Delhi, was set up in 2007 with the aim of expanding economic engagement between Indian Diaspora and India. The OIFC is potentially the first site for any Indian Diaspora member wanting to invest in India or planning to return to India.
19 'NRIs just click to access India', *Times of India*, 28 May 2007, <http://timesofindia.indiatimes.com/world/NRIs-now-just-click-to-access-India/articleshow/2080144.cms>, accessed on 27 September 2015.
20 Murti May 2013: 33.
21 Ajaya Kumar Sahoo and Johannes G. de Kruijf, *Indian Transnationalism Online: New Perspectives on Diaspora*, England: Ashgate, 2014.
22 See <https://twitter.com/IndianDiplomacy>.
23 See <http://www.youtube.com/user/Indiandiplomacy>.
24 See <http://www.youtube.com/watch?v=bE-UF9bjhrA&list=TLWrfn636l0OKaLzu1_vJ4GeezjxLDidZS>.
25 See <https://www.facebook.com/IndianDiplomacy>.
26 See <https://twitter.com/IndianDiplomacy>.
27 See <http://indiandiplomacy.blogspot.in/>.
28 Richard O'Brien, *Global Financial Integration: The End of Geography*, New York: Council on Foreign Relations Press, 1992.

29 Frances Cairncross, *The Death of Distance: How the Communications Revolution Will Change*, London: Orion, 1997.

30 Kenichi Ohmae, *The Borderless World: Power and Strategy in an Interdependent Economy*, New York: Harper Business, 1990.

31 Robert B. Reich, *The Future of Success: Work and Life in the New Economy*, New York: Alfred A. Knopf, 2001.

32 Jan Aart Scholte, *Globalization: A Critical Introduction*, London: Macmillan, 2000.

33 Thomas L. Friedman, *The World Is Flat: A Brief History of the Twenty First Century*, New York: Farrar, Straus and Giroux, 2005.

34 <https://www.youtube.com/channel/UCuLBML1ZqMKYLsze0HHwdDA>.

9

OPEN GOVERNMENT IN
SOCIAL MEDIA AGE

A cursory look at the social media profiles of poorest citizens and governmental apparatus will allow us to revisit the genealogy of the new mode of political thinking and contentious political actions triaged by cyberspace. This chapter is an introductory approach to evaluate government on social media manoeuvred on two important principles of democracy in the contemporary times: participation and deliberation. Theories of participatory and deliberative democracies are linked to open government debates. Therefore, the chapter assumes that social media initiatives of government functionaries to reach out to citizens for service deliveries ensure participatory and deliberative ideals of democracy. Extensive examples of social media platforms used by governmental apparatus are cited so as to conclude that there are open government on social media, which is different from governmental engagements in pre-Internet age.

Government deliveries and social media are important correlations. Here let us ask a few important questions! What does it mean to be 'connected' between the ruling class and the citizen in the age of social websites in a society that has great social cleavages and inequitable access to the corridors of power? What does it mean to be open in social media? Can social media provide a renewed push to open democracy movement in India? Can all citizens benefit the citizen media? Is the social media participation enhancing deliberative democracy in general and 'open politics' in particular? The focal point is whether online public spaces are democratic at all. The concern is whether social media–enabled political deliberation has any concrete political impact. The relevant question is whether social media platforms and digital technology enable modern governments to go back to founding principles at Agora, that is classical direct democracy, a democracy in which all citizens are direct participants. Is it feasible to think of governments in terms of 'for, by and of' the people, which was popularised at Gettysburg in modern times? Could democracy be more democratised by the Internet?[1]

Practices based on open government framework are flourishing in India. However, the existing open government initiatives such as open government enactments like RTI are insufficient as there are visible lack of transparency, collaboration and participation from the citizen. Therefore, technology-mediated participation and collaboration are binding for achieving open government. This volume proposes that government in general and various ministries, departments and public institutions at different levels make use of social media platforms and other open source software, all of which can configure a Government 2.0. Facebook, Twitter, YouTube, Blogger, emails, chat options and other such social media platforms can be instrumental in this process.

The rationale of Government 2.0 is to introduce a fresh needle for measuring an open government with the metrics of openness, transparency and collaboration. Existing open government indicators tend to focus either on the presence of key laws and institutions or on citizens' perceptions of government performance. The underlying argument is that conventional notions of openness, transparency and collaboration are insufficient to understand open government. The degree to which governments deal with social media is now part of how they deal with civil liberties, press freedom, privacy and freedom of expression in general.

> Dear bijugayu@gmail.com
> Welcome to the official website of the Prime Minister of India.
> We look forward to your support and active participation in good governance. Share your views and feedback to help us serve you better.
> Thank You
> P.M. India Website Management Team
> Welcome to PMO India
> no-reply@pmindia.gov.in
> Fri, Sep 26, 2014 at 5:25 PM

What one would read just above is an instance of the government embedded in the digital architecture in India. Social understanding of the seeping penetration of social media in the richly contradicting interplay of the Indian state and society (in the architecture of governance) requires a critical theory of the differential capacity of multiple players involved in the architecture of governance. A substantive reading of technology in the realm of e-governance initiatives could augment the assumption that a techno-imperialism is robbing the citizen of digital divide, hate campaigns on Internet and so on which endorse a dystopic perception of social media. On the other hand, an instrumentalist reading of technology thickens the assumption that e-government empowers the hitherto unreached social margins as social media enables quick, easy, cost free, uncensored access to governmental deliveries which endorse a utopian configuration of social media. A digital revolution is seeping across everywhere in which political deliberation and governmental engagement are tremendously changing. However, this revolution cannot be sufficiently excavated without a critical perspective that re-situates social media in the socio-political and cultural locality in which it is deployed. Therefore, a critical reflection of the email communication in the above question is placed in the framework of an infotopia of technological rationality, which assumes that citizen experiences of social media are differently situated in the context rather than testing them with universally valid premises. The email communication delivered by the administrator of the official website of Prime Minister of India from @pmindia.gov.in/en/ to many Indians and the author too got one on 26 September 2014 reflects a commonplace assumption that government is just a click away. Prime Minister of India is available at your clicks, and interact with him @pmindia.gov.in/en/, know your Prime Minister @narendramodi.in/ and enhance good governance ensuring your participation with MyGov @mygov.nic.in/ and all what one would require is just in an email @sampark.gov.in. If one goes with the link at http://pmindia.gov.in/en/social-media-updates/, one would get the social media updates of the Prime Minister in both Facebook and Twitter.

The email in question is not an isolated example. On Independence Day, Republic Day, Teacher's Day and so on, people shared their thrill over flooding greetings on Facebook, Twitter and SMSs from the office of the highest functionaries like the prime minister. Connection works more intimately in Internet age. It is now more intimate. On most national important occasions, many people share their thrill over emails from the social media team of Prime Minister of India informing, sharing and seeking help from a vast majority of connected Indians. In the online survey many people said that they did not get such messages. While interpreting their responses their curiosity about this new kind of connected public has been apparent.

Lesser participation becomes greater participation in social media age. Lesser politics, too, is bigger politics. If so, less government is more government. Social media is just making a new kind of governmental system, in which we are increasingly enthused by technological reconfiguration of government. Social technologies induce audience to become digital citizens. It helps in transforming citizen from passive to active. Here participation is redefined, as the new mantra is that non-participatory citizens become avid participants. It is enabling users with a voice that was otherwise untapped. The greatest ideal of contemporary democratic movements is participation. As a cleavage-rich society, we have challenges in meeting these requirements. India is far ahead of other national societies in making use of social media for citizen participation. People cutting across differences in caste, class, gender, regions and income are making use of social platforms.

With participatory politics attaining new proportions steered by social media, equally important is the deliberative dimension of user-generated content. Deliberative and discursive politics has a distinct trajectory on Internet. On social media, digital natives need not be 'someone' to 'someone'. Whether it is a professor delivering lectures to the students in a classroom, a couple of octogenarians figuring out their laptop's camera or fish that spin, social media has arched everyone into our social imagery. Politicians, government, citizens and activists purposefully hit into the potentialities of social media. The prediction is that poles in democracy that are between citizen and the government are reduced with social media.

Crucial to political engagement in the present day is political communication which seems to be mediated by techno-politics, i.e. the use of new technologies such as smartphones, tablets, computers and the Internet to advance political engagement and participatory politics. Historically political communication in the modern era has always been mediated by technology with the printing press, photography, film, television, Internet, radio and now social media playing crucial roles in all realms of social life. This prospective connection between technology and politics in the modern era has been highlighted, long assumed, documented and predicted in the writings of McLuhan[2] and others.

For example, just the day after taking office as thirteenth President, Pranab Mukherjee announced that he would be opening a Facebook account to receive and respond to comments and queries from the public.[3] It implies that there is a growing sense among the ruling establishment that *transparency, collaboration* and *participation* are buzzwords for open government[4] and democratisation processes. Being connected is a microcosm of how the governments across the world are starting to get with the swing of Web 2.0. Government 2.0 is integral to delivering on several agendas on which the government has been running at present. In contemporary civic life when governments deal with social media, it also means how they deal with freedom of expression, civil liberties, privacy and human rights. Then, Government 2.0 signifies manipulating emerging digital platforms, to augment government efficiency and effectiveness, while ensuring prompt service deliveries.

187

Social media is a key element of many emerging citizen engagement platforms. These platforms bestow citizens' voice and channels of communication for government; for instance, ministries and public authorities have Facebook, Twitter and YouTube pages. There are Facebook profiles of ministries' engagement with the public. Along with the ministries, there are constitutional bodies such as Election Commission that is also on Facebook, which makes citizens feel that they can be in touch with highest offices from their home, street or on travel or by any other manner.

Theoretically on the political spectre, the idea of open government is placed on liberal democratic traditions, which emphasises ideas such as 'participation' and 'deliberation'. Open government deals with a specific nature of 'democratic transition' attached with 'digital media', based on the popularity of 'online civic engagements' in the 'socio-economic transitions' in India. It outlines values of online forms of participation, deliberation and contentious politics in supporting civic engagement in Indian democracy.

Democratic rationalisation of Internet

One day in December 2015, there was a video call on my Google Hangout, which was created for ethnographic study of Internet behaviour of anonymous users. A lady was on the screen whose face was hidden from the screen. She began to unhook the area down the neck and invited spectators to comment on her naked area visible on the screen. The live show went on for five to seven minutes during which lots of comments were poured on her comment box on Google Hangout. There were five to ten spectators whose identity or whereabouts were unknown and the lady too had anonymous, fake identity. It is commonplace knowledge that plenty of pornographic materials are freely accessible on Internet. Such materials are overloaded with different genres and content qualities, say HD, to satisfy user requirements and viewer purposes. Yet, people on the group videocalling I mentioned continued watching live performance of the lady till she signed out. She did not respond to comments during and after the live show. It is sure that nothing can be traced on the Internet when she signed out, who she was, where does she come from and other vital information. But the incident is enough to prove an argument that spectatorial practices and material creation on Internet have been benefiting the underprivileged citizens. On Internet they are excavating a new citizenship and belonging.

Many questions flash out when one witnesses such an unlikely incident. Who is the lady? Where does she come from? Her caste, age, class, marital status? Is she a transgender? Is she a widow or divorcee? Is she married? Is she doing it as a revenge to someone or is it just an example of erotic practices? Does it represent any kind of rhetorical practices in the taboo-rich cleavage-strong nation where everything related to sex is screened with conservative community standard? Is she a sexual activist who makes her body a rhetorical tool? Why does she live-perform on Hangout to a group of spectators in her anonymity or is it just an example of someone releasing their libidinal energy in a manner that is otherwise impossible even to imagine?

A similar incident was narrated by Lawrence Liang in a speech on how technology is shaping a new culture[5] delivered on the occasion of the golden jubilee of India International centre, SAHMAT and Knowledge Commons. A user in a group chat set a weird picture status on his chat profile. On the tip of his finger he drew the genital of a woman with colour pencils. Many users began to chat with him thinking as if he were a woman. They asked him to live-perform for them. Liang says people are not interested on the abundant supply of pornographic materials on Internet, if they had a hyperreal experience. They have inability of consciousness to distinguish reality from a simulation of reality.

The intersection of culture of spectator practices and emergence of a new culture is deeply embedded in the socio-political locality in which the Internet is used by citizens and the state apparatus. Emergence of digital technology is creating new ways of looking at culture and the way contents in cyberspace are viewed and consumed on platforms like YouTube, Facebook and Twitter may be more like searching an infinite database. The spectatorial practices are enormously under profound cultural shifts. The implication of this shift will take time to understand at least how to relate it with the lives of the underprivileged. Digital technology is creating not only new forms but also new ways of relating to such forms. The point raised in the stories narrated above is reminding the book titled *New Cultural Histories of India*[6] by Partha Chatterjee, Tapati Guha-Thakurta and Bodhisattva Kar. There is an apparent need for a more dynamic reformulation of new cultural history of India in the present era of digital age and consumer globalisation. There is materialist turn in India's cultural realms. The contemporary urban spaces, football and cricket in politics, performance and film-making studies in south India, bar dancers in Mumbai and Mayawati's monuments in Lucknow and so on, all the visual and screen imageries of cultural artefacts and social realms seem to be profoundly undergoing a materialistic turn. Internet is relevant here. It is on this profoundly complex, fluid and ever-changing social house that a political Internet is born where marginalised and underprivileged citizens try to find their citizenship in a profoundly unconventional manner. It too is relevant for Indian democracy.

For example, authors of the book *Anxieties of Democracy Tocquevillean Reflections on India and the United States*, Partha Chatterjee and Ira Katznelson,[7] predicted the effect of democratisation process on key elements of public life such as citizenship, development, class, religion, caste, capitalism, poverty, the struggle for equality and the status of minorities. Here Internet seems to have distinct trajectories because of cyberspace where citizens' use of social media will have plenitude of meanings. India continues to remain caged in backwardness, says Dipankar Gupta, one of India's foremost thinkers on social and economic issues in his book *The Caged Phoenix: Can India Fly?*[8] Making a comparison with the developed West, Gupta underscores the point that affluence can be achieved only after living conditions improve across all social classes. There is reluctance to acknowledge the fact that structural impediments, which deny growth benefits to the majority of Indians, are an apparent challenge to democracy. The point raised is that there is a close link between growth in high-technology sectors of the Indian economy on one side and backwardness and rural stagnation on the other. To place technology, particularly Internet, is a daunting task. The question whether technology would be hijacked in favour of high-technology capitalism or in favour of backwardness and marginalisation seems not exposed at the moment or properly understood now.

For example, in the book *The Nation and Its Fragments: Colonial and Postcolonial Histories*, prominent theorist Partha Chatterjee[9] looks at the spiritual and material dimension of culture and investigates how the nationalists resolved nationalist question in favour of the spiritual ramification. Theoretically, nationalists divided culture into material and spiritual domains. Hence, there are material and spiritual aspects of culture. However, nationalists had very early resolved cultural question in favour of the spiritual aspects of life. So, religion, caste, gender, family and peasantry found their legitimacy not in the material sphere but in spiritual. The spiritual resolution to the cultural question thus created unending troubles in the imagination India as a nation state. Old cleavages thus still remain as a perennial question in India. Middle class elites first imagined the nation into being in this spiritual dimension and then readied it for political contest, all the while 'normalising' the aspirations of the various marginal groups that typify the spiritual sphere. Here one could place technology being discussed above. Why are people experimenting in technology in weirdest manner which are objectionable for social orthodoxy? Colonial state and nationalism debate was polarised on the question of national culture. The state was kept out of the inner domain of national culture, that is spiritual aspects of culture. At the same time, nationalism tried to fashion a modern national culture in India that is not western. It took place at the inner level of national culture, says Partha Chatterjee.[10] Chatterjee makes distinction between political and civil society. The wider question that he asks is whether the concept of civil society is relevant for countries like India that are marked by social exclusion, inequality and poverty. Large numbers of citizens continue to be relegated to the margins of society. Not only do they not possess any kind of status, they are not protected by law. Can technology empower them is a question that still remains to be understood. Chatterjee accordingly argues that in India civil society as a bourgeois sphere is restricted to a fairly small section of citizens, notably the middle classes who speak the language of rights. The poor, who negotiate the travails of everyday existence through the adoption of illegal means, and clear violations of the law, occupy the space of political society. Here one exposing nudity on Internet is obscene and punishable under law but not to the consciousness of the underprivileged. Though Chatterjee does not explicitly reject civil society, he sees it as irrelevant for a vast majority of Indians. And though he does not valorise political society, he seems to indicate that this space and these mediations are somehow more authentic than those of civil society.

Let me add two more difficulties that can be identified with Chatterjee's distinction between political and civil society. Do practices in 'political society', such as tapping water and electricity connections illegally, fall into the category of politics, or that of proto-politics? As Eric Hobsbawm[11] put it in his study of social banditry, certain forms of politics are, strictly speaking, proto-politics. And these can be undetermined, conservative and ambiguous. Proto-politics or semi-politics refers to those practices that seek concessions for the individual or the group. But if the objective of politics is to shape and reshape the political context in which we live, then we need a politics that has a broader vision than merely negotiating the problems of everyday life illegally. Such a politics demands that people be brought into a relationship with each other, that collective action be forged, that the universal be mediated by the particular and that citizens participate in the constitution of a public and critical discourse. State concessions to proto-political activities neither change formal institutions nor build solidarity. In fact piecemeal practices might even strengthen the power of the state. Though such forms of politics can exist in modern civil societies as well, ultimately democratic agents have to take on the responsibility of making the transition from short-sighted practices into long-term engagement with modes of power. In democracies, therefore, political society may well be a transitional space, not a permanent feature of Indian politics.

Democracy need not be centred on any universally valid premises, says Sudipta Kaviraj in his acclaimed book *The Enchantment of Democracy and Indian Politics and Ideas*.[12] He who believes that Indian democracy is peculiar on various counts unlike those in the West in terms of caste, absence of prior liberal tradition, prevalence of non-secular society, poor literacy and rising violence.

Writings of Rajani Kothari, Ashis Nandy, D.L. Sheth and others who worked partly with the language of comparative politics stretched to entirely uncommon conclusions that seriously countered Eurocentric limitations circumscribing the theorisation of Indian democracy. Acclaimed sociologist and author Dipankar Gupta argues that democracy requires 'an elite of calling' in order to deliver in substance to citizens. Ordinary politicians will not deliver to democracy. In order to make significant advances in democracy, Gupta argues that active intervention by the citizen elite, who are not concerned with short-term electoral calculations but have a vision for strengthening democracy, is a pre-condition for its success. The author cites examples for such citizen elites from Basque, Spain, which counts best on indexes of health, innovation and education.[13] The relevance of social media discussed in the book demands true test in what Gupta said as citizen elites.

Sudipta Kaviraj's *The Imaginary Institution of India: Politics and Ideas*[14] suggests that introduction of modernity from the outside, or the fact that modernity rested on foundations that were unfamiliar to Indian society, explains much of the disjuncture that continues to mark Indian politics to date. It depicts Indian society as predominantly cultural. The failure of Indian politics, for him, is the failure to comprehend the importance of culture in people's lives.

Debates on democracy are enriched with extensive literature. Robert A. Dahl's[15] *On Democracy* understands that participation, equality, information, control on agenda and inclusion are important criteria for the success of democracy (2000: 37). However, a review of democratic process across the world tells different stories. None of those prerequisites was ever satisfied in full swing anywhere in the world. Alexis de Tocqueville's *Democracy in America* (1835) observed that equality was the great political and social idea. To achieve more democracy, the ideals of equality must be fulfilled. However, it is rarely achieved in any part of the world in the strict sense of the term. Joseph A. Schumpeter's[16] *Capitalism, Socialism and Democracy* (1942) was a classic work, which predicted destruction of capitalism by asking, 'Can capitalism survive?' He believed capitalism *would* be destroyed by its successes and that it would spawn a large intellectual class that made its living by attacking the very bourgeois system of private property and freedom so necessary for the intellectual class's existence. Schumpeter believed that there are dangers to democracy that are inherent in capitalism. Government should be free in peace and security, argue Alexander Hamilton, James Madison and John Jay in *The Federalist Papers*. Five basic themes can be discerned from the words of Hamilton, Madison and Jay, including federalism, checks and balances, separated powers, pluralism and representation. In *Democracy: A Very Short Introduction*, Bernard Crick (2003) presents a short account of the history of the doctrine and practice of democracy, from ancient Greece and Rome through the American, French and Russian revolutions, and of the usages and practices associated with it in the modern world. The book argues that democracy is a necessary but not a sufficient condition for good government, and that ideas of the rule of law, and of human rights, should in some situations limit democratic claims. *Lords of the Sea: The Epic Story of the Athenian Navy and the Birth of Democracy* by John R. Hale tries to present epic battles, the indomitable ships and the men – from extraordinary leaders to seductive rogues who established Athens's supremacy – which became a source of modern debates on democracy.

The literatures on democracy are plenty. A review of literature points out the inherent contradictions in democratic life. More precisely, there are unresolved problems in the practice of democracy. The literatures cited, though not an exhaustive list, are proof that there are still underprivileged and social groups that remain outside the realm of deliberations in democracy. Technology is looked in the vantage point of emancipation that democracies are yet to provide to the underprivileged.

While leading the national movement, Gandhi was often looked at with suspicion, particularly from the landed aristocracy. It was natural for the elites to frown up on anything that was purposefully set in to torpedo the system. In the early period of its existence, even the Indian National Congress had lesser mass support. People hesitated joining the political struggle for self-rule. In the southern part of India, it was said that only quite a few had actually been present when Sree Narayana Guru installed Shivalinga (Ezhava Shiva) for lower castes at a time when there was severe oppression by caste patriarchs. History was always created by very few for the masses. At least according to Thomas Carlyle, it was the great men who created the world. Great men theory valorised the glory of leader while overlooking the real role the underprivileged played in history – the oppressed, women and minorities. Here comes the significance of democracy and technology interplay.

Any discussion on democracy in India will never be complete without referring to the book *India after Gandhi* (2007) written by Ramachandra

Guha. In the book Guha elaborates how India as an unnatural nation survives as a constitutional democracy. He believed that India as a land of diversity and contradiction is the only society to form a democracy through peaceful manner. However, the democracy we inherited is an unnatural combination. The seeds of its destruction are within. In the book *Battles Half Won: India's Improbable Democracy*, Professor Ashutosh Varshney observed that for a society deeply racked by social inequalities and hierarchy, sixty years has come quite far but needs to go further and the battle for deeper democracy is the need of the hour. The author pinpoints the fact that Indian democracy needs to be further democratised. *The State of India's Democracy* (2007) by authors Sumit Ganguly, Larry Diamond and Marc F. Plattner say that in recent decades, India has proven itself capable not only of preserving democracy but also of deepening and broadening it by moving to a more inclusive brand of politics. Political participation has widened, electoral alternation has intensified and civil society has pressed more vigorously for institutional reforms and greater government accountability. It means there are channels of expressions and spaces of inclusion in Indian democracy.

How has democracy taken roots in India in the face of a low-income economy, widespread poverty, illiteracy and immense ethnic diversity? Atul Kohli's book *The Success of India's Democracy* addresses this question. He brings together some of the world's leading scholars of Indian politics to consider this intriguing anomaly. They do so by focussing, not so much on socio-economic factors, but rather on the ways in which power is distributed in India. Two processes have guided the negotiation of power conflicts. They claim the interests of the powerful in society have been served without excluding those on the margins.

Technology is a promise. It is a hope to people that are footnoted. When democracy fails to the fault lines of social landscape, technology fills in the vacuum. To understand that, one needs to go into technology with a different methodological parameter.

Participatory democracy

Over the last couple of years, there has been reappearance of a growing interest on the idea of popular participation. Undoubtedly, the idea of participation has turned out to be the key attribute of the new democratic theory. In the well-liked and most prevailing contemporary democratic theories, citizens are placed with a negative role, in the sense that they are implicated in passively choosing between options presented to them. This is associated with the ideal that the 'elected representatives' have greater knowledge and more wisdom than their constituents and thus they should accordingly have significant autonomy in making political resolution[17] and in fact, it reflected an amended version of Benthamite utilitarianism. On the contrary, in participatory politics, representatives are taken as messengers or delegates, conveying decisions of their constituents. To Holden, participatory democracy is a modern artistic facsimile of classical direct democracy and representation is just deployed to deal with degree of trouble.[18]

Participatory process of collective decision-making has combined elements both from direct and representative form of democracy. Widely citizens have the power to decide on policy proposals and politicians presume the role of policy realisation.[19] The extent to which citizens can affect policy and determine social priorities is directly aligned with the degree to which they choose to involve themselves in the process. Even though inspired by earlier thinkers such as Rousseau or John Stuart Mill, the first theoretical formulations of 'participatory democracy' was made during the 1970s by Pateman[20] and Macpherson.[21] An excellent discussion of the main features of this model of democracy is found in David Held.[22]

Analysis of participatory politics with the online media gets a fresh theoretical framework with the writings of Osborne et al.[23] The idea is that members of a society decide independently whether to attend a meeting at a cost, where the policy decision taken will be a compromise among the attendees' ideal positions. Attendance in the meeting is based on a cost–benefit calculation that citizens compare the cost of participation with the impact their presence will have on the decisions that is a result of the compromise. Knowledge acquires wider significance in the model. In particular, it is assumed that citizens reward those legislators that implement policies proposed by the citizens' assembly by re-electing them and punish those who do not consider the assembly's proposals by not re-electing them. Participatory democracy would best enable all citizens to lead active, extended, virtuous, vigorous, peaceful, happy lives. Accordingly, to help solve the enormous problems confronting humanity in the twenty-first century, the highest priority of democratically minded society should be helping their own communities and nations create the truly democratic society that is envisioned as necessary if the world were to transform into an integrated world of interactive, interdependent, justly collaborative, truthfully democratic societies.

In many countries in the western world, the proportion of the population that participates in the electoral process has been steadily declining. At the same time, studies show that the public often trusts its elected representatives less than it does other professionals or public figures.[24] In the

West at least, apathy and cynicism seem to be as much a part of the democratic process as does participation. Meanwhile, in the developing world,
democratic governments are increasingly replacing totalitarian regimes, yet
democracy has not, in many cases, brought with it significant economic
benefits for the poor. This is an important shortcoming especially when one
considers the fact that lower socio-economic groups make up the majority
of most developing world countries' populations.

Here comes the relevance of digital media and civic engagement. In pure
direct democracy model, citizen cannot ideally participate. The space and
times concepts hinder it largely. Digital technology has largely redefined
the concepts of time and space with the categories of 'online sociality' and
'digital politics'. One of effective means to effect participation to achieve
the idea is to have more collaborative, participative, cheap, open and transparent form of political engagement.

Increasingly, technology is viewed not as a distinctively chatty toolbox
used by society but as a vital part of a shared co-evolution leading to new,
first time, forms of societal, organisational practices.[25] Moreover, digitally
interactive technologies have now become both available and affordable for
organisational, personal, public and corporate use. There is also a general
agreement that fundamental societal changes facilitated by new technologies are on the go, mainly in terms of how we correspond, cooperate, create and exchange knowledge through the medium of virtual environment.
Manuel Castells[26] and Jan van Dijk[27] explain how and why a modern post-
industrial society is changing within the new notions of the Network Society and Information Age. In parallel, an equally new conception of 'tele'
and digital democracy has emerged,[28] with special focus on the impact
of digital technologies on democratic practices, dividing commentators
and audiences – according to Pippa Norris[29] – into 'cyber-optimists' and
'cyber-pessimists'.

Equally, there seem to be two divergent views on the potential of social
media platforms. While there is a general consensus that digital information
and communication technologies have potential to maximise democratic
benefits, particularly in the area of greater participation, it is less clear as
to the 'mechanics' of such impact and as to the roles of the main parties involved – citizens, the state, the market. It is also unclear who the
chief beneficiaries are and how the interplay between technology and society (including civil society and the state) can be described and integrated
into a broader democratic theory. Finally, there is a question mark as to
whether the democratisation potential of new media is universal enough to
be applicable beyond the democratically mature developed societies and if
it is possible to apply it to non-western societies, in the ex-Soviet transition

societies having democratic deficit, diverse and plural societies like South Asia and closed societies like China and Cuba. It is equally important to look at Indian democracy with the lens of new media and the interplay between society and digital platforms.

A participatory democracy approach to digital media suggests that political decisions will be more acceptable to citizens if they are available through a collaborative, transparent, open, networked, participative process that builds community and shared understanding and, therefore, overcomes societal divisiveness and polarisation.[30] Social media can be useful in effecting collaborative, transparent, open, networked, participative politics by which a digital agora is assured to citizens to the possible extent.

Deliberative democracy

Numerous changes are taking place in the fashionable conceptions about popular sovereignty with the rise of mass democracy in the contemporary world, and the classical understanding of democracy has already become almost inadequate to explain the impending changes and challenges. There are many different versions of deliberative democracy, which is roughly classified under two main schools: the first broadly influenced by John Rawls and the second by Jurgen Habermas. In the past decades, the theory of democracy has been dominated by these two very different approaches.[31] For deliberative democrats, the essence of democratic legitimacy is the capacity of those affected by a collective decision to deliberate in the manufacture of that resolution.

Discussion is the heart of deliberation that involves conversation in which individuals are amenable to scrutiny and changing their preferences in light of persuasion (but not trickery, intimidation or manipulation) from other participants. Claims for and against courses of action must be justified to others in terms they can accept. Jurgen Habermas and John Rawls, respectively, the most influential political philosophers of the late twentieth century, have identified themselves as deliberative democrats. Deliberative democrats are uniformly optimistic that deliberation yields rational collective outcomes.

In recent years, deliberative theories of democracy have sparked a renewed interest in the role of persuasion, reasoning, and normative entreatment in democratic politics.[32] From the perspective of deliberative theories, democracy is regarded as intrinsically enhancing the legitimacy of government or governance because it ensures the (procedural) conditions for a high quality of the decision-making process with respect to regulatory choices.

Although participants expect to pursue their interests, an overall interest in the democratic legitimacy of outcomes ideally characterises deliberation.

Democracy is minimally defined as a form of governance in which policy decisions are made by a majority vote of the populace. Though useful as a rough way of classifying polities, this definition is, on closer examination, both ambiguous and radically incomplete. The main thrust of the critique of minimal democracy developed in contemporary democratic theory is that voting is not the sole political mechanism for ensuring legitimacy and that it in turn owes accountability for policy decision towards the citizens. A significant political apparatus that is missing from the minimalist view of democracy is deliberation.

In illuminating accurate, fuller or purely enhanced structured information, the mechanism of deliberation provides an opportunity for participants to arrive at more considered judgements themselves and to effect a collective decision-making by influencing the judgements of others. Its consequences may affect what happens in a voting booth or in a legislative or a judicial chamber, or in the way we approach a personal moral puzzle. The platform for a decision-making process that fails to create the opportunity for deliberation is bound to raise questions about the legitimacy of the resulting outcomes.

Deliberative democratic theory addresses a body of political theory that seeks to develop a substantive version of democracy based on public justification through deliberation. Instead of viewing it (deliberative democracy) as a political system based on discussion, deliberative democracy calls for the deliberation of citizens as reasonable equals for the legitimate exercise of authority and as a way of transforming the preferences and intentions of citizens. Theorists of deliberative democracy address some of the problems that face democratic theory in complex societies such as the plurality of values, which would, in principle, render the construction of the 'common good of democratic theory' as well as the establishment of common democratic practices difficult. The concepts of deliberation and deliberative democracy have attracted much attention in political theory over the past few years. Initially noticed as both highly idealised and unreflective of actuality and practicality, they have now shed this accusation of impracticality. As practitioners and policy makers alike have attempted to institute deliberative principles on a national and international scale, the theory attracts wider recognition.

Social media gives push to deliberative democracy movement. There are loads of questions to address in an attempt to theorise deliberative democracy such as: what kinds of participation are included in a deliberative democracy? Who participates in a deliberative democracy? What outcome does deliberative democracy yield? How are the outcomes in a deliberative democracy identified? Surely, technology is used to enhance deliberative democracy. For example, the environmental collective Greenpeace had spearheaded an advocacy against use of diesel in mobile towers. It used emails and SMSs campaigns to effect its impact on decision makers. However, the question is whether such online advocacies will have as much impact as that of protest actions like youth demonstrating street protest against government decision to enhance pension age of government servants or sustained protests – hunger strikes, rallies, fishing strike, sea siege of the plant – by people in large numbers against Koodankulam Nuclear Power Project in Tamil Nadu. Does the Facebook campaign organised by India Against Corruption carry the same effect as that was carried out by the violence and working-class agitation at Maruti Suzuki India's Manesar plant?

The focal point is whether the online public spaces are democratic at all. The perplexing concern is whether social media deliberation can have any concrete political impact and, more predominantly, whether social media is stimulating deliberation by its very nature. The deliberative implications of the online spaces are measured based on the characteristics of the medium. In contrast to other existing media, it appears that online communication is a relatively new type of communication that has elements in common with the media that preceded it (printed media, face-to-face communication, television and radio) and, meanwhile, that is different from any of these media. Compared to informal public spaces (i.e. informal political reunions, town square, face-to-face public square, bumpy street etc.), online spaces consent to a non-centralised communication of many-to-many: (1) each participant is by and large equally entitled to make comments, share, like, tweet, upload, scrap, post and raise new questions; (2) online spaces are open public spaces. In fact, they are even more open than informal discussion spaces since there are generally no geographical or temporal limitations, and online spaces are places where participants are free to express their opinions. There is, in general, no censure and limits to expressing opinions. In this context, social media platforms and their various social interactive tools can build a deliberative practice.

Open government

Open government is a needle of democratisation of democracy and, therefore, a 'questionable' qualification of every government that should be 'participatory', 'transparent', and 'collaborative'. Examples include the social media presence of government. It is at present widely acknowledged that greater openness, transparency and collaboration benefit not only citizens but also the government itself, by promoting better record management, making decisions and services more efficient and serving as a safeguard against misgovernment and corruption. The OECD defines *open government* as 'the transparency of government actions, the accessibility of government services and information and the responsiveness of government to new ideas, demands and needs'.[33] These three building blocks are seen to support a number of benefits for government and societies: improving the evidence base for policy making, strengthening integrity, discouraging corruption and building public trust in government.[34]

The term *open government* has become one of the catchphrases of twenty-first-century democracy debates. It is the ideal to which modern political leaders claim to aspire and the benchmark that journalists, citizens and civil society organisations use to challenge corrupt leaders and secretive institutions. The free flow of information from government to the public and third parties such as civil society organisations and the media and critically back from the public and third parties to government is at the heart of well-functioning open governments. Anxiety across the length and breadth of democratic polities to establish a great deal of open government initiatives calls for more citizen involvement.

The OECD's definition of *open government* refers to the 'accessibility of services and information'. Decision makers are responsive to the needs, ideas and priorities of citizens and external bodies, and provide a number of effective and accessible channels for these to be voiced.[35] In such a system, sharing information is the norm within the public sector and significant resources, training and administrative procedures are devoted to the effective dissemination of knowledge and services.[36]

Within this framework, access to information or simply the right to know remains the most developed field. For some, it simply means facilitating the flow of information from governments to citizens, exchanging old, closed decision-making practices for a system where citizens have a right to know what their leaders are doing.

Legislation to secure citizens' access to information is widely considered an important first step towards more open and participatory forms of government and a precondition for citizens' ability to scrutinise, question and contribute to decision-making.[37]

Access to information is now recognised as a human right under the Universal Declaration of Human Rights[38] and regional human right systems such as the African Charter on Human and People's Rights, the American Convention on Human Rights and the European Convention on Human Rights. Alongside access to information laws, a growing number of governments have in place additional institutions and policies that contribute to greater transparency, accessibility and accountability. These include oversight bodies such as Supreme Audit Institutions, Ombudsman and Information Commissioner Offices, whistle-blower protection schemes, public interest disclosure acts and right to observe public meetings.

It has become an all-embracing label for a more transparent, accessible and responsive governance system, where information moves freely both to and from government, through a multitude of channels.[39]

There is compelling evidence that properly implemented and enforced open government frameworks can hold a number of benefits for governments and societies.[40] A World Bank study of the impacts of transparency on governance found that greater access to information could, among other things, improve risk management, economic performance and bureaucratic efficiency in governments.

Other studies have shown how increasing government openness can contribute to a higher rate of GDP growth in OECD, reduce the incidence of corruption[41] and raise standards in public management and service delivery.[42]

A more informed and empowered public can contribute to more cohesive community relations, more active and trusting citizens and more effective public services. Accessibility and responsiveness measures can lead to better decisions and risk management, which in turn leads to more effective services and enhanced social welfare. Better access to information can also bring about a more active media, which in turn leads to informed voters and force political class more accountable.

A World Bank Institute report quotes studies by Besley and Burgess[43] that found 'regions in India where the media are more active are also regions which are the least likely to suffer from famines during droughts'. The reason is that an active media keeps voters informed of politicians' intentions and record of accomplishment, thus enabling them to vote for those who provide the best deal for citizens.

Arguments in favour of openness often include a strong normative element; the literature contains many references to open government as intrinsic to modern democracy and a basic human right.[44] Other studies have shown how increasing government openness can contribute to a higher rate of GDP growth,[45] reduce the incidence of corruption[46] and raise standards in public management and service delivery.[47]

Government 2.0

For government agencies, where store-like walk-in access is either difficult or unavailable, especially at the national level, improving citizen contact through the Internet has become an essentially enduring goal. In the twenty-first century, politics may not be televised but it is likely will be tweeted, blogged, texted, uploaded and organised on Facebook. Government agencies are embracing social media to inform and interact with the public. Citizens connected like never before will have the skill sets and passion to solve problems affecting them locally as well as nationally. Government information and services can be provided to citizens where and when they need it. Citizens are empowered to spark the innovation that will result in an improved approach to governance.

Government agencies are developing and expanding their presence via social media and a number of public sector institutions are using social media such as Twitter, YouTube, Facebook and Flickr for diverse purposes. If the town squares and public floors now include public discussion online through social media sites, democratic governments in the twenty-first century are finding civic life in unusual ways. In contemporary civic life when governments deal with social media, it also means that how they deal with press freedom, civil liberties, privacy, freedom of expression and human rights in general.

Tim O'Reilly[48] observes that the valid inspiration of Government 2.0 is the projection of government as a platform. Openness, collaboration, transparency and participation can be materialised by the social media presence of government and its various agencies. Government using social media will have profound implications both at levels of governance and civil society. Bridging the gap between citizens and institutions is the concern of every democratic society. Inclusion and accommodation are daunting challenges for a government at work.

Social media platforms hold great promise in their ability to transform governance by increasing government's transparency and its interaction with citizens. The interactive and instant capabilities and the increasingly pervasive nature of platforms can create new ways of democratic participation, pressures for new institutional structures and processes and frameworks for open and transparent government on an unprecedented scale. These potentials are profound, but come with challenges in the areas of policy development, governing and governance, process design and conceptions of democratic engagement. This document provides a selected overview of key issues, questions and best practice government initiatives regarding social media technologies.

202

Government 2.0 is the idea of the government as platform, governments designing programmes to be generative, building frameworks that enable people to build new services of their own government information and services can be provided to citizens where and when they need it.

Government 2.0 is an outline to reorganise how citizens could take part in government using social media. Social media is a central element in almost all emerging citizen engagement platforms.

Government agencies are deploying social media platforms to inform and interact with the public and this indicates the emergence of information technology innovation and the web as a platform for fostering efficiencies within government and citizen participation. Government 2.0 is the idea of the government as a platform whereby government designs programmes to be generative, building frameworks that enable people to make new services of their own through user-generated content platforms.

Government 2.0 absorbs straight citizen involvement in discussion about government services and public policy through open access to public domain information and new Internet-based technologies and, more specifically, social media. It also engages ways of working that is underpinned by openness, collaboration and engagement. Nowadays, technology of varied sorts are being used in a plethora of social spheres and a new kind of social interaction is developing. Mobile phone–enabled coordinating function has affected daily life in the form of what Ling calls 'hyper-coordination'[49] and what Rheingold calls 'smart mobs'.[50] M-governance, m-politics, m-administration and m-activism are on the burgeoning stage.

Citizens connected like never before will have the skill sets and passion to solve problems affecting them locally as well as nationally. Government information and services can be provided to citizens where and when they need it. Citizens are empowered to spark the innovation that will result in an improved approach to governance. Government 2.0 is about the use of technology to encourage a more open and transparent form of government, where the public has a greater role in forming policy and has improved access to government information (see Table 9.1).

Being open, collaborative, participant, online, deliberative and transparent implies providing the public the services they want, ahead of deciding what they want and request for it. The public should get the government at their disposal. Digital technology–embedded democratic practices entail new services to people without them having requested. Government 2.0 is also about innovating the way communication has done to support the citizen.[51] Government 2.0 simply makes it easy to access and understand government and it makes it easy for users to interact around it.[52]

Table 9.1 Government 2.0

Activities	Interactive platforms	Interactive tools
M-governance	(Cell phones for citizen engagement in government-related services, deliveries)	Post, send, enter, follow-up visit, comment, update, tweet, retweet, like, wall, share, forum, notes, reply, forward, collaborate scrap, bookmark, upload
E-governance	(Citizen services, citizen information)	
Discussion and chats among citizens	(Blogs, chat rooms, emailing lists, community pages, websites)	
Citizen access to MPs and public authorities	(Web, email, blogs)	
Online 'participatory' journalism	(web, email, SMS, MMS, blogs, micro-blogging)	
Connections and weak-tie networks	(Networking sites)	
User-generated content in broadcasting	(Social media badges in TV, radio, web, SMS, blogs)	
Social movement activity	(web, blogs, email, wikis)	
Collaboration/ cooperation	(Social network sites, emails, video sharing, photo sharing sites)	
Alternative media	(News sites, interactive news portals, blogs)	

Source: Author

Citizens have connected like never before and have the skill sets and passion to solve problems affecting them locally as well as nationally. Government information and services can be provided to citizens where and when they need it. Citizens are empowered to spark the innovation that will result in an improved approach to governance. Government 2.0 is about the use of technology to encourage a more open and transparent form of government, where the public has a greater role in forming policy and has improved access to government information.

Social media is a key element of many emerging citizen engagement platforms. These platforms give citizens new voices and provide new channels for government, workers and elected officials to talk with them; for instance, many Facebook profiles of Ministries are having widest possible engagement with the public. Along with the ministries, there are constitutional bodies like Election Commission which are on Facebook, which makes citizens feel that they can be in touch with highest offices from their home, street, on travel or by any other manner. The government maintains information on a variety of issues, and that information should rightly be considered a national asset.

Social media governments across the world

There is a new interest among governments across the world to leverage social media platforms to increase effective citizen collaboration and participation in ensuring good governance. Governments have already launched projects towards that end. Despite the efforts at leveraging social media for open government initiatives being success stories from different parts of the world, the Indian case is not much of relief to its people.

A leading case for Government 2.0 is the US model. US president Barack Obama's celebrated electoral campaigns via social media have been aide memoire.[53] In the same way, the UK government has formulated a cut-out Twitter strategy for government departments, for example, the Twitter account @BISgovuk.[54] BIS also has a YouTube[55] channel along with other digital channels.

On the same lines, government in New Zealand made regulatory changes in 2010 for its public and non-public service departments under the Public Finance Act (PFA) to use Web 2.0 platforms to incorporate interactive government as well to create citizen-generated contents.[56] Australia was one of the first countries to deploy social media and has been very aggressively making use of it through social media guidance for the agencies' staff and other stakeholders.[57]

Russia also geared up to optimise the opportunities thrown by social media especially with the launch of Facebook in January 2010 and the growing popularity of Facebook among young generation. The presidential commission for modernisation and technological development of Russia's economy through online tools has created a forum called i-Russia.ru, where citizens can post comments and connect their social networks.[58]

These stories lead one to an informed conviction that many countries across the world maintain a very good social media policy for its citizens, governance and content generation. While many countries across the world are using social media platforms for citizen engagement, how interfaces between social media and government look like in India is often confusing!

Government 2.0 initiatives in India

Several government bodies have been leveraging social media sites. The first government agency to join the social media was the Ministry of External Affairs in 2011. It currently has over 844,000 followers on Twitter[59] and the account has updates on a regular basis. In fact, the initiative has been applauded especially due to its role during the Libya crisis. Along with updating relevant information about the crisis, the profile also helped Indians trapped in Libya to return home safely. The interactive platforms in a way seem useful and hopeful for families, and this was evident from the Twitter experience of the ministry during the Libyan crisis. It has a YouTube[60] channel. The channel has uploads of the ministry that has a considerable user base also. The page has 31,260 subscribers and 2,104 video uploads by August 2016. A popular page, for example, *A La Cart!!! Food in the Streets of India,*[61] had close to five lakh views in January 2014. Its Facebook page has one 891,892 likes[62] and Twitter page has 784,115 followers and 14,476 tweets by August 2016.[63] It also has a Blogger page.[64] In fact, it means the government has been moving on to social media.

Another good example of a government body that has been effectively using social media is the traffic police in various cities, including those in Chandigarh, Bangalore, Delhi[65] and Mumbai. The Facebook page of Delhi Police is engaging and interactive.[66] It has regular traffic updates, responds to complaints and even educates citizens about road safety rules.

Recently an initiative by the Delhi Traffic Police made news; it urged its citizens to upload pictures of traffic rule offenders and successfully seized over 20,000 of them through social media campaign. Traffic police in Delhi, Chandigarh and Bangalore are leveraging Facebook to the hilt, and their initiatives have been immensely popular amongst the citizens. The Indore Police Department has been maintaining a regular blog[67] in Hindi since 2009, a Facebook[68] page, a Twitter[69] profile and a website.[70] However, Mumbai Traffic Police, which initially was active, has remained inactive.

In areas as diverse as energy, education, jobs, banking, health care and governance, there are unique opportunities to rethink how government agencies perform their mission and serve the citizens. Cloud computing, web, social media and cell phones all provide new capabilities that government agencies are beginning to harness to achieve demonstrably better results at lower cost.

Social networking sites such as Twitter and Facebook are becoming the newest tools of Government of India in guaranteeing active participation of the citizens in governance. For instance, various government departments

206

like India Post, Delhi Traffic Police, Ministry of External Affairs and MCD are bringing in the benefits of budding social media.

Indian Postal service,[71] world's largest postal network, has a Twitter[72] account for its interactions with users, and it was the first government office to open account in social networking. It has been answering queries posted by users in relation to the service and questions like how one can use the services easily. Additionally, the government department also launched an exceptional 'e post office'[73] which would add up as an e-commerce platform.

Ministries of union government have been active on social media. The Facebook account of/in the name of ministries is a testimony to the growing significance of social media to empower the democratic potential of Indian democracy: Income Tax Department,[74] Ministry of Finance,[75] Ministry of Health and Family Welfare,[76] Ministry of External Affairs,[77] Ministry of Railways[78] and Ministry of Defence.[79] There are people who feel excited to see the platforms of highest offices in a mouse click away which otherwise are impossible for them to approach. Some government officials, high-ranking politicians and even certain government agencies are making their presence felt on social media. The diplomat Nirupama Rao is an example.

With social media–embedded contentious political claims, m-governance platforms and fifth estate electoral constituencies being in full swing during election time, the Department of Information and Technology (DIT) under the Ministry of Communications and Information and Technology realised the potential of social media as a platform to reach out to people directly. The drafting of the framework and guidelines for the use of social media for the government agencies after consulting various media experts, social media consultants and lawyers was an attempt towards collaborative government and labelling government as platforms. The government has issued guidelines to its various departments about the use of social media (FGUSMGO).[80] Several politicians and government bodies have been effectively using the medium ever since cautiously.

There were efforts by the Information and Broadcasting (I&B) Ministry to integrate social media for citizen collaboration and it has requested citizens to become their 'digital volunteers' to help disseminate its messages on social media platforms. *My India initiative*[81] is a digital volunteer programme to enable the government to disseminate information to citizens, especially youth. The programme has embedded principles of participative and deliberative governance, leading to real-time engagement through social media platforms. People interested in becoming digital volunteers are expected to fill up a form and give identity proof for registration that will take about five days. Participants are expected to spread thoughts on government policies and programmes through social media presence. A digital volunteer is expected to talk about the government's programmes by sharing them on Facebook and Twitter.

I have surveyed the presence of constitutional bodies such as UPSC, Finance Commission and National Commission for SC/ST on social media. Of course there were many profiles. But it doesn't mean that they were real and verified profiles. Yet, their mere virtual presence, though non-engaging, gives heavy excitement to citizens. Their user behaviours on those profiles are indexes of their excitements. Election Commission of India,[82] Finance Commission of India[83] and National Commission for Women[84] are far more significant in ensuring more democracy since the social media accounts in the name of highest functionaries bring such towering institutions to the people and rejuvenate the spirit of democracy in essence.

For a long time, governments at various levels and its departments have been seen as faceless entities with no transparency and labelled as untrustworthy. Inspired from business success stories, governments need to do the same by communicating with its target audience: the citizens. It seems the policy makers and politicians have come to realise the potential of social media beyond using it during elections and advertising themselves.

Census 2011 utilised social media as well to ask citizens to fill in their information accurately and in full during the time of visit of an enumerator. The initiative was launched on Facebook[85] and Twitter[86] with an on-ground campaign in the offing as well. Its Facebook page had close 50,000 likes by January 2014, and its Twitter profile had over 25,000 followers in the same period.

The Planning Commission of India used its Facebook[87] page to ask users to submit their expectations and ideas for the Twelfth Five Year Plan (2012–17). However, it is now dysfunctional.

At the Govt2.in awards 2011, Ministry of External Affairs received the award for most innovative use of social media and Web 2.0 tools in government. Other recipients of the award were the Municipal Corporation of Delhi, India Post, Delhi Traffic Police, Census India 2011 and the Twelfth Planning Commission.

OGPL initiative

Open Government Platform[88] (OGPL) is a joint artefact from India and USA to prop up transparency and greater citizen engagement by making more government data, documents, tools and processes publicly accessible and obtainable. OGPL will be available as an open source platform. By making this available in useful machine-readable formats it allows developers, analysts, media and academia to enlarge new applications and insights that will help give citizens more information for better decisions. In using an open source method of development, the OGPL community will provide future technology enhancements, open government solutions and community-based technical support. OGPL has become an example of a new era of diplomatic collaborations that benefit the global community, promote government transparency and citizen-focussed applications and enrich humanity.

The government has proposed guidelines for use of social media by public institutions (FGUSMGO). The government has issued guidelines to its various departments about the use of social media. The attempt to ensure transparency, collaboration and participation through open government initiatives seems much belated. However, it can be obviously felt that a government on social media is not too far away from accomplishment. The widely held document by Department of Electronics and Information Technology document titled 'Framework and Guidelines for Use of Social Media for Government Organisations' stipulates the norms and codes to be followed by government agencies while on social media. In India, for example, government functionaries such as ministries, police departments, commissions and committees, various departments and public sector undertakings have social media presence and they engage on user interface platforms.

The Indian government has made it clear that in coming years it intends to make publicly available much of its data. In its Tenth Five Year Plan (2002–07),[89] it announced its intention for India to become a 'SMART' (Simple, Moral, Accountable, Responsible and Transparent) state. This led to many e-governance initiatives, but few of them have resulted in publicly accessible databases.

One of the most important changes in the citizen government relationship in India since its independence has been the passage of the Right to Information (RTI) Act in 2005. The government has an extensive e-government strategy, suggested in part by the National Knowledge Commission (NKC), assembled by the prime minister in 2006–09 and charged with making proposals to develop the country's knowledge infrastructure.

Digital agora

The government has become open when it is on social media platforms. It is evident from the profile page surveys of government functionaries in India. A new form of governmental deliveries appears on Internet. In the age of digital technology, the government has been seemingly available at a mouse click away. The most prestigious institutions and offices along with most important office bearers have now reached our home, computer screens and respond to us at fingertips. The positive dimension of Government 2.0 would outweigh the negatives in the long run. Social networking sites would make association and engagement with public simple and powerful, make research faster and provides mechanism for getting rid of negative publicity and most importantly in understanding public sentiment to help form public policies.

The pulse of the people has been represented on social media via big data. The state apparatus by new forms of engagements facilitated by the digital media and people, too, began to give feedback on proposals, policies, legislative enactments and governmental decisions. Now almost all government documents appear to be downloadable by citizens and that all could easily share, comment, send, check, upload and what not, nearly everything to reach millions of citizens within no time. Participatory politics, deliberative engagements and contentious actions have become almost unavoidable on social media to Indian democracy. Digital media has facilitated all necessary components of democratic engagements with much ease and vigour. However, challenges are also tangible.

The social media–powered democratic engagements formed a digital agora that will facilitate what modern democracy has lost from the ideal: Greek agora. The digital agora of India is, yet, much young since the people using digital media are comparatively lower than the majority who does not. We need to be cautious while governments appear on platforms. Now it is time to take a call for new initiatives that can refine both the penetration of Internet and the participatory politics and deliberative attempts in digital media.

Social media platforms hold great promise in their ability to transform governance by increasing transparency of government and its interaction with citizens. The interactive and instant capabilities and the increasingly pervasive nature of social media technologies can create new ways of democratic participation, pressures for new institutional structures and processes and frameworks for open and transparent government on an unprecedented scale. These potentials are profound, but they come with challenges in the areas of policy development, governing and governance, process design and conceptions of democratic engagement. This volume provides a selected overview of key issues, questions and best practice government initiatives regarding social media technologies.

Government 2.0 is more about than wikis, open data, Facebook, You-Tube, Twitter, Web 2.0, or social media. It is about the strategic use of technology to transform twenty-first-century government into a platform that is participatory, collaborative and transparent as pinpointed in the theoretical discussion on deliberative and participatory democracy mentioned elsewhere in the chapter. Social media helps facilitate this transformation, but starting a blog or Twitter account is by no means a prerequisite. Open government does not start or end with social media. It starts with a mindset to become more participatory, collaborative and transparent. While government use of social media has often been highlighted as the best example of open government, it is by no means the only example. It doesn't mean that government can be open only if social media is deployed for citizen engagement. Those who are sceptical or pessimistic about government in social media will have other exciting tools to be open without being dependent on social media.

Social media is a tool of engagement, not a revolution itself. It is a cheap and fast way to spread message to a large group of people who are sympathetic to some cause. Discussion of the political impact of social media has focussed merely on the power of mass protests to topple governments. In fact, social media's real potential lies in supporting civil society, open government and the public sphere. Government 2.0 and open government are conceptual categories to analyse the democratisation of democracy. India lags far behind in leveraging the potential of social media to achieve transparency, collaboration and participation. However, Government 2.0 is on the rise along with Politics 2.0 where Indian political classes are found making use of social media to reach out to the public. Government functionaries are opening accounts in social media platforms to be generative and collaborative. It is obvious that politicians using social media are a good sign of democratisation and participatory politics. Most of the politicians who use social media to connect with people are at their middle ages or below. It is a good sign that when Indian population will reach its youth by 2050, the real potential of engaging with them will be realisable through such platforms. In this decisive moment, social media attains political significance. Government 2.0 comes in this critical juncture as a vanguard of engaging with youth and bringing them more to democratic politics and political dialogue in far more constructive ways.

At a time when politics becomes decidedly hierarchical and feudalistic, engaging with citizens is almost an ancient ideal and remains only in principle. Formal political institutions have almost become nastiest to most of citizens in democracies in conviction. Institutionalised politics becomes an anachronism when civil society supersedes established ways of exchange and negotiation. Democratising democracies become an inevitable corollary of modern democracy and an ideal yet to achieve. Open government is an indicator of democratisation of democracy. It is, therefore, a prerequisite of every government that the government should be 'transparent', 'participatory' and 'collaborative'.

In today's networked world, the public sector and public authorities are tapping into new media platforms to increase participation, transparency and collaboration. The open government agenda, which gained impetus over the past years, looking at social media to attain it. Openness, transparency and collaboration benefit not only citizens but also the government itself. Open government promotes better record management, makes decisions and services more efficient and serves as a safeguard against misgovernment and corruption.

The chapter findings highlighted that there is considerable ambivalence in approaches to the role of social media in political processes, particularly with respect to deliberative and participatory democratic practices. It is necessary to focus attention particularly on the impacts of social media on the engagement of the poorest and most marginalised in political processes, and how to emphasise the importance for governments to enable all of their citizens to have the opportunities to participate in these new forms of political engagement. It is necessary to emphasise that technology is not an autonomous power that can inherently be used for 'good' or 'bad'. Far from it, historically, there is strong evidence that technologies have usually been shaped and used by those in power to maintain their positions of power. Scholars such as Habermas[90] and Unwin[91] have extensively documented this aspect. Social media is no way different from this historical process of technology being shaped by those in the power. The rule cannot be different for social media. It must also be noted that writers like Castells[92] had the view that whether or not social media has created a new information age, or created, a multiple, micro counter public to challenge the existing structures of power, social media in the political sphere too is shaped by those in the power structure. As a theatre in modern society social media public sphere operates as a social opposition. Democracy, however, is not a unified concept that can be easily defined. Beyond the general idea of 'the rule of the people', it is an ambiguous and abstract value that can be used in several different meanings and contexts. However, if democracy is understood more analytically as a concept or a value to be defined, discussed and contested, the chapter can assume that different normative theories of democracy – i.e. theories that seek to define the general principles and values of democracy – also imply different intellectual and normative frameworks for evaluating the roles of different media in society. So open government is truly a value in understanding the democratic potential of social media in the socio-political lace in which social media is deployed for citizen engagement.

Notes

1 Abraham Lincoln, 'Draft of the Gettysburg Address: Nicolay Copy', November 1863, Series 3, General Correspondence, 1837–1897, The Abraham Lincoln Papers at the Library of Congress, Manuscript Division, American Memory Project, Washington, DC, 2000–02, <http://memory.loc.gov/ammem/alhtml/alhome.html>.
2 Marshal McLuhan, Quentin Fiore, and Shepard Fairey, *The Medium Is the Massage*, New York: Bantam Books, 1967.
3 Cited by Shashi Tharoor in Freedom of Expression and Communications Challenges in the Age of the Internet, at India International Centre, Twentieth Rosalind Wilson Memorial Lecture delivered at the India International Centre on 28 July 2012.
4 OECD, *Effective Open Government: Improving Public Access to Government Information*, Paris: OECD Publishing, 2005a.
5 Lawrence Liang, 'Framing new technologies and cultural practices: Viewing technology in the arts and ownership', Speech delivered on the occasion of Golden Jubilee of India International Centre, SAHMAT and Knowledge Commons, 1 September 2012, <https://www.youtube.com/watch?v=cSXXvwK5bkM>, accessed on 9 May 2016.
6 Partha Chatterjee, Tapati Guha-Thakurta, and Bodhisattva Kar, *New Cultural Histories of India*, New Delhi: Oxford University Press, 2014.
7 Partha Chatterjee and Ira Katznelson, *Anxieties of Democracy Tocquevillean Reflections on India and the United States*, New Delhi: Oxford University Press, 2012.
8 Dipankar Gupta, *The Caged Phoenix: Can India Fly?*, Stanford: Stanford University Press, 2010.
9 Partha Chatterjee, *The Nation and Its Fragments: Colonial and Postcolonial Histories*, Princeton: Princeton University Press, 1993.
10 Partha Chatterjee, *Empire and Nation: Selected Essays*, New York: Columbia University Press, 2010.
11 Eric J. Hobsbawm, *Primitive Rebels*, Manchester: Manchester University Press, 1959.
12 Sudipta Kaviraj, *The Enchantment of Democracy and Indian Politics and Ideas*, New Delhi: Permanent Black, 2011.
13 Dipankar Gupta, *Revolution from Above: India's Future and the Citizen Elite*, New Delhi: Rupa Publications, 2013.
14 Sudipta Kaviraj, *The Imaginary Institution of India: Politics and Ideas*, New York: Columbia University Press, 2010.
15 Robert A. Dahl, *On Democracy*, Yale: YUP, 2000.
16 Joseph A. Schumpeter, *Capitalism, Socialism and Democracy*, New York: Harper & Row, 1942.
17 Barry Holden, *The Nature of Democracy*, New York: Barnes and Noble Books, 1974, p. 69.
18 Holden 1974: 70.

19 E. Pagés and Sánchez S. Aragone, 'A theory of participatory democracy based on the real case of Porto Alegre', *European Economic Review*, 53(1), 2009, pp. 56–72, doi:10.1016/j.euroecorev.2008.09.006.

20 C. Pateman, *Participation and Democratic Theory*, Cambridge: Cambridge University Press, 1970.

21 C. B. Macpherson, *The Life and Times of Liberal Democracy*, Oxford: Oxford University Press, 1977.

22 David Held, *Models of Democracy*, Stanford: Stanford University Press, 1987.

23 M. J. Osborne, J. S. Rosenthal, and M. A. Turner, 'Meetings with costly participation', *American Economic Review*, 90, 2000, pp. 927–943.

24 S. Hall, 'Only 51% plan to vote in elections', *The Guardian*, 25 March 2004, <http://www.theguardian.com/politics/2004/mar/25/uk.polls, accessed>, accessed on 6 September 2014; and W. Nylen, 'New political activists for disillusioned democracies: An analysis of the impact of popular participation on participants in the participatory budgets', Orçamento Participativos of Betim and BeloHorizonte, Minas Gerais, Brazil, Paper Presented for Fourth International Congress of the Union Iberoamericana de Municipalitas, Cordoba, Argentina, 12–16 October 1998.

25 J. Bach and D. Stark, 'Link, search, interact: The co-evolution of NGOs and interactive technology', *Theory, Culture & Society*, 21 (3), 2004, pp. 101–117.

26 M. Castells, *The Rise of the Network Society, The Information Age: Economy, Society and Culture*, Vol. 1, Cambridge, MA and Oxford: Blackwell, 1996/2000; M. Castells, *The Internet Galaxy: Reflections on the Internet, Business and Society*, Oxford and New York: Oxford University Press, 2001; and M. Castells and P. Himanen, *The Information Society and the Welfare State: The Finnish Model*, Oxford: Oxford University Press, 2002.

27 Jan van Dijk, *The Network Society: Social Aspects of New Media*, London: Sage Publications, 2006.

28 C. Arterton, *Teledemocracy: Can Technology Protect Democracy?*, Roosevelt Centre for American Policy Studies, Newbury Park, Beverly Hills, London, and New Delhi: Sage Publications, 1987; I. McLean, *Democracy and New Technology*, Oxford: Polity Press, 1989; B. Loader and L. Keeble (eds.), *Community Informatics: Shaping Computer-Mediated Social Networks*, London: Taylor, 2001; and E. C. Kamarck and J. S. Nye (eds.), *Governance.com: Democracy in the Information Age*, Cambridge, MA: Visions of Governance in the 21st Century and Washington, DC: Brookings Institution Press, 2002.

29 Pippa Norris, *Digital Divide: Civic Engagement, Information Poverty, and the Internet Worldwide*, Cambridge: Cambridge University Press, 2001.

30 D. Kemmis, *Community and the Politics of Place*, Norman: University of Oklahoma Press, 1990; and M. A. Shannon, 'Building trust: The formation of a social contract', in R. G. Lee and J. Schumpeter (eds.), *Capitalism, Socialism and Democracy*, New York: Harper and Brothers, 1992, pp. 229–240.

31 James Bohman and William Rehg (eds.), *Deliberative Democracy: Essays on Reason and Politics*, Cambridge, MA: MIT Press, 1997; Joshua Cohen, 'Deliberation and democratic legitimacy', in Alan Hamlin and Philip Pettit

(eds.), *The Good Polity: Normative Analysis of the State*, Oxford: Basil Black-well, 1989, pp. 17–34; John S. Dryzek, *Discursive Democracy: Politics, Policy and Political Science*, New York: Cambridge University Press, 1990; John S. Dryzek, *Deliberative Democracy and Beyond: Liberals, Critics, Con-testations*, Oxford: Oxford University Press, 2000; Jon Elster, 'Introduc-tion', in Jon Elster (ed.), *Deliberative Democracy*, New York: Cambridge University Press, 1998, pp. 8–9; James Fishkin, *Democracy and Delibera-tion*, New Haven: Yale University Press, 1991; and Amy Gutmann and Dennis Thompson, *Democracy and Disagreement*, Cambridge, MA: Har-vard University Press, 1996.

32 Gutmann and Thompson 1996.

33 OECD 2005a.

34 Ibid.; OECD, *Modernizing Government: The Way Forward*, 2005b, <http://www.ntpu.edu.tw/~pa/course/syllabus/herman/96-2Modernising%20gov.pdf>.

35 Open Society Justice Initiative, *Transparency & Silence: An Overview*, New York: Open Society Justice Initiative, 2006.

36 OECD, How and Why Should Government Activity Be Measured in 'Gov-ernment at a Glance'?, 34th Session of the Public Governance Committee, 30–31 October 2006, Château de la Muette, Paris.

37 OECD 2005b.

38 <www.un.org/en/documents/udhr>.

39 OECD 2006.

40 OECD 2005a.

41 Laura Neuman, 'Enforcement models: Content and context', The Interna-tional Bank for Reconstruction and Development/The World Bank, Wash-ington, DC, 2009, <http://siteresources.worldbank.org/EXTGOVACC/Resources/LNEumanATI.pdf>.

42 OECD 2005b.

43 R. Islam, 'Do More Transparent Governments Govern Better?', Policy Research Working Paper, World Bank Institute, Washington, DC, 2003.

44 Toby Mendel, *Freedom of Information: A Comparative Legal Survey*, Paris: UNESCO, 2003, p. 3.

45 OECD 2005b.

46 Laura Neuman and Richard Calland, *Making the Access to Information Law Work: The Challenges of Implementation*, 2007, <https://www.carter center.org/resources/pdfs/peace/americas/making_the_law_work.pdf>.

47 OECD 2005b.

48 Tim O'Reilly, 'Gov 2.0: It's all about the platform', 4 September 2009, <http://techcrunch.com/2009/09/04/gov-20-its-all-about-the-platform/>, accessed on 27 March 2013.

49 R. Ling and B. Yttri, 'Hyper-coordination via mobile phones in Nor-way, nobody sits at home and waits for the telephone to ring: Micro and hyper-coordination through the use of mobile telephones', in J. Katz and M. Aakhus (eds.), *Perpetual Contact*, Cambridge: Cambridge University Press, 2001, pp. 139–169.

50 Howard Rheingold, *Smart Mobs: The Next Social Revolution*, Cambridge, MA: Perseus, 2002.

51 Downs July 2011.

52 Kenneth Downs, 'Open Government', July 2011, <OntarioMEDI, http://www.mri.gov.on.ca/blog/index.php/2011/07/kenneth-downs/>, accessed on 22 October 2012.

53 Pamela Rutedge, 'How Obama won the social media battle in the 2012 presidential campaign', *The Media Psychology Blog*, 25 January 2013, <http://mprcenter.org/blog/2013/01/25/how-obama-won-the-social-media-battle-in-the-2012-presidential-campaign/>, accessed on 25 January 2014,

54 See <https://twitter.com/bisgovuk>, official Twitter channel of the UK Department for Business, Innovation and Skills. The Profile page says it.

55 See <http://www.youtube.com/user/bisgovuk>.

56 Log on to the link at <https://webtoolkit.govt.nz/guidance/social-media/hands-on-toolbox/#Social%20Media%20in%20Government:%20 Hands%20on%20Toolbox>, to know more about the social media government use and policy in New Zealand.

57 Log on to the link at <http://www.dss.gov.au/social-media-policy> to know more about social media policy of Government of Australia.

58 See <http://rbth.ru/articles/2011/03/24/russian_government_becomes_more_accessible_online_12611.html> to know more about social media modernisation policy in Russia.

59 See <https://twitter.com/IndianDiplomacy>.

60 See <http://www.youtube.com/user/Indiandiplomacy>.

61 See <http://www.youtube.com/watch?v=bE-UF9bjhrA&list=TLWrfn63 6l0OKaLzu1_vJ4GeezjxLDidZS>.

62 See <https://www.facebook.com/IndianDiplomacy>.

63 See <https://twitter.com/IndianDiplomacy>.

64 See <http://indiandiplomacy.blogspot.in/>.

65 See <http://www.delhitrafficpolice.nic.in/>, over nine lakh visitors as on 28 March 2013.

66 See <http://www.facebook.com/pages/Delhi-Traffic-Police/11781737 1573308>, 166,741 likes and 1,723 talking about this as on 28 March 2013.

67 See <http://indorepolice.blogspot.in/>.

68 See <http://www.facebook.com/IndorePolice>, 3,415 likes and 23 talking about this.

69 See <https://twitter.com/indorepolice>.

70 See <http://www.indorepolice.org/>.

71 See <http://www.indiapost.gov.in/>.

72 See <https://twitter.com/postofficeindia>.

73 See <http://indiapost.nic.in/>.

74 See <http://www.facebook.com/Incometaxindia>.

75 See <http://www.facebook.com/pages/Ministry-of-Finance-Government-of-India/>.

76 See <http://www.facebook.com/pages/Ministry-Of-Health-and-Family-Welfare/>.

77 See <http://www.facebook.com/MEAINDIA>.

78 See <http://www.facebook.com/pages/Ministry-ofRailways>.

79 See <http://www.facebook.com/pages/Ministry-of-Defence>.

80 Framework and Guidelines for Use of Social Media for Government Organisations, Department of Electronics and Information Technology, Ministry of Communications & Information Technology, Government of India.

81 See <http://inbministry.blogspot.in/2013/02/myindia-initiative-digital-volunteer.html>, accessed on 18 June 2014.

82 See <http://www.facebook.com/pages/Election-Commission-Of-India/140319599359151>, 6,437 likes as on 25 October 2012.

83 See <http://www.facebook.com/pages/Finance-Commission-of-India/108014979226858?ref=ts&fref=ts>, 22 likes as on 25 October 2012.

84 See <http://www.facebook.com/pages/National-Commission-forWomenIndia/100529223359125?ref=ts&fref=ts>, 45 likes as on 25 October 2012.

85 See <http://www.facebook.com/Census2011>, 38,861 likes and 252 talking about this as on 28 March 2013.

86 See <https://twitter.com/IndiaCensus2011>, 26,338 followers, 303 following and 206 tweets as on 28 March 2013.

87 See <http://www.facebook.com/TwelfthPlan/info>.

88 See <http://ogpl.gov.in/>.

89 'Tenth Five Year Plan of India', Planning Commission of India, <www.planningcommission.gov.in/plans/planrel/fiveyr/welcome.html>, last accessed on 29 September 2010.

90 Jurgen Habermas, *Knowledge and Human Interests*, 2nd edition, tr. J. Shapiro, London: Heinemann, 1978.

91 T. Unwin (ed.), *Information and Communication Technologies for Development*, Cambridge: Cambridge University Press, 2009.

92 M. Castells, 'Toward a sociology of the network society', *Contemporary Sociology*, 29 (5), September 2000, pp. 693–699.

10

SOCIAL LEARNING
Pedagogy of the oppressed

Educational potential of social media is much political. So, what does it mean to think about the 'political' of social media's educational use? As we know, India is impregnated with different social hierarchy, where access to education is taxing for underprivileged people. Social media is a natural choice for millions of people who do not have access to high-quality education and knowledge due to various historical reasons. Here, social media does not have hierarchy! Then, the question is what role social media could play in the educational scenario in India? This enquiry explores what extent social media could create Education 2.0 in the contemporary social media landscape in India. Social media holds political significance in the traditional Indian social structure that restrains education for all for various reasons, be it access, quality and equity. Facebook, Twitter, YouTube, Blogger, WordPress and LinkedIn, in particular, have greater usage in educational scenario. Social media could configure social learning in the rigid and hierarchical social structure in India that impedes the prospects of education among poorest people and minority communities, and this is the trajectory of political significance of social learning. Social media rejuvenates higher education in the days ahead and has the potential to pass across the factors that have been traditionally a hindrance to the educational attainment of masses in the context of deep-rooted social hierarchy in India.

A better description of the political potential of social learning could be meticulous if one goes through the personal social media story told by a student. It is best to begin with Sunandita Sur, a Cotton Hill College student from Odisha, who was doing a Bachelor of Arts programme. She had the view that social media changed her whole outlook about political science as a career fortune, once she was able to meet a teacher blogger from Kerala. The teacher blogger in question was the author himself. Being a member of a wealthy family, she had often encountered existential questions as a student of this social science stream, which in her native was the least option among the rich sections of the society. She often faced questions such as what did political science teach? what job opportunities does it offer? what are one learning about strikes and protest? and so on that indeed had a demoralising effect on her student life. She was even planning to drop it. However, the blogger in question was something like reinvention of her learning imagination once she got some encouraging comments from the blogger. She asked the same questions that were often confronting her in the family circle.

To her surprise, the blogger said that in the 100 intellectual survey of *Foreign Policy* magazine 2007 it was political science which had bagged seventeen members, and this number was the largest among them.[1] World Thinkers 2013 of *Prospect* magazine had nine political scientists out of a list of sixty-five.[2] Barak Obama, Bill Clinton, Henry Kissinger and Narendra Modi, among the many, had been students of this discipline. Indeed, Sunandita says that social media cultivated a new learning culture for study with information abundance and now she is more confident! This is how many ordinary students like her learnt to migrate to social media for problems that we would not get a solution otherwise. If Sunandita was able to dig up a new impetus for learning via social media, how many among us have really thought about the educational potential of social media?

Education 2.0 represents a metaphor that could have iconoclastic power which derails the hierarchical and stigmatised Indian society and thus access to education, at various levels, once unattainable for the subaltern and poor people, remains a touch away now. It was in 2009 the author started to blog at http://bijugayu.blogspot.in/ on academic topics. The blog was used as a connected learning platform over the last couple of years. It was very comfortable to post assignment and seminar topics for the students and official seminar notifications of the college funded by various academic agencies. More interestingly, the comments section was richly engaging and interactive. Getting over 500 shares for many posts on an average, the blog is one of the academic publishing hits on Internet. Students across the world have raised many questions concerning career opportunities, academic learning and so on in the comments section, contact form and live chat options in the blog. Users say, 'Thank you very much'. People say, 'Ohh you have done a good job', 'you save us', you have just summarised my whole semester', 'I got a clear idea from you, thanks', 'It is really useful . . . thank u very much' and' Thank you sir, this is what I expected'. And the comments section inflates.[3] It means lot of things to me as an academic blogger.

Professor Aijaz Ahmad, a well-known Marxist literary theorist and political commentator in India, says he stopped listening to mainstream media for news and information; instead, he often depends on web resources. Prof. Ahmad told a group of students of journalism in Chennai that while he had no reason to watch television channels, only a few facts he used in his writings came from mainstream media now. 'I get most of my facts through alternative sources, mostly on the web or through direct communication on email, Skype and others who are also involved in the act of gathering the real truths of our time', says Aijaz Ahmad.[4] The sign that guided young academics to new ideas a generation ago were limited, with higher levels of abrupt and unwritten formalities, and were exclusionary. Nowadays, the best students are using social learning skills to look for the information that matters to them.

Colleges and universities are fast embracing social media for academic purposes. In the age where crowd, mass participation, producer public and user contents shape the knowledge system, any attempt on reforming educational system cannot bring in good results until and unless an attempt to reincorporate social media into curricular and pedagogical aspects is properly made. Schools are developing connected learning methodologies to enhance erudition among kids and so they are fast adopting social networking sites in their everyday learning activities. This chapter excavates some of the lived-in experiments and social media configuration in curricular aspects in India. While doing so, the chapter would sketch the 'political' significance of new kind of pedagogy, which this chapter reformulates into a grounded label called social learning using ethnographic approaches on selected learning communities and user interfaces. The principal assertion in the chapter is that social media has destructive power which can bypass traditional impediments superimposed by the social structure which hinders access to education.

Universities, colleges, institutes and think tanks are using connected platforms that carry profound educational significance. Classrooms have begun to lengthen beyond their walls. Teachers move around to become 24-hour providers. Students have teleported learning environment to digital platforms. The fact is that connected learning appears to be more student-centric. Now, a new kind of pedagogy works for the teeming millions: the pedagogy of the oppressed. Let us call Education 2.0 the pedagogy of the oppressed.

In today's thematic world, pedagogy is increasingly gearing towards technology, particularly social media. The user-friendly interfaces in learning environment are always motivating for the black sheep, say most of the teachers contacted. Students often consider specific social media platforms as second classroom since they feel it as their comfort zone. Many students have claimed that they were using mobile platforms to download or check classroom points or prepare assignments.

Alternative media seems overcoming caste and gender and subverting oppressive social structures. It caters to the educational demand of people located on the outskirts of social margins. Projecting Internet as a liberating ideal has acquired greater popularity in this respect. Internet has no caste, gender, race, region, communal consciousness and 'linguistic extremism'. The political significance of social media lies in the apparent social stratification and structural constraints seen in the traditional Indian society. Social media acquires widest political resolution to education in respect of access, quality, cost, time, geography and parity, which conventionally remains a challenge to policy makers, government and stakeholders.

Easiness in connectivity makes social media a significant element in higher educational scenario. Education 2.0 as a term acknowledges the fact that technological developments, especially connected platforms such as Facebook, YouTube, Twitter and blogs are empowering teaching and learning processes. User-generated contents could be accessed anytime and anywhere. Certainly, my friends, your friends and their friends make easy collaboration and dissemination of information to widest possible networks of people anytime without barriers such as money, time, geography and social structure. Indeed, the interactivity motivates learners to expand knowledge through further exploration and collaboration.

Despite long years of tryst with democracy and attempts by successive governments to provide quality education to all sections of the population, women, tribes, minorities and Dalits are yet to be empowered.

Schoolchildren explore the web for study materials. Academicians say they do not need to indulge in library while browsing for massive volumes to take plentiful notes. Education experts say Internet has been facilitating guaranteed access to information. Now just think how easy Internet has altered the conventional parameters of knowledge production, dissemination and sharing. Knowledge is not just confined to reading and printing in the social media age. It is more at save, forward, share, like, upload, check and comment formats. Indeed, many educationalists believe that educational arena is in a good position to utilise social media practices to support the collective creation of knowledge amongst students and the wider community.[5] Many universities are now striving to develop ways of using social media to support these new forms of learning.[6]

Internet has been playing a principal role in streamlining administrative procedures and processes of universities and educational institutions. The official Facebook page of Calicut University in Kerala, for example, has been liked by over 13,000.[7] Users say it is useful for getting official university notifications pertaining to admission, exam and other related information. Modern universities, educational institutes and research centres

221

maintain their own websites and other social web platforms. Here they tag links and share and upload information pertaining to courses, lecture notes and videos of classroom lectures. Students and admission seekers apply for admission online which eliminates paperwork and amplifies administrative effectiveness. Students and applicants receive e-notifications regarding admission, course schedules, billing procedures and other useful information. Students can pay fees online as well as seek their examination results. Teachers prefer to receive tutorials online, which not only lends itself to faster transmission but also avoids the difficulty in reading a manuscript. In the same way, some faculties put up not only their course material on the website but their lectures also, which attract widest possible audience online such that students who were unable to attend lectures/classes can also benefit from them. In many cases, assignments, term papers and so on are useful for submitting online and teachers can share such submissions through social media platforms so that they can reach out to a larger audience instantly. The faculty and students remain connected through email and social media sites on which students receive instructions, fix appointments, send essays or assignments and so on. In fact, students who have access to Internet will facilitate a round-the-clock classroom experience.

While reputed universities and higher educational institutions deploy the conventional face-to-face lectures, there were attempts to offer online courses especially during the summer break in western universities. While such courses have the obvious disadvantage of the absence of personal interaction, they permit discussion through setting up of chat rooms and social media sites. Such online courses and discussions have often proved to be more rewarding than standard classroom interactions as they consent to students and teachers from different parts of the world to converge and meet together.

Universities and courses that facilitated greater accessibility, openness and quality to education than ever before to people who were denied such opportunities in the past are part of an ongoing movement towards smart education. While popular perception usually values a degree from a regular college over a degree from online college, the utmost benefit of an online university or college is that a student need not commute or live on campus. Online courses embedded with social media sites are helpful for students who cannot afford education while staying at campus. This is especially truer for certain kinds of courses designed to cater to the needs of students who do not have financial backup, inhospitable social systems or stumpy family support. Since specialised degrees are directly related to good employment, re-engineering e-education at tertiary level has enormous benefit. As jobs become frequently insecure in a liberalised economy and mid-life career changes more intermittent, the call for online education is increasing over time.[8]

Today, not only formal education institutions but most other work places are equipped with at least some kind of digital platforms that bring people and user content together and provide learning activities to poorest and help people construct and process information and knowledge. The producer public could re-enact their learning practices by their own instead of resorting to a top-down approach. With the availability of new technologies, common access to Internet and information, new types of social interactions mediated by technology, all of these necessitate a shift in the way that we learn and teach. Obviously online platforms for higher education has two important advantages: first, learners can take a more active part in their education, and second, learning platforms offer 'anytime, anywhere learning'.[9] The aim of online learning platforms is to provide an online learning environment that supports quality learning and teaching, and connect students, teachers and parents, anywhere and at any time (DEECD 2010).

Learners to providers

There is a clear need to thoroughly reconsider what education is and what forms it should assume in the social media age. These are issues steered by normative understanding about the essentially ethical question of what counts worthwhile learning and worthwhile education.[10] In a thought-provoking book, author and professor of economics Tyler Cowen[11] categorically links Internet with skills that could improve on autism and neurodiversity since it helps us organise and understand information with the new access to information. In this background, educators face the immediate task of integrating social media into curricular practices. In the read/write web universe, crowd is far better than the few wise or the skilled professionals. Therefore, social media can provide diversity, independence, decentralisation and aggregation, where crowd could be far smarter than elite few, says *New Yorker* business columnist James Surowiecki.[12] Quite importantly, educational institutions could have compelling reasons to reconsider the practical challenges of how to assess the collaborative wok published in connected paces by those producer public on social web.[13] In these ways, educators could also play an important role in supporting students' supposedly self-directed activities, collaborative productions and mass publications, thereby providing them with a good base in 'arranging the furniture' of technology-based learning.[14] Social media use implies that learners should be 'active co-producers' of knowledge rather than 'passive consumers' of content and that learning should be a 'participatory, social process' supporting personal life goals and needs.[15]

Many educators maintain that social media could be used successfully to support the provision of what Goodyear and Ellis[16] term 'serious student-centred learning'. The most structured implementation of social media in educational settings implies a degree of 'user-driven' education, i.e allowing learners to take more active roles in what they could learn as well as how and when they could learn it. Nevertheless, many higher educators believe that universities are capable of accommodating and benefitting from these techno-shifts in education. Some commentators have therefore begun to talk of the need to develop pedagogy 2.0, implying 'innovative pedagogies that leverage these affordances to support learner choice and autonomy'.[17] Yet, as with many previous new technologies, academic discussion and debate remain largely speculative rather than well-informed judgements.

In the 1990s, the meaning of digital communication for an average student was by any means limited only to indicate communication over the plain old telephone. In those days, sharing a course material or classroom notes or documents related to academic activities was possible only by using a photocopier or using a fax machine. Such initial digital equipment were rare at home or among ordinary people. Since then, there has been a huge rebellion in communication technologies. As Internet and mobile services have penetrated into even the most rural areas of India, people can now communicate almost at the same level as if they meet in person, but without the need to even leave their homes.

Leading western universities have found social media useful for extending their classroom and learning process through networking. The courses and classroom settings of such universities are also available via streaming videos. Harvard University has their classroom and curricular aspects on Web 2.0. See Posterous,[18] Facebook,[19] YouTube,[20] iTunes,[21] Twitter,[22] Foursquare[23] and Social Media Group.[24]

A major shift that user-generated platforms brought about in the ever-expanding educational horizon is the transformation in the relationship between learners and knowledge providers. Social media has supported a new form of knowledge consumption and construction that are epistemologically unrelated to the principles of formal and conventional practices of education and individualised instruction methods. For example, anyone, anywhere in the world can access over 1,800 open courses at MIT, which is astounding. On top of that, the challenge is the fact that teachers of all ages increasingly have to deal with students who have grown up in such a techno-enriched atmosphere that it has trained them to absorb and process information in fundamentally different ways.

Pushed by the constructivist and sociocultural learning theories, educationalists have compelling reasons to re-examine entirely the nature of learning in the light of altering relationships that social media users seemingly have with information in the digital age. In the description of a technology-enhanced 'new culture of learning', Douglas Thomas and John Seely-Brown[25] have recounted that learning that is based on principles of collective study, play and innovate rather than individualised instruction that keeps changing. Some argue that learning has fundamentally undergone changes and that the way today's student thinks and develops cognitively is fundamentally different.[26]

There is growing logic that most powerful learning is social rather than individual.[27] Current learning theories emphasise the importance of social involvement for motivation, construction of knowledge and as a source of support.[28] The co-construction of knowledge through joint action can lead to deeper understanding, and collaborative learning can develop critical thinking and shared understandings and lead to long-term retention of learning materials compared to more traditional knowledge transfer models.[29] Feedback is essential for learning, among other things, whether from teachers to students, among students and, more importantly, from students to teachers, says Hattie.[30] Blogs, wikis and discussion forums connect people online, enabling communication, collaboration and feedback, and it certainly ensures collaborative learning and co-production of knowledge.

These new ideas are reflected most overtly that learning in the social media age now rests upon the ability to access and use scattered information on a 'just-in-time' basis. In the digital age, learning is more related to an individual's ability to take over specialised information whichever is required, apt and fitting. George Siemens,[31] for example, has put it aptly that learning could be conceived in terms of the 'capacity to know more' via digital media platforms rather than relying on the individual accumulation of prior knowledge in terms of 'what is currently known'. Thus being knowledgeable and informative could be seen as the ability to nurture and keep up knowledge and information connections.[32]

We move away from thinking of knowledge as a substance that we transmit from student to teacher, to a social view of learning. Not 'I think, therefore I am', but 'We participate, therefore we are' and from 'access to information' to 'access to people'. It is more in form of from 'learning about' to 'learning to be'. Everything is becoming participative. Amazon.com and Wikipedia are great examples of how participation is integral to an industry success and collaboration in knowledge production. But it is also an example of the irony of participation. Credibility and authenticity of participative culture in the age of social media falls under the shadow of doubt.

In short, the future of higher education largely depends on Web 2.0. Social learning is based on the premise that our understanding of content has socially been constructed through conversations. The focus is not so much on what one is learning but on how one is learning.

In short, to understand the pedagogy in the age of social media practices, a shift in dominant pedagogy is required. Web 2.0 has higher application in pedagogy. In fact, Web 2.0 promotes motivation and participation, self-directed learning skills, higher-order skills, reflection and meta-cognition, networking and collaboration, and embracing diversity to enhance individual skill development. Learning 2.0 approaches support motivation, participation and reflection, empowering learners to develop self-directed learning skills, and helping them to better realise their potential. Teachers become designers, coordinators, moderators, mediators and mentors, rather than instructors or lecturers, while students have to not only assume the role of (peer) teachers, supporting each other in their learning endeavours, but also jointly create both the learning content and context, developing their own rules and strategies for cooperation and content production while endorsing inclusion and equity.[33]

A portrait of Education 2.0

The label *Education 2.0* consistently passes on to an array of en suite online platforms that can be both educationally applicable for learning atmosphere and politically a metaphor which citizens could use against social apartheid invisible in the modern Indian state. It is necessary to understand what exactly Education 2.0 looks like and what constitutes such an innovative educational practice. When directed towards learning practices, Web 2.0 impacts on four principal dimensions of the learner's experience. Two are broadly social in nature (collaboration and publication) and two are more cognitive (literacies and inquiry). These practices are more frequent on certain social media sites peculiar to Indian context that could have iconoclastic power. They are blogs, Facebook, Twitter and YouTube. They are explained in the following section of the chapter. What many people share on Facebook, tweet on Twitter, watch on YouTube, text on a chat forum, post about an academic seminar, share news about a global conference, mark a like on an educational event on social networking sites while you are by a train, a bus or flight or by some other means are all about Education 2.0.

The term *Education 2.0* refers to a range of integrated online tools that can be either Internet-based or networked. These interactive tools can include webpages, email, message boards, text and video conferencing. It is necessary to understand what exactly Education 2.0 looks like and what constitutes such an innovative educational practice. The coming days will be the days of Education 2.0 and it will have all the components of Classroom 2.0, Students 2.0 and Teachers 2.0. Education 2.0 labels the technological developments especially connected on platforms such as Facebook, YouTube, Twitter and blogs empowering teaching and learning processes.

Blog for Classroom 2.0

Navigating online search to the blog link of http://indianbloggers.org/, one would get a whole list of popular bloggers in India. Why this introduction is that everyone has an opinion on education. However, we do not know much about the educational aspect of blogging in India that is claiming a significant fragment of the huge blogosphere. Everyone one meets on Internet will have something to say about education, be it personal blog or blogs committed for some other causes.

From an educational point of view, blogs are the development of traditional learning logs for students and teachers, whether as a complement to traditional lectures or as an e-learning tool. The blog http://education. trak.in/, for example, says *everything about Indian Education, colleges, universities, guidance and information.* The importance of applications of this sort has increased due to the changes in the classroom dynamics, say Mora and Espinosa.[34] There are many uses for blogs in many fields. A study by Nardi and team has recounted five major motivations for blogging: documenting one's life; providing commentary and opinions; expressing deeply felt emotions; articulating ideas through writing and forming and maintaining community forums.[35] These motivations are not mutually exclusive and might come into play simultaneously.

More than ever, in the education field, blogs are being used to satisfy a variety of communication needs to favour e-learning practices. In a study by Leslie,[36] a matrix of some of the possible uses of weblogs in education is shown. These possible uses are analysed in a two-dimensional space: who uses the weblog (instructors or students) and for what (writing or reading). While following this same matrix, a list of possible uses is provided in a study by Lowe[37]: improving writing skills, encouraging reflective writing, reading student weblogs for assessment, sharing resources and ideas, recording progress and process, course administration, group work and so on. See Table 10.1 for the blog links of some educational institutions offering various educational content.

The use of blogs for educational purposes is a bit different. In terms of using blogs by students, it has been widely scaled for reflective journaling;

Table 10.1 Blog links

SL No	Platforms	Address
1	Department of Economics, MG College, Trivandrum	http://mgceconomicsdept.blogspot.in/
2	Kerala University Youth Festival	http://keralauniversityyouthfestival2014.blogspot.in/
3	UNIZOA, alumni association of Department of Zoology, University College, Trivandrum, Kerala, India	http://unizoa-unizoa.blogspot.in/
4	A blog that disseminates information on social science conferences, jobs, courses etc. in India and abroad	http://thesocialscienceinformer.blogspot.in/
5	Research in Centre for Studies in Science Policy	http://cssp-jnu.blogspot.in/
6	Swaraj Musings	http://gandhimgu.blogspot.in/

summarising classroom discussions, reflecting on what students learned during a class activity or project, sharing ideas for applying what they have learned to their own practice and so on. Blogs are also used by students to accomplish a number of other objectives. Moreover, blogs promote reflection and analysis. They are making students connected to a professional community of practices. They offer avenues for garnering feedback on ideas from course and community colleagues and opportunities for collaboration with colleagues. Most importantly, blogs promote a habit of writing. Further, using blogging for educational purposes provides an opportunity to take advantage of the Web 2.0 tools which students are using in their personal and often professional lives. Another benefit of introducing blogging and other Web 2.0 tools to students who are in the field of education is that they give them an opportunity to learn to use Web 2.0 tools as aids to instruction with their own students. Finally, blogging is used to introduce students to Web 2.0 tools. Web 2.0 tools can be used as vehicles for self-expression, enquiry, construction and collaboration as well as to support lifelong learning endeavours. Blogs triumph over the traditional social barriers impregnated with lives of marginalised people with access to education. These form the political value of blogs in a society that has social cleavages.

Timeline learners

Young people are natural adopters of Facebook in India and more profoundly popular among students who were born after the advent of Internet in India. Now, it is the moment of 'timeline' learners. According to reports students who used Facebook for semester courses did better in terms of course assignments than those who did not use it. Sorry to Todd Oppenheimer,[38] Facebook and computer technologies are bringing in lifestyle changes in learning behaviour. Room to Read is a global organisation seeking to transform the lives of millions of children in the developing world through a focus on literacy and gender equality in education. Its Facebook[39] profile says that 'we partner with communities across Asia and Africa to support literacy and gender equality in education'. Facebook is significant since education in India has been obviously unaffordable for people at the lower rungs of social hierarchy.

The educational potential of Facebook is unwieldy and that even outsizes the basic purposes of the platform. Professors use it for teaching notes. Students use it to share their views on everything under the sky. Students criticise the use of plastic flowers and plastic bottles of potable water used during the environmental day celebration in college. They comment on what so and so have done in politics. In fact, Facebook can help kids, students and young people develop relationship skills by gaining a better understanding of feelings of other people and their social system. When they see others sharing their personal feelings online, it is easier for them to empathise and identify with their experiences and comment with support.

Students say that they read book reviews in Amazon for doing assignment and projects, if they have a smartphone and it was because the professor has been sharing the book link in the timeline. In a country where access to quality education is unaffordable for various reasons, a cell phone is more than being connected. And if you have a desktop it is more of a luxury and if it is a gadget, you are on top of the world. India is a land of wonders as well as contradictions. The Facebook story is too much contradicting. In that regard, the educational applicability of Facebook is materialised with timelines, instant messaging, email and the ability to post videos and pictures. Most notably, anyone can post information and collaborate within the system. Recently Facebook has opened up development of downloadable applications, which could further supplement the educational functions of Facebook. It could also provide numerous other pedagogical advantages to both teachers and students.

Facebook as a networking platform connects students with each other, indirectly creating a learning community, a vital component of student education. It provides instructors opportunities by which students can help and support one another by building their courses atop the community already established by the students themselves. Reports recount that students who participated in a web-enhanced class outperformed those students in a traditional lecture format. Facebook also increases both teacher–student and student–student interactions in the form of read/ write web communications. It helps instructors connect with their students about assignments, upcoming events, useful links and samples of work outside the classroom.

The nature of social learning has been changing at a moderately rapid pace in India precipitated in part by widespread use of online social networking sites such as Facebook. Sharing photographs, revealing demographic information, displaying interests and conducting online conversations are just a few among the features utilised on Facebook. The following list provides an overview of the different ways that Facebook can be integrated into a course.

Profile Page: An instructor can choose to create a profile page for him-/ herself. The profile page can be used to communicate with students via Facebook email, IM or posting on the wall. In addition, relevant videos, images and websites can also be included. Students can also be exposed to relevant and educational Facebook groups.

Creating a Group Page for a Class: A separate page can be created specifically for a course. Students can virtually find other classmates through this page, learn about their classmates, communicate with their classmates and professor and post/discuss relevant class information. Professors can send an announcement to the entire group and set up and remind students about events.

Replacing/Duplicating Web Course Functions on Facebook: Discussions that traditionally have taken place on web course boards can also occur on Facebook discussion boards. Instant messaging functions are also available online. Instructors can post information and websites on their profile and group page for students to download and use for class.

Integration of Facebook Applications: There are a number of useful applications that will expand the functionality of Facebook for class. However, using these applications requires that students download them as well.

Facebook is not just a great way for us to find old friends or learn about what is happening on weekend; it is also an incredible learning tool. One could utilise Facebook for class projects, for enhancing communication and for engaging students in a manner that might not be entirely possible in traditional classroom settings.

Hashtag classroom

Twitter hashtag at #classroom20 navigates users to a community level feature hosted by the website at http://www.classroom20.com/, which introduces that it is a social network for those interested in Web 2.0, Social Media and Participative Technologies in the classroom. If you follow the hashtag at #ProfessorV1, you would get the whole updates on the activities at Professor V's Teaching Café,[40] which is also one of the interactive communities for the cause of education.

The point is that Twitter is a very powerful search engine just like Google. You can find good things if you are good at using it. One of those effective ways is leveraging the power of hashtags. The hashtags at #Edchat is a weekly Bammy Award–winning Twitter conversation that any educator can join to discuss and learn about current teaching trends, how to integrate technology, transform their teaching and connect with inspiring educators worldwide.

Twitter's classroom capabilities are limited only by an educator's imagination. Though many believe its limitations prevent valuable applications to an academic setting, teachers in the fray realise the microblog has potential to establish a nurturing classroom for students of all ages. Twitter can make a surprisingly useful educational tool, giving students and teachers an easy way to communicate that goes beyond office hours and classrooms. With the use of a simple hashtag (#), it becomes incredibly easy to curate tweets, giving students an easy way to follow the information that is associated with a specific class. Alternatively, teachers can create accounts or Twitter lists specific to a course that students can then follow, making it easy for them to find each other on Twitter.

There are loads of great educational hashtags that have been created that one can search out and see what other educators are providing. Are you a social studies teacher or do you need history resources? Check out #sschat. Maybe English is your taste, and then there is #engchat. Maybe you are looking for just general education resources. Then one should do a search for #edchat. If you just navigate to CybraryMan,[41] you can get plenty of educational hashtags. Twitter can be used in novel ways to make classroom interaction in an unprecedented manner. Lots of Twitter applications have educational values. Especially tweets and retweets are powerful instruments for making classroom beyond walls of the institution.

Twitter can be more effective to send reminders to students about homework and assignments, and provide relevant information for their next class. Using Twitter on a smartphone could ensure that students receive notifications and can keep pace with the latest class news. This is where

Twitter's SMS service can also come in handy. Teachers can use this to their advantage by tweeting interesting educational links for their students to read. Sending out a tweet to give students a reading assignment is an instantaneous way to keep them prepared for their class ahead of time. Teachers can easily collaborate with each other on Twitter too, exchanging ideas and teaching tools. With the use of a hashtag, it is easy for any group of people to connect on Twitter, so why not teachers? The hashtag #edchat, #edtech and more give instant access to links, thoughts and tweets from educators from all over the world.

History teachers can use Twitter to communicate with students using the voice of a historical figure, by creating a Twitter account in that person's name. Students can get a feel for what kind of language was used at the time, in a fun, interactive way. They can even be encouraged to interact with the historical figure, using the same language and style.

Creative writing professors can use Twitter as a means to encourage student creativity in a challenging format. Writers and poets use Twitter to share their micro poems with the world, using hashtags like #poetweet or #micropoem. The social network can be a great way of encouraging students to write haikus or six-word stories, a concept that began when Ernest Hemingway was challenged to write a story in six words. Twitter is the perfect tool to convey a concept or story with as few words as possible.

In a classroom setting, Twitter use can contribute to a discussion and give students and teachers a way to keep the conversation going long after the class is over. Professors have already used this method in large classrooms, with a projection screen at the front of the class, displaying the search results for the chosen hashtag for the discussion. Using an application like TweetDeck, or any desktop app with a self-updating feature, is the ideal way for tweets to be displayed during class.

Hashtag learning experiences could extend learning practices beyond the 'walls' of the classroom and they can bring about far-reaching implications since access and equity in education are disadvantageous to marginalised communities in India. They help bring in current events to the curriculum and students can become more engaging and participative than ever before. As it can connect students from across multiple sections or institutions and stream of education, indeed the political significance of Twitter in educational practices far exceeds the basic function it was thought of. Reach out to experts in the field just by a click. As it can pull the world into your classroom the power of Twitter is unbelievable.

EduTube

Kevin Kelly, the founder of *Wired* magazine, and Lawrence Lessig, Stanford law professor and Creative Commons founder, say our cultural shift today is one from book literacy to screen fluency. Here what they mean is video formats and that a new vernacular is developing in motion. It is a 'world beyond words', where TV, movies and all audio-visual work will find themselves with table of contents, abstracts, indexes and rendering them searchable within a short span of time.[42]

Video and online media are not new to education, but they offer remarkably new capabilities for educational practices. Educators are seeing new ways to express their art through technological means. The body of literature about YouTube is small but growing. Works cited on YouTube research tended to be websites, magazine articles and blogs about the website. However, a number of scholarly studies in a variety of disciplines are accumulating. Juhasz's[43] pilot 'YouTube only' classroom pointed out that mainstream reports did not take the idea of a YouTube classroom seriously, portraying the ideas and students of the class as rudimentary. Mainstream media's biases treated the class and YouTube as a joke. However, a number of studies have documented the YouTube and its socially useful and educationally applicable dimension.[44]

Professors say that they search YouTube content that can be useful teaching aid in classroom atmosphere. Indeed, educationalists believe that universities are in a good position to utilise social media practices to support the collective creation of knowledge amongst students and the wider community. Several universities are now striving to develop ways of using social media to support these new forms of learning. Leading universities have their classrooms on YouTube, for example, MIT,[45] Yale University,[46] Harvard Kennedy School,[47] Princeton University,[48] Columbia University[49] and Stanford University.[50]

Allan Collins and Richard Halverson[51] recount that educators must think about rethinking education in the age of connected platforms as they are going to bring in phantom changes in almost all levels of life. EduCanon[52] is a free web platform that simply lets teachers to slot in online video content into their lessons. Using videos from YouTube, Vimeo[53] or TeacherTube,[54] now teachers can make assignments directly on the pinnacle of that video content. In fact, screen learning makes students more interested in learning activity. More obviously, video content sharing is significant to a generation who are unnecessarily forced to pay attention to screens of various sorts, be it touch, swipe or so.

In 2012, Google launched YouTube for schools, which aimed at giving teachers an easy access to YouTubeEDU. It was an educational library replete with free, high-quality educational videos, which sort out the enormous video contents uploaded to YouTube by different educators in different points of time from different parts of the world. In effect, it became the first push by a major Internet company to bring a new form of learning into the classroom. The YouTubeEDU[55] says that 'whether you're doing research for a project, need help with homework, or just want to learn something new, YouTube EDU features some of our most popular educational videos across YouTube'.

YouTubeEDU, promoted by the company officials, is a YouTube section devoted to academic content. Calling this new site 'a free, self-organizing, democratic website containing the entire world's knowledge', YouTubeEDU promises an environment in which 'any qualified teacher can contribute and absolutely anyone can learn'. It features lectures and other materials from hundreds of colleges and universities, including Stanford, Harvard and MIT. The Google+[56] tagline of the YouTubeEDU says, 'Where anyone anywhere can learn or teach anything'.

Google organised an interactive session on YouTube for Education in October 2013 at the Google office in Gurgaon, India. Google launched Google Teacher Academy (GTA) on 27–28 November 2014, which is a professional development experience designed to help primary and secondary educators from around the globe to get the most from innovative technologies. YouTube is not the only Internet site offering higher education lectures and courses. One competitor is Big Think, which bills itself as 'a global forum connecting people and ideas'. Its experts include Paul Krugman, the Nobel Prize–winning professor from Princeton University, as well as Billy Collins, former US poet laureate and dozens of other professors, politicians and business leaders speaking on various topics. For example, viewers can see a presentation on how the Supreme Court works or an explanation of the future of the US government's bank rescue plan.

Another website, Education for All, offers more than videos with its courses. The site provides syllabus materials that accompany courses, plus reading lists. The link for a course on financial markets, taught by Robert Schiller, a professor of economics at Yale University, even added copies of the exams and solutions as well as a discussion forum for viewers. The site also includes a complete set of four Chinese-language courses available with a package of downloadable textbooks and audio recordings of dialogues.

Then there is Academic Earth, a site that also offers video courses and lectures from some of the nation's top scholars. Founded by Richard Ludlow, a Yale graduate, Academic Earth's mission is to 'give everyone on earth access to a world-class education'. It draws material from Harvard, MIT, Princeton, Stanford, Yale and Berkeley, and says that 50 per cent of its users come from outside the USA. Like many other educational sites, it has a Facebook page and a presence on Twitter.

Learning through video sharing platforms has many advantages. It ensures mobility and makes distance learning easy. Increased and easy access to video sharing apps makes YouTube and other video hosting platforms more befitting for the idea of education at door steps. In that sense, video hosting platforms and its use for educational purposes are relevant for overcoming the barriers of rigid social structures. Certainly, YouTube-based educational practices offer a ray of hope to communities on the social walls of social hierarchy. It is more of a political choice.

Education 2.0: reflections on the Indian scenario

Internet and social media practices have greater potential in breaking time and distance barriers to facilitating collaboration and knowledge sharing among geographically dispersed student communities in India. There are various kinds of ICT applications and Internet platforms holding relevance to education, such as email, teleconferencing, audio conferencing, radio broadcasts, interactive voice response system, television lessons, audiocassettes, CD-ROMs and interactive radio counselling. They are used in the educational scenario for different purposes in different parts of India.

Web 2.0 platforms for higher education collaboration and networking are popular in India as the Internet penetration increases. A study by Suil Tyagi[57] in the National Capital Territory of India about the use of social media among faculties found that despite many fears and challenges, user-generated content holds greater significance to a stratified society like India. Social media acquires greater role in quality enhancement in India. It brings down quality disparity between rural and urban India. Indira Gandhi National Open University (IGNOU) uses radio, television and Internet technologies, for instance, Subscribe E-Resources,[58] IGNOU Homepage,[59] Virtual Classrooms,[60] IGNOU Online[61] and IGNOU WIKi.[62]

Using Internet and television, the Government adopted the National Programme on Technology Enhanced Learning (NPTEL) (2007): a concept similar to the open courseware initiative of MIT and is an initiative of seven IITs and IISc for creating e-contents. It hosts a YouTube Channel[63] having 157,716 subscribers and 87,734,135 video views, a Facebook page[64] and so on. Eklavya initiative has been using Internet and television channels to promote distance learning, for example, Eklavya Technology

Channel[65] in India since 2007. It is a distant learning joint initiative between the IITs and IGNOU. It hosts a Facebook page.[66]

Twitter, Facebook and YouTube are frequently deployed Web 2.0 platforms of premier institutes in India, especially IITs, IIMs and NITs. For instance, IIT Gandhinagar has Facebook, YouTube and Twitter pages. IIM Calcutta has been managing its YouTube, Facebook, Twitter and LinkedIn pages. Libraries too have developed collaborating and publishing platforms on social media sites. A library blog has been created to keep up to date the students, faculty and other staff members of BUEST[67] (Baddi University of Emerging Sciences and Technology). Hundreds of colleges and their teaching departments have plenty of platforms for different kinds of users to collaborate and network and to constitute a twenty-four-hour classroom learning experiences.

Seminar, symposium, workshop and academic events are updated through social media sites. Blogs are intensely popular to network and inform, for example, Blogger titled 'The Social Science Informer'.[68] Admission to various colleges are notified by specific blogs,, for example, 'Admissions to various Courses in India',[69] i.e. a blog that collaborates and networks for latest admission notification to various courses in India, offered by universities, colleges and other higher education institutions in India.

In addition, m-learning has begun sweeping the Indian educational scenario. Mobile devices, including PDA, handheld tablets, mobile phones, smartphones and Symbian, are popular for teaching-learning purposes. It makes education portable, impulsive, efficient and thrilling. By this, students are able to record the lectures, multimedia materials, provide feedback, read e-books, access Internet and practical exercises and use software for educational activities, says a study by Mitra and Ganguly.[70]

The Government of Rajasthan invests heavily on ICT infrastructure building for development of Education 2.0. The state's Information Technology Department plans to launch its own education on social network like YouTube and Facebook for learning. Educational institutions such as HLC International, St Patrick's School, Chennai Public School (CPS) and Rosary Matriculation Higher Secondary School are using sites like YouTube, Facebook, Twitter and Ustream to interact with students, parents, alumni and well-wishers, says a *Times of India* report.[71] Portals such as Studyplaces.com and Tutorvista are functioning as information exchanges for students. Web portals such as 100percentile.com provide online examinations. The mathguru.com offers solved questions on the CBSE mathematics curriculum, says Lokesh Mehra of Cisco.[72]

India benefits much from the Internet and social media platforms since they hold greater promise to cut across a plenty of variables that historically turned hostile towards the educational opportunities of a very large portion of its population. In this context, focus is moving on to four identified social media platforms. These platforms are critical in the context of India. These platforms can claim a significant stake in the higher education space in India. The Higher Education 2.0 beseems realisable in the Indian context by a wider application of the following social media platforms: Facebook, Twitter, YouTube and Blogs, which hold a significant influence on creating Education 2.0 in the Indian context.

Fostering networks and communities is an essential element of a learning platform. It has been recognised for some time that principals, teachers, students and parents can connect and form communities organised around relationships and ideas. Through an online community, members can reflect, comment and contribute to conversations, equally. The conversations become 'learning activities' that can involve 'experts', as well as all members of the community.

The need for communication tools in the learning process has often been underestimated by educators in India, especially those who feel comfortable with the traditional, instructive ways of teaching should come of age. More recently, an increasing number of learning environments have been transforming into digital forms in the higher education scenario. This is a hope and perhaps our educators would realise the significance of platforms.

Conclusion

The political significance of social media lies in the visible social stratification and structural constraints seen in the tradition-bound Indian society. Education 2.0 acquires political potential in respect of a rigid social structure that hampers mobility due to factors such as gender, geography, caste, rituals and beliefs. It also holds political consequence in respect of qualitative aspects such as access, quality, cost, time and parity, which conventionally remains a challenge to policy makers, government and stakeholders.

Historically, education has been inaccessible to scores of social groups in India. Moreover, education has been literally elitist since it is afforded by higher castes in the social hierarchy. Ever since independence, there have been attempts to bring down education to every doorstep transcending all kinds of structural barriers. To achieve this cherished goal visualised in the national freedom struggle, the Constitution and many subsequent statutory enactments, we have embraced special provisions and reservations for people at the social frontiers.

Developing younger population and providing them education to meet the human resources requirement require a political solution. However, education remains unattainable for a large section among them. Many sections of Indian population have no access to good education. Many things remain barriers to their access to education. Women, religious minorities, sexual minorities and Dalits are still out of mainstream educational infrastructure in the nation. Their worries need to be wiped out. Besides this, barriers to education such as quality, access and cost are still hampering the prospects of good education to many sections. Here, it is more useful since students and young people are heavily immersed in Web 2.0 platforms (i.e. blogs, social network sites, YouTube, Twitter, virtual worlds, podcasts, wikis, Facebook, video sharing and photo sharing). They are constructing online lives that impeccably bond with their offline world. Indeed, Internet is playing an increasingly important role in the academic life of students.

It is apparent that Education 2.0 seeks to answer loads of challenges that the educational domain in India has faced for the six decades or more. More than that, new media–embedded education destroys a range of variables that makes attainment of education more difficult. Minority social groups in India are, in fact, due to social factors such as gender, caste, geography, quality, access and cost, unable to leverage opportunities of higher education. Digital media thus resurfaces with the potential to wipe out the structural barriers to educational setting in India. This is because Internet has no caste, gender, race, class and so on. This means Education 2.0 has political potential since it reflects the pedagogy of the oppressed. This form of education has more reasons to be popular among marginalised communities than the mainstream. Hope the government facilitates initiatives in this regard in the coming days.

Notes

1 Chidanand Rajghatta, 'Seven Indians among top 100 intellectuals', *Times of India*, 6 May 2008, <http://timesofindia.indiatimes.com/world/us/Seven-Indians-among-top-100-intellectuals/articleshow/3013408.cms>, accessed on 18 August 2014.
2 'World Thinkers 2013', Prospect magazine, May 2013, <http://www.prospectmagazine.co.uk/features/world-thinkers-2013>, accessed on 18 August 2014.
3 See <http://bijugayu.blogspot.in/2011/07/public-administration-meaning-nature.html#.U_FNRaMZrPw>.
4 See Aijaz Ahmad cited in *The Hindu*, 'Social media, both an opportunity and a challenge', Chennai, <http://www.thehindu.com/news/national/tamil-nadu/social-media-both-an-opportunity-and-a-challenge-says-aijaz-ahmad/article6187512.ece>, accessed on 8 July 2014.
5 J. Kimmerle, J. Moskaliuk, and U. Cress, 'Wiki-supported learning and knowledge building', *Journal of Computer Assisted Learning*, 25 (6), 2009, pp. 549–561.

6 G. Conole and P. Alevizou, 'A literature review of the use of web 2.0 tools in higher education', A report commissioned by the Higher Education Academy, The Open University, Milton Keyne, August 2010.

7 See <https://www.facebook.com/calicutuniversitypro/info>, accessed on 21 August 2014.

8 Sanat Kaul, 'Higher Education in India: Seizing the Opportunity', Working Paper 179, Indian Council for Research on International Economic Relations, New Delhi, May 2006.

9 *Emerging Technologies for Learning*, Vol. 2, Coventry: British Educational Communications Technology Agency, 2007, <http://www.becta.org.uk/>.

10 P. Standish, 'Preface', *Journal of Philosophy of Education*, 42 (3–4), 2008, pp. 349–353.

11 Tyler Cowen, *Create Your Own Economy: The Path to Prosperity in a Disordered World*, Connecticut: Tantor Media, 2009.

12 James Surowiecki, *The Wisdom of Crowds: Why the Many Are Smarter Than the Few and How Collective Wisdom Shapes Business, Economies, Societies and Nations*, New York: Anchor, 2004.

13 K. Gray, C. Thompson, J. Sheard, R. Clerehan, and M. Hamilton, 'Students as web 2.0 authors', *Australasian Journal of Educational Technology*, 26 (1), 2010, pp. 105–122; and C. Buckley, E. Pitt, B. Norton, and T. Owens, 'Students' approaches to study', *Active Learning in Higher Education*, 11 (1), 2010, pp. 55–65.

14 C. Crook, 'Theories of formal and informal learning in the world of web 2.0', in S. Livingstone (ed.), *Theorising the Benefits of New Technology for Youth*, Oxford: Oxford University Press, 2008, pp. 30–37.

15 M. Lee and C. McLoughlin, *Web 2.0-Based e-Learning*, Hershey, PA: Information Science Reference, 2010.

16 P. Goodyear and R. Ellis, 'University students' approaches to learning', *Distance Education*, 29 (2), 2008, pp. 141–152.

17 Lee and McLoughlin 2010: 1.

18 See <http://harvardsocial.posterous.com/>.

19 See <https://www.facebook.com/Harvard>.

20 See <http://www.youtube.com/user/Harvard>.

21 See <http://itunes.harvard.edu/>.

22 See <http://twitter.com/#!/Harvard>.

23 See <https://foursquare.com/harvard>.

24 See <http://abcd-socialmedia.scribo.harvard.edu/>.

25 D. Thomas, and J. Seely-Brown, *A New Culture of Learning*, Charleston, SC: Createspace, 2011.

26 Josh McHugh, 'Connecting to the 21st century student', 2011, <http://www.edutopia.org/ikid-digital-learner#>, accessed on 11 February 2011.

27 M. Kalantzis and B. Cope, *New Learning: The Science of Education*, Port Melbourne: Cambridge University Press, 2008.

28 S. Schaffert and W. Hilzensauer, 'On the way towards personal learning environments: Seven crucial aspects', e-Learning Papers No. 9, Barcelona, 2008, <http://www.elearningeuropa.info/main/index.php?page=home>.

29 K. Kreijins, P. Kirschner, and W. Jochems, 'Identifying the pitfalls for social interactions in computer supported collaborative learning environments:

A review of the research', *Computers in Human Behavior*, 19 (3), 2003, pp. 335–353.

30 J. Hattie, *Visible Learning: A Synthesis of over 800 Meta-Analyses Relating to Achievement*, London: Routledge, 2009.

31 G. Siemens, 'Connectivism: A learning theory for the digital age', 2004, <www.elearnspace.org/Articles/connectivism.htm>.

32 M. Chatti, J. Amine, and C. Quix, 'Connectivism', *International Journal of Learning Technology*, 5 (1), 2010, pp. 80–99.

33 See Learning 2.0: The Impact of Web 2.0 Innovations on Education and Training in Europe Report by Institute for Prospective Technological Studies.

34 Sergio Lujan Mora and Susana de Juana Espinosa, 'The use of weblogs in higher education: Benefits and barriers', <http://gplsi.dlsi.ua.es/proyectos/webeso/pdf/inted07.pdf> (see 0912f50647a5a6fd9b000000), accessed on 2 August 2012.

35 B. A. Nardi, D. J. Schiano, M. Gumbrecht, and L. Swartz, 'Why we blog', *Communications of the ACM*, 47 (12), December 2004, pp. 41–46.

36 S. Leslie, 'Matrix of some uses of blogs in education', *EdTechPost*, October 2003, <http://edtechpost.ca/wordpress/2003/10/09/Matrix-of-some-uses-of-blogs>.

37 A. J. Lowe, 'Blog use in teaching – Dragster activity', *Internet*, <http://www.webducate.net/dragster2/examples/bloguse/>, accessed on 2 August 2012.

38 Todd Oppenheimer, *The Flickering Mind: The False Promise of Technology in the Classroom and How Learning Can Be Saved*, 1st edition, New York: Random House, 2003.

39 See <https://www.facebook.com/roomtoread/timeline>.

40 See <http://teachingcafe.ning.com/>.

41 See <http://www.cybraryman.com/edhashtags.html>.

42 Kevin Kelly, 'Becoming screen literate', *New York Times Magazine*, 21 November 2008, <http://www.nytimes.com/2008/11/23/magazine/23wwln-future-t.html?ref=magazine>; and Lawrence Lessig, *Remix: Making Art and Commerce Thrive in the Hybrid Economy*, New York: Penguin Press, 2008. Lessig predicts that television and movies will be 'bookified'. Television, movies and audio-visual works will soon have tables of contents, indexes and abstracts to accompany them; they will become searchable to the minute, if not the second or the frame, and have – in the holiest of holy grails – information about rights provenance defined and embedded for both legacy and new work.

43 A. Juhasz, 'Why not (to) teach on YouTube', in G. Lovink and S. Niederer (eds.), *Video Vortex Reader: Responses to YouTube*, Amsterdam: Institute of Network Cultures, 2008, pp. 133–140.

44 J. Burgess and J. Green, *YouTube*, Cambridge: Polity Press, 2009; L. Manovich, 'The practice of everyday (media) life', in G. Lovink and S. Niederer (eds.), *Video Vortex Reader: Responses to YouTube*, Amsterdam: Institute of Network Cultures, 2008, pp. 33–44; X. Cheng, D. Dale, and L. Jiangechuan, 'Understanding the characteristics of internet short video sharing: YouTube as a case study', 2007, <http://arxiv.org/PS_cache/arxiv/pdf/0707/0707.3670v1.pdf>, accessed on 2 May 2009; and P. G.

Lange, '(Mis)conceptions about YouTube', in G. Lovink and S. Niederer (eds.), *Video Vortex Reader: Responses to YouTube*, Amsterdam: Institute of Network Cultures, 2008, pp. 87–99.

45 See <http://www.youtube.com/user/MIT>.

46 See <http://www.youtube.com/user/YaleCourses>.

47 See <http://www.youtube.com/user/HarvardKennedySchool>.

48 See <http://www.youtube.com/user/princetonuniversity/videos>.

49 See <http://www.youtube.com/user/columbiauniversity>.

50 See <http://www.youtube.com/user/StanfordUniversity>.

51 Allan Collins and Richard Halverson, *Rethinking Education in the Age of Technology: The Digital Revolution and Schooling in America*, New York: Teachers College Press, 2009.

52 See <https://www.educanon.com/>.

53 See <https://vimeo.com/>.

54 See <http://www.teachertube.com>.

55 See <http://www.youtube.com/education>.

56 See <https://plus.google.com/+YouTubeEDU/posts>.

57 Suil Tyagi, 'Adoption of Web 2.0 technology in higher education: A case study of universities in National Capital Region, India', *International Journal of Education and Development Using Information and Communication Technology (IJEDICT)*, 8 (2), 2012, pp. 28–43.

58 See <http://www.ignou.ac.in/ignou/footer/Subscribed%20E-Resources>.

59 See <http://www.ignou.ac.in/>.

60 See <http://www.ignouonline.ac.in/VirtualClass.htm>.

61 See <http://www.ignouonline.ac.in/>.

62 See <http://ieg.ignou.ac.in/wiki/index.php/Main_Page>.

63 See <http://www.youtube.com/user/nptelhrd>.

64 See <http://www.facebook.com/pages/National-Programme-on-Technology-Enhanced-Learning-NPTEL/160344787335526>.

65 See <http://www.tv14.net/eklavya-technology-channel/>.

66 See <http://www.facebook.com/pages/Eklavya-Technology-Channel/103383429716685?v=desc>.

67 See <http://buestlibrary.blogspot.in/>.

68 See <http://thesocialscienceinformer.blogspot.in/>.

69 See <http://admissionsindia.blogspot.in/>.

70 See <http://bcjms.bhattercollege.ac.in/mobile-communication-devices-as-a-tool-of-educational-process-a-brief-reference-to-indian-scenario/>.

71 Kamini Mathai, 'Schools use social media to connect with parents', *Times of India*, 22 August 2011, online, accessed on 21 April 2013.

72 See <http://www.cisco.com/web/IN/about/leadership/enabling_onlineeducation.html>.

11

CULTURAL VOCABULARIES
IN POLITICAL INTERNET

This chapter briefly identifies cultural vocabularies in the political Internet on the background of the data analysed for discussions across various chapters. It is an in-depth examination of certain identified vocabularies of interest to political Internet. Social science of Internet has recently produced many cultural vocabularies. Such vocabularies excavated in this book as part of the political Internet was born in relation to the power of Internet in dismantling the old social cleavages in our social architecture. Unfortunately such vocabularies did not figure out prominently in the social studies of Internet. Therefore, this chapter fills in the gap. A social study of Internet-related vocabularies and its linkages with social and political life of the nation is attempted in the chapter. Considering the possibilities of Internet-related vocabularies of interest to social studies of technology, it may be useful to revisit vocabularies of political Internet in a convenient manner. Primarily, what figures out at the outset is Internet of Things (IoT). What kind of changes IoT would bring into cultural vocabularies of activism and political engagement? Will new kinds of techno-rich resistance vocabularies reconfigure lived-in realities of underprivileged people. Can new resistance vocabularies of social media age do away with oppressive social system coming out of social structure? The following is an attempt to track them, though not substantively but literally.

An IoT is going to surround people in the twenty-first century. Internet is everywhere! Every realm of life is closely connected to Internet, thus making techno-social life an entirely different form of existence. Technologies are reaching out to transform the lives of girls, underprivileged, women, Dalits and those living in isolated and remote communities just like a medical support. In this context, prediction goes like this: the number of things connected to Internet is more than the number of people connected to it. So a technology-saturated world is awaited in the days ahead. Device-obsessed people have become the new kind of citizens of techno-republics. In days ahead, gadgets and platforms will become more familiar than life partners. Google search, Facebook, WhatsApp, Twitter and so on will have indispensable use in almost all aspects of life. Whether security, transport and logistics, job opportunities, insurance, language, health care, reading, education, sporting, food safety, document management or security, almost everything is closely connected to Internet. The predictions and statistics are beyond understanding in the near future. The change and its impacts are far-reaching.

Long-distance love is then the future of romance. Adultery is to have a different meaning. Sex is going to have an expanded meaning, which might also include cybersex as real sex. Devices from remote places monitor security. Transportation is made easier by long-distance-controlled devices. Territories are surveilled by unmanned army of robots and technical applications controlled from a single place located in a remote corner of the nation. Technologies are used to locate people and objects in distance. Tele-operation and telepresence are then the hallmark of future mode of doing things. Tele-medicine will become an advantage to all other forms of medical support systems. Economy is likely to be influenced by virtual economy. Politics is likely to be engaged by thematic virtual publics. Amid such phantom advances of technology in everyday life, more techno-rich cultural vocabularies to mean many things we traditionally used to mean in the physical social world are currently in use. Metaphors are retreating and allegories are boomeranging.

Kevin Ashton first used the term *Internet of Things* in 1999. While referring to this, one might understand that it is a big market. Reports predict incomprehensible numbers about IoT. The global IoT market is awesome. It will grow to $1.7 trillion in 2020 from $655.8 billion in 2014. No layman could understand what this fuss is all about. However, life is going to be embarrassed by it. The number of IoT-connected devices such as cars, washing machines, refrigerators and everything in between will grow from 10.3 billion in 2014 to more than 29.5 billion in 2020.[1] The impact of IoT on life is immense. It influences almost all layers of social life. Politics, economy, culture and so on will look different. Here the concern in this chapter is all about resistance. Not that nature of resistance will look different but it is that the cultural vocabulary associated with almost everything will change to new kind of meaning making.

Prediction is that IoT is bigger than the Industrial Revolution. Internet is more complex than human society. Possibilities of these cultural shifts are not properly understood. Internet is full of unexplored continents. It is still a vision in part and a reality in part. However, one thing is very clearer. Amid enticing cultural vocabularies in the age of Internet, 'big data' is amazing.

Data are massive in digital age, so *big data* is a catchphrase used to describe a massive volume of both structured and unstructured data. It is too large to process using traditional database and software techniques. It consists of billions to trillions of records of millions of people in the digital age. They derive all from different sources, for example, media/entertainment, web, sales, health care, customer contacts centre, life sciences, social media, video surveillance, transportations, mobile data and retail. Big data is typically loosely structured that is often incomplete and enormous. Therefore, they could be accessible for multiple functions. Corporates have been using it for brand marketing. Politicians use it for voter engagement. Governments use it for citizen engagement.

Big data analytics is relevant, which refers to the process of collecting, organising and analysing such large sets of data to discover patterns and other useful information. Big data analytics helps to understand information contained within the data. It also helps identify the data that are most important to the business and future business decisions. Mostly, big data analysts want the knowledge that comes from analysing the data. Big data and IoT are not only useful for doing business; they are also useful for government, citizen activism, public sphere, contentious politics, social capital and civil society. In short, they have greater applicability in democratic engagements.

Technology writer Andrew Keen has been warning of privacy issues for the last couple of years. While appraising the unethical act of selling of privacy to third-party entities, he had in mind Facebook and its flawed privacy policies. An important dimension of such massive data retrievable in the digital age is that they could be used for other set of data, whereby assumptions and inferences are possible. Inferences drawn up could have other applications. Thus the name *big data*. Big data is such that business, government and private individuals use it for particular purposes. Times ago, governments, research agencies and private firms were using citizen information for various purposes. While doing so, they collected data by means of sample sources. It means collecting citizen data was difficult in many respects: be it access, time, cost and credibility. Inferences thus drawn were not reliable in many scales. Data are important anyhow now and before. Problem of data in the age of big data is that of abundance whereas it was paucity in the past. Therefore, what makes big data unique is that they are huge, rich, accessible, quick, cheap and credible. They are just a touch, click or swipe away.

Citizens migrating to connected space have larger political significance. They digitalise every human act. Knowingly or unknowingly, in doing so, they engage in a political act. Every tweet matters. All timeline update counts. Each post has significance. Every share speaks. Emotions are digitalised. Pleasure and pain are teleported to Internet. From birth to death, citizens engage through the bits. Everybody does it. If so, no matter what religion, caste, language and gender one belongs, one is part of a constant connection. One could call it connected space, i.e. a world of connection in IoT, which forms big data. Big data and connected space have vicinal political significance. Together they give shape to big democracy, big politics, big protest, big citizens, big activism and big government.

IoT, connected space and big data are at the heart of participation, which is at the centre of big democracy. Democracy too is about participation. Digitalisation of every human act empowers democracy. Government gets data. It gathers citizen perception just by a click. Big data gives an innovative push for deliberative politics. Big democracy operates at various scales. One important dimension is open government. Good government is about transparency. It is about engagement. As information sharing is democratised on Internet, connected space facilitates open government. Government could be more engaging, interactive and participatory and could be a touch away. It could be in the monitor, accessible even while on travel and instantly set on contact, thus the term *open government*. It enriches big democracy because big data makes massive data easily manageable and be documented in the age of IoT.

Not only government is changing from the vantage point of transparency, many institutional apparatuses are also changing. Institutional apparatus traditionally thought to be inaccessible and undemocratic are becoming more popular in IoT. Diplomacy, one of the most elitist businesses of government, has become citizen-friendly. Social media has a role in it. Diplomats, diplomatic institutions and foreign policy concerns have become more citizen-friendly, thus the term *Internet diplomacy*. Expatriates are more connected with home country. Government makes home more intimate to them. Connected space makes feeling for home more intimate on Internet. How could ordinary citizens in India make amateur success stories if otherwise no technology was for their benefit? It is only because they get support of expatriates that intimacy gets new expressions.

Apart from institutional apparatus, democracy gets vivid expressions in the form of the new way of digital protest. Clicktivism, the new way of citizen involvement in connected age, democratises the political processes. Gone are the days when citizen marched to street or town square to communicate a grievance. In the past, demonstrations, marches, rage, picketing, 'bandhs' and so on were non-party forms of political engagements by citizen. In the connected age, unlike those of past, class, gender, sexuality and so on are not effective tools of mobilisations. There are new codes and coders on Internet. Protest and collective action are different now. Today, democratic way of citizen protest is digital, thus the term *clicktivism*.

Mouse charmers are the new sort of citizen. Cyber intimacy is defining their new solidarity. They engage the polity in Twitter, Facebook, You-Tube, blogs and other similar social media platforms. They are new sort of citizens. The less social become more social on Internet for the reason that it is more political for them. Less involved become more involved. Less participation becomes more participation. Touchscreen, swipe pads or push-button beeps give new identities. They speak less and act more. On connected spaces, intimacy is the essence of citizenship unlike the case with previous media.

Intimate speaking works better on connected space. Intimate citizenship is such that people once introverted or expelled from mainstream find their space in the connected public. They find intimate citizenship. Profound changes take place in the realm of conventional boundaries of citizenship. Reproductive technologies revolutionised birth of citizens. Test-tube babies and surrogate mothers are a few among them. Sexualities have undergone tremendous changes. Lesbians, gay transgenders and others are catering to new identity formations. They all give call for redefinition of conventional citizenship. Digital citizenship is the latest entrant in this feat. Cyber intimacy is the identity of new citizenship on connected space. One may call it intimate citizenship.

Democracy is about participation, engagement and deliberation. Under-privileged, subalterns and minorities are away from democratic engage-ments for various reasons. Caste oppressions, gender discriminations, regional imbalances and cultural antagonisms all get vivid expressions in modern India and thus pose serious threats to democratic life. People think that it would bring solutions to our old problems. Social media has been an iconoclastic allegory for underprivileged Indians. They believe that it could beat casteism, religious dogmas, communal sensitivities, gender oppressions and elitism of the traditional media. Therefore, for the under-privileged, social media has had a symbolic value that could be an image-breaking genie and is a political choice, whereby it could bring solutions to old problems. Political campaigners use 'friend power' to reach voters on the assumption that politically less engaged citizens are more likely to be convinced by one of their friends than by a standard political message. Social websites are like eco-chambers. They just make echo; it reverberates in the fortified friendship circles and weak-tie networks. It is in the sense that the messages and communications do not go for many; they go to friends and those who subscribed to them. Indeed, it is apt to call it per-sonalisation of communication channels.

246

Public sphere 2.0

Social media gives way to a quickly traceable public sphere or rekindles public interest in the public sphere imagination. An uncensored public sphere is the immediate outcome of political Internet. It is easily accessible to people who were previously unable to access it. It provides easy access for politicians. It helps them easily understand what citizens think. They quickly come to know what is happening in the public sphere during an election campaign or any other important occasions; thus they are strategising on electioneering. It is replica of voter attitudes as it mirrors moods, mindsets, aspirations and dreams of the population. Underprivileged people use it to form opinion and censure political class. Social media represents the democratic aspirations of the young voters as young voters patently deploy social media platforms such as Facebook and Twitter. Internet caters significantly to the causes of subaltern people. Dalits often use it to beat caste discrimination and question social cleavages and caste colonies. Women find intimate citizenship on it. The public sphere 2.0 is queering and sexual revolution is seeping across cyberspace. A public sphere on Internet is born to the fault lines of our ancient social structure.

People power

User profiles and respondents on the social media have people power. Power of people on Internet is amazing. Put it differently, power of people on social media is more powerful than those in power. People on the social margins are exposed to the mainstream just because of Internet. It gives an inclusive public sphere something like a town square. Internet has a huge role in bringing power back to the people. Through providing a platform for people to come together and share views and opinions, Internet encourages people to take action on issues that matter to them. The web also provides a huge community to listen to their voice so there is no need to knock on every door! Many platforms are out there, which give power to people.

Therefore, people power does work! Web allows a broader range of people to get involved. With a few clicks of the mouse, thousands of us who might otherwise not have participated get their voices heard through the petition sites or some other platforms. Social networking sites such as Facebook are also key in gaining attention and developing discussion about the political campaigning.

Internet has revolutionised people power. By harnessing the power of the web to reach millions of people from all around the globe, people are getting their voices heard through platforms such as online petitions, encouraging real change. Internet is also allowing us to re-establish meaningful connections with other human beings just like the young people involved in the uprisings in North Africa and the Middle East. The key to all of this is communication. Internet provides a platform encouraging the free expression of opinions on issues and people across the world feel passionate about it. Be it on Facebook or an online petition, the huge audience that Internet provides makes it a valuable tool for transforming society and culture.

'Friend power'

'Friend power' is amazing at least according to the underprivileged, who are now able to make use of friendships for doing political activism. There are some peculiarities to political deliberation in social connections. One could call political deliberation in social connections as 'friend power' in politics. 'Friend power' facilitates political deliberation to the advantages of citizens – think of Dalits, women, minorities, backward class population and others who were once not in the mainstay of political democracy.

'Friend power' on social media platforms hugely benefits politics. People are roaming around social connections. People benefit out of social technologies in many realms of life. It is high time that we placed a more watchful eye on the benefits derived out of political deliberation in the Indian society, which is notorious for the social cleavages and social obscurantism prevailing for centuries. *People power, mass power, town square of the world* and such terms are most popular among social media enthusiasts to charge this phenomenon. All right; but amid all such terms one thing that is distinctly reflected is the new power of social media in political processes in India. A brief sketch of that trend and the sort of mechanism that makes 'friend power' in politics is so demanding. A discussion on 'friend power' is listed in the chapter on 'friend power' in resistance.

A compelling political connotation of Internet has come in the way of facilitating offline events. As politicians and activists are sending messages across a wide spectrum of viewers, chances of them reaching to millions in one click in less than a second make social media a more efficient political communication channel dearest to political class. The 2014 electoral campaign made successful use of social media, including blogs, tweets, text messaging, emails and search engine advertising by the use of micro-target. Voters received phone calls from their local candidates requesting support. Facebook messages were used for engaging voters. Now boundaries of field of politics in offline and online are meaningless as both are overlapping in our perception. Politically traditionally engaging voters are now finding it comfortable to make social media a new loudspeaker.

Micro-target

The importance of social media comes in the way voter data are used to hit 'micro-target' and how messages are sent to particular groups of users during political campaign. People increasingly feel that they are getting a personal touch from the political class. The fact is that politicians send them private messages on Facebook or email or cell phones. Social media gives them a new kind of intimate speaking.

One influential aspect that cyberspace puts upon our political imagination is SoMe Effect, or, put otherwise, social media effect. Social websites and their political power seem unquestionable. Many-to-many communication is possible through social media. It is on the assumption that people formerly known as the audience are now at the centre of social media–driven deliberations. Chief hit in that line of development is in the electoral process. It tips off new propositions in electioneering strategy. With a new hypothesis, election strategists and experts propose a number of correlations pertaining to social media. They map out the distinct correlation between social media and election interfaces. The general election scenario in 2014 was a test case. Perhaps it aired out the future too. One may call it the SoMe Effect.

Social media gives power to political actors, in particular smaller parties or lesser known candidates. They get power to evade mass-media filters. The newly born AAP is a testimony, specifically their prize-winning government formation in Delhi Assembly election in 2013, at least. In particular, this power of social media allows lesser known candidates and political parties to communicate directly with citizens as well as reduce their dependence on traditional intermediaries such as journalists and media monopolies.[2] The monopoly of the big media is gone. Now social media is the new medium. It helps people voice what they were not allowed in big media.

Repository of political information

Social media is a repository of political information as journalists and broadcasters are fast moving on to the nebulous social media environment for political news and sources of storytelling. Majority of Narendra Modi's electioneering, political competition and rhetoric against opponents have been viral. They spread across and beyond social media sites. Shashi Tharoor put most of his campaign tactics over the platforms. Most senior BJP leadership signed up Facebook and Twitter accounts particularly during General Election 2014 anticipating its potential to bring in voters to polling booth. Carefully, Twitter's data were integrated with TV channels during 2014 election season. Here the real-time online data were beautifully presented with dynamic imageries, arranged by day or week. Furthermore, twenty-nine million Indians viewed the election on Facebook. Facebook decided to roll out a new app called 'I'm a voter' worldwide after its successful pre-test in Indian election and indeed, the 'app' got over four million clicks by the Indian voters on the 'I'm a Voter' button during the parliamentary elections, said a report by Reuters on 19 May 2014.[3] Facebook, on the day of the elections, also issued a notice reminding its Indian users that it was Election Day and encouraged them to share the fact that they voted. Such enormous social data used extensively by television and other traditional mediums to boost their election coverage have become flashpoint in general election. Twitter debate show #YourVote2014 on Headlines Today was popular. CNBC-TV18 has been using the iElect app by TCS in association with Twitter India. With the help of Frrole and Twitter, the *Times of India* developed a Social News Hub. Thus, TV channels have leveraged Twitter and Facebook in all possible ways. Indeed, it was a political table.

Social data

Social data decide the future of Indian electoral scenario. As Neil Postman[4] said, information appears at random, heading for no one, but in huge size and at high velocity and disconnected from theory, sense or principle. Everybody uses this data, in particular broadcasters. This correlation between social data and social election will be deciding the future dimension of politics in India. Social data significantly changed the face of General Election 2014 in India as more and more people migrated to platforms. Now the success of any candidate in election is influenced by social election and social votes. At the same time, let us ask who contributes to social data. Rural Indians, poor citizens, marginalised people and other minorities have greater stakes in this.

Tweetivism

The hyper polarised caste, communal, heteronormative and gendered nation is obsessed with a seven-letter word: Twitter. It is a connector for the people who are expelled from social mainstream just because of their identity. It is easy to follow your likes and unfollow your dislikes. Follow, tweets and retweets are important in the cleavage-rich Indian landscape. They are political for people on the social margins. Connection works like an alternate public sphere. Twitter makes connection possible. Opportunities are important in a world of lesser opportunities. Whose use is more political when communication opportunities in Twitter are exposed to people? It is those who were once denied a space for communication. More particularly, it is the women, lower caste groups, Dalits and marginalised communities who make use of connection for political contentions as well to find an alternate space. On Internet, people do not have any oppressive identifiers or torments from social cleavages. Twitter hosts production mills of a new sort of cultural vocabulary politicising our tastes, identities, consumer preferences, dissent and personal choice. Often use of such a cool technology signifies a potential political act.

Very few countries could match with India where use of hashtags, tweets and so on is more political. When social cleavages are more rigid, Twitter use gives rise to kinds of Dalit Twitter, feminist Twitter, queer Twitter and so on. When communicative spaces in mainstream society are more colonised, Twitter gives rise to an inclusive communicative public. It gives a quick and accessible public sphere. With the use of hashtags, political life is made possible on the go and fast. Hashtags like 'occupy nights' are energising feminists. Hashtags like 'I am in Periods' are powering more confidence in women. Hashtags on themes reflecting anti-rape, anti-caste, anti-censorship and anti-rightist campaigns tell why Twitter use is political for ordinary Indians.

People often follow profiles that tweet about cool life tips, cookery tips, car maintenance, beauty tips and so on. Often they get updates on profiles that give tips on personality, health care, fitness, smart money, education, spirituality and so on. But beyond the coolness of Twitter profiles' following, there are elements that make it a relevant place for doing activism. It is relevant for being political. When we follow such profiles, one thing cannot be overlooked: the political question involved in choosing a private profile. Your Twitter profile is political in India that tells why profile picture is questioning many things. Profile description is political because that portrays your ideological position in a cleavage-rich society.

Over the last couple of years, the entrenched patriarchal nation has been home to a new sort of battles that has an entirely different ecology and modus operandi. It is called tweetivism. Women began to oppose male-dominated ruthless culture through the window of opportunities on Twitter. Subalterns have been resisting hegemony of the dominant in it. Regions and peripheries protest exploitation by the centre through this new activist ecology. Now the battle is between journalists, film stars, sport stars, political class and business tycoons on one side and common man on the other side. However, the battlefield is amazing. It is the Twitter landscape. Whose tweets, hashtags and following are more political, which decide the social agenda of the day? Answers, though not definitive, are visible in Twitter. But this new reconfiguration of political contentions receives little attention in the political imagination of the nation.

A new class of speakers and audience make tweetivism the cultural vocabulary of the resistance in the age of the Internet. Activists like Meena Kandasamy are a new class of speakers who tweet. There is a new class of audience who is interested in retweets. Some section of this Twitter land is home to hashtag activists. The direction of Twitter republic in India disturbs many. More importantly, Twitter is used to challenge oppressive systems and inactions of the authority. The DNA, a news portal, initiated an online campaign on Twitter to spread messages against growing violence against women.[5] Just see the Twitter profile Being Feminist I surveyed. Being Feminist has 4,742 tweets, 836 followers, and 34 following by August 2016. It is a feminist group consolidated on cyberspace.[6] Such groupings on solidarity are what make tweetivism so profound. In doing so, they are not alone. They join force with groups having similar interest along with analogous groups articulating other interest gather a loose coalition of alliance. They form an important force to reckon with. They easily spread, communicate and influence. You might call it tweetivism.

Tweetivism, the mechanics of a new breed of speakers deciding the agenda of a new breed of audience, creates the hybrid of activism mediated by cool technology. Over the last few years, Twitter hashtags like #DelhiGangRape, #StopThisShame, #DelhiProtests, #Amanat, #Nirbhaya and #Damini have served as anchors to inform, educate and galvanise mass support. Twitter messages ('tweets' in the jargon) are like public telegrams. No more than 140 characters in length sent from any computer or mobile phone, they make a new form of networked public and 'cool politics'. Anyone with an account (there are 100m and rising) can send a public message to anyone else by placing the @ sign before a username or a # sign before a topic.

People often dub it as a celebrity class. The 140-character world is much small by any standards for anyone who believes in the big. However, for many from films to sports and business to politics, this 140-character world is much more than mere connection. If you are one, certainly, a look at the other side of Twitter gives a new narrative setting in India's socio-political ecology. At least according to Shobhaa De, writer and socialite, when she was the target of Shiv Sena and MNS protest for saying something related to Mumbai, in the wake of the decision on bifurcation of Andhra Pradesh, Twitter is more than mere celebrity class. She (@DeShobhaa) tweeted:

Shobhaa De @DeShobhaa 30 Jul 2013
Maharashtra and Mumbai??? Why not? Mumbai has always fancied itself as an independent entity, anyway. This game has countless possibilities.
Retweets 307 Favorites 152

11:49 PM-30 Jul 2013

Shobhaa De, though not an ordinary Indian, was stalked for making a comment on a public issue that is more sensitive to some sections of Indians. The sensibility behind online troll pertaining to her was that Shobhaa De is a woman. Therefore, the comment was gendered and sexist. But patriarchal rule in India is wary of women using Internet.

Ordinary citizens find it painful and even empowering while speaking on Twitter. At least according to Ravi Srinivasan, a Puducherry-based industrialist and volunteer of anti-corruption movement, who was arrested under the draconian provisions of Section 66-A of the Information Technology Act, 2008, and could be facing a three-year term in jail. The reason was a tweet from him (@ravi-the-indian) that provoked Karti Chidambaram, the son of the then finance minister P. Chidambaram.

Ravi Srinivasan
@ravi-the-indian
got reports that karthick Chidambaram has amassed more wealth than vadra
Retweets 418 Favorites 60

5:33 AM-20 Oct 12

Notably, ordinary citizens and well-informed activists who are fond of Twitter and find it engaging often have contradicting experiences in their everyday life. At least for Meena Kandasamy, a Chennai-based poet and activist who faced a flood of Twitter abuse in April 2012 after a tweet that said her support for a beef eating food festival in Osmania University, which was intended to build support for the addition of beef to the campus canteen. Certainly, it was an attempt to reinterpret Brahmanic narratives about Indian society and people.

It was in 2009 that Twitter became very popular following a controversy by Shashi Tharoor. The controversy was following announcement of austerity measures by the union government. A journalist asked Tharoor

253

(@ShashiTharoor) a question in Twitter. Unfortunately, the label 'cattle class' created a big controversy in public realm.

> Kanchan Gupta @KanchanGupta
> @ShashiTharoor Tell us Minister, next time you travel to Kerala, will it be cattle class?
> 15 Sep 2009
> Shashi Tharoor @ShashiTharoor
> Follow
> @KanchanGupta absolutely, in cattle class out of solidarity with all our holy cows!
> > 5 Retweets 117 favorites 12:17 AM- 15 Sep 2009

What do India's powerful politicians fulfil in Twitter? We Just identify here a few leading politicians using Twitter. In August 2014, Narendra Modi had 5.62 million followers, Shashi Tharoor with 2.29 million followers and 2.18 million for Arvind Kejriwal; now Twitter has become an important vehicle of change in India. Probably they represent three leading political lines, which stand in opposition to each other. However, it is interesting to investigate what these three different lines of Twitter profiles on Internet engage for the nation, in terms of their ideology, policy and for future. Just see a Modi tweet that became viral on Internet.

> Narendra Modi
> Narendra Modi @narendramodi
> India has won!
> > 70,415 Retweets 46,376 favorites 12:09 PM-16 May 2014

The shift towards a new political communication represents validation of new patterns of political consumption associated with an 'aspirational' middle class that has become increasingly taken as a model of progressive politics. In the nine-phase voting process that spanned six weeks, with millions exercising their right to vote, what does a Twitter election look like? It looks like this: Twitter India said that the platform witnessed more than 56 million election-related tweets from 1 January 2014 till 12 May 2014, when the polls got over. Twitter points out that: Each of the poll days saw between 5.4 lakh and 8.2 lakh election-related tweets. Narendra Modi became a clear winner even before election results were announced, on Twitter with 11.1 million tweets about him, accounting for 20 per cent of all election-related traffic. Aam Aadmi Party found mention in 8.2 million or 15 per cent of election-related tweets, followed by the BJP at six million or 11 per cent. Arvind Kejriwal, head of AAP, was mentioned in 5 million (9 per cent) tweets; Indian National Congress 2.7 million (5 per cent) and Rahul Gandhi 1.3 million (2 per cent) were also on the top 10 list. Terms like *Election 2014*, *Varanasi*, *Amethi* and *Lok Sabha* were also trending terms during the 16th Lok Sabha polls. There were 76,000 tweets on 16 May 2014 congratulating Narendra Modi on the hashtag #Congrats NaMo. #CongratsNaMo trended worldwide for almost 10 hours. There were over 320,000 tweets using @narendramodi talking about Modi or talking to him (which is probably a record for the number of mentions received on one Twitter handle). Fifty-six million tweets were sent out till August 2014 with the total 'reach' (including tweets, retweets and quotes) standing at 267 billion, as per data released by the US-based firm.

The Twitter public is a site of major significance for anyone interested in understanding not only the operating logic of the social media age but also the contemporary dynamics of urban politics, media culture, political communication, public culture and social change. In the Indian case specifically, an account in Twitter must be informed by India's great cultural diversity, its rigid social structure, its dense and contested social cleavages, its vibrant audio-visual image culture and its complex arrangements of civil and political society. Now, the story of the Twitter politics in India is also widely perceived as being part of a wider political narrative through which Indian democracy is variously described as digital politics, social politics, net politics, cyber politics and so on.

Campaign personalisation

Politicians are very close in the age of technology. They are very near and knock at our doorsteps right away. How is it possible? It is, among other things, facilitated by connection technologies. One significant development is the personal appeal brought into political campaign during electioneering. Electioneering is more intimate now. Politicians communicate to the voters personally. Voters engage their representatives instantly and more closely. The increasing personalisation of modern election campaigns is going to benefit the poorer sections of Indians. Personal relationship is more important in the age of constant connection. The success of any politician is largely decided by the social media strategy he or she adopts. Social media strategies tend to give more emphasis on the individuals than collectivities. Online campaigning places more importance to personalities and personal relationships, even in party-oriented electoral systems. Tweets, connections or timeline updates keep followers and friends constantly in touch with politicos and the political parties.

It is very easy to communicate instantly. Voters are easily informed about whatever the candidate is currently doing as part of the campaign. Photographs, audio speeches or videos of the candidate at events are posted on social media sites directly. Social media is used for building brand images to politicians. It is sued for building a personal appeal and more sentimental images of candidates and politicians during election time. Emotional appeal is more vibrant in personalisation of electoral processes. Such aspects can make messages more likely to be shared with others in a more advantageous way. Tweets that have content that is more emotional are real change makers. Timeline updates that have personal touch and intimacy are real game changers.

Many politicians use social media. Twitter is a favourite platform for political communicators. Primarily, social media acts as a private broadcast channel for the politicos. It is also a one-directional communication, where politicians speak what they want the public to know. Put it otherwise, social media gives shape to a 'homestyle information provision strategy'. Personalised campaigns are informal communication.

Majority of tweets by politicians are essentially broadcasting information. They are primarily aired with the aim of mobilising supporters. Politicians could enter directly into a real interactive conversation or exchange with voters. Sure, this strategy is not without risks. Resources are required to keep up the interaction effective. In addition, the chance of encountering people opposed to a candidate's position is much greater. Politicians need to be prepared to deal with these so-called 'Internet trolls'. Anyway, campaign personalisation in a greater degree democratises the institutions of electoral politics.

Wall battalions

A Facebook community in Karnataka campaigned against tax imposed on private vehicles registered outside the state and approached the high court seeking amendment in the Motor Vehicles Act. Facebook groups for organic farming spread the value of agriculture among tech-savvy younger India at a time when government interventions, massive policy initiatives and campaigns fail to control climate change, environmental degradation and river pollution. Online library communities spread value of reading culture, which within a few days brings in books at your doorsteps just by a few clicks. A Facebook group formed in protest against moral policing motivated a nationwide Kiss of Love campaign. Lesser participation makes bigger changes possible.

In the era of digital sociality, Facebook is the bona fide vehicle of uprisings for feminists, Dalits, displaced and others. Timeline speak go viral. Facebook, for instance, is aplenty with networks for women's cause in India, and sentiments both for and against women resurface in these platforms. For instances, see the Facebook pages such as Feminist India[7] and Voices of Indian Women.[8] Being Feminist[9] says it as a site to promote feminism and women's rights and share experiences of being feminists. As a distinct social space, women make use of Facebook as an alternative social space since the conventional public sphere is gendered and hostile towards female sex.

Among the political parties, verified Facebook pages of BJP has 9.3 million likes, 3.9 million likes for Indian National Congress (INC) and 2.8 million likes for Aam Aadmi Party on August 2016. In 2014 twenty-nine million people in India had 227 million interactions (posts, comments, shares, and likes) regarding the elections on Facebook from the day general elections were announced to the day polling ended.

Certainly, the use of social media in democratic politics and in particular Facebook was a path-breaking event in the electoral history in India. Without a doubt, Facebook has been important in incorporating the apolitical generation into the democratic process. It provides them a medium where they post and share their notions and indeed lament their aversion to political class. At the same time, it gives them a space that politicises them into core issues of democracy. However, much deeper issues need to be thoroughly investigated. Despite all the hue and cry over Facebook, scores of stories remain untold.

General Election 2014 had more from the crowd class: Facebook indeed, among the platforms. Facebook swallowed up a bigger stake than other social media platforms. Undeniably, the role of Facebook in the 16th General Election was impulsively promising also. However, there is a more important question beyond facts and figures about social media presence of the political actors. How they can translate greater presence of citizens on the fifth estate into polling booth? Success and survival of any political actor depends on answering that question.

To understand Facebook's role in General Election 2014, it is pertinent to draw an analogy that better helps sum up the nebulous Facebook election landscape. Apparently, Facebook configured fifth estate electoral processes at four parallels: political parties, political leadership, online electoral campaign and apolitical e-state voters.

Facebook India scrolls up news feed related to political events in the country, i.e. Facebook Indian Political Interest Lists.[10] This news feed lists out a whopping list of links to political parties and political leadership.

The page had only over 500 likes and over 100 shares by mid-March 2014. The pages did not have much likes, followers and commenters. Navigation on the link will take users towards verified pages of political parties and politicians.

There are many more in the list on the verified Facebook roll of political parties.[11] Facebook India has hosted a roll of verified official Facebook pages of Indian Political parties. The Facebook roll streams news of so and so verified party pages.

Bharatiya Janata Party (BJP)[12] had 2,829,848 likes by mid-March 2014 and its cover page said, 'Let us work together to make Mission 272+ a reality.' In fact, BJP has larger follower base on Facebook. Just in one hour, a post in the page[13] on 19 May 2014 got an average of over 4,116 shares. On the same day a wall post got over 21,000 likes on the page.

Indian National Congress had[14] 2,107,693 likes and its cover page says, 'voice, opportunity, transparency and empowerment'. However, the page has a growing user base. On 19 May 2014, a post in the page got over 10,000 likes in seven hours.

Nationalist Congress party had 220,312 likes by March 2014. Many parties are on the roll list of Facebook India that provides link to potential online political parties. However, the Aam Aadmi Party is active and maintain state-wise and even city-wise Facebook pages for the party.

In addition, political leaderships have their verified Facebook pages. Indian Political Leaders List is a page hosted by Facebook India for General Election 2014 and it has the official verified links to almost all leading politicians in India.[15]

Navigate to the Indian Political Leaders List that directs users to pages of political class; for instance, the Facebook page of Narendra Modi has over 35 million likes. The profile when I surveyed for this chapter grabbed over 18,000 likes, over 900 comments and over 700 shares within one hour of each post on 20 March 2014 when I surveyed it. To the best of my knowledge, this was the average response for every post he made.

Every wall post of Narendra Modi went viral and likes went spiralling hour after hour. Arvind Kejriwal with over 4.7 million likes emerged as a major contender for fifth estate constituencies. Arun Jaitley with five and a half lakh likes, Milind Deora with 57,000 likes by March 2014 and almost all politicians across all ages migrating to Facebook signify the growing desire for bringing change through technology.

Politicians on Facebook act as timeline warriors. They use it as loud-speaker. Every timeline warrior thus makes public their ideology, principles, vision and style statements on the Facebook cover page. The cover page politics even signifies the growing implication of a new loudspeaker that makes a tidal wave in the way we do politics. Milind Deora, for instance, states on his cover page how his motto would lead his politics: Principle, Access and Action.

Facebook organised Candidates 2014. Facebook tied up with 'News-laundry' for a Facebook Talks Live event called Candidates 2014. Analo-gous to US electoral strategies in online spaces, it was a town hall format where people engaged their leaders through Facebook and a live audience asked questions to political leaders who could play a role in the formation of the next government. It also took a leading national TV channel as its leading channel partner.

Facebook users were able to pose questions directly to key political con-tenders for the 2014 General Election with the launch of a special initiative: Facebook Talks Live. In the run-up to the 2014 Lok Sabha election, users of Facebook were able to discuss the electoral agenda of country's top politicians including West Bengal chief minister Mamata Banerjee, AAP leader Arvind Kejriwal and Uttar Pradesh chief minister Akhilesh Yadav, among others.

Eminent journalist Madhu Trehan moderated the session by asking questions on behalf of Facebook users. It was livestreamed on the website besides being broadcast on an identified private TV channel.

India Election Tracker[16] is a Facebook app hosted on the Facebook India page. The app has three major sections: (1) Follow the Facebook Talks Live, (2) Election issues–related poll and (3) Leading candidates and par-ties at a glance. The page has 143,363,057 likes.

Most important element of Facebook success in India's electoral poli-tics was its positive impact on apolitical voters. The depoliticised young voters are transformed into vigilant political actor on fifth estate con-stituencies during 16th parliamentary election in 2014. On Facebook profiles, the largely apolitical young voters from here and there and in particular from cities in India began to speak like self-appointed guard-ians of justice. On Facebook, depoliticised generations of young India seem speaking like game changers during election time. The political comments of apolitical voters on fifth estate had passed through contro-versies and cyber wars.

It was found that during elections, social media profiles of young users I surveyed – fake, annymous, profiles with malicious intentions – have been united in saying that this time let us make a different game. There was euphoria over the political power of social media power success among young voters. The game changer is social media and in particular the Facebook. Young voters are co-opted into political process and democratic dialogue by the connection opportunities provided on Facebook. Considering the political significance of Facebook in politicising apolitical voters during parliamentary election in 2014, there is no denying the fact that it is an important platform for democratic engagements.

Perhaps General Election 2014 was an election that saw the rise of the Aam Aadmi Party, increasing campaigns against corruption and NOTA debates. Meanwhile the recipe for a non-Congress, non-BJP entity, the Third Front, a name synonymous with general elections in India comprising eleven Left and secular parties offering themselves as an alternative to the Congress and BJP while side-stepping the contentious leadership issue, came to the forefront.

With Narendra Modi in the race for prime ministership and Arvind Kejriwal with potential for game changing in the heat, the 16th General Election had many peculiarities. Among these, the increasing popularity of social media constituencies and fifth estate voters are a new arrival in election strategies. Social media consolidating public opinion during election campaign has seemingly attracted the fascination of all establishments across the political spectre.

However, a vivid generation divide has become inevitable as the elder generation exhibits a higher level of scepticism whereas digital natives, i.e. those born after Internet have been internalising their touchscreens and monitors as virtual realities. The trajectory of social media as a game changer during General Election 2014 mirrors the imaginations of everyone as never before in this context.

However, there are deeper issues involved in Facebook stories. With the popularity of Facebook in electoral politics in the General Election 2014, electoral democracy in India has been undergoing a new identity shift. Political public has been fragmenting towards a kind of balkanisation. Indeed, technology takes us towards a super-saturation point as it copes up with a society that never experienced a medium of this sort before. For this medium, we have almost surrendered our culture to technology. Politicians have migrated to this space by overstepping their pitfalls. Consequently, we have made our culture to fit technology instead making technology fit our culture. These severe issues of technology use in electoral process need deeper scrutiny and thorough analysis. Hope it would.

E-signature

Signature campaigns are popular for spreading an awareness or grabbing the attention of public authority towards issues of public importance. Since feudal days, people hoped that petitioning the sovereign could have greater effects. Inviting public attention was accomplished through different methods. Repeating the method here will not serve any purpose. Rather it is significant to mention a new method which was used by people for inviting public attention on issues of public concern. It is signature campaign. Signature campaign was one among them used for attention grabbing. People could use different mechanisms for doing that, for example, tree, long banner like cloth, paper and even human body. However, it also is interesting if you look at what it means to think about signature campaign in the social media age. There is a broad collection of software programmes accessible on the Internet, which can be put up on webpage platforms to get the e-signatures of thousands of people. It is particularly a user-friendly way of collecting signatures against a crime, a policy or an issue. NGO groups are better in adopting this mode of online signature campaigns. It involves thousands of people sending an email signature or requesting information from a website at the same time, and finally the tactic becomes a collective action. Emails are more common now. E-signature campaigns are just like a shrub growth. For persuading users to join a cause, inboxes are flooded with campaign initiatives. Most of you might have come across mails, for example, to protect forests in Central India from coal mining.[17] Another one is impact of coal mining on tigers.[18] Junglistan, a cultural vocabulary in the age of political Internet, is a simulated image of a country of forests citizens living in a virtual land. They pledge to protect it from mining. They show the government that they want their forests to remain intact.[19] Another example is 'Ask Sunil Mittal to fulfil Bharti Airtel's promise @Airtel_Presence or Ask Him to Switch Off Diesel'.[20] This signature campaign used by Greenpeace which I surveyed for the chapter signifies the potential of the new kind of attention seeking activities in the age of social media.

E-signature campaign is particularly a user-friendly way of collective action; for instance, Greenpeace successfully mobilises supporters through online campaigning by way of collecting e-signatures to forward to authorities concerned for cautioning them about taking a particular decision. Movements also put a link in emails, which will send them straight through to the petition page. Internet indeed changed the whole modus operandi of collective action in novel ways. Now collective action beseems more cool for social media generation.

Emailism

Emailism has been widely used in social movement tactics to mobilise supporters. Use of email for movement mobilisation was documented in a study among global justice activists by Della Porta and Mosca.[21] Emailism is the growing use of email platforms from Google, Yahoo, Rediff, Hotmail and so on, which are used to signify slant expression of life taste. Here small bits of fringe acts in personal life or amateur acts result as individual choices, but they transform into solo political dissent. Inbox, compose, archive, sent, forward, list, trash, spam folder and an ever-expanding list of tools for connection in Gmail, Yahoo, Hotmail, Rediff and so on are more than acts of communication. Every day inboxes become graveyard of call letters from NGOs and civil society groups like Greenpeace, CRY and NBA to sensitise us on issues that are lifestyle issues.

Every day we read bulky inbox messages either as direct inline messages or as a forwarded letter. There would be solo individual heresies concerning lifestyle issues. There would be people regretting over the failure of all responsible mechanism including political class and public institutions such as judiciary and legislature. People are increasingly becoming solo protestors. They engage in lifestyle dissent in all such occasions I mentioned. Here one may forward emails for generating public awareness, type words expressing personal dissent, and send messages to a long list of recipients. All these happen just by a small click, that too within seconds. Sometimes people archive messages for future references. Sometimes, people mark some emails as important. They also trash, spam folder and so on their messages. On emails, there are nauseating stuff that otherwise make a big difference to life.

Emailism is a more disruptive form of civic engagement. It means large amounts of information in emails are sent by underprivileged people to authority, elites and influential class in anger against insensitivity towards issues of public importance. Such emails either target the accounts of ministers and public institutions or attempt to pin down a system mailing server. It is also signifying the extent of support for a specific concern.[22] Email vigilance is an incredibly useful method to be in touch with many people very swiftly, facilitating mobilisation, awareness and education. Email alert is a useful device for reaching as many people as possible cost-free and effort-free. In emailism, the sender and the recipient do not need connected at the same time in order to communicate. This means that it is particularly useful for communicating across time zones, geographies and nationalities. It is extremely quick and most messages reach their destination inboxes in a flash. Email is an exceedingly powerful medium for alerting large numbers

262

of people to new developments that enable civil society groups to respond rapidly to events and often to outpace and outflank established power structures.

Emails make writing to politicians easier. Now, emails are a new connection technology that can be used to fill the void between political class and the mass. For group purposes, the most significant development of email technology is the 'list server', i.e. a programme, occasionally called a 'ListServ' that enables people to subscribe to a discussion list and receive by email messages which the list owner or other subscribers have posted. When people send messages and respond to a list, an online discussion can develop. The number of discussion lists currently active is unknown but is certainly very large and they are a prime resource for civil society groups.

E-petition

It is equally important to admit the fact that in the age of social media, we are likely to end up as mere ivory tower or air-conditioned protestor. We do not like to risk blood on the street in cyber age. We are multitasking from the comfort zones of life. Now the question comes in. Are we feeling a sort of in situ protest? Yes, of course, but it makes sense because there are times when even fish need bicycle. Lifestyle is very much a response to the realities of state capitalism, and very much about creating networks of resistance and new ways of doing and being that help us escape the cultural, ethical and structural parameters that dominate our world.

A very important step from the online advocacy to effect a protest is to e-petition the minister/corporation/perpetrator that is to be lobbied. Movements normally can do this using e-petition software, which generally provide a space for personal comments and replies. Many online petitions include a pre-written letter, by which one has the opportunity to edit or amend. These e-letters tend to be more effective than online petition, but are probably not as effective as a volume letter. Wide opportunity to lift anti-rape activism, anti-nuclear movements, protest against use of diesel in mobile towers, anti-graft movements, human rights advocacy and so on through petitioning sites such as change. org, petitiononline.com, ipetitions.com and thepetitionsite.com have, in effect, redefined the modus operandi of non-party political domain on Internet. It is so common now to flood user inboxes with online petitions. Some issues are favourites for the digital activists. Reservation, corruption and anti-nuclear movement are some examples. Just see online petitions such as 'No to reservations in private sector and IIT/IIM/ Medical colleges',[23] 'India Against Corruption',[24] 'Abandon Koodankulam

Nuclear Project'[25] or 'Tell the Prime Minister of India to stop supporting the violence in Burma'.[26] One interesting thing is that majority of issues undertaken are middle class issues. They are undertaken by educated, employed, tech-savvy and city-dwelling Indians. But they are useful.

Internet has just ushered in a fresh age of user-friendly petitioning. Petitioning is just a click away. With access to Internet just through a tiny device, now people are in a comfortable position to become activists or dissenters or to be a committed citizen. There is a broad collection of software programmes accessible on the Internet (a lot of them free) that can post on webpage platforms to get the e-signatures of thousands of people. The protest actors are initiated more interestingly by way of e-petitioning and email writing.

In addition, Earl Jennifer[27] makes a division between online petitions performed by social movements themselves and petitions that are centralised on a specialised 'warehouse site'. Sites like ipetition.com, thepetitionsite.com and MoveOn.org are labelled as petition sites[28] and eventually become much more than a simple petition site, but incarnated as a distinct movement appealing to a new generation of politically engaged citizens.[29]

Do we know that diesel used in mobile towers by mobile companies attracts resistance from environmental groups when we read an email letter from Greenpeace? Do we know that junk food in the nearest fast-food restaurants makes us the next target of health-industrial complex that we read from the Health Law Advisor email? Do we know that political satire in our forward emails sensitise us on the illegitimacy of inactive and irresponsible political class? How often do we make sense that the daily email subscription to our inbox from 'Kafila'[30] is large enough to remind us that at home, at workplaces, at public transport, on the street a whole lot of misogyny and sexism prevails and our women are equal neither in home nor in rest of the world? Sure enough, many more, our inbox, sent, forward, trash, spam, archive, compose and so on are more than what they are.

Multiplier effects

Multiplier effects were perhaps the most important aspect of social media in the 2014 General Election. The 'network effect' produced when someone who has watched a video slides along a page or hits a tweet indeed gets further on to all of their friends or followers. Narendra Modi benefitted by this mode of multiplier effect during the election season. The 'second degree' networks (i.e. followers of followers) may represent weak social ties, but can be very large. Therefore, my friends, your friends and their friends have compartmentalised the voters for scrupulous ideologies, candidates or some other important issue raised. Liked by nearly four lakh people and shared by nearly 14,000, Narendra Modi Facebook post, for example, 'I will represent Varanasi in Lok Sabha & I look forward to this wonderful opportunity to serve Ganga Maa & work for Varanasi's development' was trending. Posted on 29 May 2014, it has been a proof to the multiplier effect in the electioneering via social media during General Election 2014. I share that you share that you share that I share that we share, possibly furthered the success and failure of many candidatures.

Homogeneity

Homogeneity was the result of Internet effect in electioneering. As Narendra Modi has been able to grab vast followers along with a couple of other big players on social media sites, homogenisation effect has already been born of Internet where we began to equate the nemesis with Obama effect of 2012. An apparent convergence of political campaigning with the net effect across the western society, indeed, has engulfed Indian electoral scenario and political communication. Now we equate electioneering in India with those in other parts of the world. We are losing an ideal, the ideal of real politics, where most important citizen issues discussed are almost lost. Now social media is just an imitation and replica of social media models across other parts of human society, which is square opposite to what prevails in India. But we adopt it, receive it and imitate it.

Rise of developmental politics

A bird's-eye view of platforms summarised that the top three trending election topics on Facebook were jobs, education and corruption. The rise of developmental politics onto platforms has significantly been inflated on Facebook, Blogger, YouTube and Twitter. YouTube politics, a mad rush among netizens to catch as much political action on YouTube as they can, seemed as if it is one of the most interesting developments pertaining to social politics in India. Traffic of political news on streaming video sites such as YouTube has been growing time after time. The content related to political speeches, television interviews and breaking news has been getting more mob watch on YouTube. Narendra Modi and Aam Aadmi Party chief Arvind Kejriwal were YouTube hits during election season 2014. However, when I surveyed the comment threads of the YouTube channels, there were comments in enormous volumes but most of them were weird and obscene.

Around 13 million people engaged in 75 million interactions regarding Narendra Modi, says Ankhi Das, the public policy director for India and South Asia at Facebook.[31] On 6 March 2014, when elections were announced, Narendra Modi had crossed 11 million fans. As the national campaign gained momentum, Narendra Modi's fan base increased by 28.7 per cent crossing 14 million fans by May 12 and he became the second most liked politician on Facebook after Obama.

Twitter as a political tool will continue as a major source of political information in the country. After general election in 2014, Twitter continued as major carrier of political news. Call it tweet politics. For example, Congress leader Ajay Maken termed Narendra Modi's new cabinet in 2014 as 'lacklustre'. He had in mind Smriti Irani, who according to him was not even a graduate but became Human Resource Development Minister. His tweets against the ministry burst into political news.

Social media sites act both as site of walled garden of friendship circle and commercial entertainment plaza. However, can social networking sites egg on social politics? What does it mean to think about how social media influenced on the result of General Election 2014? Speculations were high on the political table. People came across a surfeit of hybrid labels such as *NaMo* and *Chai pe Charcha* and it finally ended on 16 May 2014, when Mr Narendra Modi tweeted (@narendramodi) that 'India has won!' which in fact became the highest ever retweeted in India within a short span of time.

Democratic aspirations of the young voters

As young people are digital addicts, social media represents the democratic aspirations of the young voters. Social media can be used as a means to direct political messages to certain target groups. Of course, not all citizens have access to the Internet and social media, so a part of society may be excluded from political discussion on social media due to this 'digital divide'. Whilst social media cannot replace face-to-face contact with youth, it can be a useful additional tool to deliberately target young people (the age group most likely to be disengaged from politics) because they are more likely to use social media, especially SNSs. Young people aged 16 to 24 in the EU-27 are more active users of social media functions than other age groups, including creating blogs, posting content or sending messages via social media.

Thunderclap

In effect, 'thunderclap' strategy has been useful in attaining popularity and building ground support. AAP has drawn much on this strategy. The social media team of AAP is a largely informal but committed set of volunteers, followers, who rock into action to counter the right-wing ambush. The party used hashtags to promote its achievements. Within minutes, hashtags such as #AAPExposedRobertVadra and #AAPExposedNitinGadkari were trending on Twitter. Perhaps, AAP could have won. They have committed volunteers but I do not have. What comes to my mind is the story of ordinary politicians and Indians. What happens to their political user contents during electioneering? Will they go for thunderclap; if so, will they get huge followers? Could they make big hits? Time will prove it. Not General Election 2014 and it was not there then.

Astroturfing

'Astroturfing', i.e. presenting professionally prepared materials as if they were unsolicited contributions from the public, has been a turning point in the general election. The callous practice of presenting a coordinated public relations campaign under the guise of unsolicited comments from members of the public has pointed the fact that social media has been widely used for sponsored publicity campaigns. Such producer public content many times ends up muddying or even contradicting the official message that a candidate wants to put in. This was more visible during General Election 2014. Almost all mainstream political parties built their ground support on this strategy. At the same time, big players were accused of such a campaign strategy.

'Friend power' strengthens deliberative democracy in social media age. However, their field is unconventional. One may call it connected public. As a keen social media observer, I have found that such social media stories do have no sound theoretical background. People were just telling that it would bring changes, often more positive. However, what struck my mind is that there was a complete lack of citations of lived-in experiences. Poorest people do have stories on social media. One should expose them. While doing so, see how social technology is deeply infiltrating our social life. Having been exposed to such social media stories, one overarching trend that is more visible is that there are no ground-breaking theories that substantiate the positive outcome of social platforms for democracy. I am thinking about deliberation. All people I surveyed on social profiles said me that social media brings in big changes. But what changes? What comes to mind is that people support social media, but they do not cite lived-in experiences of ordinary people as examples for their claim. I am citing a few cases where one could see how social media could strengthen deliberative democracy. Many ordinary people are making wonders on social media. People sign up on to social platforms. While doing so, they are becoming part of a new system which demolishes an old one. These cases, though not representative of the social media Indians, are in no way unrepresentative of them. They are stories people told me and some stories I have been exposed to. Some stories are told by people, which they did not even share with family members. Your every click has a story to tell. They are more than just a click. They represent a cultural shift of our time.

Digital ethnographic method is used in this enquiry. While doing so, I become a YouTuber, Facebooker, Tweeter, Blogger and so on. Lots of people are referent cases in the excavation of political Internet. You and I are part of this, your friends and their friends too. They are random cases drawn on a snowball sampling. They are signalling a particular pattern of social media use. Let us call them social citizens.

Social citizens is a term I would use to analyse a particular pattern of social media use. Your every tweet counts. Every timeline update matters. YouTube like is significant. Such social media use configures a networked public. I call it connected public. Here people make intimate speak. It is special in social platforms. It is because this peculiarity is one by which ordinary Indians are able to get just by a click what Shiv Vishwanathan or Ramachandra Guha was not able to get by their regular newspaper commentaries or TV talks.

I sent a Facebook friend request to social science nomad, Shiv Vishwanathan and became a friend on Facebook. I waited long to watch any of the updates he could make. I waited and waited for long. But there was none. He updated regularly only the articles and columns he wrote for newspapers both print and online. However, no one put a like mark to the post. I too did not mark a like mark. He was not an intimate speaker and not a social citizen too. If so what makes social citizenship on connected spaces? Well, if you speak on social media give it a personal touch. Speak through heart.

Ordinary people form their micro publics on connected spaces. They are able to make intimate speak. It is one of the conditions of deliberative democracy. Social citizenship just provides intimate speak by denizens of connected spaces that create and recreate deliberative democracy. In doing so, my analytical framework is social citizenship.

Feminist historians become timeline speakers. Academic become wall eloquent. Nuns become intimate citizens. Social media enthusiasts have huge followers on Facebook profile. Ordinary women speak with personal touch. Many terms were introduced in the chapter. They were analysed and discussed in the background of the data retrieved and analysed across the chapters in the book. IoT, connected space, big data, big democracy, open government, Internet diplomacy, digital protest, clicktivism, mouse charmers, cyber intimacy, intimate citizens, people power, 'friend power', tweetivism, wall battalion, emailism, e-signature, thunderclap and so on are discussed. What connects them and is common to all? Social media! Call it political Internet.

Notes

1 Steven Norton, 'Internet of Things market to reach $1.7 trillion by 2020: IDC', *Wall Street Journal*, 2 June 2015, <http://blogs.wsj.com/cio/2015/06/02/internet-of-things-market-to-reach-1-7-trillion-by-2020-idc/>, accessed on 15 July 2015.
2 See summary of evidence in Untangling a complex media system: a comparative study of Twitter – linking practices during three Scandinavian election campaigns; H. Moe and A. Larsson, 'Untangling a Complex Media System', *Information, Communication & Society*, 16 (5), 2013, pp. 775–794. Note however, contrary evidence where major party candidates were more likely to be present on the web in Finnish elections in T. Carlson and K. Strandberg, 'The Rise of Web Campaigning in Finland', in J. Ramos and R. Davies (eds.) *iPolitics Citizens, Elections, and Governing in the New Media Era* Cambridge: Cambridge University Press, 2012; and R. Fox and J. Ramos (eds.), 'Politics in the new media era', *iPolitics: Citizens, Elections and Governing*, New York: Cambridge University Press, 2013, p. 130; and evidence showing prioritised candidates were more likely to use Twitter in the 2010 Dutch elections.
3 Gabriel Debenedetti, 'Facebook to roll out "I'm a Voter" feature worldwide', 19 May 2014, <http://www.reuters.com/article/2014/05/19/us-usa-facebook-voters-idUSBREA4I0QQ20140519>, accessed on 9 June 2014.
4 Neil Postman, *Technopoly: The Surrender of Culture to Technology*, New York: Vintage, 1993.
5 DNA, 'Delhi gang rape: Outrage on Twitter over safety of women, 18 December 2012, <http://www.dnaindia.com>, accessed on 30 April 2013.
6 See <https://twitter.com/being_feminist>.
7 See <http://www.facebook.com/FeministIndia?filter=3>, which is a Facebook network which in their own profile description says, 'Making people more aware about issues in India which can be eliminated through feminism. A place for debate and discussions. This page seeks to stop Rape

Culture (and other issues stemming from patriarchy)'. It had 788 likes and 28 talking about this as on 25 November 2012.

8 See <http://www.facebook.com/VoicesOfIndianWomen>, Voices of Indian Women is an auto-financed project born with the hope to document the clearly visible minority condition of the Indian women compared to the chauvinist society in India. It had 315 members as on 25 November 2012.

9 See <http://www.facebook.com/BeingFeminist>, and it had 15,040 likes, 4 notes and 3,514 talking about this as on 25 November 2012.

10 See <https://www.facebook.com/notes/facebook/facebook-indian-political-interest-lists/712639158756020>.

11 See <https://www.facebook.com/lists/10151862497682341>.

12 See <https://www.facebook.com/BJP4India>.

13 See <http://www.bjp.org/media-resources/press-releases/5th-list-of-candidates-for-lok-sabha-election-2014>.

14 See <https://www.facebook.com/IndianNationalCongress>.

15 See <https://www.facebook.com/lists/10151862504152341>.

16 See <https://www.facebook.com/FacebookIndia>.

17 See <http://www.junglistan.org/act>, emailed by Brikesh Singh, Greenpeace India <Greenpeace.india@mailing.greenpeace.org>, to bijugayu@gmail.com on 8 March 2012.

18 See <http://www.greenpeace.in/donate/>, emailed by Preethi Herman <Greenpeace.india@mailing.greenpeace.org>, to bijugayu@gmail.com on 12 July 2011.

19 See <http://www.greenpeace.in/junglistan/save/become-a-citizen>, emailed by Preethi.

20 See <http://www.greenpeace.org/india/en/What-We-Do/Stop-Climate-Change/>, emailed by Abhishek Pratap <Greenpeace.india@mailing.greenpeace.org>, to bijugayu@gmail.com on 20 October 2011.

21 Donatella Della Porta, 'Multiple belongings, tolerant identities, and the construction of "another politcs": Between the European Social Forum and the local social fora', in Donatella Della Porta and Sidney G. Tarrow (eds.), *Transnational Protest and Global Activism*, Oxford: Rowman & Littlefield, 2005, pp. 175–202.

22 Graham Meikle, *Future Active: Media Activism and the Internet*, New York and London: Routledge, 2002.

23 It was addressed to President of India, <http://www.petitiononline.com/petitions/ps0424/signatures?page=2>, and had 30,465 signatories as on 11 January 2013.

24 It was addressed to both President of India and Prime Minister's Office, <http://www.petitiononline.com/petitions/06042011/signatures?page=7>, and had 21,383 signatories as on 11 January 2013.

25 It was addressed to Hon'ble Prime Minister of India, CMs of Tamil Nadu and Kerala and Members of Parliament, <http://www.petitiononline.com/petitions/kankersg/signatures>, and had 375 signatories as on 11 January 2013.

26 It was addressed to Dr Manmohan Singh, <http://www.petitiononline.com/burma123/petition.html>, and had 1,659 signatories as on 11 January 2013.

27 Jennifer Earl, 'Pursuing social change online: The use of four protest tactics on the Internet', *Social Science Computer Review*, 24 (3), 2006, pp. 362–377.
28 Ibid.
29 Victor W. Pickard, 'Cooptation and cooperation: Institutional exemplars of democratic Internet technology', *New Media and Society*, 10 (4), 2008, pp. 625–645.
30 See <http://kafila.org/>.
31 Ankhi Das, 'How "likes" bring votes – Narendra Modi's campaign on Facebook', 17 May 2014, <http://qz.com/210639/how-likes-bring-votes-narendra-modis-campaign-on-facebook/>, accessed on 1 October 2014.